T0320911

# *Downsizing*

Downsizing is one of the most frequently used business strategies for reducing costs, returning firms to profit or for restructuring businesses following takeovers, mergers, and acquisitions. Downsizing measures are also set to become much more prevalent in the public sector as governments seek to restrict levels of public spending. This book is one of the first to provide a thorough study of downsizing from a global perspective. It examines the phenomenon in its entirety, exploring how it is initiated and what the process of downsizing looks like. It also looks at the effects of downsizing at a number of different levels, from the individual (e.g., motivational effects, effects on health and stress levels) to the organizational (e.g., financial outcomes, reputational and productivity outcomes). Written by an international team of experts, the book provides a comprehensive overview of downsizing that examines both the strategic and human implications of this process.

CARY L. COOPER CBE is Distinguished Professor of Organizational Psychology and Health at Lancaster University Management School.

ALANKRITA PANDEY is a Ph.D. Candidate in the Department of Management at the University of Texas at Arlington College of Business.

JAMES CAMPBELL QUICK is John and Judy Goolsby Distinguished Professor in the Department of Management at the University of Texas at Arlington College of Business.

CAMBRIDGE COMPANIONS TO MANAGEMENT

*Series Editors:*

Professor Cary Cooper CBE, Lancaster University Management School
Professor Jone Pearce, University of California, Irvine

*Advisory Board:*

Professor Linda Argote, Carnegie Mellon University
Professor Michael Hitt, Texas A&M University
Professor Peter Mckiernan, University of St Andrews
Professor James Quick, University of Texas
Professor Dean Tjosvold, Lingnan University, Hong Kong

Cambridge Companions to Management is an essential new resource for academics, graduate students and reflective business practitioners seeking cutting-edge perspectives on managing people in organizations. Each Companion integrates the latest academic thinking with contemporary business practice, dealing with real-world issues facing organizations and individuals in the workplace, and demonstrating how and why practice has changed over time. World-class editors and contributors write with unrivalled depth on managing people and organizations in today's global business environment, making the series a truly international resource.

TITLES PUBLISHED:

Brief, *Diversity at Work*
Cappelli, *Employment Relations*
Tjosvold and Wisse, *Power and Interdependence in Organizations*
Saunders, Skinner, Dietz, Gillespie, and Lewicki, *Organizational Trust*
Sitkin, Cardinal, and Bijlsma-Frankema, *Organizational Control*
Smith, Bhattacharya, Vogel, and Levine, *Global Challenges in Responsible Business*
Cooper, Pandey, and Quick, *Downsizing*

# Downsizing

## Is Less Still More?

Edited by
CARY L. COOPER
ALANKRITA PANDEY
and
JAMES CAMPBELL QUICK

CAMBRIDGE
UNIVERSITY PRESS

CAMBRIDGE UNIVERSITY PRESS
Cambridge, New York, Melbourne, Madrid, Cape Town,
Singapore, São Paulo, Delhi, Mexico City

Cambridge University Press
The Edinburgh Building, Cambridge CB2 8RU, UK

Published in the United States of America by Cambridge University Press, New York

www.cambridge.org
Information on this title: www.cambridge.org/9781107004672

© Cambridge University Press 2012

This publication is in copyright. Subject to statutory exception
and to the provisions of relevant collective licensing agreements,
no reproduction of any part may take place without the written
permission of Cambridge University Press.

First published 2012

Printed in the United Kingdom at the University Press, Cambridge

*A catalogue record for this publication is available from the British Library*

ISBN 978-1-107-00467-2 Hardback

Cambridge University Press has no responsibility for the persistence or
accuracy of URLs for external or third-party Internet websites referred to
in this publication, and does not guarantee that any content on such
websites is, or will remain, accurate or appropriate.

# *Contents*

# *Figures*

# Tables

# *Contributors*

DYNAH A. BASUIL is an Associate Professor at the W. SyCip Graduate School of Management at the Asian Institute of Management. Her research interests are in the area of strategy, particularly international business such as foreign acquisitions and human resources such as employee downsizing. Her research has appeared in the *Journal of Management* and she has presented her research at the Academy of Management meetings.

HILA CHALUTZ BEN-GAL is a Ph.D. candidate, Advanced Studies, Haifa University, Israel. She received her master's degree in management from the Heller School at Brandeis University in Boston USA and her B.A. in social science from the Hebrew University in Jerusalem. Her current research interests include organizational effectiveness, especially in the service sector, as well as the measurement of organizational and individual performance.

WAYNE F. CASCIO is Robert H. Reynolds Distinguished Chair in Global Leadership at the University of Colorado, Denver. A former SIOP President, SHRM Foundation Chair, and member of the Academy of Management's Board of Governors, he has published more than 145 journal articles and book chapters, and has authored or edited 24 textbooks, the most recent of which is *Investing in People* (2nd edn., 2011, with John Boudreau). He also authored *Responsible Restructuring: Creative and Profitable Alternatives to Layoffs* (2002), as well as the US Department of Labor's 1995 *Guide to Responsible Restructuring*. He is a two-time winner of the best paper award from the Academy of Management Perspectives for his research on downsizing and responsible restructuring.

CARY L. COOPER is Distinguished Professor of Organizational Psychology and Health at Lancaster University Management School, England. He is Chair of the Academy of Social Sciences, President of the

British Association of Counselling and Psychotherapy, Fellow of the Academy of Management, Founding President of the British Academy of Management, has honorary doctorates from a number of universities – Sheffield, Aston, Heriot-Watt – was made a Fellow of the Royal College of Physicians (and Royal College of Physicians of Ireland (occupational health)), and was Chair of the Global Agenda Council on chronic disease and well-being of the World Economic Forum (2009–2010). He is also Founding Editor of *the Journal of Organizational Behavior* and Editor-in-Chief of *Stress and Health*. In 2001, he was awarded the Commander of the Most Excellent Order of the British Empire (CBE) by the Queen for his services to occupational health.

GUANGRONG DAI is a research scientist at Korn/Ferry Leadership and Talent Consulting. He received his Ph.D. in industrial/organizational psychology from Central Michigan University and M.Ed. from East China Normal University. His main research focuses on competency modeling, 360-degree feedback, leadership development, derailment, high potential assessment, and identification.

DEEPAK K. DATTA is the Eunice and James L. West Chair of Business at the University of Texas at Arlington. He obtained his B.S. in mechanical engineering from the IIT, Kharagpur, his M.B.A. from the IIM, Calcutta, and his LL.B. from Calcutta University. He completed his Ph.D. in strategic planning and policy from the University of Pittsburgh in 1986. Professor Datta's research interests are in the areas of mergers and acquisitions, CEO (chief executive officer) selection, TMT characteristics, corporate governance, strategic decision processes, strategic human resource management, international entrepreneurship, and international business strategies. He has published over 50 articles in journals such as the *Academy of Management Journal*, *Strategic Management Journal*, *Organization Science*, *Journal of International Business Studies*, *Journal of Management*, *Journal of Management Studies*, *Management International Review*, *Journal of World Business*, and the *Human Resource Management Journal*. Professor Datta's research has been cited over 1,200 times by scholars in management and related areas.

JOHN B. DAVENPORT is a doctoral candidate in organizational leadership at Regent University. John has more than two decades of business development, research, and management experience in multiple industries, including health and safety, information technology, banking, and investment management. He is also an adjunct professor, having taught classes in business administration, finance, and leadership. His research interests include leadership dynamics within technical professions, organizational team dynamics, and secondary research interests in investment portfolio management. John's research has been published in several peer-reviewed and professional journals, including *The Journal of Financial Services Professionals*, *The CPA Journal*, and *Disclosures*. John has also presented research at numerous academic conferences, including a "best paper" award for work presented to the Institute for Behavioral and Applied Management.

KENNETH P. DE MEUSE is Vice President of Global Research at Korn/Ferry Leadership and Talent consulting, based in the firm's Minneapolis office. Previously, he was on the faculties at the University of Wisconsin – Eau Claire, Iowa State University, and the University of Nebraska at Omaha. Dr. De Meuse has written five books and published numerous articles on employee attitudes and organizational behavior in several leading professional journals. His most recent book, entitled *FYI for Talent Engagement: Drivers of Best Practice for Managers and Business Leaders*, was published in 2009. A recognized and well-respected expert on the impact of corporate change and organizational downsizing on the workforce, Dr. De Meuse has appeared on ABC News, CNN, AP Radio, and National Public Radio and has been featured in national publications such as *The Wall Street Journal*, *Business Week*, *Fortune*, *US News and World Report*, *The New York Times*, and *USA Today*. More than 100 universities and 175 corporations have contacted him regarding his research work in this area. He received his Ph.D. in industrial/organizational psychology from The University of Tennessee, his master's degree in psychology from the University of Nebraska, and his Bachelor's degree in psychology and mass communications from the University of Wisconsin.

ROCKI-LEE DEWITT is a Professor of Management in the School of Business Administration at the University of Vermont. She is a member of the University of Vermont's inaugural class of Sustainability Fellows and a member of the Food Systems Spire. She served as Dean of the University of Vermont's School of Business Administration from 2002 until 2009. Dr. DeWitt received her Ph.D. from Columbia University. Her research integrates competitive strategy and organizational justice theories to address the multi-level challenges of sustaining performance over the course of a firm's history. Her work has been published in leading journals, including *Administrative Science Quarterly*, *Academy of Management Journal*, *Strategic Management Journal*, *Journal of Management Inquiry*, *Journal of Management*, *Journal of Applied Social Psychology*, and *Journal of Experimental Social Psychology*, and also appears in a number of book chapters.

SIMON L. DOLAN obtained his Ph.D. at the Carlson Graduate School of Management, the University of Minnesota. He taught for over 20 years at the Universities of Montreal and McGill in Canada and in many universities throughout the world as visiting scholar. He is a prolific writer with over 50 books (in multiple languages) to his credit, and over 120 scholarly published papers. He has extensive consulting experience in human resource management and culture reengineering as well as coaching senior business executives. Today, he is the "Future of Work" Chair in ESADE Business School in Barcelona and the editor-in-chief of *Cross Cultural Management – An International Journal.*

NICO DRAGANO is Head of the Unit of Occupational and Social Epidemiology at the Institute for Medical Informatics, Biometry, and Epidemiology, University Duisburg-Essen. He holds a doctor's degree in sociology from the University of Düsseldorf, Germany, and a master's degree in social, political, and media sciences. He examines health effects of work-related stress and the influence of organizational and legal structures on the emergence of stress in the workplace. Respective research results are published in international journals

KYLE EHRHARDT is a doctoral student in management at the Sheldon B. Lubar School of Business, University of Wisconsin-Milwaukee. His current research focuses on employee attitudes, and in particular how work relationships and human resource practices contribute to shaping these attitudes. Kyle's recent work has been published in *Human Resource Development Quarterly* and the *International Journal of Sport Management.*

ERICH C. FEIN is a lecturer and Program Director at the Centre for Human Resource Management in the School of Management, Division of Business at the University of South Australia. Erich served as an intelligence officer and survival instructor in the US military. He received his Ph.D. in industrial/organizational psychology from the Ohio State University. His research focuses on performance management, personnel selection, leadership development, and managerial ethics. His publications have appeared in the *International Journal of Selection and Assessment*, *Research in Personnel and Human Resources Management*, and the *Journal of Management Development*.

SARAH J. FREEMAN is Associate Professor of Organizations and Strategic Management and Director of Masters Programs at the Sheldon B. Lubar School of Business, University of Wisconsin-Milwaukee. She holds a Ph.D. in organizational behavior from the University of Michigan. Her work investigates organizational change, particularly under conditions of decline or threat, as well as the implications of managerial interpretation for later action. Recently, she has looked at large-scale change in the non-profit arena, and comparative processes in non-profit and business organizations, as well as career crossover in the non-profit and private sectors.

FRANCO GANDOLFI, D.B.A. serves as Full Professor of Management and Director of the M.B.A. program in the School of Global Leadership and Entrepreneurship at Regent University, Virginia Beach. Specializing in change management and human resources management, he regularly advises firms in Australia, Switzerland, and the United States. Some of Dr. Gandolfi's current and former clients include UBS, Novartis, Deloitte, Credit Suisse, the US Marine Corps, and General Motors. Dr. Gandolfi serves on a number of international boards and committees and is an active researcher and writer. He is the principal author of five textbooks and his publication portfolio includes more than 50 peer-reviewed research articles in top-tier international journals. Dr. Gandolfi is recognized for his research work on organizational downsizing. The much-acclaimed book, *Corporate Downsizing Demystified: A Scholarly Analysis of a Business Phenomenon* (2006), has been adopted by consultants, policy-makers, and business executives around the world. He holds two master's degrees in commerce and education and a D.B.A. from one of Australia's leading Graduate Schools of Management.

KEVIN F. HALLOCK is Joseph R. Rich '80 Professor, Professor of Economics and of Human Resource Studies and Director of the Institute for Compensation Studies (ICS) at Cornell University, a Research Associate at the National Bureau of Economic Research, a Senior Fellow for Executive Compensation at The Conference Board and a member of the Board of Directors of World at Work. His research is focused on compensation and labor markets. Hallock earned a B.A. in economics, Summa Cum Laude, from the University of Massachusetts at Amherst and a Ph.D. in economics from Princeton University.

MAGNUS HANSSON, PH.D., is Assistant Professor at the Centre for Empirical Research on Organizational Control (CEROC), Örebro University, Sweden. Magnus's research has primarily been focused at studies of corporate restructuring, especially focusing on plant closures and various forms of downsizing. In Magnus's research, a particular stream has been aimed at developing explanations to the closedown effect, a productivity increase effect that occurs during the process of plant closure. He is also teaching classes of all levels, including topics such as organizational theory, management, marketing, strategy, and research methodology. Magnus's professional experience includes experience within industries such as oil and gas, telecommunications, and human resource management.

M. BLAKE HARGROVE is a graduate teaching assistant and a Dean's Fellow at the University of Texas at Arlington, where he is a Ph.D. candidate in organizational behavior. He holds an M.A. in management from Webster University. His research interests include occupational stress, business ethics, and psychological capital. In addition, Hargrove is a tenured instructor at McLennan Community College in Waco, Texas. Hargrove has 20 years of business experience in the real estate, construction, and manufacturing. Prior to his business career, he served in the US Navy as a submarine sonarman. Hargrove lives in Hillsboro, Texas with his wife of 18 years, two adolescent daughters, and an ancient dog.

JASMIN CHIA-JUNG LIN is Assistant Professor of Management in the School of Business at Robert Morris University. She received her Ph.D. in organizational studies from Southern Illinois University Carbondale.

She has experience in restaurant, publishing, and non-profit organizations. Her research focuses on top management teams, organizational downsizing, managerial behaviors, firm performance, and customer services. She has published in *Journal of Business Research*, *International Journal of Strategic Management*, *Business Studies Journal*, and *Journal of International Management Studies*.

BRIAN MARTINSON is a doctoral student at the University of Texas at Arlington. His research interests are in the areas of human capital, human resource management, and strategy, with current projects focusing on the relationship between human capital, human resources practices, employee behaviors, and firm performance.

WILLIAM MCKINLEY is Rehn Professor of Management in the College of Business at Southern Illinois University, Carbondale. He received his Ph.D. in organizational sociology from Columbia University. His research interests are organizational restructuring and downsizing, organizational decline, entrepreneurial cognitions, epistemological issues in organizational research, and the sociology, philosophy, and history of organization science. His publications have appeared in *Administrative Science Quarterly*, *Academy of Management Journal*, *Academy of Management Review*, *Academy of Management Executive*, *Journal of Management Inquiry*, *Organization*, *Organization Science*, *Organization Studies*, *Accounting, Organizations and Society*, *Advances in Strategic Management*, *Journal of Organizational Behavior*, *Journal of Management Studies*, and other journals and edited books. He currently serves as Senior Editor of *Organization Studies*.

GARY C. MCMAHAN is Associate Professor of Strategic Human Capital and Organization Ethics in Management at the University of Texas at Arlington. Dr. McMahan's primary research interest is on the strategic role of human capital in the human resource management of organizations. Dr. McMahan has published over 45 journal articles, proceedings, monographs, and book chapters. Gary serves on the editorial board of the *Journal of Applied Behavioral Science*. His research has been published in premier management journals, including *The Academy of Management Journal*, *Journal of Management*, *Journal of Applied Psychology*, *Personnel Psychology*, *Human Resource Management*, *Human Resource Management*

*Journal*, *International Journal of Human Resource Management*, and *The Journal of Business Ethics*. His 1992 paper on Strategic Human Resource Management has received over 1300 cites. Additionally, Gary has had extensive work and consulting experience, including a decade of employment with General Motors Corporation in Michigan. Dr. McMahan spent nearly two years in Austin, Texas (2000–2002) as Chief People Officer and Board Secretary of Builder Homesite, Incorporated, a consortium of the nation's premier homebuilders. He has consulted or conducted research in over 40 organizations. His consulting practice, GCM Associates, was established in 1993 and is based in Arlington, Texas.

LIOR OREN received his Ph.D. from Ben-Gurion University of the Negev in Israel and, at present, is a faculty member at Ariel University Center of Samaria and Netanya Academic College. His research achievements in fields of stress and burnout, career and organizational behavior are summarized in a number of publications in peer-reviewed journals.

ALANKRITA PANDEY is a Ph.D. candidate in the Department of Management at the University of Texas at Arlington. She has an M.B.A. from the University of Delhi and an M.S. in Human Resource Management from the University of Texas at Arlington. She teaches undergraduate courses in management process theory and human resource management at the University of Texas at Arlington. Her primary research focus is strategic human resource management with an emphasis on human capital. She has also done some research in downsizing. One of her papers was recently awarded Best Doctoral Paper in the Healthcare and Hospitality Division of the Southern Management Association. Her work has appeared in the *Journal of Management*.

JAMES CAMPBELL QUICK is John and Judy Goolsby – Jacqualyn A. Fouse Endowed Chair, Goolsby Leadership Academy at the University of Texas at Arlington and Honorary Professor, Lancaster University Management School, United Kingdom. Jim is a global leader in executive and occupational health. He was honored with the 2002 Harry and Miriam Levinson Award by the American Psychological Foundation for consulting with senior leaders and executives in creating healthy, more humane work environments. Jim has over 130 publications in ten languages. He is a fellow of the Society for Industrial and Organizational Psychology, American Psychological Association, and American Institute of Stress. UT Arlington honored Jim with a 2009 University Award for Distinguished Record of Research and a 2008 Distinguished Teaching Professorship in the Academy of Distinguished Teachers. Debra Nelson and Jim coauthor a highly acclaimed textbook series, the key title being *Organizational Behavior: Science, the Real World, and You* that is now in the seventh edition (2011). Jim is quoted and interviewed extensively in the print and broadcast media. Colonel Quick, USAFR (Ret.) served by appointment of the US Secretary of Defense on the Defense Health Board from 2008 to 2011. He is married to the former Sheri Grimes Schember.

ELENA A. RADEVA is a Ph.D. student in Management at the University of Texas at Arlington. Elena also earned her master's degree in human resource management from the University of Texas at Arlington. Elena has over ten years of diverse human resource experience and is also certified as a Senior Professional in Human Resources by the Society for Human Resource Management. Her research interests include strategic HR management, international management, organizational culture, organizational downsizing, corporate governance, social capital, and networks.

LISA M. RENZ is a doctoral candidate in organizational leadership at Regent University. She is a Sam M. Walton Free Enterprise Fellow and a Beta Phi Fellow. Lisa serves on Regent University's Board of Advisors for the M.B.A. program. She is an Executive Director for BNI. She was honored by Inside Business as a Top 40 Under 40 in 2009. She has also been honored with a Community Builder Award in 2010. In 2011, she was honored with Business Person of the Year by the Specialist Radio Hour. Lisa has been published in areas regarding entrepreneurship and marketing, and is currently researching the invasion of privacy.

JOHANNES SIEGRIST is Professor of Medical Sociology and Director of the Department of Medical Sociology and of the School of Public Health at the Medical Faculty, University of Düsseldorf/Germany. He has conducted extensive research on the influence of an adverse psychosocial work environment on health, having developed and tested the stress-theoretical model of effort–reward imbalance at work. He has contributed several hundred original publications in international and national scientific journals and books. Journals include *Journal of Occupational Health Psychology*, *Occupational and Environmental*

*Medicine*, *Social Science and Medicine*, *International Archives of Occupational and Environmental Health*, among others. His honors include membership of Academia Europaea, Fellow of the European Academy of Occupational Psychology, and Corresponding Member of the Heidelberg Academy of Sciences. His main research areas are the identification and measurement of health-adverse psychosocial working conditions, the role of work in explaining social inequalities in health, quality of work in older workers, and the impact on socially productive activities on health and well-being of retired people. Moreover, he is involved in policy efforts of improving quality of work and employment at national and international level.

MICHAEL R. STRAIN is a Ph.D. candidate in economics at Cornell University. His academic research is in labor economics, the economics of education, and public policy. He works on the creation of linked employer–employee data with the Center for Economic Studies of the US Census Bureau. He holds a master's degree from New York University, and is a graduate of Marquette University. Prior to coming to Cornell he worked in the research group of the Federal Reserve Bank of New York.

SHAY S. TZAFRIR is a senior lecturer in the Department of Human Services at the University of Haifa. He received his Ph.D. in behavioral science from the Technion – Israel institute of Technology, having also received his M.Sc. in behavioral science from the Technion. He also earned a B.A. in political science, LL.B. as well as an M.A. in political science, all from the University of Haifa. His current research interest includes the role trust plays in various organizational factors, such as strategic human resource management, organizational performance, emotion, and service quality. His articles have been published in journals such as *Industrial Relations*, *Human Resource Management*, *Journal of Organizational and Occupational Psychology*, *International Journal of Human Resource Management*, and others.

AHARON TZINER (Ph.D., Labor Studies, Tel Aviv University) is Full Professor of Management, former Dean of the School of Business Administration, present Dean of the School of Behavioral Sciences, and Vice-rector for Research at Netanya Academic College. He has published 84 refereed articles, three book chapters, and five books in the area of staffing organizations, performance appraisal, work adjustment, structure and performance of groups in organizations, and the financial value of human resource management programs and organizational behavior. He has served as an editorial member of the *Journal of Organizational Behavior* and *Human Resource Management Review* and currently is on the editorial boards of *Academy of Management Learning and Education*, *Economic Amphitheatre Journal (Romania)*, *Review of Work and Organizational Psychology* (Spain), *Canadian Journal of Administrative Sciences* and *IJMSIT*. He is a member of the Academy of Management, APA, IPA, and SIOP. He has been associated with the University of Montreal, the City University of New York, Tel-Aviv University and Bar-Ilan University. He has also held visiting appointments with the State University of New York (at Albany), the University of Minnesota, and Ben-Gurion University.

DOUGLAS WEBBER is a Ph.D. candidate in the Department of Economics at Cornell University. His research focuses on labor market flows, and how competition in the labor market impacts compensation and other employment outcomes. His research utilizes linked employer–employee data compiled by the US Census Bureau. His graduate study has been generously funded by the National Science Foundation.

# *Foreword*

Downsizing has become a fact of life throughout the world. The term downsizing has come to mean terminating employees when the organization is still viable and has work for employees to do. Historically, downsizing white-collar workers was a rare event, and these employees could reasonably expect that if they performed well they would keep their jobs as long as the organization existed. A couple of decades ago that all changed. Now downsizing is common, driven by mergers, acquisitions, recessions, incentive-driven decisions to show a short-term boost in quarterly profits, and ideologically driven market signaling. Downsizing is now done for so many different reasons that shareholders, analysts, employees, and local communities struggle to interpret and understand an organization's downsizing. Even in the public sector, once considered safe from downsizing, employees increasingly find themselves at risk for downsizing, and public-sector managers must make decisions they never expected to make. What is more, downsizing can be a traumatic, life-altering experience for everyone involved. For these reasons, it is probably one of the most important decisions that executives make. In the past few years, scholars have tried to understand this increasingly important phenomenon. Because downsizing has such powerful effects, it cries out for the systematic and dispassionate knowledge that scholarship can bring.

Cary Cooper, Alankrita Pandey, and James Campbell Quick have done an outstanding job of gathering together the leading scholars from a wide variety of disciplines focusing on the behavioral causes and consequences of downsizing. All of the chapters draw on or report carefully designed empirical research that seeks to dig deeper into the consequences of downsizing, and the reasons why executives decide to let employees go. Here readers will learn what drives the decisions to downsize, and the effects of differing ways to do it. A number of chapters address the effects of downsizing on the remaining employees, and its effects on those who have lost their jobs. Here readers will find the best of our current knowledge about downsizing. This book organizes and clarifies what we know about downsizing and is a pioneering contribution to the study of this vital subject. There is something here both for scholars interested in research on downsizing as well as for interested general readers who want to separate fact from ideology on the human and social causes and consequences of downsizing.

Jone L. Pearce
University of California, Irvine

# *Preface*

Cameron (1994) characterized the business strategy of downsizing as the most pervasive yet most understudied phenomenon in the business world. In the ensuing two decades, downsizing has been studied across various disciplines from sociology to economics, from psychology to strategic management, from finance to human resources. Each of these diverse disciplines offers a unique perspective and point of view. Our book aims to reconcile the different points of view towards downsizing by offering a comprehensive set of chapters that capture the entirety of the process, from beginning to end and with consideration of each of the many facets of the process. We have brought together leading business strategists, business practitioners, human resource experts, and psychologists into a single volume, offering the reader 13 chapters.

Datta, Guthrie, Basuil, and Pandey (2010, p. 282) define downsizing as "a planned set of organizational policies and practices aimed at workforce reduction with the goal of improving firm performance." In the book's opening chapter, Hallock, Strain, and Webber survey the job loss literature, thus providing an introduction to the concept of downsizing. Their line of discussion suggests that the employment relationship in the United States has changed over the years. They define the downsizing process even while examining alternatives like work-sharing, to typical mass layoff policies.

Downsizing comcs about through different macro-environmental or external and micro-organizational or internal causes. Cascio's chapter discusses factors such as globalization, workforce demographics, differences in regional labor costs, and industry factors at the external level, as well as firm resources, mergers and acquisitions, governance factors, CEO (chief executive officer) characteristics, and other internal factors such as HR (human resource) practices at the internal level using case studies and research from several countries. Freeman and Ehrhardt's following chapter takes the reader through the direct and indirect antecedents that may cause a firm to downsize. This chapter differentiates between reactive and proactive downsizing. Reactive downsizing has as its internal antecedents unsatisfactory firm performance, strategy, and technology, while its internal antecedents are economic cycles, globalization, and changes in regulatory environments. They describe reactive downsizing to consist of anticipations of market and other changes, streamline processes as a performance strategy, or decentralizing operations. Other factors they describe are: the desire to mimic successful firms, norms of culture or context, or downsizing becoming a practice.

The chapter by McKinley and Lin examines executive cognitions of the process of downsizing to understand how it comes about and diffuses through the organization. Executive power and experience act as moderators to perceptions about the financial effects and inevitability of downsizing. Higher levels of downsizing activity make the phenomenon institutionalized in the organization, which acts as a further influence on the kind of downsizing the organization undertakes.

Since downsizing has a profound impact on the people of the organization – who may be the victims of the downsizing, those who are left after the downsizing, or the managers who undertake the downsizing – it becomes important to consider the human element while discussing the process. McMahan, Pandey, and Martinson develop a strategic human resource management model of the process of downsizing in their chapter. According to them, the organizational-level outcomes happen through individual-level processes. Strategies such as downsizing influence human capital and then performance through the mechanism of employee in-role and targeted extra-role behaviors. Downsizing at the individual level changes perceptions of justice, trust, and commitment, and therefore changes extra-role behaviors. HR practices also play a role in these relationships. Thus, downsizing is a complex process which influences different parts of the organization and has varied impacts.

Still within the human side of the downsizing process, Tziner, Fien, and Oren discuss human motivation outcomes in their chapter related to the process of downsizing. Human needs and values, organizational culture and values, leader member exchange, and job design and fit are all factors influencing human motivation, which is also influenced by the perceptions of justice. Human motivations of individuals lead to self-regulation and outcomes, such as job engagement, citizenship behaviors, and job performance.

At the individual level, downsizing can have extremely negative impacts on health. In their chapter, Siegrist and Dragano state that downsizing acts as a health threat which disrupts habitual living and working conditions for individuals. Drawing on studies in Sweden and the United States, they explain how this threat leads to the development of survivor disease with its adverse health impacts. Burnout and physiological impacts are felt by survivors and victims alike.

In a companion chapter, Hargrove, Cooper, and Quick further explain the stress effects of downsizing on the victims, the survivors, and the manager. Downsizing is stressful to all these groups of people and has lingering impacts on their health and well-being. Perceptions of justice, of support, and how the process of downsizing is managed, all influence these perceptions of stress as do individual attitudes. Stress affects health and also work behaviors.

Downsizing is undertaken to improve financial performance and therefore its financial outcomes are an important consideration, which is the concern of Datta, Basuil, and Radeva in their chapter. They review research on downsizing and divide it into three streams dealing with the immediate market response of stock returns, the longer-term profitability measures of ROA (return on assets), ROE (return on equity), and ROS (return on sales) and the longest term productivity measures of efficiency and employee productivity. They find that these outcomes are moderated by environmental and organizational factors.

De Meuse and Dai's chapter draws on the results of a long-term study to discuss the successes of downsizing with regard to financial outcomes, thus extending the considerations offered by Datta, Basuil, and Radeva in their preceding chapter. They find that downsized firms tend to have lower profit margins and return on assets than similar non-downsized firms. They suggest better management of employees and expectations in order to ameliorate the negative effects.

Downsizing as a phenomenon is here to stay in organizations. Therefore, it becomes important to address the proper management of the process in order to maximize its financial and firm-level outcomes and to reduce the negative people outcomes. DeWitt's chapter discusses considerations such as the firm positioning itself to best leverage its resources and capabilities, retaining its appropriate relationships, managing control mechanisms, and working with key partners as key strategies.

A lot of scholarly work in the area of downsizing has focused on firms in the United States. However, it is a global phenomenon and therefore should be examined as such. The concluding two chapters in the book consider downsizing in this global context. In their chapter, Gandolfi,

Renz, Hansson, and Davenport discuss the global proliferation of downsizing through Australia, Eastern, Central, and Western Europe, Japan, Korea, and the United Kingdom, highlighting similarities and differences between the various phases of the process and its outcomes. In the final chapter, Tzafrir, Ben-Gal, and Dolan develop a multinational multi-factor cross-cultural model to explain how downsizing impacts positive stakeholder behavior. They find that values driving local firms or multinationals at the local or global level influence perceptions of trust in these firms, impacting the way the downsizing is perceived. Culture is a very essential factor in this process.

This overview of the book's 13 chapters provides a glimpse of the depth of content offered by the international team of interdisciplinary scholars and business leaders. By examining the antecedents, causes, and outcomes, the book considers the downsizing process in its entirety and viewed from myriad perspectives. In addition, we look at the business side of the enterprise, focusing on the reasons why firms downsize and the financial and reputational outcomes. We also examine the human side of organizations, emphasizing impacts on individuals and communities after the downsizing has been carried out.

We wish to thank our Cambridge University Press editorial team of Paula Parish and Philip Good for their encouragement and support throughout the development of the book.

Cary L. Cooper
Alankrita Pandey
James Campbell Quick

## References

Cameron, K. S. 1994. "Strategies for successful organizational downsizing." *Human Resource Management Journal* 33: 89–112.

Datta, D. K., Guthrie, J. P., Basuil, D., and Pandey, A. 2010. "Causes and effects of employee downsizing: A review and synthesis." *Journal of Management* 36: 281–348.

# PART I

# *Overview*

# 1 *Job loss and effects on firms and workers*

KEVIN F. HALLOCK, MICHAEL R. STRAIN, AND DOUGLAS WEBBER*

Job loss is painful. There are thousands of individual stories of workers who lose their jobs each year from all parts of the world.[1] A great deal of work across the social sciences examines the causes and consequences of job loss. This chapter addresses a small part of that work and specifically focuses on the effects of job loss on workers (including the effects on subsequent wages and on health) and on the effects of job loss on companies (including short- and longer-run corporate performance). Other questions are also considered, such as whether firms are less committed to workers and workers less committed to firms than they were in the recent past. A variety of data sources are accessed for research on job loss, and consideration is given to the alternatives to job loss and the various public policies adopted in the United States and throughout the world.

To begin, it should be noted that this chapter will not focus on other important issues related to job loss. It will not examine, in significant detail, the effects of international trade or tariffs. The chapter is also not about labor turnover that is initiated by the worker. Voluntary quits and separations are not discussed, nor are firings for cause or strictly for performance.

The chapter examines instances where companies layoff employees (temporarily or permanently, although the focus is on the latter). It examines changes in the displacement of workers over time, reasons for the changes, and the effects on workers and companies. There is also a focus on policies, consideration being given as to whether there can be improvements to what is known and done about job loss, and a discussion of how other countries handle reductions in the demand for labor.

## Introduction, data sources, and roadmap

This section outlines various important data sources for the study of job loss in the United States. It also provides an outline of the rest of the chapter.

*Description of some of the data on job loss*

A wide variety of data sets has been used to examine the causes, consequences, and characteristics of layoffs, some of which are summarized in Table 1.1. One of the most popular data sources is the Current Population Survey (CPS), administered by the Bureau of Labor Statistics (BLS), which is a common source for many labor market statistics. In addition to the survey questions relating to worker displacement in the standard monthly CPS, the BLS also makes available a Displaced Worker Supplement of the CPS, which contains detailed questions specifically tailored to worker displacement. The Displaced Workers Supplement (DWS) of the Current Population Survey (CPS) began in 1984 and is conducted every two years. Examples of the clever use of the survey include Farber (1999, 2005, and 2011).

Another commonly used data set is the Survey of Income and Program Participation (SIPP). Unlike the CPS, the SIPP contains short panels on respondents. For researchers interested in the health-related consequences of layoffs, the Health and Retirement Study (HRS) contains among the most detailed health questions of any data set. Additionally, many of the responses are verified by a doctor to avoid self-reporting bias.

For many questions related to layoffs, it is desirable to have long panels (repeated sampling of the same individuals over many years). One of the most commonly used panel data sets, the National Longitudinal Survey of Youth (NLSY), has two cohorts (beginning in 1979 and 1997) for which there are detailed surveys every other year. Another popular source, the Panel Study of Income Dynamics (PSID), currently follows about 9,000 families. Panel data sources are necessary to answer questions about the long-term impact of layoffs, since they allow repeated questions with respect to job loss, job holding, and income for the same individuals over time. Additionally, they provide researchers with additional statistical modeling choices, such as fixed-effects specifications.

This chapter also discusses some studies conducted using individually collected data. For example, data from Billger and Hallock (2005), Hallock (2009), and Farber and Hallock (2009) include all job loss announcements published in the *Wall Street Journal* for any company ever in the *Fortune* 500 covering the years 1970–2007.

Data sources, which could provide key insights into the long-term consequences of layoffs for both firms and individuals, are linked employer–employee data. In the United States, the Longitudinal Employer Household

**Table 1.1** *Data sources on job loss*

| Source | Sample size | Panel | Details |
|---|---|---|---|
| Current Population Survey | ~60,000 households | Short (1 year) | Monthly survey (March is the most commonly used month because it asks respondents about income). The standard source of US labor market data (e.g., unemployment rate). |
| Displaced Worker Survey | ~60,000 households (All CPS households are given the survey) | Short (1 year) | A supplement to the CPS given every two years. Displacement is defined as follows (via CPS website): "Persons 20 years of age and older who lost or left jobs because their plant or company closed or moved, there was insufficient work for them to do, or their position or shift was abolished." |
| Health and Retirement Survey | ~22,000 individuals | None | Main focus is on health outcomes for persons age 50 and over. Health status verified by doctor. |
| Survey of Income and Program Participation | ~14,000–37,000 households | Medium (2.5–4 years) | Main focus is on federal/state/local income transfer programs. |
| Panel Study of Income Dynamics | ~9,000 households | Long (1968–present) | Began in 1968 with 4,000 families. All descendants of the originally surveyed families are added to the sample. Detailed demographic, human capital, and work history information. |
| National Longitudinal Survey of Youth (1979) | ~13,000 individuals | Long (1979–present) | Respondents were 14–22 in 1979. Detailed demographic, human capital, and work history information. |

**Table 1.1** (*cont.*)

| Source | Sample size | Panel | Details |
|---|---|---|---|
| National Longitudinal Survey of Youth (1997) | ~9,000 individuals | Long (1997–present) | Respondents were 12–16 in 1997. Detailed demographic, human capital, and work history information. |
| Longitudinal Employer Household Dynamics | 98% of private, non-farm employment | Long (1990–present) | Linked employer–employee data. Quarterly observations of earnings and job status. Only basic demographic information is available on workers. |

Dynamics (LEHD) data cover nearly all (98 percent) private US non-farm employment, and allows researchers to follow the employment behavior of workers and firms over time. Some work on mass layoffs has already been conducted using these data (e.g., Abowd, McKinney, and Vilhuber 2009).

## *Definitions of job loss*

One complicating factor in the job loss literature is the degree of subjectivity with which job loss can be defined. From the point of view of the worker, the broadest definition of job loss is any involuntary separation from a job. This rules out voluntary quits, but includes all other job separations. Because workers who are fired for cause are often quite different from the rest of the workforce, the definition of job loss is typically restricted to layoffs.

Other important points are status (full-time/part-time) and how long the worker held the job before being laid off. For instance the DWS distinguishes between workers who are long-tenured (three or more years at the same employer) or short-tenured (less than three years).

The reason for the layoff is also of interest. Many studies restrict their sample to layoffs which result from a plant closure in an attempt to avoid potential selection bias arising from the weakest workers being the first laid off. However, this definition could also suffer from selection bias if the plant closed because the average worker quality was lower than at other plants.

From the perspective of the firm, the definition of a layoff is similarly complicated. The researcher must choose a threshold by which to define a layoff event. This can be done in absolute terms (100 workers laid off) or percentage terms (15 percent of a firm's labor force).

## *Roadmap for the chapter*

This chapter is neither intended to be an exhaustive literature review of all that is known regarding job loss nor an exhaustive literature review of the subset of topics that we choose to discuss. It is intended to be a short description of a few areas, and discussion of some work related to the effects of job loss on workers and on companies over the past several decades. The next section is an overview of job stability in the United States, including an examination of changes in job stability over time and a consideration of whether it may be the case that firms are less committed to workers and workers are less committed to firms than they were in the not-too-distant past. Reasons for and alternatives to layoffs are then discussed in the third section. Work-sharing is extensively examined in the fourth section. The fifth section begins with an examination of the timing of job loss announcements and then goes on to discuss the effects of job loss on workers' subsequent employment and wages as well as the long-term health outcomes. The results, on average, are not good news for workers who lose their jobs. The effects of job loss on companies are discussed in the penultimate section. This includes an analysis of the link between job loss announcements and CEO (chief executive officer) pay and CEO turnover and the short- and longer-run relationships between job loss and organizational performance. Concluding comments and some additional issues are discussed in the final section.

## Job stability in the United States

Is the average worker in the United States with the same employer for fewer years than in the past? An important first issue is whether job stability has actually changed in the United States. If it has, for whom and why? This section will briefly examine this literature with significant emphasis on results from the DWS.

### *Changes in job stability over time*

Henry Farber has written a series of very important papers (including Farber, 2005, 2007, 2008, 2010, and 2011) which clearly and carefully document changes in job stability over time. Some of this work considers whether one can use the DWS to actually identify all relevant job displacement (e.g., Farber, 2010), some examines general trends in job loss in the United States (Farber, 2005) and some investigates the change in long-term worker–firm attachment (Farber, 2007, 2008).

Farber (2005) examines the DWS from 1984 to 2004 and has several important findings. First, more than one-third of job losers are not employed at the next survey date (two years later). Second, about 13 percent of those who lost a full-time job are subsequently holding part-time jobs. Third, on average, those who lose full-time jobs earn about 13 percent less on their new jobs, relative to the previous one. Fourth, he estimates that including the foregone earnings increases experienced by those who did not lose their jobs, those who lose full-time jobs earn on the order of 17 percent less on their new jobs than they would have, had they not been displaced.

As for the interesting question of whether long-term employment has changed in the past decades, Farber (2007, 2008) uses data from the Current Population Survey (CPS) from 1973 to 2006 by birth cohort to examine changes in the length of employment relationships. He finds that both (a) mean tenure and (b) the fraction of workers working at least ten or at least 20 years at the same employer have each fallen,[2] particularly among male workers (as a result of growing commitment of women to the labor force and the fact that longer-term worker–firm relationships among women has, in fact, increased slightly during this period) (see Figures 1.1a and 1.1b). He also finds more of what he calls "churning," or short-term jobs, defined as the fraction of workers whose job seniority is less than one year. He concludes that younger workers are much less likely than older workers to have a long-term job with the same employer.

The growing instability of employment relationships appears to have affected employees at various organization levels, and across industries.[3]

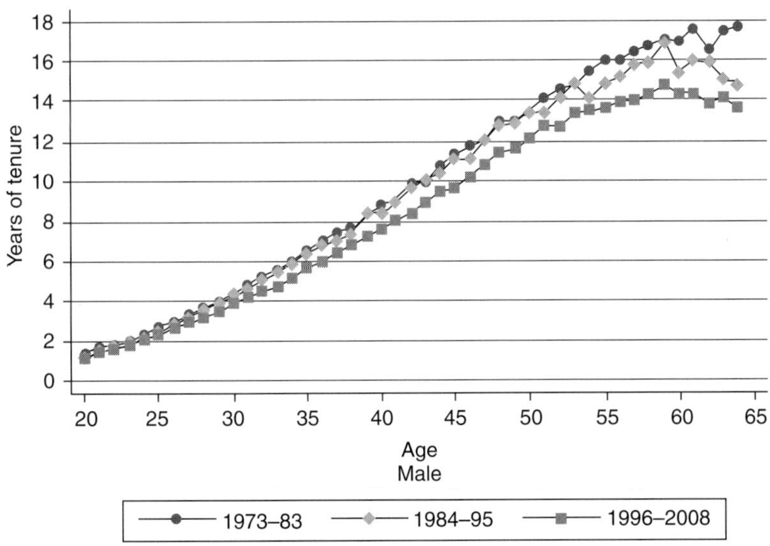


**Figure 1.1a** Mean job tenure by age and year cohort: men

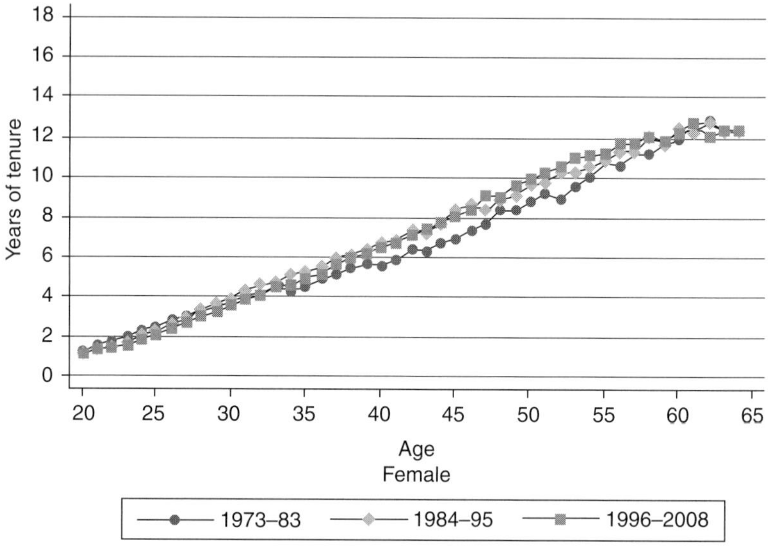


**Figure 1.1b** Mean job tenure by age and year cohort: women

For example, Cappelli (1992) studies managerial displacement. Using the DWS, he finds that, at least during the 1980s, "managers were actually more vulnerable to displacement than were other employees, suffering proportionately greater job loss from efforts to streamline and downsize organizations and from plant closings" (p. 203). Chan and Stevens (2001) consider job loss among older workers. Using the Health and Retirement Study (HRS), they find that, for workers who lose jobs after age 55, the employment rate is 20 percentage points lower than the employment rate of similar workers who were not displaced. Elder (2004) studies this area with the same data sources and provides structural estimates of a dynamic search model. He finds that "simulations indicate that both market opportunities and age-related preferences for leisure are responsible for the observed unemployment durations, but that older workers would still have relatively long post-displacement jobless spells if preferences for leisure did not vary with age."

Given Farber's clear and convincing work, job stability in the United States has clearly changed in recent decades. Long job spells are clearly much less frequent than in the previous generation, although there is some variability by gender. The next section considers reasons for and potential alternatives to layoffs.

## Reasons for and alternatives to layoffs

Why do firms execute layoffs? Are there alternatives to layoffs? Both of these questions are interesting and complicated. To begin, in this section we describe the reported reasons for job loss in more than 5,000 individual layoff events over the past 38 years (also see Hallock, 2009). In the subsection that follows, we discuss a variety of alternatives to layoffs. There also appears to be diversity in the kinds of political pressure, social sanctions, and direct economic costs to employers across countries.

### *Changes in stated (by firms) reasons for job loss*

In the past four decades, there has been a quite substantial change in the *reported* reasons for job loss. Using a sample frame that included all firms that were *ever* in the *Fortune* 500 between 1970 and 2007, data on each job loss announcement described in the *Wall Street Journal* Index were recorded. For these 5,353 instances, the complete *Wall Street Journal* article was then read and a variety of information was collected. This information includes the primary, secondary, and tertiary reasons for the layoff, the number of workers affected, and whether white- or blue-collar workers were included.[4]

Table 1.2 lists 18 reason categories for the job loss announcements. The table is arranged, for each "reason," in the following way: the first column shows data for all years, and the subsequent four columns relate to specific decades, 1970s, 1980s, 1990s, and 2000–2007. Clearly, the category "demand slump" is most frequent overall, and for each decade. However, there is a substantial amount of variation over time. To see this more clearly, in Figure 1.2 the "reasons" are grouped into six general categories: "reorganization" (reorganization, restructuring, and in-house merger), "plant closing" (leave market and plant closing), "slump in demand" (demand slump, excess supply, and structural), "cost issues" (cost control, posting losses, increase earnings, and restore profitability), "other" (increased competition, merger, bankruptcy, strike, and other), and "missing." While these groupings are, in some sense, arbitrary and other choices for groupings can easily be made, some dramatic changes over time are clearly visible in Figure 1.2. Note the scale is the same in each sub-figure, except for "slump in demand." The "slump in demand" category follows the business cycle quite closely with spikes around the times of the recessions in the early

Table 1.2 *Distribution of reasons for job loss announcements over time*

| | All years | 1970–1979 | 1980–1989 | 1990–1999 | 2000–2007 |
|---|---|---|---|---|---|
| Reorganization | 503 | 116 | 127 | 173 | 87 |
| Restructuring | 315 | 37 | 96 | 143 | 39 |
| Cost control | 619 | 103 | 162 | 222 | 132 |
| Slump in demand | 1,855 | 568 | 588 | 365 | 334 |
| Increased competition | 99 | 20 | 20 | 45 | 14 |
| Merger | 130 | 8 | 29 | 49 | 44 |
| Restore profitability | 71 | 16 | 16 | 16 | 23 |
| Bankruptcy | 40 | 2 | 8 | | 30 |
| Leaving market | 134 | 54 | 32 | 27 | 21 |
| In-house merger | 11 | 0 | 3 | 4 | 4 |
| Posting losses | 259 | 107 | 97 | 41 | 14 |
| Plant closing | 303 | 66 | 84 | 71 | 82 |
| Increase earnings | 28 | 5 | 4 | 13 | 6 |
| Excess supply | 340 | 148 | 160 | 24 | 8 |
| Structural | 30 | 13 | 9 | 8 | 0 |
| Strike | 200 | 134 | 47 | 19 | 0 |
| Other | 305 | 145 | 95 | 45 | 20 |
| Missing | 111 | 37 | 38 | 32 | 4 |

*Source*: Calculations by the authors using announcement information from the *Wall Street Journal* and data stock price data from the Center for Research in Security Prices (CRSP).

1980s and 1990s and during the end of the high-tech "bubble." It is also interesting to note that job loss announcements categorized as being due to "reorganization" have changed quite a bit as a fraction of all announcements. Announcements due to "reorganization" became progressively more prevalent during the 1980s and 1990s, when some have argued that Wall Street wanted firms to get "lean" and encouraged firms to shrink employment (more on this below). However, the number of announcements categorized as "reorganization" dropped quite a bit in the early 2000s.

One might wonder about the quality of these "reported reasons" data. After all, the information likely came from a press release, to a reporter, and then to a researcher. In order to consider the quality of the

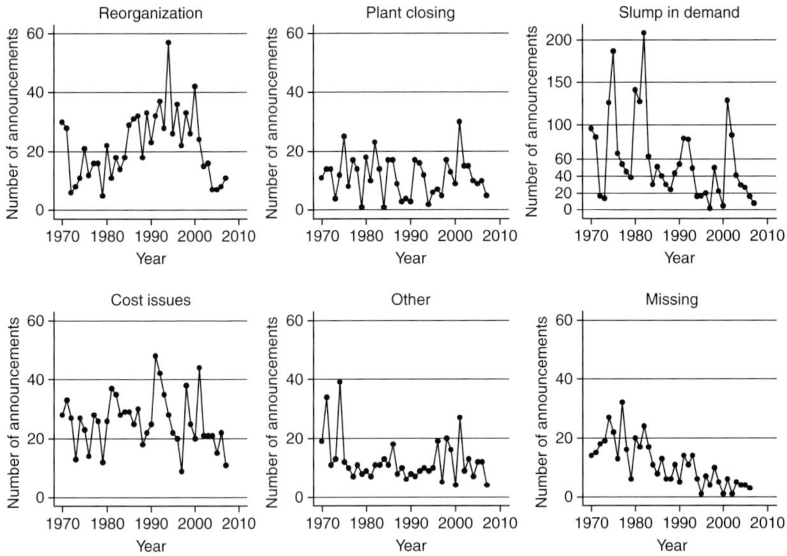


**Figure 1.2** Distribution of stated reasons for announced job loss over time

"reasons" data culled from newspaper accounts, 40 senior managers were interviewed about how they felt about the accuracy of the reasons stated in the *Wall Street Journal* in relation to the actual reasons for job loss. Many of their responses were interesting. Some felt that the reasons found in the paper were not very related to the actual reason for the announcement:[5]

No. I don't believe them. Most of it seems to be management screw-ups. (Senior Manager, Nondurable Goods Manufacturing)

Businesses absolutely manipulate the reasons in the *Wall Street Journal*. But don't necessarily put a negative connotation on this word. You do everything you can to message ... In the last year, there was almost no negative connotation of layoffs. Firms can make massive layoffs with almost no repercussions. (CEO, High Tech)

Every meeting we go to, we talk about a layoff or a downsizing, whatever the [expletive deleted] you want to call it ... Why does the CEO get any satisfaction from using the words we are compressing the size of company? Nobody ever wants to tell the truth. (Senior Manager, Durable Goods Manufacturing)

Should I have any confidence about what is said? No. Audiences are different. The *Wall Street Journal* is speaking to potential investors so the spin is to make opportunities to buy the company stock. (Senior Manager, Durable Goods Manufacturing)

No. Rarely. There is so much corporate speak[6] ... It is all spun because the constituency is the current workforce, shareholders, consumers. (Senior Manager, Nondurable Goods Manufacturing)

They won't admit poor judgment. Some truth, but it doesn't include we screwed up. (Senior Manager, Wholesale Trade)

On the other hand, most respondents felt that the articles reported in the *Wall Street Journal* were not false but that some type of "spin" was put on them:

I never feel that the stated reasons are lies or incorrect. But I do feel that they are never complete ... The PR guy's job is to describe that the glass is half full. (Senior Manager, High Tech)

I think the companies are trying to collectively manage their image and investor confidence. I think they spin the information. I always wonder what is really happening. That is the job of the reporter. I rarely think the company is lying. They just need to put the best light on it. (Senior Manager, High Tech)

Firms might take the most glamorous reason ... We would have a PR agency involved in layoffs and would craft that into what the market wanted to hear ... As with all – layoffs are a scapegoat for poor performance. Weak managers. (Senior Manager, High Tech)

Well, I think as positive sounding as we can. We try to frame it in a positive light. It is a sad story. We try to emphasize that we are trying to do right by the employees. (CFO, High Tech)

Probably not accurately. We spin it a certain way and they take it from there ... They accurately portrayed specific pieces. They spin it to make news. (Senior Manager, High Tech)

I guess, reasonably confident, that what is in the *Wall Street Journal* tells about 80 percent of the story; possibly ... Typically what you see is all true. There just may be additional details. (Senior Manager, Agriculture)

### *Alternatives to layoffs*

There are several potential alternatives to layoffs. In this section, I will discuss many of them, including wage cuts, "voluntary" time off, paid sabbaticals and work outside the firm, early retirement, and voluntary work-sharing. There is a long literature on the tradeoff between job loss and cuts in wages (see for example Bewley, 1999, who asks *Why Wages Don't Fall During a Recession?*). One option for avoiding layoffs is to cut wages. Rather than cut 10 percent of the workforce, a company could cut 10 percent from the pool of compensation, across-the-board or otherwise. This may be a viable alternative for some organizations, but it is difficult to tell at what point this would have to stop. Some companies argue that they would rather have a smaller number of fully employed staff than a higher number of staff who are not working full time and who are, therefore, upset about potential lower earnings. Some organizations have turned to temporary help agencies and outsourcing as a way to help buffer the cyclical effects of employment demand at their firms (Autor, 2003). One question is whether these are "good" jobs.

Some specific companies have tried to make attempts at alternatives to layoffs, but even these are not always sustainable. An example described in Cascio (2002) is Charles Schwab and Company, who in 2001 found their commission revenue 57 percent below a year earlier. The company tried many alternatives to layoffs: (1) delaying projects and cutting expenses such as travel and entertainment, (2) senior executives taking pay cuts,[7] (3) encouraging employees to take unused vacations and take unpaid leaves, and (4) designating certain Fridays as "voluntary" days off. In the end, the company did have to make layoffs to 2,000 of 25,000 employees, but provided generous severance.

Cisco Systems is another example described in Cascio (2002). Cisco understood the value of goodwill and the importance of treating employees who were laid off well. When Cisco cut its workforce from 38,000 to 30,500, it tried a program of paying employees one-third of their salaries and "lending" them to nonprofits for a year. This was a way for the company to keep in contact with employees in the hope of avoiding retraining costs when demand increased. Cisco made a "Great Places to Work" list during this period.

In a related case, Accenture cut 600 support staff in June 2001, but, for some staff, the company instituted partially paid sabbaticals where the firm paid 20 percent of salary and all benefits, and the employees could keep laptops, an office phone number, and e-mail. Roughly 1,000 workers took this option (Cascio, 2002).

Many universities recently are offering some staff "early retirement" incentives. In March 2009, Cornell University offered non-faculty staff, who were age 55 or older and had worked for the university for at least ten years, one year's salary plus an additional 30 percent of a year's pension contribution to retire by June. More than 400 people took the early retirement option and left the university by June 2009.

Some, including Gordon (1996), have argued for "substituting compensatory time as an alternative to time-and-a-half for overtime – meaning that workers would be able to work less some other day if they worked extra hours today" (p. 247).

Oaklander (2003) is an interesting case study of a company called Dynabil Industries, which in 2001 had 130 employees. After an "all hands meeting" called by the General Manager to discuss business performance and projection, all 130 employees filled out a questionnaire that asked them "how many days per quarter they could absent themselves from work without pay, and to do so – or not do so – completely voluntarily" (Oaklander, 2003, p. 7). They were further told their responses were non-binding. About one-third said they could not sacrifice a day. In one of the 12 blue-collar units, everyone volunteered. The fraction who did not volunteer varied from 16 percent to 75 percent by unit. Ten percent of women and 24 percent of men were willing to take more than ten days off. In all, 81 workers agreed to participate and a layoff was averted. It is not at all clear whether this could work elsewhere or whether it would work again in the same organization at some other time.

For some 60 years, Lincoln Electric has maintained a policy of guaranteed continuous employment – no permanent US employee has been laid off for "lack of work." For Lincoln Electric, employee layoffs are not just a last resort, the option is not even put on the table for discussion. Instead, merit-based bonus pay, mandatory hours reductions, and nimble project assignment are all among the tools that Lincoln Electric's leadership draws on when it needs to respond to business cycles turning south (see Koller, 2010).

Even companies with long-histories of "no layoff" policies have faced job loss.[8] An anecdote may show that it is possible to see how quickly companies turn from a strong "no layoff" or "shared sacrifice" mentality to one entirely different. One of us visited a high-tech company with roughly 1,000 workers in 2001, right after their first job loss. There were discussions of extraordinary anguish and difficulty – including the CEO crying while telling part of his workforce that they would have to go. He visited the headquarters of the same organization about six months later, when they were beginning a new round of layoffs. The senior staff had an entirely different view – and described the situation in stark, economic terms. They said that if the next round of cuts were not made, the entire company would go under. The emotion in the job loss seemed to be almost entirely gone.

## Work-sharing

Work-sharing is an alternative to layoffs and merits detailed discussion. It can be thought of as the redistribution of labor hours among people with the goal of reducing involuntary unemployment. As an example, consider a firm where all workers earn the same salary. The firm falls on hard times and needs to reduce its payroll by 20 percent. One way to do this is to layoff 20 percent of its workforce. Under a work-sharing arrangement, however, the firm can instead cut the hours of *every* worker by 20 percent – for example, by telling workers to stay home on Fridays. This way, no worker loses his or her job, and the firm does not have to incur the costs of the layoff and of hiring and training when demand increases.

Under this arrangement, workers are losing money. Governments can supplement this lost income under programs known as short-time compensation (STC) where workers receive a prorated amount of unemployment insurance benefits to cover the reduction in pay associated with lost hours. For example, Reid (1982) studies an experimental Canadian program put in place in 1977 which resulted in layoffs being avoided in 24 firms. Instead of laying off a portion of their workforce, these firms reduced the hours of *all* employees, and the experimental program allowed the workers to receive unemployment insurance (UI) benefits for the day or so each week they were not working. Reid concludes that most workers favored the plan because they received, in the typical case, an extra day off per week at the cost of a 5 percent of their after-tax income,[9] and that employers favored the plan because they avoided the costs associated with layoffs.

These programs exist in 17 US states, though they are seldom used. MacCurdy, Pearce, and Kihlthau (2004) point out, for example, that less than 1 percent of California companies with UI claims participated in an STC program. Among the reasons they suggest for the low take-up rate are that workers may not want STC since it "imposes reductions in pay that can be avoided by acquiring alternative full-time" employment.

Such work-sharing unemployment insurance (WSUI) plans are relatively much more popular overseas, and can be found in Austria, Belgium,

Canada, the Czech Republic, Denmark, Finland, France, Germany, Hungary, Ireland, Italy, Japan, Luxembourg, the Netherlands, New Zealand, Norway, Poland, Portugal, the Slovak Republic, Spain, Switzerland, and Turkey (Hijzen and Venn, 2011).

What is one possible explanation for the cross-country variance in the use of work-sharing? Van Audenrode (1994) builds an implicit contract model with unemployment insurance to study the relationship between STC and hours flexibility. He shows that STC has to be relatively more generous than traditional UI systems in order to get workers to accept variable hours. Studying ten OECD countries, the evidence supports his model. He finds that in countries with the most generous STC programs hours respond quickly to changes in the need for labor. He concludes that overall labor adjustments in these countries are as flexible as in the United States because hours adjustments compensate for firing restrictions. He suggests that the failure of STC programs in the United States and Canada is caused by the fact that these programs were insufficiently generous.

In the remainder of this section on work-sharing, we will discuss three issues. The first is a general description of work-sharing plans. The second is the effect of work-sharing on employment. The third is the role of work-sharing in the 2008–2009 recession, with a detailed discussion of the features of current work-sharing programs in OECD countries.

## *Varieties of work-sharing*

The goal of work-sharing from a social perspective is that it might be able to reduce the number of workers who are involuntarily unemployed. This goal can be pursued under a number of different work-sharing programs. Dreze, Persson, and Miller (1986) present a work-sharing taxonomy consisting of three parts: (1) trading jobs, (2) sharing jobs, and (3) trading hours for jobs.

Perhaps the most common form of trading jobs is early retirement plans. The United Kingdom introduced such a program in 1976, allowing older workers to leave their jobs early and to receive an allowance from the government until the age of normal retirement, provided that their employer replaces them with an unemployed worker. This program was considered to be quite successful. Belgium offered a similar program starting in the late 1970s, but required that the replacement worker be an unemployed person under the age of 30. France offered a similar program around that time. Studying these and other early retirement programs, Dreze *et al.* (1986) offer two conclusions. The first is that the mandatory replacement provision is necessary to achieve job creation. The second is that these programs should be popular with older workers, provided that the rate of income replacement is high enough.

Dreze *et al.* (1986) examine early retirement on a part-time basis – progressive retirement – as a type of job sharing. In 1982, the United Kingdom introduced a policy where a worker could retire early on a half-time basis, with the other half of the worker's hours being picked up by an unemployed person. In 1983, the French adopted a similar program. Both programs were extremely unsuccessful. In the United Kingdom, for example, after 12 months of operation the program covered only 578 jobs.

By trading hours for jobs, Dreze *et al.* (1986) mean a statutory decrease in the number of hours per week worked by workers, with the goal of increasing the number of employed persons. Belgium and France experimented with such policies in the late 1970s and early 1980s with little success. With the exception of firms operating on a continuous basis with multiple shifts, policies which decreased hours per week *without* mandatory new hiring did not lead to a short-run reduction in unemployment. The authors conclude that early retirement with mandatory replacement is the most promising short-run approach to work-sharing.

## *Effect of work-sharing on employment*

On the surface, it seems that the effect of work-sharing on employment would be unambiguous: work spread over more people would result in higher employment. But is this the case?

The Canadian province of Quebec gradually decreased its statutory standard workweek for hourly wage non-union workers from 44 hours to 40 hours over a period of three years, starting in 1997. The goal of this policy change was to incentivize firms to hire more workers – prior to the policy change, a Quebec firm would have to start paying time-and-a-half at 45 hours, but after the policy change time-and-a-half pay would begin at 41 hours. Notably, the policy change did not include a requirement that Quebec firms increase the wages of current workers in order to compensate them for their lost hours. Skuterud (2007) studies the effects of this policy change, and finds that it was associated with a 20 percent reduction in weekly hours worked beyond 40. However, the policy did *not* lead to an increase in employment, either at the province or industry levels.

Given this evidence, where does the intuition break down? Work-sharing will *necessarily* increase employment if the amount of work that needs to be done is fixed. But this assumes that the amount of work needed to be done *is* fixed. Hunt and Katz (1998) challenge this assumption. Suppose that, as Skuterud (2007) describes, a policy were enacted which reduced the standard hours per week of work. If this implies an increase in the marginal cost of production at the pre-policy-change level of output, then optimal output will fall, and with it the demand for labor. In addition, this will be reinforced by the substitution effect – firms will substitute away from the now-more-costly input, labor, and towards capital. Thus, both hours and employment could actually *fall*, much less rise, due to work-sharing.

There is evidence that something like this happened in Germany. Beginning in 1985, West German unions began to reduce the standard workweek – the maximum number of hours per week which do not require overtime pay – in an effort to reduce the number of unemployed workers. Using industry-level data and cross-industry variation in standard hours reductions, Hunt (1999) finds that work-sharing may have reduced employment in the period 1984–1994.

The goal of increasing employment is especially important during a recession. We now turn to the effects of work-sharing on employment in such a macro-economic environment.

## *Work-sharing and the 2008–2009 downturn*[10]

Hijzen and Venn (2011) study the effect of short-time work schemes on employment and average hours of OECD countries during the 2008–2009 recession. They conclude that work-sharing prevented many workers from joining the ranks of the unemployed, particularly in Germany and Japan.

Twenty-two OECD countries either set up new short-time measures or adjusted existing measures in response to the recession. In Belgium, Turkey, Italy, Germany, and Japan – the OECD countries with the highest take-up – between 3 and 6 percent of all employees in 2009 participated in a short-time program. Across countries, the goods producing and construction sectors had the highest take-up rates at the end of the last decade, while financial, business, social, and personal services had the lowest. Most OECD countries had a work-sharing UI system in place prior to the recession – new programs were introduced in Poland, the Netherlands, Hungary, the Czech Republic, the Slovak Republic, Mexico, and New Zealand.

The main features of these programs are work-sharing requirements, eligibility requirements, conditionality requirements, and generosity. There is intercountry variation across all these dimensions.

Work-sharing requirements specify the range of hours reduction required for STC eligibility. Austria, Canada, Denmark, Finland, Germany, Hungary, Ireland, Korea, the Netherlands, Norway, the Slovak Republic, Spain, Switzerland, Turkey, and the United States all have a minimum permissible reduction in weekly working hours for short-time workers. The Slovak Republic's requirement is a mere 4 percent, while Denmark, Ireland, and Norway all require hours reduction of 40 percent. The majority of countries allow a maximum hours reduction of 100 percent – that is, a temporary layoff.

Eligibility requirements set conditions on firms and workers. For example, of the 24 OECD countries studied by Hijzen and Venn (2011), every country except Denmark, Ireland, the Netherlands, and New Zealand require that firms provide justification of economic need in order for their workers to receive short-time compensation. Explicit agreements between workers and firms are often required. Some countries require that the participating worker be eligible for standard unemployment insurance benefits. Conditionality requirements are relatively less common. Examples include compulsory training for the worker, firm commitments not to fire workers receiving short-time compensation, and job-search requirements for the worker.

A natural measure of the generosity of a work-sharing UI program is the ratio of the income a STC worker receives to his normal income. There is variance in this measure within countries due to the minimum and maximum hours reductions discussed previously. In France and Korea, a worker can receive 100 percent of her normal wage under STC. The lowest ratio is about 0.3, and is found in Ireland. Apart from Ireland and Poland, this ratio is larger than 0.6 for all countries. Workers in 18 countries can enjoy a ratio of over 0.9, given a certain hours reduction.

It is interesting to compare within-country ratio of UI income to normal income under STC and the same ratio under a standard UI program. In almost every country, a worker receives more money under STC than the standard unemployment benefit. Portugal is the only country where the standard UI benefit exceeds the work-sharing benefit, but even there the UI benefit is only greater when hours have been reduced by more than 55 percent.

An additional component of generosity is the length of time a worker can receive short-time compensation. The median length of time across these countries is 12 months. Finland has no limit. As of 2009, Japan has the second longest duration, at 28 months. Five countries have a maximum duration of two years. Eight countries have a maximum duration of less than ten months. The responsiveness of the maximum duration to the recession is often striking. Turkey, for example, more than tripled its maximum duration, from less than four months pre-recession to 12 in 2009. Most dramatically, Austria went from a maximum duration of three months to a maximum duration of 24 months.

To identify the effect of short-time compensation, Hijzen and Venn (2011) employ a differences-in-differences estimation strategy, using variation in labor-adjustment patterns and in the intensity of use of STC across countries and time. They conclude that STC had an important impact on job preservation during the recession, particularly in Germany and Japan.

## What are the effects of job loss on workers?

Given that job loss is so widespread, it is important to understand the effects of job loss on individuals and families. For public policy reasons, it is particularly important to understand the size of the effects. If, post-job-loss, workers quickly find new jobs, have wages and benefits near the same level, and have no longer-term negative effects on themselves or their families, then we might think differently about job loss than if there were ill effects from job loss. Uchitelle and Kleinfield (1996) and Uchitelle (2006) describe interesting and moving personal stories of those who have lost jobs. The rest of this section uses larger data sets (including administrative data) to describe effects on subsequent work and wages, and on happiness and health. The next subsection begins with a description of the timing of job loss.

### *Timing of job loss announcements*

It is interesting to consider whether firms manipulate the timing of announcements to their advantage and whether the timing of

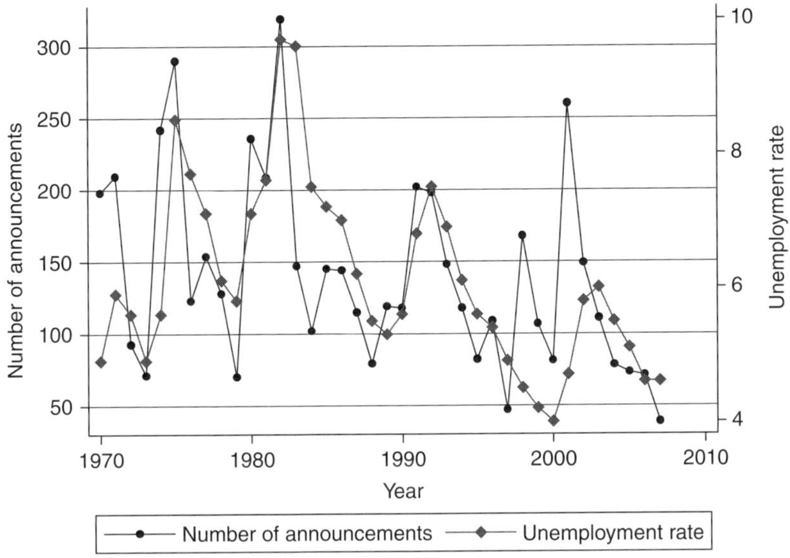


**Figure 1.3** Number of layoff announcements and unemployment rate, by year

announcements has changed over time. Figure 1.3 shows the distribution of job loss announcements by any firm ever in the *Fortune* 500 for each of the 38 years from 1970 to 2007. The number of job loss announcements tracks the unemployment rate quite closely, except for the first two years in the sample and, for some reason, for the five years around the year 2000. Note that these are announcements, and are not weighted by the number of people in the announcement. Nevertheless, it is remarkable that the two series track each other so well.

Given that we know something about the frequency of job loss announcements over time, it is interesting to consider whether companies have an incentive to manipulate the timing of announcements.[11] Yermack (1997) provides evidence that senior managers may manipulate the timing of the release of news in their companies for their own benefit. He argues they do this, in particular, to game stock options. In interviews with a set of 40 senior managers in companies, Hallock (2006) investigated whether there might be manipulation of the timing of announcements. It is surprising that so many admitted such manipulation of timing:

I've never been a part of something like that but I would assume there is potential to do it. I imagine you time it just right to drive the stock price. I think firms game options. (Senior Manager, High Tech)

Yes. There are discussions like that. Our quarterly earnings release and conversation with analysts is day $x$ so the announcement is day $x + 1$. (Vice President, Agriculture)

People see patterns of announcements depending on the timing [of options]. (Senior Manager, Nondurable Goods Manufacturing)

At the same time, there were other managers who found the idea of manipulating timing deplorable:

No gaming. [Layoffs] can be absolutely devastating. One woman was lying on my floor screaming and crying. (Senior Manager, Nondurable Goods Manufacturing)

You make them when you have to make them. There has to be a catalyst event. It is a human decision. It is hard. We cut [a large percentage] of employees ... It is deplorable to manipulate for short-term financial gain. (CEO, Mining)

It was interesting to see that some managers felt that they could be flexible in when they made layoff announcements. They mentioned that if the firm was having a terrible year, then they could "take a bath" and let workers go before the end of the fiscal year. This was so they could begin the new year with a "clean slate."

Our fiscal year starts on [*X*] of each year. We may make sure that all employees are out for the end of the fiscal year so we can have everyone out and lower costs for the next year. (Senior Manager, Durable Goods Manufacturing)

Fiscal year? I don't know. This business of taking a one-time charge. In [*X*] or the first weeks of [*Y*]. You report 2000 results plus exceptional one-time charge for severance and then you go into next year clean. (Vice President, Durable Goods Manufacturing)

A few managers noted that they did not want to let workers go near "the holidays."

No one wants to do it at Thanksgiving or Christmas. (Senior Manager, High Tech)

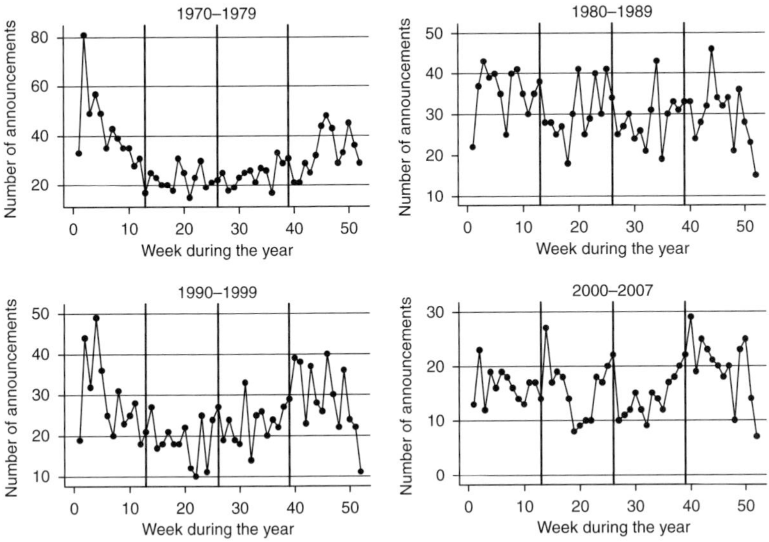


**Figure 1.4** Frequency of announced layoffs by week in the year

There is always a year-end crisis . . . So take the charge at the end of the year to make next year get better. Is that appropriate to be laying people off around the holidays? (Senior Manager, Nondurable Goods Manufacturing)

We didn't want to have layoffs in December for emotional reasons, not financial . . . We don't want to lay people off at Christmas. That just [expletive deleted]. (Senior Manager, High Tech)

This leads one to consider whether the timing of announcements during the year varies over time. Figure 1.4 shows the distribution of when the announcements occurred during the year, by decade. The period from 1970 to 1979 and the period from 2000 to 2007 are quite different in this regard. Notice that the figure for the 1970s has an "inverted U" shape; that is, there is a spike in announcements early in the year and another run-up in the final weeks of the year. The period from 2000 to 2007, on the other hand, appears "flatter"; that is, announcements seem to be timed more evenly throughout the year. This is consistent with the idea that layoff announcements are potentially more routine now than they were in the past. Figure 1.5 shows the distribution of the day of the week the layoff announcements appeared in the *Wall Street Journal*, by decade. The period from 2000 to 2007 is strikingly different from the other

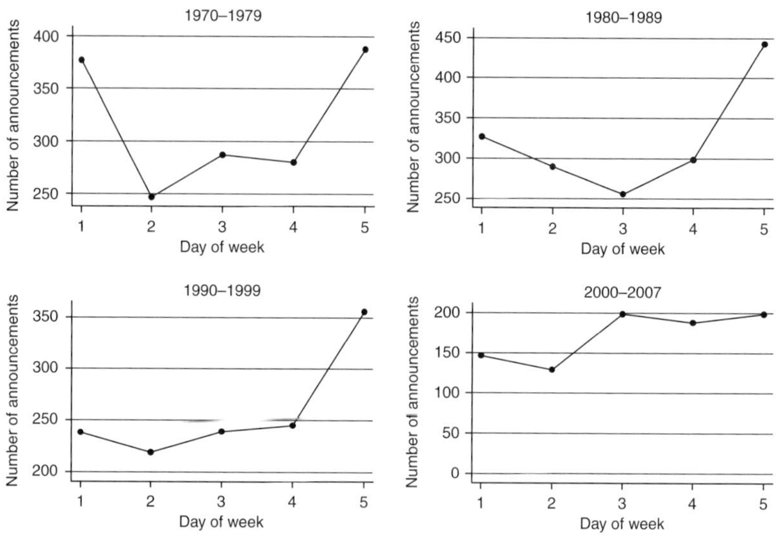


**Figure 1.5** Frequency of job loss announcements by day of week they appeared in the *Wall Street Journal*

periods in that the announcements are as likely to appear on any day of the week. This is in striking contrast to previous decades.

## *Effects on subsequent work and wages*

Important considerations when workers lose jobs are how quickly they find new ones, and do the new jobs have similar compensation and benefits. A large body of literature documents the large and long-lasting negative effects of job loss on workers' subsequent employment and earnings.

In the seminal paper on the issue of earnings losses after displacement, Jacobson, LaLonde, and Sullivan (1993) use administrative data from Pennsylvania during 1974–1986 on workers' earnings histories with details about their companies to consider the magnitude and the time pattern of wages for displaced workers. The administrative data are a very large sample, which allows the authors to apply techniques from the program evaluation literature. The authors find that high-tenured workers leaving "distressed" firms suffer long-term losses on the order of 25 percent of their wages. Interestingly, they also find that, on average, wage losses begin before workers lose their jobs, depend on local labor market conditions and industries, and are significant even in cases where workers find jobs in similar companies.

In a follow-up to Jacobson *et al.* (1993), Couch and Placzek (2008) perform a very similar analysis for a different state (Connecticut) and for a more recent time period. While their results are somewhat similar, there are some interesting differences. While Jacobson *et al.* (1993) find long-term (six years post-displacement) effects of 25 percent lower earnings, Couch and Placzek (2008) estimate effects of 13–15 percent. Couch and Placzek (2008) find immediate effects of about 33 percent and Jacobson *et al.* (1993) estimate immediate effects on the order of 40 percent. Couch and Placzek (2008) argue that the larger effects estimated in Pennsylvania are due to the fact that there was a very high fraction of unemployment insurance recipients in Pennsylvania during the time of that study.[12]

A host of other papers estimate earnings losses following displacement using a variety of sources, including the DWS (e.g., Topel, 1990; Farber, 1997; Carrington, 1993; Neal, 1995), the Panel Study of Income Dynamics (PSID) (e.g., Ruhm, 1991; Stevens, 1997), the Health and Retirement Study (HRS) (e.g., Couch, 1998; Chan and Stevens, 2004), and the National Longitudinal Survey of Youth (NLSY) (e.g., Fairlie and Kletzer, 2003). In general, these studies find smaller negative effects on wages post-displacement than administrative studies. Given the potential biases from survey data, this is an interesting finding. Von Wachter, Hildreth, and Handwerker (2009) try to reconcile differences between the administrative and survey results using a unique match of the Displaced Worker Supplement (DWS)[13] and administrative records in California. When they use a common method to account for measurement error in survey wages that are correlated with demographics of workers, they find earnings estimates are similar across the two data sources.

Some authors have taken a different approach to considering effects of job loss on wages. Two examples are Stevens (1997) and Hanner (2005). Using the PSID, Stevens finds that much of the persistence in the effects of negative earnings losses post-displacement is due to additional job losses in the years following the initial displacement. Hanner (2005) examines the effects of job loss on the distribution of earnings using, among other methods, quantile regression. He finds that, in his sample, while mean earnings fall by 22 percent, the 5th percentile of income falls 45 percent, and a significant number of workers experience gains following displacement.

In a more recent paper, Von Wachter, Song, and Manchester (2007) investigate very long effects of displacement during the early 1980s recession on earnings using administrative data from 1974 through 2004. They find that workers who permanently left an employer between 1980 and 1995, for which they had worked a long time, had very large and continuing earnings losses as many as 20 years later. They attribute the losses to reductions in employment and in pay for those who continue to work.

## *Effects on happiness and health*

Independent of the issue of earnings losses following displacement is the important issue of the effects of job loss on health and happiness of those who are displaced from work. There is a rich literature in applied psychology on the effects of job loss on the "survivors" of layoffs[14] that we will not cover in this chapter. More recent work by economists (and others) is focusing on the effects of job loss on health, both physical and emotional, for displaced workers.

Much of the work in the area finds the overall health of displaced workers may be substantially compromised as a result of job loss. Two papers have alternative findings to this. With a provocative title, Ruhm (2000) asks "Are recessions good for your health?" He concludes the paper by stating, among other things, "Surprisingly the answer appears to be yes" (p. 647). Primarily relying on fixed-effects models with US states as the unit of observation, Ruhm (2000) finds that total mortality and eight of his ten sources of mortality move with the business cycle.[15] Another study finds no negative effects on stress following job loss. Browning, Dano, and Heinesen (2006) study men in Denmark from 1981 to 1999 and find no evidence that being displaced from a job is related to being hospitalized for a stress-related disease.

Given the potential problems with using state-level data to consider these sorts of questions, Sullivan and Von Wachter (2007, 2009) consider similar issues and study the relationship between job loss, career outcomes, and mortality for individuals using administrative data.

They match quarterly earnings and employment records to death certificates and find that job displacement leads to a 15–20 percent increase in death rates during the subsequent 20 years. They calculate that if this rate continued beyond the estimation period, this would translate into a loss in life expectancy for someone at age 40 of 1.5 years! They go on to suggest that "factors correlated with a decrease in mean earnings and a rise in the standard deviation of earnings have the potential to explain an important fraction of the effect of displacement on mortality" (Sullivan and Von Wachter, 2007, p. 1). Additionally, Dooley, Catalano, and Wilson (1994) use individual panel data and find an increase in depression following job loss.

The effects on workers, from loss of earnings to potentially serious health outcomes, are substantial. If outcomes for workers are negative, and there is significant evidence that they are, it is important to consider the potential effects on companies. This is the subject of the next section.

## What are the effects of job loss on firms?

Many authors carefully document trends in worker attachment and job loss (e.g., Farber, 2008, 2010), the personal stories of displaced workers (e.g., Uchitelle, 2006), or the effects of job loss on workers' subsequent outcomes, including earnings (e.g., Jacobson *et al.*, 1993) and health (e.g., Sullivan and Von Wachter, 2009). While these studies are critically important to understanding the effects of job loss on workers, a distinct literature has been building more recently that aims to consider the effects of job loss on *firms*. In the first instance, it would seem reasonable that firms let workers go because it is in the best interest of the firm (or the firm, obviously, would not have done it).[16] However, what would we think if, upon further investigation, we found that job loss is bad for workers and their families, and it is bad for firms? This section aims to investigate the effects of job loss on companies. The effects include the outcomes for CEOs, for short-run stock prices, for company stock prices and viability in the longer run, and for productivity. Most of the analysis is necessarily confined to publicly traded companies in the United States.

### *The effect of mass layoffs on CEO pay*

There is a massive literature on executive compensation in the United States that may have been driven, in part, by access to data. Much of this work is focused on the extremely important goal of determining the link between the pay of the company CEO and the performance of the firm (e.g., Murphy, 1985). The aim of this section is to consider another potential correlate of CEO pay – job loss. Starting in the middle of the 1990s, the popular press (Cappelli, 2005) and some policy groups (Anderson and Cavanagh, 1994) became very interested in the relationship between job loss in companies and executive compensation – do executives profit at the same time (or in the wake of) their employees are losing their jobs?

Hallock (1998) investigates the relationship between the compensation of CEOs of companies and whether those companies lay off workers. The paper uses data from three main sources. First, is the CEO compensation data collected from *Forbes Magazine*'s annual CEO compensation issues.[17] Three measures of compensation examined in the paper are salary plus bonus, salary plus bonus plus other (including such measures as savings plan contributions and the value of memberships to clubs), and total compensation (the sum of salary, bonus, other, and also the value of stock options exercised). The second data on company characteristics are obtained from Standard & Poor's Compustat and from The University of Chicago's Center for Research in Security Prices (CRSP). Finally, information on layoffs is from Pro Quest's *Newspaper Abstracts*. Abstracts from the *Wall Street Journal* were searched for the words "layoff," "laid off," "downsize," "plant closing," or "downsizing." The number of abstracts found from 1987 through 1995 was 3,470

In order to determine whether there is a simple relationship between layoff announcements and CEO pay, Hallock (1998) plots the number of layoff announcements in the *Wall Street Journal* and median CEO total compensation against time, and finds that both grow over the sample period. Since, as pointed out by Rosen (1992) and others, CEO pay is very strongly related to company size, Hallock (1998) also plots the fraction of companies announcing at least one layoff and the real median CEO total compensation against the size of the company, as measured by market value of equity (Figure 1.6). The smallest 10 percent of companies are in market value of equity decile 1, the next 10 percent of companies are in decile 2, all the way up to the largest 10 percent of companies in decile 10. It is clear from the figure that larger companies pay more *and* are more likely to announce a layoff in a given year.

A more formal analysis of layoffs and CEO compensation reveals that the apparent relationship may be nothing more than a mere statistical association. Table 1.3 shows the results of regressing the log of CEO total compensation[18] on whether the company had a layoff in the previous year. The results of this regression appear in column (1) of Table 1.3. The coefficient on lagged layoff is 0.378 (translating into a percentage gain of roughly 46 percent), and it is highly statistically significant. This is a large effect, and taken at face value suggests that the pay premium to CEOs for making large layoffs is quite high.

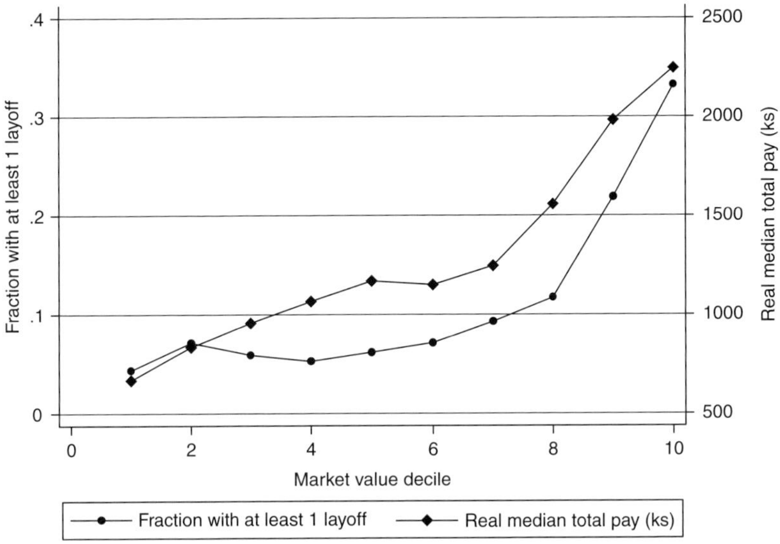


**Figure 1.6** Fraction of firms announcing at least one layoff and median total compensation by market value of equity decile

However, taking into account the importance of firm size (as evidenced by Figure 1.6) and other firm-specific characteristics, column (2) repeats the specification of column (1) with additional controls: lagged log market value of equity, lagged one-year stock return, age of the CEO and its square, seniority of the CEO and its square, and yearly indicator variables. The coefficient on lagged layoff declines substantially to 0.134 but is still statistically significantly different from zero. Finally, in a specification controlling for individual firm effects (column 3), the coefficient on lagged layoff is negative and not statistically significantly different from zero. So, once firm-specific effects are controlled for, the CEO pay premium for laying off workers disappears. Note, however, that many CEOs hold many times their annual income in stock and stock options in their firms (Hallock and Torok, 2008). Therefore, in order to continue this investigation, it is sensible to consider the relationship between job loss announcements and stock prices.

## *Mass layoffs and profitability or value in the very short run*

There are many reports in the popular press of large layoffs at firms in the United States and around the world. There is also a great deal of

Table 1.3 *Effects of layoffs on CEO pay*

| | Dependent variable: log total CEO compensation[a] | | |
|---|---|---|---|
| | (1) | (2) | (3) |
| $(\text{Any layoff})_{t-1}$ | 0.378*** | 0.134*** | -0.050 |
| | (0.048) | (0.044) | (0.036) |
| Log (market value of equity) | ____ | 0.319*** | 0.534*** |
| | | (0.012) | (0.033) |
| $(\text{Annual return})_{t-1}$ | ____ | 0.149*** | 0.070*** |
| | | (0.034) | (0.026) |
| Other regressors[b] | no | yes | yes |
| Company indicators | no | no | yes |
| $R^2$ | 0.019 | 0.252 | 0.693 |

Notes:
[a] Total compensation is the sum of salary, bonus, other compensation, and exercised options.
[b] Other regressors are age of the CEO and its square, seniority of the CEO, and its square and yearly indicators variables.
*** significantly different from 0 at the 1% level.
Sample size is 3,242. Standard errors are in parentheses.

*Source*: Hallock (1998).

discussion about the potential effects of these layoffs on companies executing layoffs. Some argue that the layoffs are necessary to maintain the financial health of the company. A host of studies linking job loss announcements to short-term stock prices have been written in the past few decades.[19] Following on from early work (Farber and Hallock, 2009) that used data on the stock price reaction to layoffs' announcements for any firm ever in the *Fortune* 500 from 1970 to1999, here we report information on the stock price reaction to layoff announcements for any firm ever in the *Fortune* 500 any year during the 38-year period from 1970 to 2007 (refer back to Figure 1.3 for the distribution of the number of these announcements each year during the period).

The sample frame for this chapter is every company that was *ever* in the *Fortune* 500 from 1970 through the end of 2007. For example, if a firm only joined the *Fortune* 500 in 1985, data were collected not only for 1985 but for every year in which the company was publicly traded. The *Wall Street Journal* Index was read for each company to locate any record of a job loss of any kind in any of these companies. After that, the complete article for each layoff event was then read.[20] This yields a sample of 5,353 unique job loss announcements made by *Fortune* 500 firms during the 28 years from 1970 to 2007 (refer back to Figure 1.3 for the distribution of the number of these announcements each year during the period).

In order to calculate the short-term stock price reaction to layoff announcements, a simple event study method is used (see, for example, MacKinlay, 1997). We assume that the market became aware of the job loss announcement very near to the time of the printing in the *Wall Street Journal*.

We calculate cumulative average excess returns using value-weighted return data from the Center for Research in Security Prices (CRSP) at the University of Chicago. Let $t$ index time in trading days and let $i$ index the companies. In the first-stage $R_{it}$, the daily stock return for the company, is regressed on $R_{mt}$, the value-weighted return for the market. This regression is run for some period in the past:[21]

$$R_{it} = \alpha_i + \beta_i R_{mt} + \eta_{it}.$$

Next, for days around the event, the daily abnormal (or excess) returns can be calculated as follows:

$$ER_{it} = R_{it} - (\hat{\alpha}_i + \hat{\beta}_i R_{mt}),$$

where $\hat{\alpha}_i$ and $\hat{\beta}_i$ are estimated in the earlier equation. One can think of the excess return, $ER$, as the part of the movement in the stock return of company $i$ that is not correlated with overall market movement in stock returns and presumably reflects unexpected firm-specific factors.

Excess returns can be calculated for many days around the "event window." In this chapter, all calculations are based on a three-day window (the day before, the day of, and the day after the event).[22] Figure 1.7 displays the average cumulative excess returns over a three-day window for each of the 38 years from 1970 to 2007. It is clear from the figure that the share price reaction to job loss announcements was negative in the 1970s and seems to have flattened out by the middle to end of this decade.

One might ask whether the stock price reactions reported in Figure 1.7 may have been influenced by "other" news in the companies. For example, perhaps earnings were announced on the same day as the layoff. In order to isolate the effect of layoff announcements, the second line in Figure 1.7 repeats the analysis after removing any announcement that is within 30 days of another layoff, earnings announcement, stock split announcement, or dividend announcement for the same company. It is clear from the figure that this does not markedly alter the main findings.

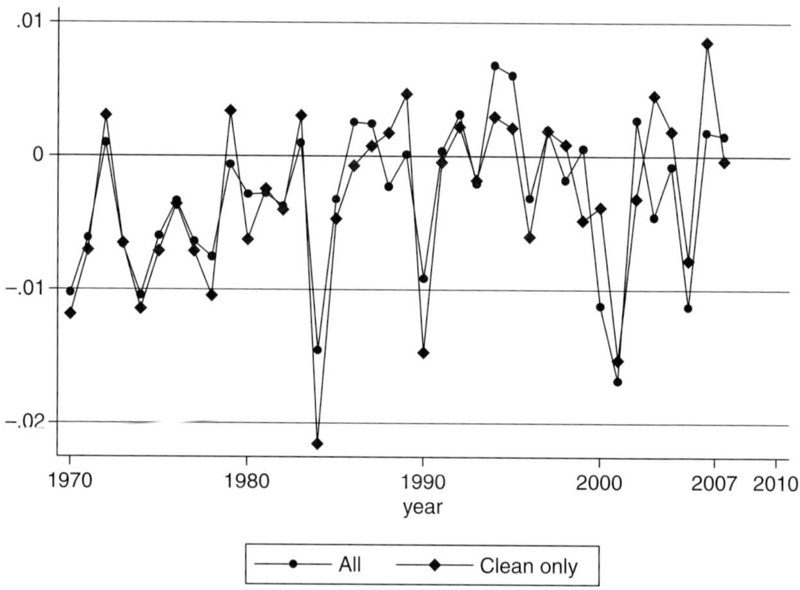


**Figure 1.7** Cumulative average excess returns (one day before to one day after the layoff)

In addition to considering the average effect of job loss announcements on stock prices, one might also want to consider the distributional consequences on stock prices. Figure 1.8 is an attempt to investigate this issue. This figure reports the distribution of the returns by decade for the years 1970–1979, 1980–1989, 1990–1999, and 2000–2007. The figure shows a wide diversity in the returns by decade, with no marked differences in the spread of the distribution over time.[23]

Regression analysis shows that the stock price reaction to job loss announcements has, indeed, changed over time (Table 1.4). The table reports the results from regressions of the three-day cumulative excess returns on indicators for decade (the excluded decade is 1970–1979) and "reasons" for the layoffs (the reasons reported earlier are condensed into five categories: reorganization, plant closing, demand slump, cost, and other (the excluded category is "missing reason"). From column (1), one can see that the excess returns in the 1970s (the constant term since the 1970s are the excluded category) were −0.654 percent. The returns in the 1980s were higher (less negative), the returns from the 1990s still higher, and the returns in the 2000s not statistically significant from those in the

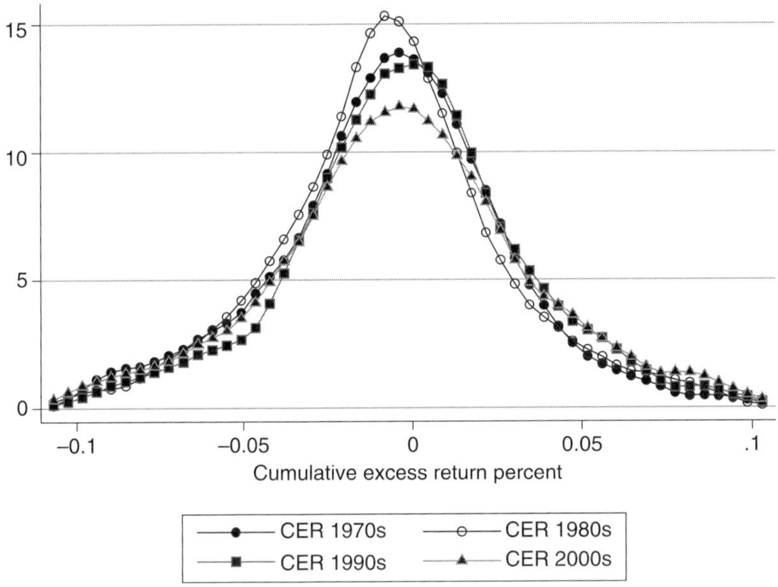


**Figure 1.8** Distribution of cumulative excess returns by decade

1970s. Furthermore, changes in the mix of reasons for job loss announcements over time are not the explanation for the change in the returns to job loss announcement over time (column 2). The final columns of Table 1.4 report the results for each decade separately. Of note is the fact that the stock price reaction to job loss announcements for the "reorganization," "cost," and "other" reasons are strongly positively significant. Farber and Hallock (2009) explore many other reasons for the change in the stock price reaction to job loss announcements for an earlier period (that does not include data after 1999) and find that reasons, industry changes, type of worker (e.g., salaried versus not) do not explain the kinds of changes seen in Figure 1.7.

## *Mass layoffs, productivity, profitability, and value in the longer run*

Perhaps more important than considering the effects of job loss on the short-term stock price reaction of firms is to consider the long-term effects of job loss on company viability and profitability.[24] The problem, of course, is that this is a much more difficult question to answer.[25] We

Table 1.4 *Are excess price reactions to layoffs explained by "reasons" or time?*

| | (1) | (2) | (3) | (4) | (5) | (6) |
|---|---|---|---|---|---|---|
| | 1970–2007 | | 1970–1979 | 1980–1989 | 1990–1999 | 2000–2007 |
| Constant | −0.654*** (0.132) | −0.403 (0.327) | −0.269 (0.494) | −0.046 (0.562) | 0.683 (0.721) | −2.061** (1.022) |
| 1980–1989 | 0.423** (0.186) | 0.311** (0.126) | | | | |
| 1990–1999 | 0.664*** (0.199) | 0.458*** (0.135) | | | | |
| 2000–2007 | −0.109 (0.235) | 0.083 (0.174) | | | | |
| Reason indicators | | | | | | |
| Reorganization | | 0.456 (0.344) | 0.223 (0.558) | 0.348 (0.606) | −0.154 (0.751) | 2.472** (1.105) |
| Plant closing | | 0.192 (0.329) | 0.313 (0.559) | 0.389 (0.631) | −1.182 (0.848) | 1.664 (1.127) |
| Demand slump | | −0.206 (0.342) | −0.244 (0.508) | −0.298 (0.578) | −0.881 (0.746) | 1.440 (1.057) |
| Cost | | −0.004 (0.342) | −0.427 (0.539) | −0.027 (0.604) | −0.536 (0.756) | 2.009* (1.087) |
| Other | | 0.327 (0.343) | 0.106 (0.520) | 0.297 (0.609) | −0.165 (0.783) | 2.181* (1.113) |
| p-value Decade = 0 | 0.001 | 0.004 | | | | |
| p-value Reason = 0 | | 0.0001 | 0.095 | 0.054 | 0.065 | 0.131 |
| $R^2$ | 0.003 | 0.007 | 0.003 | 0.004 | 0.005 | 0.005 |
| N | 4,907 | 4,907 | 1,515 | 1,515 | 1,183 | 694 |

*Note*: Standard errors are reported in parentheses. Observations are weighted by the inverse of the standard error of the cumulative excess return. The base category is the 1970–1979 period due to "missing" reasons.

*** Significantly different from 0 at the 1% level.

** Significantly different from 0 at the 5% level.

* Significantly different from 0 at the 10% level.

can imagine that firms would not reduce headcount if it were not in the best interests of the company. However, increasing the time period over which we can study the "long-term" effects also increases the probability that some confounding effects will be introduced into the analysis.

A classic example of a study of the longer-term effects of downsizing on corporate value is Dial and Murphy (1995). The authors describe an extraordinary change at General Dynamics that began in 1991. The company hired a new management team and committed to a strategy of creating shareholder value in the face of a potentially serious fall for demand for defense-related products. They also specifically tied compensation of senior managers to the creation of shareholder wealth.[26] The senior managers began a strategy of extraordinary downsizing and restructuring which led to sizeable compensation to the managers. Total employment at General Dynamics when the new CEO, William Anders, was hired in 1991 was 98,150. Total employment at General Dynamics at the end of 1993 was 26,800. During that same time period, executives at General Dynamics were rewarded and shareholders had gained a return of 553 percent. Clearly, there was more going on at General Dynamics than simply a new compensation package for managers and layoffs. Nevertheless, this is an extremely interesting case study. The CEO, Anders, had the following to say regarding whether resources from shareholders should have been used to help retrain workers who lost their jobs: "I do not see that we have a special obligation to our employees. This is an issue of excess human capacity that had to leave the defense industry. We trained our people to have specific skills and paid for that training. Then we paid them for their skills" (Dial and Murphy, 1995, p. 303).

Firms presumably downsize because they believe that downsizing will lead to better performance. An important measure of performance is productivity. If laid-off workers contributed relatively little to productivity, then we would expect productivity to rise after a layoff. It is reasonable to think that this is also the expectation of firms that choose to downsize. Is this happening?

Using plant-level data from the Longitudinal Research Database (LRD), Baily, Bartelsman, and Haltiwanger (1996) study productivity growth in the US manufacturing sector during the 1980s, a period marked by extensive downsizing. They find, "in contrast to the conventional wisdom," "that plants that *increased* employment as well as productivity contribute almost as much to overall productivity growth in the 1980s as the plants that increased productivity at the expense of employment" (emphasis added).

Using the same methodology as Baily *et al.* (1996), Collins and Harris (1999) applied the UK Annual Census of Production (ACOP) to study the UK's motor vehicle manufacturing sector, and found that "successful" downsizers – firms which decreased employment and increased productivity – had higher productivity growth, but that firms which were "unsuccessful" downsizers – firms which decreased employment and productivity – had very low relative productivity growth.

An alternative way to investigate the relationship between downsizing and productivity is to study the effects of employment protection. If firms want to downsize but are unable to do so due to legal and regulatory constraints, then we might expect firm performance to be hurt as a consequence of the presence and enaction of employment protection.

Autor, Kerr, and Kugler (2007) use variation in the cost of dismissing employees brought on by the adoption of wrongful discharge protection by US state courts from the late 1970s through the early 1990s to study the relationship between employment protection and productivity. Using establishment-level data from the US Census Bureau, they find that wrongful discharge protection led to a reduction in employment flows and that the short-run rise in adjustment costs led to a decrease in total factor productivity. Bassanini, Nunziata, and Venn (2009) confirm this basic finding by studying the impact of job protection legislation on industry-specific productivity growth, employing a differences-in-differences strategy using panel data from 11 OECD countries. They find that layoff restrictions reduce productivity growth in industries where such restrictions are more likely to be binding.

A possible channel through which employment protection could decrease productivity is through the effort of "survivors" – those employees who remained employed by the firm after the firm downsized. Ichino and Riphahn (2005) study the effect of employment protection on a particular form of worker effort: worker absenteeism. They use weekly observations for male and female workers hired for white-collar jobs by a large Italian bank in the mid 1990s. For the first 12 weeks of employment, these workers are on probation; after 12 weeks, the workers enjoy employment protection. The average numbers of days absent from work per week more than triples for men and shows a sizable increase for women after employment protection kicks in.

Joel Brockner and coauthors have extensively studied the effects of downsizing on survivors' effort, with mixed findings. Studying the effect of layoffs on survivors using a laboratory experiment, Brockner, Greenberg, Brockner, Bortz, Davy, and Carter (1986) find evidence in support of "positive inequity theory" – the idea that by surviving a layoff, a worker will perceive her "outcome-to-input ratio" to be larger than her laid-off coworkers, will experience guilt, and will consequently increase her work effort. Likewise, Brockner, Grover, O'Malley, Reed, and Glynn (1993), using evidence from both the lab and the field, find that the work effort of survivors increases with perceived threat of a future layoff.

Brockner, Grover, Reed, and DeWitt (1992) argue that the change in work effort of survivors brought on by a layoff is driven by perceptions about job insecurity. Using survey data of employees of a national retail chain, they find that the pre- to post-layoff change in reported work effort follows an inverted U pattern over job insecurity – if survivors feel either very secure or very insecure about their employment probability, then the change in work effort is relatively low, whereas if survivors feel moderately secure, then the change in work effort is relatively high. They hypothesize that survivors who feel very secure may be complacent, that survivors who feel very insecure may feel helpless, and that workers who feel moderately secure may feel empowered to affect their outcome.

An interesting example of studying the longer-term effects of job loss is Cappelli (2000), who examines downsizings. He specifically defines "downsizing as reductions in jobs driven by the desire to improve operating efficiencies" and distinguishes that from "layoffs typically associated with shortfalls in demand." Cappelli uses data from the National Center on the Educational Quality of the Workforce (EQW) of the US Census Bureau, which is an establishment-level survey of employment practices. He considers the relationship between downsizing and several outcomes, including sales per worker, labor costs per worker, or labor costs as a percentage of total costs. The results do not all point to the same conclusion and the issues are, obviously, difficult. Unfortunately, the study did not include a measure of accounting profit or organization value in the data. Nevertheless, one of Cappelli's interesting conclusions is that "At least in the mid 1990s, when these data were collected, job reduction decisions seem not to have been dominated by factors associated with shortfalls in demand. Whether this situation represents something distinct about that period – one of economic expansion when the level of excess capacity in establishments may have been too small to drive job cuts – or something more fundamental is a question for further research" (p. 511).

One study that specifically measures the relationship between employment change and firm performance in the longer run is Cascio, Young, and Morris (1997).[27] The authors use 5,479 instances of changes in employment and investigate the relationship between these employment changes and return on assets (their measure of profitability) and return on common stock. However, as opposed to much of the current discussion, Young and Morris examine the total employment change in a firm that is not limited to layoffs (that is, some of the job loss could be voluntary on the part of the worker and, in addition, if one worker leaves and another takes her place, this would be undetected). With these limitations in mind, the authors find that companies that just lowered employment performed no better than other companies. On the other hand, companies that downsized and "restructured assets"[28] had both higher returns on assets and returns on stock than their industry competitors.

The data on employment change in Cascio, Young, and Morris (1997) are from Standard & Poor's CompuStat. Our understanding is that the employment data in CompuStat are missing for a reasonably high percentage of the observations. Further, the employment data are not audited (like accounting data)[29] so these results should be regarded with some caution.

## *The relationship between mass layoffs and CEO turnover*

Another firm outcome that can be studied with respect to job loss is CEO turnover.[30] Are job loss announcements and CEO turnover in large companies positively or negatively related? Which comes first? Are some CEOs hired to lay people off? Billger and Hallock (2005) examine some of these issues using data over a 31-year period on job loss announcements and CEO turnover. They find that CEO turnover is significantly related to one or more job loss announcements the previous year. This relationship has also changed over the decades (with a stronger effect in the 1970s than in later decades). They consider different types of layoff announcements separately. Layoffs that are associated with negative stock price reactions (that is, the market thought they were a "bad" idea) are more likely to lead to CEO turnover than those associated with positive stock price reactions (that is, the market thought they were a "good" idea), especially earlier in the sample.

## Concluding comments

Job loss is extremely difficult for individuals, families, and organizations. This chapter provides an overview of just some of the issues related to job loss, including changes in stability of jobs over time in the United States, the issues of timing of job loss, reasons for job loss and alternatives, work-sharing and short-time compensation programs, the relationship between job loss and subsequent wages and health of workers, and the effects of job loss on companies. Our own opinion is that things have changed quite a bit in this area in recent years. Cappelli (2005) notes "For employees, economic downturns are now more catastrophic, because more workers are laid off more quickly with less chance of being rehired, while those who remain employed find their employment conditions worsening. But upturns are now more advantageous, as employers bid not only for entry-level help, as they have in the past, but also for experienced workers" (p. 110).

There are several findings about job loss and its effects on firms and workers in this chapter. First, it is clear that there has been a marked change in stability of jobs in the United States. A decline in job stability alone does not necessarily mean bad news for workers. In fact, increased job change could be good for workers. However, additional evidence suggests that on average, this is not the case. Second, there appears to have been a shift in the *types* of layoffs that have occurred in the past 40 years in the United States. For example, job loss specifically due to "deficient demand" seems to be less prevalent than in the past. Third, a host of evidence shows a significant and negative impact of job loss on workers, both in terms of employment and earnings, and in terms of health and happiness. Fourth, the very short-term stock price reaction to job loss announcements has changed markedly over time and is now quite modest. The longer-term impacts of job loss on company performance are less clear and more work needs to be done in this area. But if companies are not markedly improved by shedding workers, why does it happen? Fifth, a look overseas reveals that many countries handle job loss in a very different way than the United States.

Finally, there have been many public policy proposals on, and suggestions for, improving the economy and dampening the effects of job loss. Evidence suggests that much more work needs to be done in this area to form a scientific base for designing effective evidence-based policy. Nevertheless, it is clear from the subset of the papers in the literature studied here that the nature of the worker–firm relationship has changed quite a bit in the last few generations – a change that has negatively impacted the lives of workers and produced modest, if any, benefits for firms.

Will things ever be the way they used to be? Will the next recession be different? Are things different now than they were just a few years ago – did the so-called Great Recession further change the relationship between firms and workers? Has the employment contract, in fact, changed in the past few generations? It seems that the balance of evidence suggests that the answer to this last question is yes.

## Notes

* We are grateful to David Autor, Sherrilyn Billger, Kristin Butcher, David Clark, Henry Farber, Felice Klein, Harold Oaklander, Tim Taylor, and Olga Yakusheva for many helpful suggestions on work leading to this paper. Michelle Arthur, Sara Christopher, John Deke, Erica Field, Charles Fields, Clayton Reck, Martha Schniepp, and Kristen Stanton provided excellent research assistance in collecting some of the data. This paper draws on, among others, Hallock (2006) and Hallock (2009) for which permission has been granted from Emerald Group Publishing Limited and The American Economic Association, respectively to use portions in this work.

1. See Uchitelle (2006) and Uchitelle and Kleinfield (1996) for examples.
2. Farber (2008a) finds that the drop in average job tenure and in long-term employment are primarily in the private sector and that there are some increases in long-term employment in the public sector.
3. Also see Brown, Haltiwanger, and Lane (2006) and Davis, Haltiwanger, and Schuh (1996).
4. Billger and Hallock (2005) and Farber and Hallock (2009) use the first 30 years of this 38-year data set. See those papers for more detail on the data construction.
5. These quotes were earlier reported in Hallock (2006).
6. O'Neil, Lenn, and Caimano (1995) note that middle managers' anger over layoffs "was directed at top managements' willingness to accept superficial slogans to justify the harsh reality of layoffs and corporate restructuring."
7. Charness and Levine (2000) find that people rate layoffs as "more fair" if the CEO voluntarily "shared the pain." They also find that people view layoffs due to "reduced demand" as more fair than those due to "employee

suggestions." They suggested that "companies should not punish employees for their efforts" (p. 381).

8. See Tuna's (2008) article in the *Wall Street Journal*: "No-layoff policies crumble."
9. Of course, the higher the maintained income, the more expensive the program per participant.
10. This section is based on Hijzen and Venn (2011).
11. The discussion here follows Hallock (2006) closely. The quotes from managers, below, are directly from that source.
12. Eliason and Storrie (2006) study long-term effects of displacement in Sweden using linked employer–employee data. They find that workers in Sweden also suffer long-term losses in the short and long (four years) run.
13. Also see Kletzer (1989) for an interesting investigation of the role of previous job tenure on earnings after job loss.
14. See, for example, Brockner (1992), Brockner, Greenberg, Brockner, Bortz, Davy, and Carter (1986), Brockner, Grover, Reed, DeWitt, and O'Malley (1987), Brockner, Konovsky, Cooper-Schneider, Folger, Martin, and Bies (1994), Illes (1996), and Mishra and Spreitzer (1998). Muirhead (2002) makes the business case for educational training for displaced workers.
15. Also see Martikainen, Mäki, and Jäntti (2007) who study the relationship between unemployment and mortality for Finnish men. They find "no excess mortality ... among those who, at baseline, were employed at workplaces that had experienced reductions in employment" (p. 1070).
16. Note, however, that some have argued for a broader view of goals of corporations. Blair and Gomoroy (2008) recently wrote "In the rush to globalization, the United States has tossed aside a crucial principle that guided the economic prosperity of the twentieth century: corporate leaders have a responsibility to their country, their community, and their employees that goes beyond maximizing share value."
17. The reporting on CEO compensation is more detailed now than it was when that paper was published. There were major changes in how executive compensation is reported in 1992 and again in 2006.
18. The results do not differ significantly if another form of compensation is considered instead.
19. See, for example, Farber and Hallock (2009), Abowd *et al.* (1990), Blackwell, Marr, and Spivey (1990), Caves and Kreps (1993), Gombola and Tsetsekos (1992), Gunderson, Verma, and Verma (1997), Hallock (1998), Kalra, Henderson, and Walker (1994) and Ursel and Armstrong-Stassen (1995).
20. See Farber and Hallock (2009, p. 2) for more details on how the data were constructed for the earlier period. The same structure was used to collect the data reported on here.

21. The period from 60 days before to 30 days before the event is used. Various changes to this interval have no noticeable effect on the results.
22. Changes to this window length have no material effect on the results.
23. One might think that one reason for the shift toward zero in the stock price returns to job loss over time are due to the fact that news is no longer "newsworthy." Hallock and Mashayekhi (2006) investigate the share price reaction to a variety of corporate news announcements. They do not find evidence that is consistent with the "news is no longer newsworthy" hypotheses.
24. One possibility would be to do a longer-run event study of job loss announcements on abnormal returns such as Desai and Jain's (1999) analysis of spinoffs.
25. Brown, Haltiwanger, and Lane (2006) discuss churning, workforce quality, and firm productivity from a more macro-perspective.
26. The authors note that "Laying off employees and leaving communities is personally painful for managers (particularly those with long company tenures). It is relatively easy to provide incentives for growth: Managers intrinsically enjoy opening new plants, hiring new workers, and announcing new investment programs. In contrast, few managers enjoy downsizing: it's simply less fun than growing" (Dial and Murphy, 1995, p. 266).
27. Wayhan and Werner (2000) study the long-term impacts of job loss for a sample of companies who reduced employment in 1991 or 1992. They find that workforce reductions improve financial performance, and that the effect is stronger in the short-run.
28. They define "asset downsizers" as companies where the decline in employment was more than 5 percent and the decline in plant and equipment exceeded the change in employment by more than 5 percent.
29. See Hallock (1998) for more detail.
30. Of course, CEO turnover can be voluntary. In much of the literature on CEOs, however, turnover is thought to be a negative outcome.

## References

Abowd, J., McKinney, K., and Vilhuber, L. 2009. "The link between human capital, mass layoffs, and firm deaths," in T. Dunne, J. B. Jensen, and M. J. Roberts (eds.), *Producer Dynamics: New Evidence from Micro Data*. Chicago: University of Chicago Press for the National Bureau of Economic Research, pp. 447–472.

Abowd, J., Milkovich, G., and Hannon, J. 1990. "The effects of human resource management decisions on shareholder value." *Industrial and Labor Relations Review* **43**(3): 203s–236s.

Anderson, S. and Cavanagh, J. 1994. *Workers Lose, CEOs Win.* Washington, DC: Institute for Policy Studies.

Autor, D. 2003. "Outsourcing at will: The contribution of unjust dismissal doctrine to the growth of employment outsourcing." *Journal of Labor Economics* **21**(1): 1–42.

Autor, D. H., Kerr, W. R., and Kugler, A. D. 2007. "Does employment protection reduce productivity? Evidence from US states." *The Economic Journal* **117**(June): F189–F217.

Baily, M. N., Bartelsman, E. J., and Haltiwanger, J. 1996. "Downsizing and productivity growth: Myth or reality?" *Small Business Economics* **8**(4): 259–278.

Bassanini, A., Nunziata, L., and Venn, D. 2009. "Job protection legislation and productivity growth in OECD countries." *Economic Policy* **24**(58): 349–402.

Bewley, T. F. 1999. "Layoffs," in T. Bewley, *Why Wages Don't Fall During a Recession*. Cambridge, MA: Harvard University Press, pp. 218–262.

Billger, S. M. and Hallock, K. F. 2005. "Mass layoffs and CEO turnover." *Industrial Relations* **44**(3): 463–489.

Blackwell, D., Marr, M. W., and Spivey, M. F. 1990. "Plant closing decisions and the market value of the firm." *Journal of Financial Economics* **26**(2): 277–288.

Blair, M. and Gomoroy, R. 2008. "Leadership is more than profit." *Huffington Post*, September 5.

Brockner, J. 1992. "Managing the effects of layoffs on survivors." *California Management Review* **34**(2): 9–27.

Brockner, J., Greenberg, J., Brockner, A., Bortz, J., Davy, J., and Carter, C. 1986. "Layoffs, equity theory, and work performance: Further evidence on the impact of survivor guilt." *Academy of Management Journal* **29**(2): 373–384.

Brockner, J., Grovner, S., Reed, T. F., and DeWitt, R. L. 1992. "Layoffs, job insecurity, and survivors' work effort: Evidence of an inverted-U relationship." *Academy of Management Journal* **35**(2): 413–425.

Brockner, J., Grover, S., Reed, T., DeWitt, R., and O'Malley, M. 1987. "Survivors' reactions to layoffs: We get by with a little help from our friends." *Administrative Science Quarterly* **32**: 526–541.

Brockner, J., Grover, S., O'Malley, M. N., Reed, T. F., and Glynn, M. A. 1993. "Threat of future layoffs, self-esteem, and survivors' reactions: Evidence from the laboratory and the field." *Strategic Management Journal* **14**(summer): 153–166.

Brockner, J., Konovsky, M., Cooper-Schneider, R., Folger, R., Martin, C., and Bies, R. J. 1994. "Interactive effects of procedural justice and outcome negativity on victims and survivors or job loss." *Academy of Management Journal* **37**(2): 397–409.

Brown, C., Haltiwanger, J., and Lane, J. 2006. "Economic turbulence: What who, and how much?" in C. Brown, J. Haltiwanger, and J. Lane, *Economic Turbulence: Is a Volatile Economy Good for America*? Chicago, IL: University of Chicago Press, pp. 10–22.

Browning, M., Dano, A. M., and Heinesen, E. 2006. "Job displacement and stress related health outcomes." *Health Economics* **15**: 1061–1075.

Cappelli, P. 1992. "Examining managerial displacement." *Academy of Management Journal* **35**(1): 203–217.

Cappelli, P. 2000. "Examining the incidence of downsizing and its effect on establishment performance," in D. Neumark (ed.), *On the Job: Is Long-Term Employment a Thing of the Past*? New York: Russell Sage Foundation, pp. 463–516.

Cappelli, P. 2005. "The path to the top: Changes in the attributes and careers of corporate executives, 1980 to 2001." *Harvard Business Review* **83**(1): 25–32.

Carrington, W. J. 1993. "Wage losses for displaced workers: Is it really the firm that matters?" *Journal of Human Resources* **12**(2): 243–275.

Cascio, W. 2002. "Responsible restructuring – alternative strategies," in W. Cascio, *Responsible Restructuring: Creative and Profitable Alternatives to Layoffs*. San Francisco, CA: Berrett-Koehler Publishers, pp. 49–70.

Cascio, W. F. 2002. "Restructuring in perspective," in W. Cascio, *Responsible Restructuring: Creative and Profitable Alternatives to Layoffs*. San Francisco, CA: Berrett-Koehler Publishers, pp. 3–15.

Cascio, W. F., Young, C. E., and Morris, J. R. 1997. "Financial consequences of employment change decisions in major US corporations." *Academy of Management Journal* **40**(5): 1175–1189.

Caves, R. E. and Kreps, M. B. 1993. "Fat: The displacement of nonproduction workers from US manufacturing industries." *Brookings Papers on Economic Activity, Microeconomics* **2**: 227–273.

Chan, S. and Stevens, A. H. 2001. "Job loss and employment patterns of older workers." *Journal of Labor Economics* **19**(2): 484–521.

Chan, S. and Stevens, A. H. 2004. "How does job loss affect the timing of retirement?" *Contributions to Economic Analysis and Policy* **31**(3).

Charness, G. and Levine, D. I. 2000. "When are layoffs acceptable? Evidence from a quasi-experiment." *Industrial and Labor Relations Review* **53**(3): 381–400.

Collins, A. and Harris, R. I. D. 1999. "Downsizing and productivity: The case of UK motor vehicle manufacturing 1974–1994." *Managerial and Decision Economics* **20**(5): 281–290.

Couch, K. A. 1998. "Late life displacement." *The Gerentologist* **38**(1): 7–17.

Couch, K. and Placzek, D. W. 2008. "The earnings losses of displaced workers revisited." *American Economic Review* **100**(1): 572–589.

Davis, S.J., Haltiwanger J.C., and Schuh, S. 1996. *Job Creation and Destruction*. Cambridge, MA: MIT Press.

Desai, H. and Jain, P.C. 1999. "Firm performance and focus: Long-run stock market performance following spinoffs." *Journal of Financial Economics* **54**: 75–101.

Dial, J. and Murphy, K.J. 1995. "Incentives, downsizing, and value creation at general dynamics." *Journal of Financial Economics* **37**(3): 261–314.

Dooley, D., Catalano, R., and Wilson, G. 1994. "Depression and unemployment: Panel findings from the Epidemiologic Catchment Area study." *American Journal of Community Psychology* **22**(6): 745–765

Dreze, J.H., Persson, T., and Miller, M. 1986, "Work-sharing: Some theory and recent European experience." *Economic Policy* **1**(3): 561–619.

Elder, T.E. 2004. "Reemployment patterns of displaced older workers." Paper presented at Federal Reserve Bank of Chicago Conference on Job Loss: Causes, Consequences and Policy Responses.

Eliason, M. and Storrie, D. 2006. "Latent or lasting scars: Swedish evidence on the long-term effects of job displacement." *Journal of Labor Economics* **24**(4): 831–856.

Fairlie, R.W. and Kletzer, L.G. 2003. "The long-term costs of job displacement among young workers." *Industrial and Labor Relations Review* **56** (4): 682–698.

Farber, H.S. 1997. "The changing face of job loss in the United States: 1982–1995." *Brookings Papers on Economic Activity: Microeconomics*, pp. 55–142.

Farber, H.S. 1999. "Alternative and part-time employment as a response to job loss." *Journal of Labor Ecnomics* **17**(October): s142–s169.

Farber, H.S. 2005. "What do we know about job loss in the United States: Evidence from the Displaced Workers Survey, 1984–2004." *Federal Reserve Bank of Chicago Regional Review*, pp. 13–28.

Farber, H.S. 2007. "Is the company man an anachronism? Trends in long term employment in the US, 1973–2006." Industrial Relations Section Working Paper No. 518, September, Princeton University, Princeton, NJ.

Farber, H.S. 2008. "Employment insecurity: The decline in worker-firm attachment in the United States." Industrial Relations Section Working Paper No. 530, July, Princeton University, Princeton, NJ.

Farber, H.S. 2010. "Job loss and the decline in job security in the United States," in K. Abraham, J. Spletzer, and M. Harper, *Labor in the New Economy*. Chicago, IL: University of Chicago Press for NBER, pp. 223–266.

Farber, H.S. 2011. "Job loss in the great recession: Historical perspective from the displaced worker survey, 1984–2010." National Bureau of Economic Research Working Paper, 17040.

Farber, H. S. and Hallock, K. F. 2009. "The changing relationship between job loss announcements and stock prices: 1970–1999." *Labour Economics* **16**(1): 1–11.

Gombola, M. J. and Tsetsekos, G. P. 1992. "Plant closings for financially weak and financially strong firms." *Quarterly Journal of Business and Economics* **31**(3): 69–83.

Gordon, D. 1996. "Can we take the high road?" in David Gordon, *Fat and Mean: The Corporate Squeeze of Working Americans and the Myth of Managerial Downsizing*. New York: Free Press, pp. 238–253.

Gunderson, M., Verma, A., and Verma, S. 1997. "Impact of layoff announcements on the market value of the firm." *Relations Industrielles/Industrial Relations* **52**(2): 364–381.

Hallock, K. F. 1998. "Layoffs, top executive pay, and firm performance." *The American Economic Review* **88**(4): 711–723.

Hallock, K. F. 2006. "Layoffs in large US firms from the perspective of senior management." *Research in Personnel and Human Resource Management*, Vol. XXV. Amsterdam: Elsevier, pp. 137–179.

Hallock, K. F. 2009. "Job loss and the fraying of the implicit employment contract." *Journal of Economic Perspectives* **23**(4): 69–93.

Hallock, K. F. and Mashayekhi, F. 2006. "Are formal corporate news announcements still newsworthy? Evidence from 30 years of data on earnings, splits, and dividends." Working Paper, Cornell University.

Hallock, K. F. and Torok, J. 2008. *Top Executive Compensation in 2008*. New York: The Conference Board.

Hanner, D. 2005. "Changes in the distribution of earnings following a job displacement: An application of quantile regression in a panel data setting." Working Paper, University of Illinois at Urbana-Campaign.

Hijzen, A. and Venn, D. 2011. "The role of short-time work schemes during the 2008–09 recession." *OECD Social, Employment and Migration Working Papers*, no. 115. http://dx.doi.org/10.1787/5kgkd0bbwvxp-en

Hunt, J. 1999. "Has work-sharing worked in Germany?" *Quarterly Journal of Economics* **114**(1): 117–148.

Hunt, J. and Katz, L. F. 1998. "Hours reductions as work-sharing." *Brookings Papers on Economic Activity* **1**: 339–381.

Ichino, A. and Riphahn, R. T. 2005. "The effect of employment protection on worker effort: Absenteeism during and after probation." *Journal of the European Economic Association* **3**(1): 120–143.

Illes, L. M. 1996. "The announcement," in L. M. Illes, *Sizing Down: Chronicle f a Plant Closing*. Ithaca, NY: Cornell University Press and ILR, pp. 5–17.

Jacobson, L. J., LaLonde, R. J., and Sullivan, D. G. 1993. "Earnings losses of displaced workers." *American Economic Review* **83**(4): 685–709.

Kalra, R., Henderson, G. V. Jr., and Walker, M. C. 1994. "Share price reaction to plant-closing announcements." *Journal of Economics and Business* **46** (5): 381–395.

Kletzer, L. 1989. "Returns to seniority after a permanent job loss." *American Economic Review* **79**(3): 536–543.

Koller, F. 2010. *Spark: How Old-Fashioned Values Drive a Twenty-First-Century Corporation: Lessons from Lincoln Electric's Unique Guaranteed Employment Program*, PublicAffairs™, a member of Perseus Books Group

MacKinlay, A. C. 1997. "Event studies in economics and finance." *Journal of Economic Literature* **35**(1): 13–39.

MaCurdy, T., Pearce, J., and Kihlthau, R. 2004. "An alternative to layoffs: Work sharing unemployment insurance." *California Policy Review* (August): 1–11.

Martikainen, P., Mäki, N., and Jäntti, M. 2007. "The effects of unemployment on mortality following workplace downsizing and workplace closure: A register-based follow-up study of Finnish men and women during economic boom and recession." *American Journal of Epidemiology* **165**(9): 1070–1075.

Mishra, A. K. and Spreitzer, G. 1998. "Explaining how survivors respond to downsizing: The roles of trust, empowerment, justice, and work redesign." *Academy of Management Review* **23**(3): 567–588.

Muirhead, S. 2002. "Compassionate downsizing: Making the business case for educational training for transitioned employees." Executive Action No. 31, The Conference Board.

Murphy, K. J. 1985. "Corporate performance and managerial remuneration: An empirical analysis." *Journal of Accounting and Economics* **7**(1–3): 59–76.

Neal, D. 1995. "Industry-specific human capital: Evidence from displaced workers." *Journal of Labor Economics* **13**(4): 653–677.

O'Neill, H. M., Jeffrey Lenn, D., and Caimano, V. F. 1995. "Voices of survivors: Words that downsizing CEOs should hear [and executive commentary]." *The Academy of Management Executive (1993–2005)* **9**(4): 23–34.

Oaklander, H. 2003. "Innovative workforce restructuring." Alliance for the Prevention of Unemployment (APU).

Reid, F. 1982. "UI-assisted worksharing as an alternative to layoffs: The Canadian experience." *Industrial and Labor Relations Review* **35**(3): 319–329.

Rosen, S. 1992. "Contracts and the market for executives," in L. Werin and H. Wijkander (eds.), *Contract Economics*. Oxford: Blackwell.

Ruhm, C. 1991. "Are workers permanently scarred by job displacements?" *American Economic Review* **81**(1): 319–324.

Ruhm, C. 2000. "Are recessions good for your health?" *Quarterly Journal of Economics* **115**(2): 617–650.

Skuterud, M. 2007. "Identifying the potential of work-sharing as a job-creation strategy." *Journal of Labor Economics* **25**(2): 265–287.

Stevens, A. H. 1997. "Persistent effects of job displacement: The importance of multiple job losses." *Journal of Labor Economics* **15**(1): 165–188.

Sullivan, D. and von Wachter, T. 2007. "Mortality, mass-layoffs, and career outcomes: An analysis using administrative data." NBER Working Paper No. 13626.

Sullivan, D. and Von Wachter, T. 2009. "Job displacement and mortality: An analysis using administrative data." *Quarterly Journal of Economics* **124**(3): 1265–1306.

Topel, R. 1990. "Specific capital and unemployment: Measuring costs and consequences of worker displacement." *Carnegie-Rochester Series on Public Policy* **33**: 181–214.

Tuna, C. 2008. "No-layoff policies crumble." *Wall Street Journal*, December 30, p. B2.

Uchitelle, L. 2006. "The shock, Part I" and "The shock, Part II," in Louis Uchitelle, *The Disposable American: Layoffs and Their Consequences*. New York: Knopf, pp. 80–97.

Uchitelle, L. and Kleinfield, N. K. 1996. "The price of job loss," in *The Downsizing of America*, Times Books, pp. 3–36.

Ursel, N. and Armstrong-Stassen, M. 1995. "The impact of layoff announcements on shareholders." *Relations Industrielles/Industrial Relations* **50**(3): 636–649.

Van Audenrode, M. A. 1994. "Short-time compensation, job security, and employment contracts: Evidence from selected OECD countries." *Journal of Political Economy* **102**(1): 76–102.

von Wachter, T., Song, J., and Manchester, J. 2007. "Long-term earnings losses due to job separation during the 1982 recession: An analysis using longitudinal administrative data from 1974 to 2004." Working Paper, Social Security Administration.

Von Wachter, T., Hildreth, A., and Handwerker, E. 2008. "Estimating the 'true' cost of job loss: Evidence using matched data from California 1991 –2000." Center for European Studies (CES) Working Paper 9–14, Harvard University, Cambridge, MA.

Wayhan, V. B. and Werner, S. 2000. "The impact of workforce reduction on financial performance: A longitudinal perspective." *Journal of Management* **26**(2): 341–363.

Yermack, D. 1997. "Good timing: CEO stock option awards and company news announcements." *Journal of Finance* **52**(June): 449–476.

# 2 *How does downsizing come about?*

WAYNE F. CASCIO

Employment downsizing, the planned elimination of positions or jobs, is a defining characteristic of modern life in organizations. It may be reactive (in response to a change in economic or organizational conditions) or proactive (executed in anticipation of such changes). In the most recent economic recession, downsizing was global in scope, with 8.5 million layoffs in the United States and more than 50 million worldwide. As Datta, Guthrie, Basuil, and Pandey (2010) have noted, in these turbulent economic times even countries that traditionally have avoided layoffs (e.g., South Korea, Japan, Taiwan, and Hong Kong) embraced the practice. Export-oriented and labor-intensive firms in China, and firms in both manufacturing and services industries in Britain, Canada, Australia, New Zealand, South Africa, South America, and Eastern Europe participated as well. Not surprisingly, therefore, employment downsizing has attained the (dubious) status as one of the most high-profile, significant, and pervasive management issues of our time. Over the past three decades, downsizing has occurred in virtually all industries and sectors of the economy, and it has affected business, governments, and individuals around the world (Cascio, 2010a; Gandolfi, 2008).

Although employment downsizing is a multifaceted phenomenon, characterized by antecedents, implementation, and consequences, this chapter addresses just three issues: what it is, what causes it, and some things we still do not know (i.e. directions for future research). The chapter does not consider other aspects of downsizing, such as its costs, consequences, or alternatives to it, that provide a more complete picture of the full scope of this phenomenon. For more on those issues, see other chapters in this volume or consult Cascio (2002, 2010), Datta *et al.* (2010), or De Meuse, Marks, and Dai (2011).

## What is downsizing?

Downsizing is a broad term that refers to reductions in a firm's use of financial, physical, human, or information assets. In fact, in its broadest sense, downsizing may be viewed as a complete strategic transformation intended to change an organization's design, its work processes, corporate culture, values, attitudes, and mission (Kets de Vries and Balazs, 1997). Downsizing is sometimes used as a synonym for the term "organizational restructuring," but technically there are important differences between these terms. Organizational restructuring refers to planned changes in the formal patterns of operations and command. It need not result in a smaller workforce. Employment downsizing, on the other hand, always results in a smaller workforce, for it refers specifically to a reduction in a firm's use of its human assets. Sometimes known as a "reduction in force" (RIF), it may be accomplished through attrition, early retirements, voluntary severance agreements, or layoffs (Cascio, 2010a).

The definition of employment downsizing provided at the beginning of this chapter – the planned elimination of positions or jobs – may be considered "bare bones." Cameron (1994) and Datta *et al.* (2010) offered more holistic definitions: "a set of activities undertaken on the part of the management of an organization and designed to improve organizational efficiency, productivity, and/or competitiveness" (Cameron, 1994, p. 192); and "a planned set of organizational policies and practices aimed at workforce reduction with the goal of improving firm performance" (Datta *et al.*, 2010, p. 282). This chapter relies on the latter definition as a contextual framework for the material that follows.

## What causes employment downsizing?

At a broad level, there are two broad classes of causes that have been proposed in the academic literature: external and internal. External causes focus on macro-environmental factors, including institutional- and industry-specific ones. Internal causes focus on organizational factors, such as a firm's performance or strategy. This section reviews relevant literature in each of these areas.

### *External or macro-environmental causes of employment downsizing*

It might appear obvious that declining customer demand is a key cause of employment downsizing, and several studies support this hypothesis (Baumol, Blinder, and Wolff, 2003; Filatotchev, Buck, and Zhukov, 2000; Hillier, Marshall, McColgan, and Werema, 2006; Wagar, 1997;

Yu and Park, 2006). In these instances, firms react to declines in demand by reducing their workforces. Such declines in demand may be long term, as in the newspaper industry, or short term, as is often the case in economic recessions. As Pfeffer (2010) has noted, the majority of layoffs that took place in the most recent recession – at financial-services firms, retailers, technology companies, and many others – were not the result of a broken business model. Rather, they were a response to temporary drops in demand. Many organizations fully expected to start growing (and hiring) again once the recession ends. Unlike firms in industries that are shrinking or disappearing, these firms cut jobs to minimize the effect on profits, not to ensure their survival.

In the case of proactive downsizing though, the "declining demand" hypothesis cannot explain management's rationale for downsizing. Many of today's job cuts are not about large, sick companies trying to save themselves, as was often the case in the early 1990s (e.g., IBM, Sears). They are also about healthy companies hoping to reduce costs and boost earnings by reducing head count (e.g., Goldman Sachs and AOL). They are about trying to preempt tough times instead of simply reacting to them. These kinds of layoffs are radical, preventive first aid that address an overarching question: "What do we need to do now in order to thrive in the future? (Morris, 2001; Zatzick, Marks, and Iverson, 2009).

Proactive downsizing may also help to explain why other studies (e.g., Budros, 1997, 2000, 2002; Yoo and Mody, 2000) did not find any significant relationships between economic conditions and employee downsizing; indeed, Budros found that firms in the utility and industrial sectors often engaged in employee downsizing during economic peaks (Budros, 2000). Findings consistent with this stream of research also indicate that industry deregulation and privatization often trigger employee downsizing (Budros, 1997, 2002; Redman and Keithley, 1998). This is particularly true in the context of manufacturing firms, and also in the context of societies that are transitioning toward capitalism, such as China (*South China Morning Post*, 2002).

In addition, studies grounded in institutional theory generally indicate that firms are more likely to engage in significant employee reductions when there are increased levels of downsizing among referent firms in the population (Ahmadjian and Robinson, 2001; Budros, 1997, 2000, 2004; Tsai, Wu, Wang, and Huang, 2006). Institutional theory holds that organizations are subject to pressures within an institutional field, and that acquiring legitimacy requires firms to conform to institutional norms by adopting prevalent management practices (DiMaggio and Powell, 1983). As Datta *et al.* (2010) have noted, when viewed from this perspective, employment downsizing can be seen as an outcome of the institutionalization process; that is, organizations seek legitimacy by mimicking downsizing practices implemented by those firms viewed as being "successful" and "legitimate."

Another way to view such mimicry among rival firms is to conceptualize employment downsizing as a *cloning response*. Indeed a study of downsizing over a 15-year period found a strong "adoption effect" – firms copied the behavior of other firms to which they had social ties (Pfeffer, 2010). Sometimes, this seems to be the only choice if a company wants to remain competitive when competitors reduce wages to cut costs. Relatedly, there is also a tendency – known as the *vividness heuristic* – to give undue attention and weight to particularly vivid or newsworthy examples of downsizing (Surowiecki, 2007). Here is how that process works.

Companies that have reaped dramatic benefits from downsizing and redesigning business processes, such as General Electric (GE) and Procter & Gamble, become templates for how the process works – disregarding thousands of companies that cut payrolls but continued to struggle. Executive overconfidence exacerbates this problem. A chief executive officer is far more likely to see himself or herself pulling off what Jack Welch did at GE than to recognize the probability that layoffs will make only a trivial difference.

Conversely, arguments have been advanced that downsizing is the result of de-institutionalization of existing practices (e.g., the employment-for-life policies that had been practiced by large firms in Japan). However, abandonment of an institutionalized practice in favor of a new practice comes at the cost of diminished legitimacy, and such costs must be weighed against the benefits of abandonment. From an institutional-theory standpoint, organizations may find safety in the number of firms adopting the new practice, allowing them to abandon the existing practice without incurring high costs (Ahmadjian and Robinson, 2001).

### *Institutional actions to prevent downsizing: The case of Germany*

In some cases, an institutional actor, such as a government, can take steps to forestall or prevent employment downsizing. Germany's actions during the most recent economic recession (and historically, well before that) are a case in point.

Actually, there were two government-sponsored programs that showed the world how to survive an economic recession. The first was a *Kurzarbeit* (literally, "short work") policy, under which companies were encouraged to place workers on reduced schedules, rather than lay them off. While the worst recession since World War II pushed up unemployment in the United States to 10.1 percent, a 27-year high, in Germany the rate fell to 7.5 percent, a 17-year low and well below the 10.1 percent average for the Euro zone (Blackstone, 2010). Although almost half a million jobs were saved, there is a tradeoff, for as the global economy recovers, hiring in Germany could stall, and that might slow down economic growth as consumers spend less.

Under *Kurzarbeit*, companies can temporarily move employees onto shorter work schedules when demand is weak. The companies pay only for the hours worked, while the government provides up to 67 percent of the workers' remaining wages. The program supported up to 1.5 million employees at some 63,000 companies, according to the Federal Labor Agency.

The short-work idea dates back more than 100 years, to 1910, when the government compensated workers who faced a slump in the fertilizer and potash industry. In 1924, when unemployment reached 11 percent, the government introduced nationwide short-work policies similar to those used today. *Kurzarbeit* critics argued that Germany was only delaying, at great cost, the inevitable pain that needed to occur after such a severe recession. Moreover, the hit to efficiency and long-term growth would outweigh any benefit from artificially cushioning the rise in joblessness. As it turned out, the critics were wrong, as a rapid rise in demand for German exports from emerging markets in Latin America and Asia, particularly China, fueled a 9 percent rise in German GDP, at an annualized rate, during the second quarter of 2010 (Blackstone, 2010).

A second policy tool used in Germany also helped contain unemployment. That tool is the work-policy account, which allows companies to reduce employees' working weeks during downturns. Later, as demand picks up, the companies do not have to pay overtime. Rather, employees work the hours they lost during the downturn and get paid ordinary wages. Trumpf, a maker of machine tools, electronics, and lasers, has such an agreement with its unions. Employees work up to 250 hours more than contractually agreed when business soars, and up to 250 fewer hours when demand is low.

When orders at Trumpf collapsed in November 2008 Trumpf exhausted this 500-hour buffer, then switched about 3,200 of its 4,500 workers in Germany onto the government's short-work program. According to the company's executive vice-president, "It was our top priority to keep our core workforce and to preserve knowledge and experience … We had layoffs in foreign markets with less flexibility, such as Spain, Poland, and partly, the US" (Vits and Randow, 2010, p. 13). Short-time labor does help to withstand a temporary loss of work in a crisis, but it is not a cure-all. As one German economist noted, "There is no job-market miracle" (Rees, in Vits and Randow, 2010, p. 13).

## *Globalization and global competition*

At its core, the globalization of business refers to the free movement of capital, goods, services, ideas, information, and people across national boundaries. Markets in every country have become fierce battlegrounds where both domestic and foreign competitors fight for market share. For example, Coca-Cola earns more than 80 percent of its revenues from outside the United States! The top five of the 500 largest firms in the world (Wal-Mart, ExxonMobil, Royal Dutch Shell, BP, and General Motors) gross almost $1.5 trillion; the top five in profits (ExxonMobil, Royal Dutch Shell, UAL, BP, and Citigroup) make more than $131 billion in profits; and the top five biggest employers (Wal-Mart, State Grid "China," China National Petroleum, US Postal Service, and Sinopec) employ more than 6 million people (Cascio, 2010b).

What does this mean for job creation and destruction (that is, employment downsizing) in western markets? Begin by considering that global trade connects the fate of every industry and laborer, no matter how small or seemingly self-sufficient, to the decisions of bureaucrats in China, shipbuilders in Korea, and bankers everywhere. Cheap labor and plentiful resources, combined with ease of travel and communication, have created global labor markets. This has affected the global distribution of job creation and destruction. Here are several examples (Gogoi, 2010).

- At heavy-equipment maker Caterpillar, Inc. more than half of the 15,000 people hired in 2010 were outside the United States. United Parcel Service (UPS) is also hiring more aggressively overseas. For both companies, sales in international markets are growing twice as fast as sales in domestic ones.

- At fiber and chemicals giant DuPont, the number of US employees shrank by 9 percent from 2005 to 2009; during the same time period, it grew 54 percent in the Asia-Pacific region.
- Among Coca-Cola's 93,000 global employees, fewer than 13 percent of them were in the United States in 2009, down from 19 percent five years earlier. This trend is unlikely to reverse course anytime soon, as the company completes a three-year, $2 billion investment in China, and a five-year, $1 billion investment in the Philippines.
- In the aggregate, according to the Economic Policy Institute, American companies created 1.4 million jobs overseas in 2010, compared with fewer than one million in the United States. Those additional 1.4 million jobs would have lowered the US unemployment rate to 8.9 percent (from 9.8 percent).

Why is this happening? The short answer is the rise of the middle class in developing countries such as India, China, and Brazil. Companies are striving to meet the growing demands of global consumers, and that often means that they need to locate factories and operations close to those consumers. In light of that demand, many of the products manufactured overseas (and the jobs created to fulfill that demand) are not coming back to the United States. Fully half the revenue of the Standard & Poor's 500 (S&P 500) companies has come from outside the United States in recent years. Indeed, by 2015, the number of consumers in Asia's middle class will equal the number in Europe and North America combined.

## *Differences in regional labor costs*

One reason for plant closings in the United States, and the attendant downsizing of the US workforces that accompanies them, is differences in regional labor costs. Consider the worldwide auto industry, for example. In Germany, wage and benefit costs averaged $58.50 per hour in 2009, while in the United States the comparable costs were $33 an hour. Compare those figures to autoworker wages in Poland ($8.83), Mexico ($3.30), and China ($3.00) (*Bloomberg Business Week*, 2010). Similar regional differences in labor costs help explain the migration of operations in manufacturing and even high-end services (financial services, engineering, tax preparation, health care, information technology, research and development) to lower-cost sites.

### Industry factors

In their 2010 review, Datta *et al.* cited research supporting the conclusion that the tendency to downsize and the level of downsizing are influenced by industry conditions. Support for this view came from Coucke, Pennings, and Sleuwaegen (2007) in their study of employee layoffs in Belgian firms. They found that manufacturing firms were more likely to downsize than firms in service industries. Those findings were consistent with Budros' (1997, 2002) observation that downsizing was more prevalent among manufacturing firms than among non-manufacturing firms. Budros (2004), however, observed that the relationship depended on the timing of the downsizing event, with manufacturing firms downsizing in the early phase of the study period (1979–1983) and non-manufacturing firms doing so in the later phase (1983–1995).

In an earlier study involving Canadian firms, Wagar (1997) found that the level of downsizing varied across different sectors of the service industry, with employee reduction in the education and health sectors being harsher than that in the communications, finance, and retail sectors. In the most recent economic recession (2007–2009) however, the health care and education sectors lost many fewer employees. Surprisingly, Datta *et al.* (2010) found that research on the role of other industry factors (e.g., industry capital intensity, industry research and development expenditures, and advertising intensity, concentration, and rivalry) was conspicuous by its absence.

### Workforce demographics

Earlier we defined downsizing as "the planned elimination of positions or jobs." This is an intentional strategy designed to reduce the size of an organization's workforce. One way to do that is to offer early retirement incentives (ERIs) to older workers. From an organizational viewpoint, managers often assume that early retirement opens up promotional opportunities for younger workers, but one research study found that it is difficult to predict accurately how many older workers will take an ERI. Typically, about one-third of those offered ERIs accept them, although there is a great deal of variation (Feldman, 2007). On the positive side, poor performers are more likely to take ERIs because they lack confidence about future pay increases (Cascio, 2010a).

Globally, workforce demographics are shaping the contours of tomorrow's workplaces. Consider that in 2011 the median age of workers in the United States is 36.8 (Blow, 2011), but it will rise to 40 by 2030. At that same time, however, Japan's will rise to 52. If large numbers of baby boomers delay their retirements, then more firms may have to offer ERIs to encourage older workers to leave, to curtail the hiring of younger workers, or to put existing ones into "holding patterns" until promotional opportunities increase. These trends are not limited to the United States. In the United Kingdom, currently 30 percent of the workforce is over age 50 (Dixon, 2003). Countries in the European Union project the number of employees over age 50 to increase to nearly 25 percent by 2020 (*Economist*, 2006). Fully, 41 percent of the Canadian workforce is projected to be between the ages of 45 and 64 by 2021 (Lende, 2005). In China, the working-age population will begin to shrink after 2020. Finally, small European nations with low birth rates, such as Austria, Belgium, Denmark, Norway, and Sweden, will drop off the list of the 30 biggest economies by 2050 because they will not have enough working-age people to maintain dominant positions (Coy, 2011a). Rather than downsizing, they are likely to adopt strategies to encourage the retention of older workers. Among these developed countries, their continued success will depend more than ever on creativity.

At the other end of the spectrum, consider that more than three-quarters of India's population, a population that is on track to exceed China's by 2028 (Coy, 2011a), is under age 40 (Misra, 2007). Among the three nations with the fastest-growing working-age populations between 2010 and 2050 – Saudi Arabia, Egypt, and Israel – their median ages in 2011 are 24.9, 24.0, and 29.3, respectively. The workforces in those nations may well drive economic growth (Coy, 2011b).

## *Investments in technology and stock market incentives*

A trend that began more than 20 years ago may actually be causing more downsizing today. That trend is the high investment in labor-saving machinery and information technology. According to economist Allen Sinai, the capital–labor ratio – total capital invested as a percentage of hours worked – may help explain why at least some companies do not feel a strong need to rehire downsized workers. Capital spending boosts productivity, and, in the short run at least, often eliminates the need for extra workers on the factory floor or in the office. When the ratio rises, as it did by 29 percent between 1990 and 2008 according to the Bureau of Labor Statistics, companies are spending more on labor-saving machinery than on workers. The ratio for capital spent on information-processing technology rose even faster, 310 percent from 1990 to 2010. To many companies, therefore, buying equipment may be cheaper than hiring people (Power, 2010). Empirical evidence supports this hypothesis. Thus Budros (2004) found that firms that make large investments in labor-saving technologies have higher downsizing rates than those that make smaller investments in such technologies.

At a broader level, consider two types of workers: creators and servers (Kessler, 2011). Creators drive increases in productivity, for they write computer code, develop "apps," design chips, create life-saving drugs, and run search engines. Servers, on the other hand, service the creators (and other servers) by building homes, providing food, or offering legal advice. Machines, computers, and changes in how businesses operate have already replaced many servers. Bank tellers, telephone operators, stockbrokers, and stock traders are just a few examples. Over time, however, evidence indicates that technology creates more jobs than it destroys (Attewell and Rule, 1984; Kessler, 2011).

The stock market may play an important role too. By 1990, the doctrine of maximizing shareholder value had gained wide acceptance among publicly traded companies in the United States. At the same time, executive compensation was firmly linked to boosting the stock price. The logical connections between reductions in headcount and increases in stock prices are well known to executives. The economic rationale behind this can be described as follows (Cascio, 2010a).

Firms all over the world undertake downsizing with the expectation that they will achieve economic benefits. The belief that there are only two ways to make money in business – cutting costs or increasing revenues – leads to this expectation. Anyone who pays a mortgage knows that future costs are more predictable than future revenues. Payroll expenses are fixed costs, so by cutting the payroll – other things remaining equal – firms should reduce expenses. Reduced expenses translate into increased earnings. Increased earnings, in turn, drive stock prices higher.[1]

According to economist Allen Sinai, "We are the only country where the mantra of maximizing shareholder value is so intense" (Power, 2010, p. 13). Reducing the role that stock options play in compensation (as is happening in many companies in the United States), thereby changing incentives for executives to maximize their own income and to please shareholders at all costs, could make executives less likely to downsize employees as deeply as they have in the past.

## *Summary of macro-environmental antecedents of downsizing*

In this section, we consider a number of such antecedents, but this list is by no means exhaustive. They include the following: reactive downsizing in response to declining demand, proactive downsizing in an attempt to cut costs and boost earnings, mimicry among rival firms, abandonment of an institutionalized practice (e.g., lifetime employment at large firms), globalization and global competition, differences in regional labor costs, differences in industry conditions, workforce demographics, investments in technology, and stock market incentives. Internal factors may also lead to employment downsizing, and we consider some of the most important ones in our next section.

## *Internal or organizational factors as causes of employment downsizing*

In the language of organizational strategy, internal strengths and weaknesses are known as "resources" and "capabilities." A firm's resources and capabilities add value by allowing it to exploit opportunities or to neutralize threats (Barney, 1995). This is the resource-based view of the firm. A key premise underlying much of the research in this area is that the primary objective of employee downsizing is more efficient utilization of human resources. The organizational efficiency perspective draws on the resource-based view of the firm to argue that employee downsizing, with attendant cost savings, is a viable strategy in redressing organizational performance declines (Datta *et al.*, 2010). That same perspective has also been used to justify downsizing in the aftermath of mergers and acquisitions (M&As). When similar firms merge, consolidation of operations generates redundancies in staffing, undercutting financial performance. In such a context, employment downsizing represents a vehicle by which the merged entity can eliminate slack and realize operational synergies (O'Shaughnessy and Flanagan, 1998).

We consider this topic further in our next section.

## *Mergers and acquisitions*

US companies slashed spending, shut factories, and fired workers in 2008 and 2009 in an effort to cope with the worst recession since the 1930s. In the process, they accumulated record amounts of cash – almost $2.5 trillion by early 2011. The combination of high levels of cash and cheap financing emboldened chief executives to approve deals aimed at boosting growth in a sluggish economy. In the aggregate, such activities pushed global mergers and acquisitions to a four-year high (Black, 2011; Damouni and Kim, 2011).

Conventional wisdom says that one of the major reasons for undertaking mergers and acquisitions is to gain economies of scale. The restructuring that frequently follows a merger, including downsizing, typically results from efforts to reduce overlap and duplication in the newly created firm. After all, the new firm needs only one payroll department, one billing department, and one information-technology platform. Beyond that, some individuals just do not fit, or cannot adapt to the culture of the new firm (Society for Human Resource Management Foundation, 2010). It seems logical, therefore, to expect some degree of downsizing to result from M&As. Several studies have found that to be the case (Conyon, Girma, Thompson, and Wright, 2002; Lehto and Böckerman, 2008), but others did not (Budros, 1997, 2004; Wagar, 1997). To reconcile these disparate findings, De Meuse *et al.* (2011) offered a more nuanced view of when M&As might be expected to result in employment downsizing, and when they may not.

Corporate M&A may or may not result in downsizing activities. Companies purchase each other for a variety of different reasons, such as gaining market share, acquiring talent, patents, or distribution routes, securing property and resources, obtaining new product lines, attracting additional customers, and numerous other motives. The amount of downsizing that transpires largely depends upon the nature of the acquisition. If the M&A involves the purchase of a company with a similar product-line (a so-called "horizontal merger"), it often denotes an integration of workforces. Efficiencies of scale and purchase power for raw materials typically come into play. In those instances, employees in support departments such as human resources (HR), marketing, procurement, accounting, and finance frequently are cut. Companies do not need to maintain two marketing departments. In contrast, if the M&A entails the purchase of a firm involved in the manufacturing process (e.g., provider of raw materials) or a company used to distribute the product, then very little downsizing may occur. Such "vertical mergers" usually keep intact the workforces of both companies. Likewise, "conglomerate mergers" generally have little impact on reducing the size of the workforce. The primary motive of these M&A purchases is to diversify shareholder value (e.g., an oil company buys a steel mill, or an electronics firm acquires a shipyard). (De Meuse *et al.*, 2011, p. 730)

In short, horizontal mergers and acquisitions may well result in downsizing, but vertical or conglomerate M&As typically do not. The lesson is clear: all M&As are not created equally.

Aside from the type of merger or acquisition, two other findings related to employment downsizing and M&As are worthy of note. In the first, Conyon, Girma, Thompson, and Wright (2004) found that hostile mergers were more likely to be accompanied by significant post-merger employment reductions than friendly transactions. Second, in a study involving the effects of acquisition premiums, Krishnan, Hitt, and Park (2007) found that when acquiring firms paid higher acquisition premiums to target firm shareholders, it typically led to greater workforce reductions in the post-acquisition phase.

## *Firm governance*

According to agency theory, or at least one variant of it, the normal behavior of a CEO (chief executive officer) is self-protective. CEOs will make decisions to solidify their positions and to maximize the rewards that they personally receive (Miller, 1995). Thus agency theory incorporates the political motivations that are an inevitable component of the corporate world (Ellig, 2002). From this perspective, as Datta *et al.* (2010) have noted, weak governance mechanisms lead managers to engage in activities that further their own interests at the expense of those of shareholders (Eisenhardt, 1989; Fama and Jensen, 1983). On the one hand, therefore, managers have a disincentive to downsize because of the benefits they derive from running larger and more complex organizations. On the other hand, however, effective monitoring (e.g., independent boards and greater institutional ownership) can mitigate agency problems and contribute to greater willingness on the part of managers to seek efficiency enhancements via employee reductions. Likewise, institutional shareholders and holders of large blocks of shares, given their significant ownership stakes and voting power, are likely to be more aggressive in monitoring management and requiring top management to employ downsizing options if they believe that doing so will enhance firm value.

In addition to monitoring, agency theory arguments also emphasize the role of incentive mechanisms in addressing agency problems. Thus when the interests of managers are closely aligned with those of shareholders (via equity ownership and/or a compensation structure), they are more likely to seek efficiency enhancements from employee reductions. Do empirical findings support these predictions?

In an early study, Bethel and Liebeskind (1993) found that firms with shareholders that controlled large blocks of stock experienced higher levels of employee downsizings than those without such large blocks of shareholdings. Filatotchev *et al.* (2000), in their study of layoffs among firms in Russia, Ukraine, and Belarus, did not replicate that finding. They found that although outside private ownership results in higher levels of employee downsizing, greater managerial ownership has the opposite effect. In a related finding, Stavrou, Kassinis, and Filotheou (2007) reported that firms with high levels of family ownership engaged in less severe downsizing.

Research on the role of governance in the context of downsizing has also examined the role of board independence and board size in downsizing decisions. Findings suggest that firms with independent boards (that is, a greater proportion of independent directors) are more likely to engage in downsizing (Perry and Shivdasani, 2005), but that board size has no effect. However, Yawson (2006) observed that the propensity to downsize is lower among firms with larger boards.

## *Characteristics of CEOs*

With respect to CEO demographic characteristics and downsizing decisions, one theoretical argument for the incidence and level of employee downsizing is the upper-echelons perspective (Hambrick and Mason, 1984; Hallock, 1998). According to this line of thinking, managers' demographic characteristics (e.g., tenure, age, functional background) represent proxies for their cognitive orientation and knowledge base and, consequently, influence strategic decisions such as downsizing.

Does the functional background of the CEO play any role in downsizing decisions? Budros (2000, 2002, 2004) found that the incidence of downsizing was higher in firms that had CEOs with finance or operations backgrounds. However, this relationship was contingent on industry type, with a finance background being associated with downsizing only in the context of firms in the financial sector (but not the industrial or utility sectors). In terms of CEO age and tenure, Hallock (1998) found that neither of these had any effect on the adoption of employee downsizing. We might also add that decisions to downsize a workforce are rarely made by a single individual, and that the backgrounds or personal characteristics of top-management teams might be a more appropriate unit of analysis.

### *HR practices*

It might appear obvious that a firm's HR practices are related to its propensity to adopt employee downsizing as a strategy. Specifically, what about firms that focus on creating high-involvement workplaces – those with management strategies that give employees the skills, information, and motivation to be competitive? Evidence indicates that layoffs at such workplaces can be markedly more detrimental than layoffs at an average company (Zatzick and Iverson, 2006). At the very least, firms should ensure that their downsizing initiatives are aligned with their approach to talent management to send a consistent message to employees (Zatzick, Marks, and Iverson, 2009). As an example of that, consider the approach taken by SAS Institute, Inc., rated the number 1 best employer in America in 2009 and 2010 (*Fortune*, 2011).

SAS Institute is a statistical-analysis software company based in Cary, North Carolina, that is well known for its extensive employee benefits and no-layoff policy. In 2006, SAS consolidated two marketing departments, which resulted in the elimination of 72 positions (Kirshnan, 2006). All affected employees were given the opportunity to apply for other positions in the organization or to take generous severance and early retirement packages. SAS conducted the downsizing in a manner that was consistent with its commitment-oriented philosophy, which was essential for helping employees to understand the strategic decisions made (Bowen and Ostroff, 2004).

### *Summary*

This chapter has identified 15 potential causes or antecedents of employment downsizing, 11 of which stem from external factors and four of which are internal. Table 2.1 shows these factors in summary form.

Table 2.1 *Causes of employment downsizing*

| External | Internal |
|---|---|
| Macro-environmental factors | Organizational factors |
| Declines in demand | Horizontal mergers/ acquisitions |
| Industry deregulation/privatization | Corporate governance practices |
| Anticipated changes in the economic environment | CEO demographic characteristics |
| Downsizing among competitors (cloning response) | HR practices |
| Abandonment of institutionalized practices | |
| Globalization/global competition | |
| Differences in regional labor costs | |
| Industry conditions | |
| Workforce demographics | |
| Investments in technology | |

A reasonable question to examine at this point is the generalizability of these antecedents across countries or cultures. On the surface, it might appear that important differences in the propensity to downsize employees might be attributable more to individualistic than to collectivist cultures. Individualistic cultures emerge in societies that are complex (many subgroups with different attitudes and beliefs) and loose (relatively few rules and norms about what is correct behavior in different types of situations). Collectivism emerges in societies that are simple (individuals agree on beliefs and attitudes) and tight (many rules and norms about what is correct behavior in different types of situations) (Triandis, 1998). As we noted earlier, however, in the 2007–2009 global financial crisis, even countries that traditionally have avoided layoffs (e.g., South Korea, Japan, Taiwan, and Hong Kong) embraced them.

With respect to industry deregulation and privatization, we know that there were many layoffs in the United States when industries such as telecommunications, airlines, and trucking were deregulated. Likewise, massive downsizing has occurred in China, Cuba, and Eastern European countries as formerly state-owned enterprises transitioned to private ownership. These trends suggest that external factors that precipitate employment downsizing may trump cultural taboos against it.

While many factors may contribute to the decision to downsize employees, a single individual rarely makes such decisions unilaterally. It may well be that the beliefs of top managers as a group about the role of people in their enterprises account for significant variability in decisions to downsize employees. Do they see employees as assets to be developed, as the source of innovation and renewal, or simply as factors of production, as costs to be cut? Evidence indicates that managers act very differently in the former case than in the latter (Cascio, 2002), and there is wide variability in such beliefs across countries. Finally, institutional barriers (e.g., legal constraints, as in many Western European nations) may reduce the propensity to downsize employees, even when organizations are confronted with many of the external and internal factors shown in Table 2.1.

## Suggestions for future research

Perhaps the single most vexing issue with respect to understanding the relative effects of antecedent conditions on downsizing decisions is the under-specification of predictive models. When models are under-specified they fail to include variables that can add predictive power and deepen our understanding of a phenomenon. That often leads to inconsistent findings in the research literature, and it also limits the ability to generalize findings across time or contexts.

In the case of downsizing antecedents, important moderating conditions, such as macro-environmental (exogenous) variables as well as internal organizational factors (endogenous variables) are not often included. A principal exogenous variable is the effect of industry conditions (Guthrie and Datta, 2008), a variable considered in the literatures on strategic management and industrial organization to have important effects on the incidence as well as the effectiveness of organizational initiatives. Features such as capital/labor intensity (e.g., consulting firms versus oil refineries), industry competition, market power, and changes in technology are important variables that, if included, can deepen our understanding of the antecedents of decisions to downsize. With respect to the financial outcomes of downsizing, for example, Cascio, Young, and Morris (1997) showed the powerful effect of including industry-adjusted returns in order to provide a fuller understanding of the true effects of downsizing. Other important exogenous variables are culture – national or organizational – privatization, deregulation, and institutional frameworks that vary across international samples.

In terms of endogenous variables, two important ones are the timing and spacing of downsizing decisions over time. Others include managerial actions or internal organizational events, such as cutbacks in expenditures for capital investments, or patterns of significant reductions in net operating expenses over time relative to changes in revenues. Inclusion of variables like these requires the use of qualitative as well as quantitative methodologies. Both can and should play useful roles in future research on the antecedents of downsizing.

Downsizing in the United States in the 1970s, 1980s, and the early 1990s largely affected manufacturing enterprises, with more than 7 million manufacturing jobs lost since the late 1970s (Perry, 2011). More recently, however, service jobs in sectors such as information technology, financial services, engineering, education, and travel have been hard hit. This is not surprising, given that in the United States about 85 percent of non-farm jobs are in services. Are the factors that lead to downsizing decisions in the service sector any different from those that precipitated downsizing in manufacturing? We just do not know.

Another endogenous variable that is likely to have a significant effect on the decision to downsize is firm strategy. As an example, consider a firm that competes through innovation. Is it less likely to downsize employees when times get tough than one that competes through cost leadership? While the answer might seem obvious, it would be helpful to be able to cite research that examines this issue systematically.

While the innovator focuses on product leadership and cycle time, the cost cutter emphasizes operational excellence and doing more with less of everything – including fewer people. For the innovator, people are a source of competitive advantage; for the cost cutter, people are an expense to be minimized (Cascio, 2006). To illustrate the difference in philosophy, consider the approach of Steve Jobs, the deceased former CEO of Apple, Inc., to managing in difficult economic times:

> We've had one of these before, when the dot-com bubble burst. What I told our company was that we were just going to invest our way through the downturn, that we weren't going to lay off people, that we'd taken a tremendous amount of effort to get them into Apple in the first place – the last thing we were going to do is lay them off. And we were going to keep funding. In fact, we were going to up our R&D budget so that we would be ahead of our competitors when the

downturn was over. And that's exactly what we did. And it worked. And that's exactly what we'll do this time. (Morris, 2008)

Unfortunately, much research on the antecedents of downsizing fails to consider firm strategy, or other firm attributes, such as size, age, or ownership and governance structure.

A final antecedent variable that researchers might profitably examine is compensation level and its impact on downsizing decisions. Perhaps the most high-profile example of this is now-defunct Circuit City, the electronics retailer that decided it needed to get rid of its 3,400 highest-paid (and almost certainly most productive) sales associates to cut its costs. When it did, customer service, innovation, and productivity all fell in the face of a smaller and demoralized workforce. As the company lost more ground, it did more layoffs, as the cycle continued. Once the death spiral started, it was hard to stop. Fewer people with fewer skills in the Circuit City stores permitted competitors such as Best Buy to gain ground; Circuit City filed for bankruptcy in 2008 and closed its doors in March 2009 (Pfeffer, 2010).

The Circuit City example illustrates the need for longitudinal studies that incorporate qualitative as well as quantitative methods. Relatedly, as Pfeffer (1998) has argued, firms that "follow the herd" in terms of employment boom-and-bust cycles will fall into the trap of "buying high and selling low" in the labor market, yielding higher compensation costs relative to those firms that follow more stable employment patterns. This issue, though critically important, remains largely unexplored in the research literature.

## *Implications for policy and practice*

Much research has been conducted over the past two decades on the antecedents and outcomes of employment downsizing. This chapter has focused only on antecedents, forces that may lead to decisions to downsize employees. Faced with declining demand, competitors that are downsizing employees, changing industry conditions or workforce demographics, just to name a few forces that drive downsizing decisions, it is easy to decide that reducing the workforce is in an organization's best interests. But wait. Before acting in haste, consider answers to questions such as the following.

Why does employment downsizing make sense for the organization? What is the business case for it? What is the problem that the organization is trying to solve? If the problem is short-term cash flow, are there alternative ways to cut costs? Do prospective layoffs include hard-to-find skill sets? When the economy turns around, as it will, will your organization be faced with the problem of trying to re-recruit people with the very same skill sets that you laid off? How will the downsizing affect high performers who are difficult to replace? What are the short-term payoffs, and what long-term threats to the organization's strategic success might be associated with employment downsizing? Do the long-term benefits associated with such a strategy outweigh its short-term costs?

Regarding firm policies and practices, researchers could make less equivocal statements about both of these if they had a more comprehensive understanding of the internal as well as external antecedents of employment downsizing, and if they could map important variables that might mediate decisions to downsize. While an admirable goal to strive for, this kind of multi-level, longitudinal research is difficult to do. Nevertheless, we now know the kind of research that needs to be done, and data are available to populate such models. The challenge remains for researchers to seize those opportunities. Companies, managers, employees, and society will all benefit in very practical, meaningful ways from the insights that such research can provide.

### *Note*

1. The key phrase above is "other things remaining equal." Many organizations define workers only in terms of how much they cost and fail to consider the value they create. For this reason, other things often do not remain equal, so many of the anticipated benefits of employment downsizing do not materialize.

## References

Ahmadjian, C. L. and Robinson, P. 2001. "Safety in numbers: Downsizing and the deinstitutionalization of permanent employment in Japan." *Administrative Science Quarterly* **46**: 622–654.

Attewell, P. and Rule, J. 1984. "Computing and organizations: What we know and what we don't know." *Communications of the ACM* **27**: 1184–1192.

Barney, J. B. 1995. "Looking inside for competitive advantage." *Academy of Management Executive* **9**(4): 49–61.

Baumol, W. J., Blinder, A., and Wolff, E. N. 2003. *Downsizing in America: Reality, Causes, and Consequences.* New York: Russell Sage Foundation.

Bethel, J. E. and Liebeskind, J. 1993. "The effects of ownership structure on corporate restructuring." *Strategic Management Journal* **14**: 15–31.

Black, T. 2011. "S&P 500 cash hoards shrink for first time since 2009." February 16. Downloaded from http://www.bloomberg.com/news/print/2011-02-16/cash-hoards-shrink-at-s-p-500-for-first-time-since-09-as-obama- woos-ceos.html, February 17, 2011.

Blackstone, B. 2010. "Jobs data vindicate Germany's work plan." *The Wall Street Journal*, October 28, p. A13.

*Bloomberg Business Week*. 2010. "The gulf in auto wages." September 12, p. 82.

Blow, C. M. 2011. "The seeds of change." *The New York Times*, February 18, p. 2.

Bowen, D. E. and Ostroff, C. 2004. "Understanding HRM-firm performance linkages: The role of the 'strength' of the HRM system." *Academy of Management Review* **29**(2): 203–221.

Budros, A. 1997. "The new capitalism and organizational rationality: The adoption of downsizing programs, 1979–1994." *Social Forces* **76**: 229–250.

Budros, A. 2000. "Organizational types and organizational innovation: Downsizing among industrial, financial and utility firms." *Sociological Forum* **17**: 307–342.

Budros, A. 2002. "The mean and lean firm: Causes of involuntary and voluntary downsizing strategies." *Sociological Forum* **17**: 307–342.

Budros, A. 2004. "Causes of early and later organizational adoption: The case of corporate downsizing." *Sociological Inquiry* **74**: 355–380.

Cameron, K. S. 1994. "Investigating organizational downsizing: Fundamental issues." *Human Resource Management* **33**: 183–188.

Cascio, W. F. 2002. *Responsible Restructuring: Creative and Profitable Alternatives to Layoffs*. San Francisco, CA: Berrett-Kohler.

Cascio, W. F. 2006. "Decency means more than 'always low prices': A comparison of Costco to Wal-Mart's Sam's Club." *Academy of Management Perspectives* **20**(3): 26–37.

Cascio, W. F. 2010a. *Employment Downsizing and Its Alternatives*. Alexandria, VA: Society for Human Resource Management Foundation.

Cascio, W. F. 2010b. *Managing Human Resources: Productivity, Quality of Work Life, Profits* (8th edn.). New York: McGraw-Hill.

Cascio, W. F., Young, C. E., and Morris, J. R. 1997. "Financial consequences of employment-change decisions in major US corporations." *Academy of Management Journal* **40**: 1175–1189.

Conyon, M. J., Girma, S., Thompson, S., and Wright, P. W. 2002. "The impact of mergers and acquisitions on company employment in the United Kingdom." *European Economic Review* **46**: 31–49.

Conyon, M. J., Girma, S., Thompson, S., and Wright, P. W. 2004. "Do wages rise or fall following merger?" *Oxford Bulletin of Economics and Statistics* **66**: 847–862.

Coucke, K., Pennings, E., and Sleuwaegen, L. 2007. "Employee layoffs under different modes of restructuring: Exit, downsizing or relocation." *Industrial and Corporate Change* **16**: 161–182.

Coy, P. 2011a. "If demography is destiny, then India has the edge." *Bloomberg Businessweek*, January 23, pp. 9, 10.

Coy, P. 2011b. "A message from the street." *Bloomberg Businessweek*, February 13, pp. 58–65.

Damouni, N. and Kim, S. 2011. "Confident, cash-rich CEOs drive M&A to 4-year high." Downloaded from www.reuters.com/assets/print?aid=USTRE71D7ER20110214, February 14, 2011.

Datta, D. K., Guthrie, J. P., Basuil, D., and Pandey, A. 2010. "Causes and effects of employee downsizing: A review and synthesis." *Journal of Management* **36**: 281–348.

De Meuse, K. P., Marks, M. L., and Dai, G. 2011. "Organizational downsizing, mergers and acquisitions, and strategic alliances: Using theory and research to enhance practice," in S. Zedeck (ed.), *Handbook of Industrial and Organizational Psychology*, Vol. III. Washington, DC: APA Books, pp. 729–768.

DiMaggio, P. and Powell, W. 1983. "The iron cage revisited: Institutional isomorphism and collective rationality in organizational fields." *American Sociological Review* **48**: 147–160.

Dixon, S. 2003. "Implications of population ageing for the labour market." *Labour Market Trends* **111**(2): 67–76.

*Economist*. 2006. "Turning boomers into boomerangs." February 16, pp. 65–67.

Eisenhardt, K. M. 1989. "Agency theory: An assessment and review." *Academy of Management Review* **14**: 57–74.

Ellig, B. 2002. *The Complete Guide to Executive Compensation*. New York: McGraw-Hill.

Fama, E. F. and Jensen, M. C. 1983. "Agency problems and residual claims." *Journal of Law and Economics* **26**: 327–350.

Feldman, D. C. 2007. "Late-career and retirement issues," in H. Gunz and M. Peiperl (eds.), *Handbook of Career Studies*. Thousand Oaks, CA: Sage, pp. 153–168.

Filatotchev, I., Buck, T., and Zhukov, V. 2000. "Downsizing in privatized firms in Russia, Ukraine, and Belarus." *Academy of Management Journal* **43**: 286–304.

*Fortune's 100 Best Companies to Work For*. 2011. Downloaded from http://money.cnn.com/magazines/fortune/bestcompanies/2011/index.html, March 7, 2011.

Gandolfi, F. 2008. "Reflecting on downsizing: What have managers learned?" *SAM Advanced Management Journal* **73**(2): 46–56.

Gogoi, P. 2010. "Where are the jobs? For many companies, overseas." December 28. http//finance.yahoo.com on January 4, 2011.

Guthrie, J. P. and Datta, D. K. 2008. "Dumb and dumber: The impact of downsizing on firm performance as moderated by industry conditions." *Organization Science* **19**: 108–123.

Hallock, K. F. 1998. "Layoffs, top executive pay, and firm performance." *American Economic Review* **88**: 711–723.

Hambrick, D. C. and Mason, P. A. 1984. "Upper echelons: The organization as a reflection of its top managers." *Academy of Management Review* **9**: 193–206.

Hillier, D., Marshall, A. P., McColgan, P., and Werema, S. 2006. "Employee layoffs, shareholder wealth and firm performance: Evidence from the UK." *Journal of Business Finance and Accounting* **34**: 467–494.

Kessler, A. 2011. "Is your job an endangered species?" *The Wall Street Journal*, February 17, p. A19.

Kets de Vries, M. F. R. and Balazs, K. 1997. "The downside of downsizing." *Human Relations* **50**(1): 11–50.

Kirshnan, A. 2006. "Worker shuffles at SAS again." Available at www.news-observer.com.

Krishnan, H. A., Hitt, M. A., and Park, D. 2007. "Acquisitions premiums, subsequent work force reductions, and post-acquisition performance." *Journal of Management Studies* **44**: 709–732.

Lehto, E. and Böckerman, P. 2008. "Analyzing the employment effects of mergers and acquisitions." *Journal of Economic Behavior and Organization* **68**: 112–124.

Lende, T. 2005. "Older workers: Opportunity or challenge?" *Canadian Manager* **30**(1): 20–23.

Miller, D. J. 1995. "CEO salary increases may be rational after all: Referents and contracts in CEO pay." *Academy of Management Journal* **38**(5): 1361–1385.

Misra, S. 2007. "Socio-economic trends in India: Implications for HR Policies." Presentation, Indian School of Business, January, Hyderabad, India.

Morris, B. 2001. "White-collar blues." *Fortune*, July 23, pp. 98–110.

Morris, B. 2008. "America's most admired companies: Steve Jobs speaks out." *Fortune*, March 6. Downloaded from http://money.cnn.com/galleries/2008/fortune/0803/gallery.jobsqna.fortune/index.html

O'Shaughnessy, K. C. and Flanagan, D. J. 1998. "Determinants of layoff announcements following M&As: An empirical investigation." *Strategic Management Journal* **19**: 989–999.

Perry, M. J. 2011. "The truth about US manufacturing." *The Wall Street Journal*, February 25, p. A13.

Perry, T. and Shivdasani, A. 2005. "Do boards affect performance? Evidence from corporate restructuring." *Journal of Business*, **78**: 1403–1431.

Pfeffer, J. 1998. *The Human Equation: Building Profits by Putting People First*. Boston, MA: Harvard Business School Press.

Pfeffer, J. 2010. "Lay off the layoffs." *Newsweek*, February 15. Available at www.newsweek.com/id/233131.

Power, C. 2010. "Machines don't get paid overtime." *Bloomberg Businessweek*, August 8, p. 13.

Redman, T. and Keithley, D. 1998. "Downsizing goes east? Employment restructuring in post-socialist Poland." *International Journal of Human Resource Management* **9**: 274–295.

Society for Human Resource Management Foundation. 2010. "Once the deal is done: Managing a merger." DVD produced by the Society for Human Resource Management Foundation, Alexandria, VA.

*South China Morning Post*. 2002. "China warns of 20 million urban jobless." April 30, p. 1.

Stavrou, E., Kassinis, G., and Filotheou, A. 2007. "Downsizing and stakeholder orientation among the *Fortune* 500: Does family ownership matter?" *Journal of Business Ethics* 7: 149–162.

Surowiecki, J. 2007. "It's the workforce, stupid!" *The New Yorker*, April 30. Downloaded from www.newyorker.com, May 2, 2007

Triandis, H. C. 1998. "Vertical and horizontal individualism and collectivism: Theory and research implications for international comparative management," in J. L. Cheng and R. B. Peterson (eds.), *Advances in International and Comparative Management*. Greenwich, CT: JAI Press, pp. 7–35.

Tsai, C., Wu, S., Wang, H., and Huang, I. 2006. "An empirical research on the institutional theory of downsizing: Evidence from MNC's subsidiary companies in Taiwan." *Total Quality Management and Business Excellence* **17**: 633–654.

Vits, C. and Randow, J. 2010. "The price of saving jobs in Germany." *Bloomberg Businessweek*, August 8, pp. 12, 13.

Wagar, T. 1997. "Factors affecting permanent workforce reduction: Evidence from large Canadian organizations." *Canadian Journal of Administrative Sciences* **14**: 303–314.

Yawson, A. 2006. "Evaluating the characteristics of corporate boards associated with layoff decisions." *Corporate Governance: An International Review* **14**: 75–84.

Yoo, H. and Mody, B. 2000. "Predictors of downsizing in the US local telephone industry." *Information Society* **16**: 23–33.

Yu, G. and Park, J. 2006. "The effect of downsizing on the financial performance and employee productivity of Korean Firms." *International Journal of Manpower* **27**: 230–250.

Zatzick, C. D. and Iverson, R. D. 2006. "High-involvement management and workforce reduction: Competitive advantage or disadvantage?" *Academy of Management Journal* **49**: 999–1015.

Zatzick, C. D., Marks, M. L., and Iverson, R. D. 2009. "Which way should you downsize in a crisis?" *MIT Sloan Management Review* **51**(1): 78–86.

# 3 *The antecedents of downsizing*

SARAH J. FREEMAN AND KYLE EHRHARDT

In this chapter, we identify and address factors which may, either directly or indirectly, influence a firm's decision to downsize. Generally speaking, downsizing has received scholarly attention since the mid 1980s. At that time, downsizing was associated primarily with decline (Whetten, 1980), and writers assumed that when organizations implemented downsizing, for example through involuntary layoffs, they were responding either to organizational decline or to cyclical drops in demand (Cappelli, 2000). Research on the phenomenon was conducted largely in US manufacturing firms by organizational scholars, and in local government operations by researchers in public administration.

In the intervening quarter century, research and theorizing on all aspects of downsizing have burgeoned. Concomitantly, the focus of downsizing research has widened: downsizing is not necessarily associated with decline, and it goes beyond layoffs – it encompasses other tactics and activities as well, including planned attrition, early retirements and buyouts, and may or may not involve organizational redesign and large-scale restructuring (Freeman, 1999). Downsizing research picked up steam in the late 1980s and early 1990s with the advent of widespread reductions in the salaried work forces of many organizations. Ever since, downsizing – framed both as a response to environmental conditions and as a proactive management strategy – (Cameron, Freeman, and Mishra, 1993) has continued unabated. It accompanied the shift to a knowledge economy and the globalization of competitive pressures; continued through the economic recovery and expansion of the late 1990s and early twenty-first century; and, more recently, was apparent in the near collapse of the economic system in the United States and much of the rest of the developed world.

At the same time, the geographic range of this practice has expanded tremendously. In the past, downsizing was regarded primarily as an

American phenomenon, while workforces elsewhere in the world enjoyed a tradition of lifetime employment and/or rigorous legal protection for jobs (Alakent and Lee, 2010; Datta, Guthrie, Basuil, and Pandey, 2010). Now, a brief scan of recent scholarly literature on downsizing reveals studies using samples in Australia, Belarus, Belgium, Canada, China, Finland, France, Hong Kong, Indonesia, Ireland, Israel, Japan, the Netherlands, the Philippines, Russia, South Korea, Spain, Taiwan, Thailand, and the United Kingdom – and, in all likelihood, this only scratches the surface of downsizing's reach.

With economic challenges continuing globally, downsizing as a topic has once again gained some urgency. Nearly 9 million jobs were lost in the United States alone during the 2007–2009 recession (Barker and Hadi, 2010; Zumbrun and Chandra, 2011); during that period, US payrolls fell nearly 6 percent (Bivens, 2010). At the time of this writing, US unemployment had just recently fallen below 9 percent for the first time since May 2009. But why do organizations downsize? Empirical investigations have indicated that, on the whole, the outcomes of downsizing – for organizations, as well as for employees – are equivocal at best. Thus, inquiry into its organizational and environmental antecedents is worthwhile.

Before proceeding with our discussion of downsizing's antecedents, it is useful to clarify the definition of downsizing. For the purposes of this chapter, downsizing consists of a set of managerial activities that reduces the number of employees in an organization on the whole, or in some part of an organization specifically. Moreover, in contrast to early characterizations of downsizing (e.g., Whetten, 1980), scholars now recognize that downsizing is distinct from decline. Specifically, downsizing indicates an intentional act – it does not happen *to* an organization but rather is something the organization and its management choose to undertake, even when undertaken in response to circumstances in the external environment. In addition, downsizing is purposive; it is aimed at organizational improvement, whether in the form of efficiency, effectiveness, or some combination thereof (Freeman and Cameron, 1993).

## Antecedents of downsizing

At first glance, it may appear obvious why organizations undertake downsizing: in response to a cyclical or structural contraction in demand

(Cappelli, 2000), or in order to balance productive capacity with demand. However, empirical evidence and managerial rationales offered indicate this is not always the case. Although early experience in the United States associated any kind of organizational shrinkage with decline (Zammuto and Cameron, 1985), beginning in the mid 1990s researchers began to take note that healthy, profitable, even growing firms increasingly engaged in downsizing (Cameron, 1994; McKinley, Sanchez, and Schick, 1995). No longer necessarily a sign of environmental contraction or managerial missteps, downsizing was even hailed at times as a sign of proactive leadership and responsible stewardship of organizational resources (Cameron, 1994). During 1994, for instance, ten oil companies went through restructuring, cost-cutting, and downsizing initiatives. In 1995, American Express announced record quarterly earnings and, less than a week later, announced plans for a major workforce reduction. Moreover, by 1996, during a period of general economic expansion, downsizing had achieved a level of ubiquity that led the *New York Times* to run a week-long special series on the practice (*New York Times*, 1996). Clearly, any stigma formerly associated with downsizing had become detached.

Drawing on existing downsizing research, we can identify four broad classifications of factors that may contribute to management's decision to downsize the organization. However, it is important to point out that specific factors present within these overarching classifications are commonly interrelated, as well as sometimes overlapping.

The first category of downsizing antecedents reflects "causes" of downsizing: that is, either events or changes in the internal or external context of an organization that lead, more or less directly, to a managerial decision to engage in downsizing. Because the decision to downsize on account of these "causes" represents individuals' reactions to the internal or external environment, we classify this group as factors associated with reactive downsizing. In essence, events inside or outside the organization lead to downsizing activity as a response, which would not have occurred otherwise, in an attempt to reposition the firm with respect to competition, profitability, or other aspects of performance. The second classification of downsizing antecedents may be conceived as contextual factors, which act as moderators affecting the likelihood of an organization's downsizing. These factors include characteristics of the firm itself, firm leadership, as well as

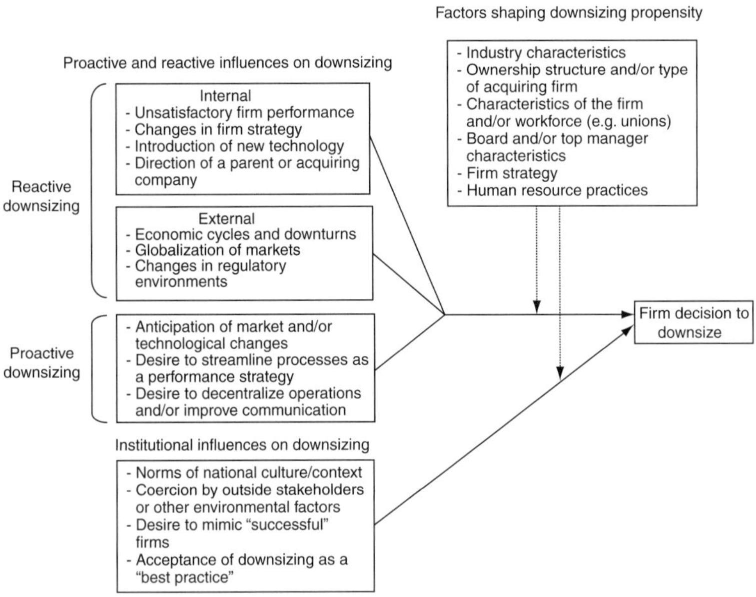


**Figure 3.1** A framework for understanding the antecedents of downsizing

additional influences independent of the organization. In short, we understand that these predictors do not cause downsizing directly, but rather influence firms' propensity to downsize. The third category of downsizing antecedents reflects goals that are associated with proactive downsizing. The definition of downsizing offered above indicates that it consists of purposive managerial action. That said, what is the goal of that action, especially without unsatisfactory performance or some precipitating event? This assumes that smaller size, in and of itself, is not management's intention, but that management hopes to achieve some other set of outcomes via downsizing. Finally, the fourth classification concerns institutional forces and/or pressures which may influence firm leadership to engage in downsizing practices.

In the following sections, we discuss each of these four classifications of downsizing antecedents, as well as highlight previous research that has addressed the individual factor's role in shaping downsizing decisions. Figure 3.1 provides an organizing framework that guides this discussion and review.

## *Causes and reactive downsizing*

As noted above, factors both internal and external to the firm may influence firm leadership's reactive downsizing decisions.

### Internal causes of downsizing

A great deal of prior research has found an association between firms implementing downsizing and unsatisfactory performance, as indicated by accounting or financial measures. The most thoroughly documented of these is the relationship between downsizing and profitability, measured in a variety of ways. For example, layoffs were found to be more likely among Japanese firms that had lower return on assets (ROA) during the late 1980s (Kang and Shivdasani, 1997). Also, firm losses predicted both moderate and severe downsizing among Japanese firms in the 1990s (Ahmadjian and Robinson, 2001). Likewise, Budros found low profitability to be associated with downsizing among financial firms (Budros, 2000), as well as a decline in profitability as predictive of downsizing among the *Fortune* 100 from 1979 to 1995 (Budros, 2002, 2004). In a qualitative study of companies in Taiwan, Tsai, Wu, Wang, and Huang (2006) found that either declining or stagnant profitability led to downsizing. In both Korea and the United States, lower profitability, measured by both ROA and income per employee, was associated with downsizing by public firms (Budros, 1997; Yu and Park, 2006). Hillier, Marshall, McColgan, and Werema (2007) found that declines in ROA were associated with the use of involuntary layoffs among public firms in the United Kingdom during the 1990s. Lower return on equity (ROE) has also been associated with the likelihood of layoffs (Coucke, Pennings, and Sleuwaegen, 2007; Iqbal and Shetty, 1994).

Researchers have also investigated extensively the relationship between downsizing and other indicators of firm performance. Declines in shareholder value have often been found to lead to downsizing (Budros, 1997, 2000, 2004; Perry and Shivdasani, 2005), as have high current ratio and inventory levels (Iqbal and Shetty, 1994) and lower asset turnover (Yu and Park, 2006). In addition, a number of researchers have found that firms with high debt levels are prone to downsizing when confronted with financial distress (Coucke *et al.*, 2007; Gittell, Cameron, Lim, and Rivas, 2006; Hillier *et al.*, 2007; Ofek, 1993). Low or declining productivity and lower capacity utilization have also been associated with layoffs (Alakent and Lee, 2010; Gittell *et al.*, 2006; Yoo and

Mody, 2000). Finally, several researchers have found a relationship between downsizing and declines in sales or market share (Ahmadjian and Robinson, 2001; Alakent and Lee, 2010; Budros, 1997; Iqbal and Shetty, 1994; Osterman, 2000).

Critical strategic and/or operational changes within a firm may additionally lead to downsizing decisions. Investigating data from a large sample of Canadian firms that downsized in the early 1990s, Wagar (1997) found that major changes in strategy were associated with severe (but not mild or moderate) workforce reductions, and that the introduction of new, labor-saving technology within the firm was associated with downsizing of all levels. Yoo and Mody (2000) also found a positive relationship between downsizing and the introduction of new technology as part of a firm's core operations. Specifically, using a sample of US-based telephone companies, the authors found that increased levels of digitalization invoked a meaningful influence on both short-term and long-term employment reductions within this industry between 1988 and 1995. Furthermore, the effect of digitalization was significant even after controlling for a variety of additional antecedents of downsizing, for example performance factors such as productivity level. Finally, the introduction of information technology has been found to be associated with decreasing firm size (Brynjolfsson, Malone, Gurbaxani, and Kambil, 1994), although its ultimate impact depended on the level of centralization of decision-making authority within the organization (Pinsonneault and Kraemer, 1997).

For subsidiary companies, an organizational decision to downsize may additionally be driven by a mandate from the parent firm (Ahmadjian and Robbins, 2005; Tsai *et al.*, 2006). Similarly, a downsizing edict may also transpire in cases where one firm is acquired by another. Several researchers have observed a link between mergers and acquisitions and subsequent downsizing (Budros, 2000, 2002; Lehto and Böckerman, 2008; Siegel and Simons, 2010). Further, even the mere threat of a takeover may precipitate downsizing (Hillier *et al.*, 2007). The relationship between mergers and acquisitions and downsizing appears especially strong under certain circumstances, for instance when the acquisition occurs across national borders (Budros, 1997; Lehto and Böckerman, 2008), is hostile or contested (Conyon, Girma, Thompson, and Wright, 2002), involves a private equity firm as the acquirer (Rodrigues and Child, 2010), includes a target firm with low operating efficiency (O'Shaughnessy and Flanagan, 1998), and/or requires the acquiring firm to pay a higher acquisition premium (Krishnan, Hitt, and Park, 2007).

In the end, virtually all internal causes of downsizing relate to a gap between the desired and actual performance levels of the firm. Although these performance gaps may themselves stem from a variety of causes, in the relationships detailed above downsizing comes about as a reaction to factors internal to the firm. It is aimed at lowering the firm's cost structure, thereby improving profitability, adapting to sales declines, increasing operating efficiency, and so forth.

**External causes of downsizing**

Events in the external environment can also lead to downsizing. Most commonly, economic cycles and severe market collapse have been associated with downsizing (Appelbaum, Lavigne-Schmidt, Peytchev, and Shapiro, 1999). For instance, the advent of the Asian financial crisis was found to increase the likelihood of downsizing, even in societies with a tradition of permanent employment (Alakent and Lee, 2010; Mellahi and Guermat, 2009), ultimately leading to the downfall of this tradition. Additionally, Wagar (1997) found that declines in market demand were associated with mild, moderate, and severe downsizing, while Filatotchev, Buck, and Zhukov (2000) found that declines in overall industry output predicted downsizing. However, it should be pointed out that some evidence does exist to the contrary; that is, instead of downsizing occurring as a result of economic slumps, economic upturns may also bring about downsizing decisions. Supporting this counterintuitive notion, for example, Budros (1997) found an association between downsizing and economic cycles, which suggested that the downsizing rate was higher during periods of economic expansion (cf., Budros, 2000).

Globalization of markets has also been associated with downsizing (Appelbaum *et al.*, 1999), as have increases in foreign competition (Budros, 1997). In addition, changes in the regulation of markets and industries, usually resulting in greater competition and demands for efficiency, are associated with downsizing. Budros (1997, 2002), for example, found that industry deregulation was likely to be accompanied by downsizing. Similarly, but in a quite different environment, other researchers found an association between changes in the funding and oversight of failing school districts and downsizing (Boyne and Meier, 2009). In state-run economies, a shift toward market pressures has been associated with downsizing among both private and state-run organizations (Dong and Xu, 2009; Redman and Keithley, 1998). Similarly, privatization of formerly nationalized industries and state-run businesses has been attended by downsizing in an attempt to increase organizational efficiency (Filatotchev *et al.*, 2000; Redman and Keithley, 1998; Rodrigues and Child, 2008; Vicente-Lorente and Suárez-González, 2007). All external causes of downsizing discussed above reflect either the contraction of an environmental niche or increased competition – that is, a shift to a less munificent, and often more complex, environment.

All in all, the above review identifies numerous internal and external factors that may lead directly to managerial decisions to engage in downsizing, including factors associated with firm performance, firm strategy, the external environment, technology, and the modern realities of the global marketplace, among others. In the next section, we shift focus onto factors that may shape a firm's inclination to undertake downsizing.

## *Moderators: Factors influencing firms' propensity to downsize*

In addition to those factors that have been found to lead to downsizing, researchers have investigated many more that – although they do not cause downsizing per se – are associated with it as antecedents. We describe these here as moderators, although researchers have not always modeled them as such. Just as the relationship between causes that precipitate downsizing and actual downsizing activity is not determinate, these characteristics also do not predict with certainty that, given a precipitating event, organizations will undertake downsizing. However, their strong association with downsizing indicates that these characteristics influence the likelihood that organizations' management will be willing to initiate downsizing, whether in response to unsatisfactory performance, to external demands, or as a proactive approach to organizational improvement.

### Industry characteristics

Several researchers have identified industry sectors and characteristics that are associated with a greater or lesser likelihood of downsizing. First, organizations in different industry sectors demonstrate varying proclivities for undertaking downsizing. Wagar (1997) found that both the use of workforce reductions and the level of those reductions (mild, moderate, or severe) varied by industry sector. Specifically, while companies in the Canadian retail and service sectors did not implement downsizing to a significant degree, those in the communication/transportation, finance, health care, and education sectors undertook mild to moderate downsizing between 1990 and 1992. Similarly, Belgian firms in the service industry were less likely to implement workforce reductions, while those in manufacturing were more likely (Coucke *et al.*, 2007). On the other side, Finnish construction, hospitality, and other service firms undergoing mergers were more likely to experience employment reductions than were those in manufacturing and the utility industry (Lehto and Böckerman, 2008). Similarly, among firms exposed to the Asian economic crisis, industry sector was a significant predictor of the adoption of downsizing (Mellahi and Guermat, 2009).

Budros has investigated the effects of industry sector and characteristics most extensively. For example, he found that industry culture, defined as either competition-oriented (manufacturing and retail) or service-oriented (financial services and utilities), predicted the downsizing rate within an industry, with those in competition-oriented industries more likely to adopt downsizing (Budros, 1997). In addition, he found that manufacturing firms were more likely to downsize in the early phases of an economic downturn, but less likely to in the later phases, and that the likelihood of a focal firm's downsizing was related to the percentage of firms with the same two-digit SIC (standard industrial classification) code that had downsized (Budros, 2004). Budros also identified several moderating effects of industry in relationships between downsizing and other predictors. Low profit and declining shareholder value led to downsizing in the financial sector, but not in the industrial or utility sectors. Mergers and acquisitions increased the likelihood of downsizing in the industrial sector, but not for organizations in the financial or utility industries. CEO functional background predicted the adoption of downsizing for financial companies, but not for industrial companies or utilities (Budros, 2000).

### Ownership structure

Several aspects of a firm's ownership structure have a demonstrated influence on the likelihood of organizations' downsizing. The existence of large ownership blocks, distinct from institutional ownership, is associated with a greater propensity to engage in downsizing (Bethel and Liebeskind, 1993; Budros, 1997; Filatotchev *et al.*, 2000).

However, firms in which family members owned at least 5 percent of outstanding shares were less likely to downsize (Stavrou, Kassinis, and Filotheou, 2007).

Researchers have found conflicting results on the effects of managerial ownership; while greater levels of managerial ownership were associated with a lower likelihood of downsizing (Filatotchev *et al.*, 2000), changes in managerial ownership (Filatotchev *et al.*, 2000) and increases in the number of shares held by the CEO (Hsieh and Davidson, 2008) increased the likelihood of firms' downsizing. Foreign ownership of a firm was also found to increase the likelihood of engaging in downsizing among firms in Korea (Alakent and Lee, 2010), Japan (Ahmadjian and Robinson, 2001), and Spain (Vicente-Lorente and Suárez-González, 2007). This effect was moreover unrelated to the home country of the parent company. However, Ahmadjian and Robbins (2005) found that membership in a large corporate group (*keiretsu*) among Japanese companies increased the likelihood that they would undertake downsizing.

Acquisition by a private equity firm has been associated with the likelihood of downsizing; however, this association has further been shown to be contingent on the acquirer's strategy for extracting value from the target (Rodrigues and Child, 2010). When the acquirer's value-creation strategy focused on extracting maximum value from the target over the short term, downsizing was likely. However, when the acquirer focused instead on renewing and developing firm assets over the long term, downsizing was less likely to occur. Although this finding is framed in terms of value-creation strategy, it may also indicate the influence of short-term versus long-term orientation among those making the downsizing decision. When attention is focused – whether by predilection or by circumstances – on short-term profitability rather than long-term growth, downsizing is more likely to occur.

**Board and firm characteristics**

Many researchers have established relationships between the adoption of downsizing and characteristics internal to the organization. Perry and Shivdasani (2005) found that a higher percentage of outsiders on the board was associated with greater likelihood of downsizing; Yawson (2006) confirmed this result, and also found positive relationships between smaller board size and higher director compensation and downsizing.

Firm age has often been included as a control variable when predicting the likelihood of layoffs, but empirical studies have produced conflicting results. While Ahmadjian and Robinson (2001) found a positive relationship between firm age and the likelihood of downsizing among Japanese firms, other researchers have found negative relationships among US (Osterman, 2000) and Belgian (Coucke *et al.*, 2007) firms. Consistent effects have generally been found for organization size: larger firms are more likely to undertake downsizing across a span of timeframes and settings (Ahmadjian and Robinson, 2001; Budros, 1997; Coucke *et al.*, 2007; Hallock, 1998; Kang and Shivdasani, 1997; Wagar, 1997). Still, even findings for the influence of organizational size have not proven universal – as Alakent and Lee (2010) demonstrated, during the Asian financial crisis of the late 1990s, larger firms were less likely to downsize.

Despite the cyclical downsizing executed in unionized manufacturing settings of the industrial age, more recently unionization has functioned to inhibit downsizing (Alakent and Lee, 2010; Osterman, 2000). Similarly, an organization's commitment to employee job security has, not surprisingly, been associated with lower levels of downsizing (Wagar, 1997). Several dimensions of strategy have also been associated with firms' propensity to engage in downsizing. High levels of diversification have been found to be associated with greater likelihood of downsizing (Hillier *et al.*, 2007), as has a cost leadership strategy when compared with product differentiation strategy (Coucke *et al.*, 2007).

Some aspects of human resource management practices have been associated with downsizing. For example, Yoo and Mody (2000) found that higher employee compensation levels predicted greater use of downsizing. The use of high performance work systems, interestingly, has a positive relationship with the implementation of downsizing (Iverson and Zatzick, 2007; Osterman, 2000; Zatzick and Iverson, 2006). These are practices that seek to create employee involvement, and include training and performance incentives. Understandably, these practices can identify opportunities for workforce reductions, and – just as understandably – tend to be associated with less use of harsh tactics, such as layoffs, compared to buyouts, early retirements, and attrition. Finally, where a strong and positive firm reputation has been associated with a lower likelihood of downsizing (Ahmadjian and Robinson, 2001; Zumbrun and Chandra, 2011), prior experience with downsizing apparently makes it easier to undertake this practice yet again (Alakent and Lee, 2010; Cascio, 2002).

A number of CEO and top management team characteristics have been associated with the adoption of downsizing as well. CEO tenure has been found to have a negative relationship with downsizing in that newer CEOs are more likely to undertake downsizing (Budros, 2004; Hallock, 1998), although Budros (2000) found this to be true in industrial firms, but not in financial or utility firms. Similarly, younger CEOs were more likely to implement downsizing (Budros, 2002, 2004). Budros also investigated the association of CEO functional background and implementation of downsizing, and found significant effects, but they depended on the framing of the dependent variable. Looking at the downsizing adoption rate, he found that CEOs with a finance background were more likely to adopt downsizing in financial firms, though not in industrial firms or utilities (Budros, 2000). When investigating employment declines via involuntary layoffs, he found that CEOs with operations backgrounds were more likely to downsize (Budros, 2002). When he divided his study time period into early (1979–1986) and late (1987–1995) phases, the effect of CEO functional background was not significant in the early phase, but CEOs with finance or accounting backgrounds were more likely to undertake downsizing in the later phase.

Finally, personality characteristics of the CEO, specifically risk aversion and self-centeredness, have also been associated with downsizing. Carmeli and Sheaffer (2009), in fact, posited a causal relationship here, with the relationship between personality characteristics of the CEO and the decision to downsize mediated by firm decline. Their findings support the role of CEO personality in influencing the likelihood of downsizing, although they found that industry decline exhibited larger effects. In addition, social cognitions among senior managers, in particular the espousal of reengineering and endorsement of downsizing, have been associated with the implementation of downsizing (Tsai *et al.*, 2006; Zhao, Rust, McKinley, and Edwards, 2010). Mutual trust has been shown to have an effect on individuals' propensity to downsize as well. Within the top management team and between the company and external stakeholders (e.g., customers and suppliers), high trust levels are associated with greater use of downsizing; high levels of trust between management and employees, on the other hand, are associated with less use of downsizing (Mishra and Mishra, 1994).

In summary, a variety of firm characteristics, industry characteristics, ownership and board structure considerations, and distinctions among firm leaders may contribute toward shaping a firm's propensity to engage in downsizing. We address depictions of downsizing as a proactive practice in the following section.

## *Goals and proactive downsizing*

In contrast to characterizations of downsizing as a reactionary decision by firm management, some theorizing and research point to downsizing as a proactive strategy aimed at enhancing organizational effectiveness. From this perspective, whereas a reactive viewpoint positions downsizing as inescapable for firms on account of technological advances, continued cost-cutting, and the pressures for efficiency and competitiveness that accompany economic cycles and advances in globalization (Appelbaum *et al.*, 1999; Zammuto and Cameron, 1985), a proactive viewpoint concerns firms' anticipation of such pressures, thereby positioning downsizing as a potentially useful means for dealing with these challenges a priori. In this sense, although research on proactive downsizing often addresses the same environmental and internal pressures that lead to reactive downsizing, distinctions exist in terms of how the decision to downsize is presented.

### Downsizing as a mechanism for improvement

The difference between reactive and proactive downsizing might be akin to that between losing weight and promoting health. In a proactive approach to downsizing, action will more likely focus on overall organizational improvement and change. Therefore, downsizing is apt to be a byproduct of other changes. For example, Cameron and his colleagues (Cameron, 1994; Cameron, Freeman, and Mishra, 1991, 1993) found that a small subset of organizations, about 25 percent, sometimes used downsizing as a means of improving organizational processes and performance. Here, when organizations sought to remove hierarchy, it was not because additional layers of management added to overall firm costs (although they do); instead, the identified problem was that hierarchy impedes organizational functioning. In these cases, goals for downsizing went beyond cost-cutting and productivity improvement, and included streamlined processes, improved communication, and decision-making pushed closer to the location of information or implementation.

In addition, when a proactive approach was undertaken, larger-scale changes – more radical downsizing and restructuring, elimination of departments and major organizational subunits – were likely to follow, although there was also less use of harsh measures, such as involuntary layoffs (Freeman, 1999). Enthusiasm for this radical redesign, the streamlined processes, and enhanced organizational functioning even seemed to lead, somewhat oddly, to the violent metaphors associated with the reengineering movement (Hammer and Champy, 1993a, 1993b).

Downsizing may further serve as a proactive strategy for working toward externally focused organizational goals. For instance, under some circumstances, firms that downsize in an effort to improve their competitive position or address globalization may not be doing so under duress, but rather as one aspect of continuous improvement. In other cases, downsizing may follow from benchmarking "excellent" companies – the highly visible, successful, and prestigious exemplars that set the standards for best practices (McKinley, 2001; Tsai *et al.*, 2006). General Electric's Workout program became widely known, admired, and, ultimately, imitated in its approach to removing excess processes and waste – and with them, headcount – from diverse business processes, ranging from manufacturing light bulbs to generating invoices. Around the same time period, proponents of the "lean" organization model (Womack, Jones, and Roos, 1990; Womack and Jones, 1996), which is derived originally from Toyota's manufacturing system, maintained that it was possible for most organizations to produce more and higher quality products and services with fewer resources of all kinds (Kinnie, Hutchinson, and Purcell, 1997). In this vein, the varying positive aims of reengineering, total quality, and lean production came to be associated with proactive, goal-driven downsizing.

### Concerns for the utility of proactive downsizing

On the one hand, the practices identified in the preceding discussion explain the advent of healthy, profitable companies undertaking downsizing, along with downsizing as continuous improvement and downsizing as a way of life (Cameron, 1994). On the other hand, the hazy distinctions in many cases between causes and goals, between reacting to poor performance and anticipating a need to react, and therefore between reactive and proactive downsizing, raise important questions related to the antecedents of downsizing.

First, it is legitimate to question how much apparently proactive downsizing is management "spin," presenting management as positive and in control, and how much is truly proactive. Second, for most of the causal and moderating relationships discussed in prior sections, the evidence is far from conclusive. Although some well-designed studies have yielded significant links between downsizing and a range of internal and external events and circumstances, others fail to find a relationship among those same factors. For example, while it was noted above that employee compensation levels showed a positive relationship with downsizing (Yoo and Mody, 2000), this relationship was not upheld by other research (Budros, 2000; Iqbal and Shetty, 1994). Additionally, although workforce unionization has recently been associated with less use of downsizing (Alakent and Lee, 2010; Osterman, 2000), an earlier study did not find a significant relationship between these variables (Wagar, 1997). Moreover, even the most widely upheld antecedent of downsizing, firm financial performance, has not been universally supported (Iqbal and Shetty, 1994; O'Shaughnessy and Flanagan, 1998; Stavrou *et al.*, 2007; Yoo and Mody, 2000). Other examples abound.

Without a doubt, these disparate results are due in part to downsizing's reach across geography and organization type, as well as to the numerous approaches to downsizing and the variety of contextual factors that may influence implementation of this practice. As with most complex organizational phenomena, it is difficult to find precisely equivalent conditions for comparison, and equally difficult to specify and collect sufficient data on models that control for all potentially relevant factors. However, the outcomes of downsizing have also been questioned. Stock price boosts turn out to be short-lived (Bruton, Keels, and Shook, 1996; De Meuse, Vanderheiden, and Bergmann, 1994; Worrell, Davidson, and Sharma, 1991); copious dysfunctions, such as poor morale, lack of trust, and risk aversion, overtake the workforce (Cameron *et al.*, 1991; Cascio, 1993); even the hoped-for gains in productivity and profitability are elusive, according to both scholarly and practitioner studies (American Management Association, 1996; Cascio, 1993; Cascio, Young, and Morris, 1997; Society for Human Resource Management, 2002; Tomasko, 1993). These results ultimately call into question whether proactive downsizing may truly serve as a useful undertaking for firms in many circumstances. As such, managers wishing to engage in organizational downsizing as a proactive strategy may be hard-pressed to find any conclusive evidence altogether supporting their decision. Despite this, however, proactive downsizing in the workplace remains a prevalent strategy for many firms.

## *The role of institutional forces*

In this section, we give particular attention to the usefulness of institutional factors for explaining a firm's decision to downsize. Ultimately, institutional factors as downsizing antecedents have been suggested at numerous levels. For instance, at a country level, the institutional norms of national cultures provide permission for or prohibition against downsizing. To this end, Mellahi and Guermat (2009) found strong country effects in comparing the adoption of downsizing during the Asian financial crisis among a large sample of firms in Indonesia, Thailand, and the Philippines. Still, even in contexts where downsizing stands in contrast with prevailing institutional norms, the discontinuous change brought about by something like a financial crisis can lead to the unraveling of existing norms (Alakent and Lee, 2010; Tsai *et al.*, 2006), and often to their replacement by new standards and expectations.

Beyond country-level considerations, however, institutional factors hold their greatest influence on a firm's decision to downsize when considered at the industry and organizational levels. According to institutional theory, institutional rules take on the qualities of myths in dictating how organizations should be structured and behave (Meyer and Rowan, 1977). They specify prevailing standards for "correct" action, to which organizations must adhere to maintain their legitimacy. Important to our discussion, institutional rules are unrelated to demonstrated economic rationality or technical efficiency. Instead, they require conformity to behavioral norms, necessary to obtain the social acceptance of the organization's field, which would include other organizations in its industry, as well as the financial community, business press, and others on which the organization depends for resources and approval.

The adoption of organizational downsizing, spreading throughout the United States and to much of the rest of the world, indicates such a process is taking place, as prior national and industry norms are replaced by a supra-national belief in the utility, even necessity, of downsizing. As these norms take hold, downsizing activity itself may be viewed as evidence of good management, and commentators seldom demand confirmation of its efficacy. For instance, as "lean and mean" has turned into an organizational ideal (Kinnie *et al.*, 1997; McKinley *et al.*, 1995), downsizing became a taken-for-granted means of achieving this end, despite acknowledgement of the organizational and individual pain it entails. Theorists have argued for and researchers have found the presence of all three types of isomorphic forces predicted by institutional theory in the diffusion and acceptance of organizational downsizing (Budros, 1997; McKinley, Zhao, and Rust, 2000). These three forces are commonly identified as coercive, mimetic, and normative isomorphism.

Coercive downsizing is evident in the demands for leanness placed on firms by the stock market, for example in both the United States (Budros, 1997; McKinley *et al.*, 1995) and United Kingdom (Kinnie *et al.*, 1997). From the mid 1980s through the early 1990s, numerous headlines and articles in prominent outlets such as the *Wall Street Journal*, *New York Times*, *Fortune*, and *Newsweek* promoted layoffs as "absolutely necessary," touting firms as "lean and green" (where "green" refers to the color of money), and referring to skyrocketing stock prices – although, as indicated above, research showed that stock prices rose only briefly if at all. Simultaneously, the senior managers who executed downsizing decisions were hailed as "heroes" and held up to be emulated (see Budros, 1997; McKinley *et al.*, 1995; Tomasko, 1993; and Useem, 1993 for examples.)

Evidence exists as well for mimetic downsizing, as firms seek to boost their standing and improve performance by imitating the behavior of other firms in their field. For instance, Budros found that *Fortune* 100 firms were more likely to adopt downsizing when it was prevalent in their industry (Budros, 1997), as the cumulative percentage of *Fortune* 100 firms that had already downsized increased (Budros, 2000), and as the cumulative percentage of downsizing firms with the same two-digit SIC code increased (Budros, 2004). Ahmadjian and Robinson (2001) found similar support for mimicry among Japanese firms in that the amount of downsizing by a focal firm's industry peers predicted its downsizing, and Tsai *et al.* (2006) found that the more benchmarking Taiwanese senior managers did, the more they were motivated to downsize. From this perspective, downsizing appears to have attained the status of a management fad (Abrahamson, 1991), with one organization after another playing follow the leader – even when it was not always clear where they were leading.

Finally, "downsizing is effective" appears to have achieved the status of conventional wisdom (McKinley *et al.*, 2000), corroborating the operation of normative forces. When "best practices" are spread through consultants, the business press, educational institutions, and professional associations to the extent they become expected practice, normative factors are at work. Budros (2000) found that the cumulative number of articles on downsizing in the *Harvard Business Review* predicted downsizing among the *Fortune* 100. In addition, as McKinley *et al.* (1995) pointed out, even the teaching of cost accounting practices in US business schools can lead to a cycle of outsourcing and downsizing, as remaining overhead is distributed over fewer activities, making each seem more expensive. In turn, these cycles generate new industry standards for headcount, employees per business line, and so forth.

Organizational experience of the last several decades typifies conditions under which institutional forces are strongest. The environment is complex and ambiguous, and demands for performance are ceaseless. The relationships between means and ends, and the ways that core technologies can be tweaked to increase performance are unclear. As globalization, competition, and technological change ramp up, organizational performance contingencies become even more uncertain. These uncertainties are exacerbated in organizations that rely heavily on knowledge work – on the work performed at corporate headquarters, in research and development units, in teams generating knowledge about new markets, caring for clients and patients, and so on – the work that exemplifies organizations to a great extent in advanced economies. When the relationship between inputs and outputs is equivocal and performance standards are difficult to ascertain, institutional forces will hold greater sway (McKinley *et al.*, 1995; Meyer and Rowan, 1977). Under these circumstances, organizations are more likely to look to the industry and other exemplars to determine what to do. In particular, managers will seek, even unconsciously, advice from the environment on how to behave. However, when managers seek guidance from the actions of successful organizations, it is a lot easier to know what they did than to know whether it worked (Davis, 2010), let alone how it worked.

The proliferation of consultants and media outlets, as well as the existence of interlocking boards and professional organizations, facilitates the diffusion of management fads in uncertain times (Abrahamson, 1991). On top of that, several circumstances divorce senior management from the human consequences of their downsizing decisions, perhaps making it easier to deliver the deathblow. As noted above, new CEOs, foreign owners, and new acquirers are all more likely to undertake downsizing in an organization. At the same time, longer tenured CEOs, managerial owners, family owners, and senior managers who enjoy high trust with the employee base are all less likely to undertake downsizing. To this end, it is conceivable that distance between downsizers and company victims or survivors makes it easier to engage in downsizing and to ignore whatever personal stake the decision-maker would have had otherwise.

## Future research directions and concluding remarks

The discussion above illustrates the wide variety of perspectives brought to bear and factors suggested as influencing firms' decisions to downsize. However, it also points to gaps in our understanding, which need to be addressed. One avenue worth pursuing would be better identification of downsizing as a truly proactive approach, as opposed to management spin on reactive approaches. For instance, when downsizing is used proactively, what other activities are likely to accompany it? And, if downsizing is indeed used proactively at times, what makes it more or less successful? What goals is it aimed at, and under what circumstances or with what tactics does it lead to their attainment? Each of these questions points to the need to achieve a better understanding of the cognitive processes managers engage in when making the decision to downsize. Researchers should consider such factors in an effort to move our understanding forward.

Second, with a few notable exceptions, most downsizing research has been conducted in the developed world. As downsizing continues to reach into a broad variety of new national contexts, however, it would be worthwhile to further expand the current lens by increasing our investigation of this phenomenon in emerging economies. For instance, if downsizing can actually serve as a proactive strategy for growth, how should it be applied in these national contexts? Moreover, how might downsizing influence these economies, especially as they are still in development? Generally speaking, whether proactive or reactive, do the most effective approaches to downsizing, and those that generate the least dysfunctional outcomes, vary across different settings?

Finally, while this chapter focused on antecedents of downsizing, we echo the call of Datta *et al.* (2010) that the influence of downsizing antecedents should be examined beyond just the decision to downsize as an outcome. To this end, only by incorporating extended longitudinal models that include the results of downsizing efforts can we capture the full, and perhaps nuanced, influence of specific downsizing strategies in shaping the future of the firm.

Bearing in mind these important areas for future research, our understanding of what factors contribute in bringing about a decision to downsize has progressed considerably over the previous three decades. In short, downsizing has moved from an unfortunate economic imperative to something organizations simply must take on, to an accepted way of doing business. During this time, there is good evidence that the reasons behind downsizing have shifted from economically oriented to socially oriented action. But reasons are ultimately not causes in the sense of determinate relationships. The conflicting evidence reminds us that downsizing, as indicated in the definition offered at the beginning of this chapter, is a choice, not an imperative. If downsizing has, indeed, become a kneejerk response to difficult circumstances – a simple demonstration of action – we need to consciously investigate our mental models and wonder about what is next.

## References

Abrahamson, E. 1991. "Managerial fads and fashions: The diffusion and rejection of innovations." *Academy of Management Review* **16**: 586–612.

Ahmadjian, C. L. and Robbins, G. E. 2005. "A clash of capitalisms: Foreign shareholders and corporate restructuring in 1990s Japan." *American Sociological Review* **70**: 451–471.

Ahmadjian, C. L. and Robinson, P. 2001. "Safety in numbers: Downsizing and the deinstitutionalization of permanent employment in Japan." *Administrative Science Quarterly* **46**: 622–654.

Alakent, E. and Lee, S. 2010. "Do institutionalized traditions matter during crisis? Employee downsizing in Korean manufacturing organizations." *Journal of Management Studies* **47**: 509–532.

American Management Association. 1996. *Downsizing on the Downsizing: 1996 AMA Survey*. New York: American Management Association.

Appelbaum, S. H., Lavigne-Schmidt, S., Peytchev, M., and Shapiro, B. 1999. "Downsizing: Measuring the costs of failure." *Journal of Management Development* **18**: 436–463.

Barker, M. M. and Hadi, A. A. 2010. "Payroll employment in 2009: Job losses continue." *Monthly Labor Review*, Bureau of Labor Statistics, March 2010, 23–33.

Bethel, J. E. and Liebeskind, J. 1993. "The effects of ownership structure on corporate restructuring." *Strategic Management Journal* **14**: 15–31.

Bivens, J. 2010. *Budgeting for Recovery: The Need to Increase the Federal Deficit to Revive a Weak Economy*. Economic Policy Institute, Briefing Paper No. 253.

Boyne, G. A. and Meier, K. J. 2009. "Environmental change, human resources and organizational turnaround." *Journal of Management Studies* **46**: 835–863.

Bruton, G. D., Keels, J. K., and Shook, C. L. 1996. "Downsizing the firm: Answering the strategic questions." *Academy of Management Executive* **10**: 38–43.

Brynjolfsson, E., Malone, T. W., Gurbaxani, V., and Kambil, A. 1994. "Does information technology lead to smaller firms?" *Management Science* **40**: 1628–1644.

Budros, A. 1997. "The new capitalism and organizational rationality: The adoption of downsizing programs, 1979–1994." *Social Forces* **76**: 229–249.

Budros, A. 2000. "Organizational types and organizational innovation: Downsizing among industrial, financial, and utility firms." *Sociological Forum* **15**: 273–306.

Budros, A. 2002. "The mean and lean firm: Causes of involuntary and voluntary downsizing strategies." *Sociological Forum* **17**: 307–342.

Budros, A. 2004. "Causes of early and later organizational adoption: The case of corporate downsizing." *Sociological Inquiry* **74**: 355–380.

Cameron, K. S. 1994. "Strategies for successful organizational downsizing." *Human Resource Management* **33**: 189–211.

Cameron, K. S., Freeman, S. J., and Mishra, A. K. 1991. "Best practices in white-collar downsizing: Managing contradictions." *Academy of Management Executive* **5**: 57–73.

Cameron, K. S., Freeman, S. J., and Mishra, A. K. 1993. "Downsizing and redesigning organizations," in G. P. Huber and W. H. Glick (eds.), *Organizational Change and Redesign*. New York: Oxford University Press, pp. 19–63.

Cappelli, P. 2000. "Examining the incidence of downsizing and its effect on establishment performance," in D. Neumark (ed.), *On the Job: Is Long-Term Employment a Thing of the Past*? New York: Russell Sage, pp. 463–516.

Carmeli, A. and Sheaffer, Z. 2009. "How leadership characteristics affect organizational decline and downsizing." *Journal of Business Ethics* **86**: 363–378.

Cascio, W. F. 1993. "Downsizing: What do we know? What have we learned?" *Academy of Management Executive* 7: 95–104.

Cascio, W. F. 2002. *Responsible Restructuring: Creative and Profitable Alternatives to Layoffs*. San Francisco, CA: Berrett-Koehler.

Cascio, W. F., Young, C. E., and Morris, J. R. 1997. "Financial consequences of employment-change decisions in major US corporations." *Academy of Management Journal* **40**: 1175–1189.

Conyon, M. J., Girma, S., Thompson, S., and Wright, P. W. 2002. "The impact of mergers and acquisitions on company employment in the United Kingdom." *European Economic Review* **46**: 31–49.

Coucke, K., Pennings, E., and Sleuwaegen, L. 2007. "Employee layoff under different modes of restructuring: Exit, downsizing or relocation." *Industrial and Corporate Change* **16**: 161–182.

Datta, D. K., Guthrie, J. P., Basuil, D., and Pandey, A. 2010. "Causes and effects of employee downsizing: A review and synthesis." *Journal of Management* **36**: 281–348.

Davis, G. F. 2010. "Job design meets organizational sociology." *Journal of Organizational Behavior* **31**: 302–308.

De Meuse, K., Vanderheiden, P., and Bergmann, T. 1994. "Announced layoffs: Their effects on corporate financial performance." *Human Resource Management* **33**: 509–530.

Dong, X. and Xu, L. C. 2009. "Labor restructuring in China: Toward a functioning labor market." *Journal of Comparative Economics* **37**: 287–305.

Filatotchev, I., Buck, T., and Zhukov, V. 2000. "Downsizing in privatized firms in Russia, Ukraine, and Belarus." *Academy of Management Journal* **43**: 286–304.

Freeman, S. J. 1999. "The gestalt of organizational downsizing: Downsizing strategies as packages of change." *Human Relations* **52**: 1505–1541

Freeman, S. J. and Cameron, K. S. 1993. "Organizational downsizing: A convergence and reorientation framework." *Organization Science* **4**: 10–29.

Gittell, J., Cameron, K., Lim, S., and Rivas, V. 2006. "Relationships, layoffs, and organizational resilience." *Journal of Applied Behavioral Science* **42**: 300–329.

Hallock, K. F. 1998. "Layoffs, top executive pay, and firm performance." *American Economic Review* **88**: 711–723.

Hammer, M. and Champy, J. 1993a. *Reengineering the Corporation: A Manifesto for Business Revolution*. New York: Harper Collins.

Hammer, M. and Champy, J. A. 1993b. "Reengineering work: Don't automate, obliterate." *Harvard Business Review* (July/August): 104–112.

Hillier, D., Marshall, A., McColgan, P., and Werema, S. 2007. "Employee layoffs, shareholder wealth and firm performance: Evidence from the UK." *Journal of Business Finance and Accounting* **34**: 467–494.

Hsieh, C. and Davidson, W. N. 2008. "Layoffs, equity-based compensation, and CEO ownership." *Journal of Academy of Business and Economics* **8**: 142–146.

Iqbal, Z. and Shetty, S. 1994. "A multivariate analysis of employee layoffs." *American Business Review* **12**: 15–21.

Iverson, R. D. and Zatzick, C. D. 2007. "High-commitment work practices and downsizing harshness in Australian workplaces." *Industrial Relations* **46**: 456–480.

Kang, J. and Shivdasani, A. 1997. "Corporate restructuring during performance declines in Japan." *Journal of Financial Economics* **46**: 29–65.

Kinnie, N., Hutchinson, S., and Purcell, J. 1997. "Downsizing: Is it always lean and mean?" *Personnel Review* **27**: 296–311.

Krishnan, H. A., Hitt, M. A., and Park, D. 2007. "Acquisition premiums, subsequent workforce reductions and post-acquisition performance." *Journal of Management Studies* **44**: 709–732.

Lehto, E. and Böckerman, P. 2008. "Analysing the employment effects of mergers and acquisitions." *Journal of Economic Behavior and Organization* **68**: 112–124.

McKinley, W. 2001. "Prescriptions for managers: Are there hidden costs?" *Academy of Management Review* **26**: 17–18.

McKinley, W., Sanchez, C. M., and Schick, A. G. 1995. "Organizational downsizing: Constraining, cloning, learning." *Academy of Management Executive* **9**: 32–42.

McKinley, W., Zhao, J., and Rust, K. G. 2000. "A sociocognitive interpretation of organizational downsizing." *Academy of Management Review* **25**: 227–243.

Mellahi, K. and Guermat, C. 2009. "The adoption of downsizing during the Asian economic crisis." *Asian Business and Management* **8**: 225–245.

Meyer, J. and Rowan, B. 1977. "Institutionalized organizations: Formal structure as myth and ceremony." *American Journal of Sociology* **83**: 340–363.

Mishra, A. K. and Mishra, K. E. 1994. "The role of mutual trust in effective downsizing strategies." *Human Resource Management* **33**: 261–279.

*New York Times*. 1996. "The downsizing of America." March 3–March 9.

O'Shaughnessy, K. C. and Flanagan, D. J. 1998. "Determinants of layoff announcements following M & As: An empirical investigation." *Strategic Management Journal* **19**: 989–999.

Ofek, E. 1993. "Capital structure and firm response to poor performance." *Journal of Financial Economics* **34**: 3–30.

Osterman, P. 2000. "Work reorganization in an era of restructuring: Trends in diffusion and effects on employee welfare." *Industrial and Labor Relations Review* **53**: 179–196.

Perry, T. and Shivdasani, A. 2005. "Do boards affect performance? Evidence from corporate restructuring." *Journal of Business* **78**: 1403–1431.

Pinsonneault, A. and Kraemer, K. L. 1997. "Middle management downsizing: An empirical investigation of the impact of information technology." *Management Science* **43**: 659–679.

Redman, T. and Keithley, D. 1998. "Downsizing goes east? Employment re-structuring in post-socialist Poland." *International Journal of Human Resource Management* **9**: 274–295.

Rodrigues, S. B. and Child, J. 2008. *Corporate Co-Evolution: A Political Perspective*. Chichester, West Sussex: John E. Wiley & Sons.

Rodrigues, S. B. and Child, J. 2010. "Private equity, the minimalist organization and the quality of employment relations." *Human Relations* **63**: 1321–1342.

Siegel, D. S. and Simons, K. L. 2010. "Assessing the effects of mergers and acquisitions on firm performance, plant productivity, and workers: New evidence from matched employer–employee data." *Strategic Management Journal* **31**: 903–916.

Society for Human Resource Management. 2002. *2001 Layoffs and Job Security Survey*. Alexandria, VA: Society for Human Resource Management.

Stavrou, E., Kassinis, G., and Filotheou, A. 2007. "Downsizing and stakeholder orientation among the *Fortune* 500: Does family ownership matter?" *Journal of Business Ethics* **72**: 149–162.

Tomasko, R. 1993. *Rethinking the Corporation: The Architecture of Change*. New York: Amacom.

Tsai, C., Wu, S., Wang, H., and Huang, I. 2006. "An empirical research on the institutional theory of downsizing: Evidence from MNC's subsidiary companies in Taiwan." *Total Quality Management and Business Excellence* **17**: 633–654.

Useem, M. 1993. *Executive Defense: Shareholder Power and Corporate Reorganization*. Cambridge, MA: Harvard University Press.

Vicente-Lorente, J. D. and Suárez-González, I. 2007. "Ownership traits and downsizing behavior: Evidence for the largest Spanish firms, 1990–1998." *Organization Studies* **28**: 1613–1638.

Wagar, T. H. 1997. "Factors affecting permanent workforce reduction: Evidence from large Canadian organizations." *Canadian Journal of Administrative Sciences* **14**: 303–314.

Whetten, D. A. 1980. "Sources, responses, and effects of organizational decline," in J. R. Kimberly and R. H. Miles (eds.), *The Organizational Life Cycle*. San Francisco, CA: Jossey-Bass, pp. 342–374.

Womack, J. and Jones, D. 1996. *Lean Thinking*. New York: Simon & Schuster.

Womack, J., Jones, D., and Roos, D. 1990. *The Machine that Changed the World*. New York: Rawson Associates.

Worrell, D. L., Davidson III, W. N., and Sharma, V. M. 1991. "Layoff announcements and stockholder wealth." *Academy of Management Journal* **34**: 662–678.

Yawson, A. 2006. "Evaluating the characteristics of corporate boards associated with layoff decisions." *Corporate Governance: An International Review* **14**: 75–84.

Yoo, H. and Mody, B. 2000. "Predictors of downsizing in the US local telephone industry." *Information Society* **16**: 23–33.

Yu, G. and Park, J. 2006. "The effect of downsizing on the financial performance and employee productivity of Korean firms." *International Journal of Manpower* **27**: 230–250.

Zammuto, R. F. and Cameron, K. S. 1985. "Environmental decline and organizational response," in L. L. Cummings and B. M. Staw (eds.), *Research in Organizational Behavior*, Vol. VII. Greenwich, CT: JAI Press, pp. 223–262.

Zatzick, C. D. and Iverson, R. D. 2006. "High-commitment management and workforce reduction: Competitive advantage or disadvantage?" *Academy of Management Journal* **49**: 999–1015.

Zhao, J., Rust, K. G., McKinley, W., and Edwards, J. C. 2010. "Downsizing, ideology, and contracts: A Chinese perspective." *Chinese Management Studies* **4**: 119–140.

Zumbrun, J. and Chandra, S. 2011. "A US recovery built on low-paying jobs." *Bloomberg BusinessWeek*, February 28–March 6, pp. 14–15.

PART II

# *Human outcomes*

# 4 *Human motivation and performance outcomes in the context of downsizing*

AHARON TZINER, ERICH C. FEIN, AND LIOR OREN

Human motivation is defined as the psychological force that generates complex cycles of goal-directed thought and behavior. Such thought and behavior is ultimately directed toward the achievement of the fundamental goal of inclusive fitness (Bernard, Mills, Swenson, and Walsh, 2005), where individuals strive to match their internal needs to actual or potential resources in their life space. Motivation is what animates us, what prompts us to launch actions, to reach decisions, to make choices, and to persist in the pursuit of courses of action until their completion. Accordingly, scholars studying human motivation intend to unveil the processes by which an individual's internal, psychological forces in conjunction with external, environmental forces determine the direction, intensity, and persistence of personal behavior aimed at goal attainment (Kanfer, 2009). In preparing this chapter, we have chosen to focus specifically on the complex interplay between endogenous forces, such as internal drives and beliefs, and exogenous forces, such as changes in the stability of rewards, within the work environment. Furthermore, because the study of motivation is extremely vast, we have currently chosen to restrict ourselves to focusing solely on work motivation within work environments. It is definitely included in the immense field of human motivation and it provides a key determinant of reactions to downsizing in organizations.

One recent and dramatic example of how a work environment may rapidly change is the traumatic closure of Deutsche Post World Net operations in Wilmington, Ohio, which has received considerable national media attention in the United States. At the beginning of the Global Financial Crisis in 2007, the DHL division of Deutsche Post World Net employed approximately 8,000 workers in Wilmington, Ohio, which was the seat of US domestic air shipping operations. By 2008, DHL announced the phased closure of shipping activities and by the end of operations approximately 7,500 employees were laid off (Lynch, 2008). Although only a portion of the laid off employees were from Wilmington, the layoffs still effectively devastated the local economy (Driehaus, 2008). Household income losses from the direct elimination of DHL jobs have been estimated at over $135 million for Clinton County, which contains Wilmington, and neighboring Highland County (Nolan, 2008). Because tax revenues were decimated, Wilmington's hospital lost 7 million dollars and was forced to close its pediatric clinic, which had served children from local low-income families (Pelley, 2009).

The sense of betrayal expressed by the community was extreme, mostly due to the considerable financial investment of the city in assisting the expansion of public goods such as roads and facilities to assist DHL, not to mention the past loyal service of thousands of veteran employees. Now two years later, as revealed in national television coverage, the Wilmington community as a whole has changed its beliefs about employee–employer relationships (Pelley, 2009). For example, some former DHL employees have decided to relegate need satisfaction through work to a secondary place in their lives after activities such as religious participation and community service (N. Campbell, personal communication, April 14, 2010).

Here we review the definition of work motivation as "a set of energetic forces that originate within the individual as well as in his environment to initiate work-related behaviors, and to determine its form, direction, intensity and duration" (Pinder, 2008, p. 11). It thus follows that work motivation results from the interaction of an individual's characteristics and outward environment components, both societal and work-organizational (Latham and Pinder, 2005). We find the Wilmington example useful because it displays the interplay of endogenous and exogenous factors as motivational forces. For example, Wilmington employees were noted for extra role performance as late as 2008, delivering up to 99 percent of packages on time, even after learning about the end of DHL operations; but this ethic may change considerably with strong evidence of employer unreliability and the estimated loss of 20 percent of the region's businesses (Lynch, 2008).

## Human needs and personality

A need can be thought of as type of psychological force which organizes "perception, apperception, intellect, conation and action in such a way as to transform in a certain direction an existing, unsatisfying situation"

(Murray, 1938, p. 123), and according to McClelland and colleagues such psychological processes may surface as reoccurring concerns for particular goal states (McClelland, Atkinson, Clark, and Lowell, 1976) So, the concept of need denotes a state of disequilibrium, of deficiency, which generates a state of internal tension along with the energy required to activate and fuel the course of action aimed at seeking the gratification, the reinforcement likely to reduce and eliminate this state of deficiency. Several need-based theories have been advanced throughout the years, including contributions by Herzberg and colleagues (Herzberg, Mausner, and Snyderman, 1959), Atkinson (1964), Alderfer (1972), and McClelland *et al.* (1976). They all posit that the forces which ignite and sustain motivation, namely the purposeful behavior to reduce the internal state of tension, are needs.

However, as important as needs may be to energize motivation, Latham and Pinder (2005), in their recent review of the theoretical progress of understanding work motivation, suggest that personality traits precede needs. And historically traits have long been considered a primary factor in needs arousal (Allport, 1951). For example, Hung-Wen (2010) argues that individuals high on self-monitoring are motivated to meet expectations of others. Specifically, in individuals high on the personality trait self-monitoring, a conformity-based need evolves to meet others' expectations and to be liked by others. Moreover, people high on conscientiousness apparently need to feel competent and maintain autonomy and control over courses of action. This possibly explains why Mount and Barrick (1998) have found that conscientiousness features high on jobs requiring autonomy. Somewhat related is the construct of goal orientation, which can be described as a relatively stable dispositional trait and is currently the dominant approach in the study of achievement motivation (DeShon and Gillespie, 2005). Individuals who possess a performance goal orientation strive to demonstrate high competence via task performance and tend to avoid challenges and to show deterioration of performance and even withdrawal in the face of obstacles. Alternatively, mastery/learning goal orientation is related to striving to understand something new or to increase the level of competence in a given activity and involves seeking challenging tasks and maintaining effective striving under difficult conditions. From an organizational perspective, performance orientation is needed when deadlines must be met and, in contrast, a mastery/learning orientation is needed while developing new products or facing organizational challenges.

Recent research also suggests that systems of related traits may offer better explanations for motivational processes. For example, Fein and Klein (2011) have recently offered evidence that a composite trait composed of facet-level traits predict self-regulation outcomes better than conscientiousness and any individual facet-level trait.

## Individual values

Latham and Pinder (2005) assert that values emanate from needs and ultimately affect goals. They are similar to needs in their capacity to initiate and sustain purposeful behavior. Whereas needs are innate, values are acquired through the socialization process, and are thereby influenced by cultural values. Pinder suggests that values are connected to needs through the choices that individuals make when selecting from opportunities in the environment that will serve to meet their needs (Pinder, 2008). In this sense, values can be considered standards or qualities that are perceived by individuals to potentially satisfy their needs and, therefore, guide decision-making, goal generation, and action (Kilmann, 1981).

The study of values is important to organizations because knowing about individual- and group-level value structures can help managers understand and predict attitudes, motivational processes, and other important organizational outcomes (Meglino and Ravlin, 1998). Many types of connections between values and work-related behaviors have been documented (Dawis, 1991; Rokeach, 1973) and individual-level value constructs have played important roles in need-based theories of motivation, such as self-determination theory (Deci and Ryan, 2002). Also, values-based constructs are critical to theories of person–organization fit (Edwards, 2004) and in explaining general congruence patterns between employee values and attitudes from a cross-cultural perspective, both on the level of individual value structures and in the collective sense of shared values, such as in Hofstede's studies of values-based elements of national culture (Hofstede and Peterson, 2000; Hofstede, 2001).

## Cultural values

National culture helps to determine which personal values should be pursued and what sort of gratification should be sought. They set normative standards to judge and select among alternative behaviors and courses of action (Latham and Pinder, 2005). For example, effects of cultural values can be seen in the shaping of motives derived from concepts of the self, such as in the degree of challenge inherent in goal levels and the degree of approach versus avoidance tendencies in self-regulatory processes (Erez, 2008).

The term culture has numerous meanings and definitions. For example, culture has been defined as unstated standard operation procedures or ways of doing things (Triandis, 1994); as the collective programming of the mind; and as the characteristic profile of a society with respect to its values, norms, and institutions (Hofstede, 2001). Although there is no standard definition of culture, many emphasize that culture is shared, is adaptive or has been adaptive at some point in the past, and is transmitted across time and generations (Triandis, 1994; Gelfand, Erez, and Aycan, 2007).

Research using a variety of typologies has shown that national cultural values are related to organizational phenomena (e.g., Hofstede, 2001). Despite the fact that there are many cultural frameworks to choose from, Hofstede offers the most influential framework for differentiating nations in relation to their cultural values. His work has guided cross-cultural research for over 20 years (e.g., Hofstede, 2001). It comprises the five dimensions: power distance, individualism–collectivism, masculinity–femininity, uncertainty avoidance, and long-term orientation. Recently, Minkov (2007) introduced two additional dimensions: indulgence versus restraint, and monumentalism. Parenthetically, Taras, Kirkman, and Steel (2010) have documented relatively large effect size between cultural values and outcomes, such as organizational citizenship behavior (OCB). Consistent with the person–situation interactionist perspective, we should look into the context (situation) components, which may or may not entertain correspondence (or fit) with personal values. Because of space limitation we focus primarily on organizational culture, job design characteristics, and the relationships between the employee and his or her superior, such as Leader–Member Exchange (LMX) theory, as constituents of the work context.

## Organizational culture

Organizational culture affects organizational behavior and may be proposed as an additional potential moderator within motivational processes. For example, in earlier studies researchers concluded that organizational culture is partly responsible for turnover intentions, especially job challenge (Carmeli, 2005). In addition, there is evidence that perceptions of organization politics, which can be highly salient aspects of organizational culture, are positively related to intentions to exit the organization and negatively related to OCBs (Chang, Rosen, and Levy, 2009). Organizational culture is viewed in the literature as a multifaceted abstraction with several dimensions that have varying degrees and directions of impact on employees' behavior (e.g., Sheridan, 1992; Song, Tsui, and Law, 2009). Past research has suggested that elements of organizational culture are important, at least as a cultural force, in determining organizational performance (Lee and Yu, 2004). For example, several studies (e.g., Handy and Katz, 1998) found that workers in non-profit organizations, such as teachers and nurses, showed a strong commitment to the philosophy of their organization and were motivated by affiliation, altruism, professional efficacy, and personal growth versus extrinsic rewards. In one of our recent studies (Tziner, Shultz, and Fisher, 2008) we used cultural dimensions that can be grouped into those oriented toward the individual and those oriented toward the organization.

Findings show that organizational culture plays a vital role in generating commitment and enhancing performance. In particular, innovative and supportive cultures were shown to have a strong positive effect on commitment and job satisfaction, while bureaucratic cultures had a negative effect (Lee and Kamarul, 2008). Cultures that emphasize group values are likely to experience a better quality of work life (Goodman, Zammuto, and Gifford, 2001). Values that cultivate loyalty and commitment to the organization, respect for the individual, security, and teamwork encourage retention (Sheridan, 1992). Since organization-oriented cultures foster entrepreneurial norms, they do not offer as much security and stability as do individual-oriented cultures. Security and stability promote loyalty and the willingness to sacrifice. Teamwork and supportiveness place emphasis on interpersonal relationships and generate emotional support for group members, which in turn may lead to positive psychological outcomes. Jehn (1997) reported that supportiveness had a positive effect on members' satisfaction in teams. Innovativeness encourages group members to take advantage of their skill and knowledge to challenge the status quo, to debate task-related issues from their own perspectives, and to question decisions and task procedures. Attention to detail boosts the members' inclination to make use of their information, skills, and knowledge to analyze various aspects of group tasks (Chuang, Church, and Zikic, 2004).

## Leader–member exchange (LMX)

Although there is much evidence regarding how some organizational contextual factors, such as job design and organizational climate, can impact motivation, there is very little research that addresses the direct role of leadership processes in influencing work motivation (Zaccaro, Ely, and Nelson, 2008). However, it seems likely that leadership processes can affect work motivation across a number of areas, which include effects on motivational states and goal generation processes (Zaccaro *et al.*, 2008). Because the LMX approach focuses on the quality of the relationship between leaders and group members, we feel it has strong potential in explaining how leaders may influence the motivational states of subordinates. A distinctive feature of the LMX approach is its focus on the dyadic relationship maintained by superiors and their subordinates. Rather than asserting that managers exhibit the same leadership style with all their subordinates, LMX posits that managers develop and maintain unique relationships with different employees. Employees who enjoy high LMX relationships with their superiors typically benefit from more opportunities, emotional support, and cooperative interactions in comparison with those maintaining low-quality LMX relationships (Liden and Graen, 1980). Substantial research has consistently demonstrated that these relationships impinge upon important subordinate attitudes and behavior (e.g., Ilies, Morgeson, and Nahrgang, 2005; Weismal-Manor, Tziner, Berger, and Dickstein, 2010, Tziner *et al.*, 2008).

As LMX is premised on the notions of social exchange (Blau, 1964) and reciprocity (Adams, 1965), subordinates offered high quality LMX are expected to feel compelled to reciprocate by working harder in exchange for the preferential treatment they receive from their manager. According to norms of reciprocity, the positive effect, respect, loyalty, and obligation, which are characteristic of high-quality LMX, should prompt employees to make more valuable contributions to their organization's viability and effectiveness. In other words, it may be expected that subordinates who enjoy high-level LMX will "pay back" their managers by engaging in discretionary behavior that benefits their manager and organization, even though it defies the organization's rules and norms (which are perceived as hampering its functioning and effectiveness).

## Job design and fit

The content of the job provides reinforcement or rewards to the employee's work-related values. For instance, Bretz, Ash, and Dreher (1989) reported that employees with a high need for achievement tend to be attracted to jobs that encourage and reward competitive effort and accomplishments. Hackman and Oldham (1976) asserted that any job's content can be analyzed with respect to five core dimensions: *skill variety* – the extent to which a job requires carrying out a variety of different activities that entails the use of diverse abilities, knowledge, and skills; *task identity* – the extent to which the job necessitates the completion of an entire identifiable part of work (to complete duties, missions) resulting in a definite, observable outcome; *task significance* – the extent to which the job has a notable impact on the lives or functioning of others; *autonomy* – the extent to which the job provides latitude, discretion of action in planning what has to be done, according to which priority, using what sort of procedures and knowledge, and so forth; *feedback* – the extent to which employees get information about the effectiveness of their work from the performance itself (no need for external appraisal), for instance a device maker knows if he or she has succeeded or not in assembling the machine or instrument by whether the device functions or not.

Hackman and Oldham further assert that these core dimensions generate feelings of meaningfulness of work, a sense of responsibility for outcomes, and knowledge of the results. These feelings have the potential to satisfy work-related needs and values, thereby leading to raised motivation. Alternatively, if the job is deficient with respect to these core dimensions, the motivation is anticipated to be lower. We note that more recent research suggests that interactions between work characteristics, individual differences, and organizational systems are an important route for advancing the utility of job design approaches to motivation (Parker and Ohly, 2008).

In the study of work relationships, the concept of congruency between individual and contextual characteristics, or *fit*, has played a major role in the further understanding of this notion. Fit denotes a harmonious relationship between the individual and his/her work environment, the extent to which the individual is fitted to the work environment and vice versa, and a reciprocal complementary relationship between an individual and the environment (Lofquist and Dawis, 1978, p. 45). Holland (Holland and Rayman, 1986) has also contributed largely to the elaboration of the meaning of the fit concept. In his view, different personality types require different work environments. For instance, enterprising types flourish in enterprising environments because such environments provide the outlets and reinforcements they need. Also, Tziner (1987), Tziner and Falbe (1990), and recently Brown and Trevino (2009) have convincingly empirically demonstrated the beneficial effects of fit. Last, Greguras and Diefendorff (2009) documented the positive effects of different types of fit. They showed that different types of fit (i.e., person-organization fit; person-group fit) satisfy different psychological needs.

## Organizational justice

Justice-related consequences include some of the most important outcomes studied by management researchers. For example, perceptions of unfair or unjust treatment have been associated with many harmful effects, including negative health outcomes, intentional deviant behaviors, and withdrawal behaviors (Pinder, 2008). To explain the power of justice-related phenomena, we must recognize that employees in organizations tend to constantly examine the actions taking place within the organization, in an attempt to determine whether an action was fair, or, in other words, whether justice exists within the organization. To this end, they explore according to three types of criteria:

- The first criterion relates to practical implications, that is personal gain or loss, which derive from the employee's feeling that the decisions reached were just and right. This fairness is examined in the distributive justice theory (Adams, 1965).
- The second relates to the way in which the decision to take action was made: the employee assesses whether the processes that led to the decision were fair (Thibaut and Walker, 1975; Leventhal, 1980).

- The third relates to the approach adopted during planning and application (i.e. the treatment employees receive during implementation, their feeling that the organization imparted new information and treated them sensitively and fairly). This fairness is examined in the Interactional Justice Theory (Tyler and Bies, 1990).

## *Perceived distributional justice*

Leventhal (1980) says that the rule of distribution is "the individual's belief that fairness exists when allocated procedures satisfy certain criteria," or, in other words, the beliefs of the individuals regarding the suitable distribution of resources in the company, and particularly material awards. Reward distribution will be considered fair if it is based on the assumption that the method of exchange is fundamentally based on human life cycles (Adams, 1965); justice, according to this perception, is the perceived fairness of rewards that people receive in the exchange. Distributive justice in an organization relates to the perceived fairness of resource allocation in the organization (Miller and Lee, 2001), or fairness as perceived by employees *vis-à-vis* the management's distribution of resources in the organization (Cropanzano, Prehar, and Chen, 2002).

The outputs of an organization, perceived by employees as rewards, are the resources the organization gives them, inter alia: power, prestige, authorities, responsibilities, wages, etc. (Adams, 1965). The inputs the employees bring into the exchange may be education, intelligence, training, seniority, and investment in work (Adams, 1965). The theory of distributive justice focuses on the level of results-rewards the organization grants employees, versus the input which employees invest in the organization. The theory also assumes that people aspire to expand, as far as possible, the gap between the inputs they invest and the outputs they receive (Folger and Cropanzano, 1998). The basis upon which people develop their perception of justice, or injustice, of a given action is grounded in a comparison (balance) between their input and output, and the perceived ratio of input and output of others, who are perceived as similar or comparable to them.

$$\frac{\text{Compensation minus Cost (of B)}}{\text{Input (B)}} \quad \begin{matrix} < \\ > \\ = \end{matrix} \quad \frac{\text{Input minus Cost (of A)}}{\text{Input (A)}}$$

This comparison indicates the expectation of resource allocation according to the equity principle: the input–output ratio of people perceived as comparable should be equal, and the measure of rewards should be compatible with the measure of input. In other words, the reward given to employees should be compatible with their investment (Ritzman and Tomaskovic-Devey, 1992). Hence, individuals who share similar characteristics should expect equal awards.

## *Perceived procedural justice*

The idea of procedural justice originates in the sphere of law – for the results of a trial to be fair, the procedure adopted must be fair (for example, laws relating to testimonies). The principle is common in the workplace as well. It relates to perceived fairness in the process of organizational decision-making. Procedural justice examines the degree of importance individuals attribute to the way in which decisions are reached. People in organizations are careful about reaching decisions in a fair manner, and also want others to regard their decisions as fair. In procedural justice, the emphasis is not on the results of the decision, but on the process/way in which the decision was reached (the extent of sharing in the decision, transparency, bias, attention, understanding). The reason for this is simple: both individual employees and the organization as a whole stand to gain when the organization operates in accordance with fair procedures.

Procedural justice comprises subjective aspects – the way in which a specific procedure is perceived – and objective aspects – the way in which a specific procedure is carried out de facto. In certain situations, a contradiction, or a partial or full overlap may transpire between subjective and objective aspects. Hence, implications regarding the way in which the situation can be changed will be different. Procedural justice relates to the perception of fairness, the way in which decisions were reached *vis-à-vis* the distribution of resources (Leventhal, 1980; Folger and Cropanzano, 1998). Thibaut and Walker published a study in 1975 in which they examined how perceptions of justice were formed in experiments that sought to find non-violent solutions during conflict. They argue that distributive justice devoid of a process is possible only if the conflicting parties reach a full and spontaneous agreement about the method of distribution (such as a specific resource), which is indeed an extremely hypothetical situation!

In addition, Sheppard, Lewicki, and Minton (1992) argued that procedural justice is a prerequisite for distributive justice.

### *Perceived interactional justice*

The two prominent scholars in the field of interactional justice, Tyler and Bies (1990), regard interactional justice as the dimension that compliments procedural justice. In their view, Thibaut and Walker's study (1975) focused on the quality of decisions made as a result of the process, that is the abilities of the project to produce justice. Tyler and Bies (1990) argue that the process has additional aspects. The interactional aspect, or the attitude of decision-makers to subordinates, is one of the parameters used when people make decisions about the degree of justice performed, regardless of formal procedure; a similar argument was voiced by Bies and Moag (1986). The second aspect relates to the fact that decision-makers enjoy unreserved freedom of action when they interpret formal procedures when managing processes, so that if, for example, we observe two judges conducting legal proceedings, we will notice differences between the ways in which they perform (Tyler and Bies, 1990). Tyler and Bies (1990) identify five criteria that relate to perceived fairness that are affected by the way in which decision-makers manage the process:

- The first relates to considering or recognizing the viewpoints of subordinates – subordinates who are asked to voice their opinion, expect it to serve as an important element in decision-making. Subordinates, who are asked to express their opinion, but ultimately feel that they have been ignored, will feel manipulated and may regard the entire process as corrupt and unfair.
- The second relates to the bias of decision-makers – subordinates believe that decision-makers should be neutral and free of any personal interest, focusing only on the fairness of the procedure. For this reason, anything regarded as prejudicial will immediately arouse subordinates' suspicion regarding the procedure's fairness.
- The third relates to the consistency of the implementation of the decisions regarding subordinates – the expectation that the approach to all (or all cases) will be equal, or at least similar. The behavior of decision-makers, which is perceived as arbitrary and inconsistent, will impair perceived procedural justice.

- The fourth relates to the timing of the report on the decision – people tend to suspect delayed reports, if there is no significant reason for the postponement, and this may impair the sense of justice.
- The fifth relates to the report on a decision taken – the report contains the explanation for the decision and the reason for its acceptance. Since numerous decisions in the world of business are made discreetly, the report can serve as the starting point for the subordinates' evaluation of the correctness of the process, and consequently its fairness. This criterion deals with information about the process given to subordinates for assessment, and through which they evaluate the intention of decision-makers, and, hence, their evaluation of the fairness of the process (Tyler and Bies, 1990).

Thus, Tyler and Bies (1990), in addition to the formal and cognitive aspect of procedural justice, which Thibaut and Walker (1975) proposed, note the human aspect, which adds feelings such as anger, frustration, and bitterness that may develop as a result of the attitude demonstrated by the decision-makers towards their subordinates. The five criteria mentioned above relate to two main dimensions of interactional justice: interpersonal justice – which deals with the nature of the employee-organization relationship – and informational justice – which deals with the nature of the information conveyed to the employees. These two dimensions reflect, each in its own way, the degree of respect that employees feel they command from the organization and its employers.

## Key work attitudes

Work attitudes are linked to beliefs through positive and negative evaluations. Specifically, individual attitudes are formed as people weigh the degree of positive and negative evaluative beliefs they hold towards particular attitude objects (Pinder, 2008). In the work environment, common and important attitude objects include people's job, workgroup, and supervisor, as well as the organization as a whole. Individuals can even form attitudes regarding their career or profession and work in general. Throughout the last century, two particular work-related attitudes have proven to be critical to understanding motivational processes in organizations: work or job satisfaction and organizational commitment (Kanfer, 2009). In particular, successful goal attainment is conducive to attitudes of work satisfaction and organizational commitment, whereas an unsuccessful outcome yields the opposite result. Numerous studies have been devoted to investigating job satisfaction and organizational commitment – two work attitudes which appear to be empirically distinct (e.g., Brooke, Russell, and Price, 1988). Interest in these two constructs undoubtedly stems from the growing body of evidence which indicates that they may affect the success or failure of organizations (Harter, Schmid, and Hayes, 2002; Chen and Francesco, 2003). We have reached the point where we can sum up the entire exposition of this chapter with the following diagrammatic display.

## *Motivation and downsizing*

Downsizing, can be defined as "the planned elimination of positions or jobs" (Pinder, 2008, p. 341) and is now a harsh fact of life in most organizations. Cascio, Young, and Morris (1997) consider downsizing to be a significant intentional reduction in workforce through mass layoffs. Similarly, Freeman, and Cameron (1993) describe downsizing as an intentional management action involving a reduction in workforce through a combination of organizational actions, such as hiring freezes, layoffs, and induced attrition, which are designed to improve a company's competitive position. Downsizing may be a consequence of global competitive pressures, enhancements in technology, and a demanding customer-driven market (Freeman, 1999; Ulrich, 1998). As a result, many companies have found that staying in business means downsizing (Kim, 2009). The experience of living with the possibility of redundancy, and watching others leave, has become part of the working experience. The *New York Times* national survey (Fisher, 2005) found that since 1980 a family member in one-third of all US households has been laid off.

The laid-off worker – the 'victim' (Jahoda, 1982) – has been the subject of extensive study for some time. Those leaving are often provided with outplacement services, personal counseling, paid time-off for job hunting, and sometimes are offered elaborate early retirement incentives. Both long- and short-term effects have been investigated in the study of downsizing. Here the effects over time are potentially more serious than the short-term stress felt by victims of downsizing. For example, over the long run, victims of downsizing can often experience financial hardship (sometimes through having to accept positions of lower quality), social strain with families and friends, as well as the adoption of negative career and work attitudes, which may be very resistant to change.

Many senior executives assume, erroneously, that the relief of not being on the "hit list" overshadows any negative feelings surviving employees have about the consequences of the downsizing process. Indeed, until recently, researchers have paid little attention to the effects of layoffs on the survivors – those who remain in downsized organizations and can either facilitate or impede the desired outcomes of the downsizing (Brockner, 1986, 1992; Greenhalgh, 1982; Davy, Kinicki, and Scheck, 2001). In practice, we still know little about the reactions of those who remain as opposed to layoff victims (Devine, Reay, Stainton, and Collins-Nakai, 2003).

Understanding the effects of downsizing on the survivors is problematic because, unless it is done as a cash-flow driven exercise (Demarie and Keats, 1996; Hitt, Keats, Harback, and Nixon, 1994), it is usually accompanied by other organizational changes, such as outsourcing (Maertz, Wiley, LeRouge, and Campion, 2010), intensification of work, or technological job-related changes. For example, Sahdev (2004) studied downsizing in two organizations. In the first organization, a manufacturing company, the (successful) downsizing was accompanied with job redesign that empowered the workers; whereas in the second organization, a credit card company, the (unsuccessful) downsizing was accompanied with greater reliance on technology.

Comprehensive review of the downsizing literature found that the impacts of downsizing on survivors have been more negative than positive. At the individual level, the survivor syndrome is the most written about outcome of downsizing to date. It is described as "a mixed bag of emotions often exhibited by remaining employees following an organizational downsizing" (Doherty and Horsted, 1995, p. 26). The reactions shown by survivors include emotions such as anger, insecurity, a perception of unfairness, mistrust, depression, powerlessness, guilt, and reduced risk taking and motivation, as well as low levels of morale, commitment, and psychological attachment to the organization (Armstrong-Stassen and Latack, 1992; Brockner, 1986; Cody, Hegeman, and Shanks, 1987; Kets de Vries and Balazs, 1997; Kettley, 1995), and high levels of stress (Allen, Freeman, Russell, Reizenstein, and Rentz, 2001) that results, also, from the threat of future layoffs (Brockner, Wiesenfeld, Stephan, Hurley, Grover, Reed, DeWitt, and

Martin, 1997). In addition, increase in turnover intention was found among survivors (Armstrong-Stassen and Cameron, 2003). Voluntary turnover may be especially damaging for organizations, especially in the critical period after a downsizing event (Trevor and Nyberg 2008).

## Downsizing and turnover

Trevor and Nyberg (2008) suggested that studying voluntary turnover among downsizing survivors, who have been earmarked as the employees most worth keeping (Martin and Bartol, 1985), is especially important. However, only one study (Batt, Colvin, and Keefe, 2002) has tested whether downsizing predicts voluntary turnover rates. In their study, they used the unfolding model of turnover (Lee, Mitchell, Wies, and Fireman, 1996) that describes how turnover decisions can be functions of "shocks," defined as a "very distinguishable event that jars employees toward deliberate judgments about their jobs and, perhaps, to voluntarily quit their job" (Lee and Mitchell, 1994, p. 60). Downsizing is an unpleasant shock that prompts fear and resentment. It is possible, however, that, despite the attitudinal fallout, downsizing survivors will appreciate what they have, feel relatively safe, and expect more varied work and organizational success. General support was found for organizational commitment as a mediator of the relationship between downsizing and turnover intentions. They also found that several HR practice dimensions moderated downsizing effects: HR practices associated with perceived procedural justice buffered downsizing effects, maybe because employment outcomes (e.g., pay) received over the long term are – given their large impact on material gains – seen as more important than a single short-term outcome. In addition, procedural justice perceptions fuel optimism regarding these critical long-term outcomes.

The second HR practice is job embeddedness, which is the level to which employees are bound in a social web (both on and off the job) that keeps them attached to their organization (Lee, Mitchell, Sablynski, Burton, and Holton, 2004; Mitchell, Holtom, Lee, Sablynski, and Erez, 2001). Such practices may be benefits plans, sabbaticals, on-site childcare, hiring for organizational fit, or flexitime. The heightened sense of attachment, in turn, would constrain downsizing-driven reduction in current employment utility and reduce downsizing effects on turnover rates. In contrast, HR practices that enhance alternative employment utility by helping to provide better external job opportunities (e.g., a career resource center, formal employee assessment to identify development opportunities, formal succession planning, a transfer policy to support learning) will enhance turnover by making the job market easier.

## Downsizing and productivity

Although there is plenty of evidence suggesting that job insecurity has negative effects on workers' health and attitudes (e.g., Kuhnert, Sims, and Lacey, 1989, Roskies and Louis-Guerin, 1990; Sverke, Hellgren, and Naswall, 2002), the relationship between job insecurity and performance is less clear. In their meta-analysis on the causes and consequences of job insecurity, Sverke *et al.* (2002) found no main effect for job insecurity on performance. This may be because job insecurity leads to enhanced performance in certain contexts, but to decreased performance in other contexts, or because of problems measuring productivity. For example, in a laboratory experiment, Probst (2002) found that participants were more productive when threatened with layoffs, but those increased outputs were rated as lower in quality and accompanied by more safety violations.

Brockner (1988) proposed that work effort may decline following a layoff. Furthermore, Greenhalgh and Rosenblatt (1984) contended that survivors will likely withhold efforts because the company is perceived as a "sinking ship." In contrast, Grunberg, Anderson-Connolly, and Greenberg (2000) found that lower-level employees, who were close to the layoff victims, reported favorable reactions, including less use of sick time and higher levels of work effort, perhaps as a strategy to avoid drawing attention to themselves. Brockner, Grover, Reed, and DeWitt (1992) suggested that a survivor's level of job insecurity is based on perceived external threat and perceived control. Greenhalgh and Rosenblatt (1984) conceptualized insecurity as the multiplicative function of threat severity and powerlessness. Job insecurity, especially at a moderate level (Brockner *et al.*, 1992) can cause workers to increase effort as a strategy to cope with lack of control and feelings of helplessness in the workplace.

Several researchers have claimed that organizational cost-cutting and downsizing tend to inhibit innovation and creative behavior due to an increase in risk-averse thinking (Cascio, 1993) and behavioral rigidity (Cameron, Sutton, and Whetton, 1988). In Amabile and Conti's (1999) study, 754 employees during organizational downsizing reported that the work environment for creativity significantly declined. Specifically, the employees reported significantly less freedom, challenge, access to resources, supervisory encouragement, work-group support, and organizational encouragement.

Probst, Stewart, Gruys, and Tierney (2007) found, in a laboratory experiment, that subjects threatened with layoffs increased their performance, but were significantly less likely to be able to solve a creative problem-solving task than their counterparts in the control group. Also, in a field study, job insecurity was negatively related to creativity. In addition, individuals who perceived their jobs to be insecure were less likely to engage in counterproductive work behaviors than individuals who reported feeling relatively more secure in their positions.

Employees in job insecurity and layoff conditions experience considerable stress, frustration, and anxiety (e.g., Brockner, Konovsky, and Cooper-Schneider, 1994a; Jacobson, 1987). Research suggests that stressful working conditions may contribute to employees engaging in counterproductive work behaviors (Burroughs, Bing, and James, 1999), including withdrawal behaviors, such as absenteeism and tardiness (Chisholm, Kasl, and Eskenazi, 1983; Gupta and Beehr, 1979), interpersonal aggression, hostility, sabotage, and complaints (Chen and Spector, 1992). Research suggests that individuals may engage in counterproductive work behavior in an attempt to regain control over their environment (Bennett, 1998). Lim (1996) found that employees with higher levels of perceived job insecurity were more likely to engage in 'noncompliant job behaviors' (Puffer, 1987). In contrast, it may be that employees in insecure job situations engage in less counterproductive work behavior because they fear the consequences.

## Individual differences

Armstrong-Stassen and Cattaneo (2010) found that older workers are especially vulnerable in downsizing. They also found that organizations that had downsized were significantly less likely to have human resource practices specifically tailored to the needs of older workers and to have a less supportive training and development climate for older workers. Concerning older workers, Kim (2009) found a negative correlation between organizational tenure and turnover intentions among survivors, explained by greater psychological attachment to the company or more company-specific skills due to their longevity. It seems that another possibility may be that they have fewer alternatives.

Concerning personality traits, Brandes, Castro, James, Martinez, Matherly, Ferris, and Hochwarter (2008) found among managerial employees, survivors of a corporate downsizing, positive correlations between cynicism and work effort. The writers argue that cynical layoff survivors distrust management and have higher expectation of losing work and, therefore, view increased work effort as the best way to cope (Fleming, 2005). Carver, Scheier, and Weintraub (1989) described increasing one's effort as a manifestation of active coping, when faced with uncertainty. Also Probst (2002) theorized that employees will choose to exert effort when the potential for job loss is great. This may also be explained by the expectancy theory (Vroom, 1964). The writers also suggest, in their intriguing study, that management actions of the past 15 years have created a "legacy of cynicism and resistance following changes which have been driven or forced as inevitable or fashionable, and which have increased working pressures and stress without clear benefits" (Buchanan, Claydon, and Doyle, 1999, p. 20). Barling, Dupre, and Hepburn (1998) reported that parental job insecurity perceptions affected children's subsequent work beliefs, including the level of alienation and cynicism brought to the job. In short, the new generation of workers fosters cynical attitudes toward their employer even prior to starting their careers. Cynicism develops when employees believe that their organization lacks integrity, is deceitful, and cannot be counted on to keep its word (Dean, Brandes, and Dharwadkar, 1998). Once established, it represents a confirmed (e.g., learned) expectation regarding expected treatment (Wanous, Reichers, and Austin, 2000). Kanter and Mirvis (1989; Mirvis and Kanter, 1992) showed that about 43 percent of the US workforce was principally cynical and that confidence in business has fallen from 70 percent to 15 percent.

Finally, we come to the point where recommendations for future research and management applications are warranted. We suggest that in respect to future research, there are two key areas that deserve further attention: organizational justice-based concepts and process and stress phenomena and related outcomes. We believe these areas are important because large numbers of studies on downsizing have stressed the key roles of justice-based concepts and stress phenomena in determining individual reactions to downsizing, and in fact note that

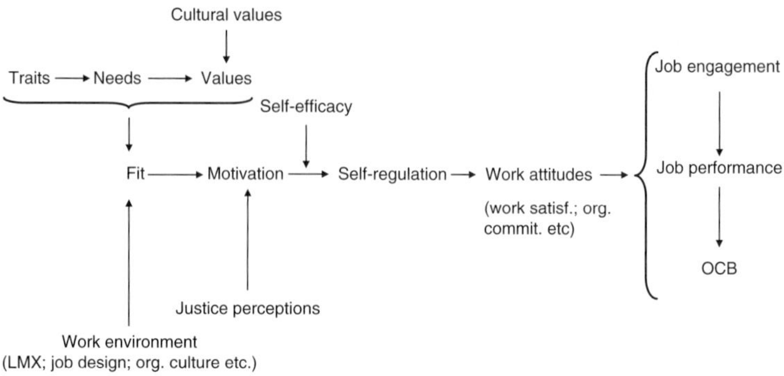


**Figure 4.1** The conceptual model guiding the chapter's argumentation and reasoning

these elements may work together in powerful ways (Brockner and Greenberg, 1990; Burroughs, Bing, and James, 1999; Chen and Spector, 1992; Davy, Kinicki, and Scheck, 2001; Jacobson, 1987). We recommend that future research refine and test models that link justice perceptions and related concepts to stress-related outcomes using key job attitudes, such as job satisfaction and organizational commitment, as potential mediators and moderators. Some of these connections appear in our model presented in Figure 4.1, and have also been suggested by previous research (Sauter, Murphy, and Hurrell, 1990).

In addition, we suggest that researchers examine a number of areas within human resource management for applications to mitigate the negative effects of downsizing. The key area that we suggest provides the most fruitful ground for such HRM applications is the performance management system. The notion of using performance management systems to renegotiate psychological contracts has been recommended in the literature (Storey and Sisson, 1993). However, this recommendation comes with the caveat that employees must feel that the managers engaged in performance management activities have a genuine relational interest in engaging employees (Stiles, Gratton, Truss, Hope-Hailey, and McGovern, 1997). In addition to this, we recommend that HRM interventions include boosting the frequency of performance management interactions between supervisors and staff (Aguinis, 2009). It would also be worthwhile to assess what non-financial rewards might look more attractive in a downsizing environment (Westacott, 2010).

Examining and improving patterns of organizational communication is also an important area for application in organizations that experience downsizing. Organizational communication includes aspects of performance management, but also relates to broader patterns of communication that occur outside of formal or informal performance management channels. We recommend that organizations take seriously the findings that suggest patterns of appropriate organizational communication have strong effects on justice perceptions (Bies, 2001; Bies and Moag, 1986). In particular, opportunities for two-way communication and thorough explanations for downsizing (Brockner, Konovsky, Cooper-Schneider, Folger, Martin, and Bies, 1994b) are likely to produce better fairness perceptions and better relationships within organizations after downsizing (Kim, 2009).

In conclusion, it seems that studying the motivation of workers after organizational downsizing should include a wide range of behaviors, from retaliation and resignation, through regular performance to investing higher efforts in the job. In addition, although (almost) no study found positive correlations between downsizing and positive work manifestation such as engagement, which is not surprising, it may also be interesting to study those behaviors among new workers, who were recruited following downsizing, instead of workers who were sent home. In this sense, it will be interesting to see whether the effects of downsizing on motivation are epidemic.

## References

Adams, J. S. 1965. "Inequity in social exchange," in L. Berkowitz (ed.), *Advances in Experimental Social Psychology*, Vol. II. New York: Academic Press, pp. 267–299.

Aguinis, H. 2009. *Performance Management*. New Jersey: Pearson.

Alderfer, C. P. 1972. *Existence, Relatedness, and Growth: Human Needs in Organizational Settings*. New York: Free Press.

Allen, T. D., Freeman, D. M., Russell, J. E. A., Reizenstein, R. C., and Rentz, J. O. 2001. "Survivor reactions to organizational downsizing: Does time ease the pain?" *Journal of Occupational and Organizational Psychology* **74**: 145–164.

Allport, G. W. 1951. "Basic principles in improving human relations," in K. W. Bigelow (ed.), *Cultural Groups and Human Relations*. Oxford: Bureau of Publications, Teachers Co, pp. 8–28.

Amabile, T. M. and Conti, R. 1999. "Changes in the work organization for creativity during downsizing." *Academy of Management Journal* **42**: 630–640.

Armstrong-Stassen, M. and Cameron, S. 2003. "Nurses job satisfaction and turnover intentions over a six-year period of hospital downsizing and amalgamation." *International Journal Public Administration* **26**: 1607–1620.

Armstrong-Stassen, M. and Cattaneo, J. 2010. "The effect of downsizing on organizational practices targeting older workers." *Journal of Management Development* **29**: 344–363

Armstrong-Stassen, M. and Latack, J. C. 1992. "Coping with workforce reduction: The effects of layoff exposure on survivor reactions." Academy of Management Review, Best Papers, pp. 207–211.

Atkinson, J. W. 1964. *An Introduction to Motivation.* Oxford: Van Nostrand.

Barling, J., Dupre, K. E., and Hepburn, C. G. 1998. "Effects of parents' job insecurity on children's work, beliefs and attitudes." *Journal of Applied Psychology* **83**: 112–118.

Batt, R., Colvin, A. J. S., and Keefe, J. 2002. "Employee voice, human resource practices, and quit rates: Evidence from the telecommunications industry." *Industrial and Labor Relations Review* **55**: 573–594.

Bennett, R. J. 1998. "Perceived powerlessness as a cause of employee deviance," in R. W. Griffin, A. O'Leary-Kelly, and J. M. Collins (eds.), *Dysfunctional Behavior in Organizations: Violent and Deviant Behavior*. Stamford, CT: JAI Press, pp. 221–239.

Bernard, L. C., Mills, M., Swenson, L., and Walsh, R. 2005. "An evolutionary theory of human motivation." *Genetic, Social and General Psychology Monographs* **131**: 129–184.

Bies, R. J. 2001. "Interactional (in)justice: The sacred and the profane," in J. Greenberg and R. Cropanzano (eds.), *Advances in Organizational Justice*. Stanford, CA: Stanford University Press, pp. 89–118.

Bies, R. J. and Moag, J. F. 1986. "Interactional justice: Communication criteria of fairness," in R. J. Lewicki, B. H. Sheppard, and M. H. Bazerman (eds.), *Research on Negotiations in Organizations*. Greenwich. CT: JAI Press, pp. 43–55.

Blau, P. 1964. *Exchange and Power in Social Life*. New York: Wiley.

Brandes, P., Castro, S. L., James, M. S. L., Martinez, A. D., Matherly, T. A., Ferris, G. R., and Hochwarter, W. A. 2008. "The interactive effects of job insecurity and organizational cynicism on work effort following a layoff." *Journal of Leadership and Organizational Studies* **14**: 233–247.

Bretz Jr., R. D., Ash, R. A., and Dreher, G. F. 1989. "Do people make the place? An examination of the fit and attraction–selection–attrition hypothesis." *Personnel Psychology* **42**: 561–581.

Brockner, J. 1986. "Layoffs, equity theory and work performance: Further evidence of the impact of survivor guilt." *Academy of Management Journal* **29**: 373–84.

Brockner, J. 1988. "The effects of work layoffs on survivors: Research, theory and practice," in B. M. Staw and L. L. Cummings (eds.), *Research in Organizational Behavior* **10**: 213–255.

Brockner, J. 1992. "Managing the effects of layoffs on others." *California Management Review* **34**: 9–27.

Brockner, J. and Greenberg, J. 1990. "The impact of layoffs on survivors: An organizational justice perspective," in J. S. Carroll (ed.), *Applied Social Psychology and Organizational Settings*. Hillsdale, NJ: Lawrence Erlbaum Associates, pp. 45–75.

Brockner, J., Grover, S., Reed, T. F., and DeWitt, R. L. 1992. "Layoffs, job insecurity, and survivors' work effort: Evidence of an inverted-U relationship." *Academy of Management Journal* **35**: 413–425.

Brockner, J., Konovsky, M., and Cooper-Schneider, R. 1994a. "Interactive effects of procedural justice and outcome negativity on victims and survivors of job loss." *Academy of Management Journal* **37**: 397–409.

Brockner, J., Konovsky, M., Cooper-Schneider, R., Folger, R., Martin, C., and Bies, R. J. 1994b. "Interactive effects of procedural justice and outcome negativity on victims and survivors of job loss." *Academy of Management Review* **37**: 397–409.

Brockner, J., Wiesenfeld, B., Stephan, J., Hurley, R., Grover, S., Reed, T., DeWitt, R. L., and Martin, C. 1997. "The effects on layoff survivors of their fellow survivors' reactions." *Journal of Applied Social Psychology* **10**: 835–863.

Brooke Jr., P. P., Russell, D. W., and Price, J. L. 1988. "Discriminant validation of measures of job satisfaction, job involvement, and organizational commitment." *Journal of Applied Psychology* **73**: 139–145.

Brown, M. E. and Trevino, L. K. 2009. "Leader–follower value congruence: Are socialized charismatic leaders better able to achieve it?" *Journal of Applied Psychology* **94**: 478–490.

Buchanan, D., Claydon, T., and Doyle, M. 1999. "Organisation development and change: The legacy of the nineties." *Human Resource Management Journal* **9**: 20–37.

Burroughs, S. M., Bing, M. N., and James, L. R. 1999. "Effects of personality and job stressors on affective reactions and aggressive work behaviors." Paper presented at the American Psychological Association and the

National Institute for Occupational Safety and Health Interdisciplinary Conference on Work, Stress, and Health, March, Baltimore, MD.

Cameron, K. S., Sutton, R. I., and Whetton, D. A. 1988. *Readings in Organizational Decline: Frameworks, Research and Prescriptions*. Cambridge, MA: Ballinger.

Carmeli, A. 2005. "The relationship between organizational culture and withdrawal intentions and behaviors." *International Journal of Manpower* **26**: 177–207.

Carver, C., Scheier, M., and Weintraub, J. 1989. "Assessing coping strategies: A theoretically based approach." *Journal of Personality and Social Psychology* **56**: 267–283.

Cascio, W. 1993. Downsizing: What do we know? What have we learned? *Academy of Management Executive* 7: 95–104.

Cascio, W. F., Young, C. E., and Morris, J. R. 1997. "Financial consequences of employment-change decisions in major US corporations." *Academy of Management Review* **40**: 1175–1189.

Chang, C., Rosen, C. C., and Levy, P. E. 2009. "The relationship between perceptions of organizational politics and employee attitudes, strain, and behavior: A meta-analytic examination." *Academy of Management Journal* **52**: 779–801.

Chen, P. Y. and Spector, P. E. 1992. "Relationships of work stressors with aggression, withdrawal, theft, and substance use: An exploratory study." *Journal of Occupational and Organizational Psychology* **65**: 177–184.

Chen, Z. and Francesco, A. 2003. "The relationship between the three components of commitment and employee performance in China." *Journal of Vocational Behavior* **62**: 490–510.

Chisholm, R. P., Kasl, S. V., and Eskanazi, B. 1983. "The nature and prediction of job related tension in a crisis situation: Reaction of nuclear workers to the Three Mile Island accident." *Academy of Management Journal* **26**: 385–405.

Cody, A. M., Hegeman, G. B., and Shanks, D. C. 1987. "How to reduce the size of the organization but increase effectiveness." *Journal of Business Strategy* **8**: 66–70.

Cropanzano, R., Prehar, C. A., and Chen, P. Y. 2002. "Using social exchange theory to distinguish procedural from interactional justice." *Group and Organization Management* **27**: 324.

Davy, J. A., Kinicki, A. J., and Scheck, C. L. 1991. "Developing and testing a model of survivor responses to layoffs." *Journal of Vocational Behavior* **48**: 302–317.

Dawis, R. V. 1991. "Vocational interests, values, and preferences," in M. D. Dunnette and L. M. Hough (eds.), *Handbook of Industrial and*

*Organizational Psychology*, Vol. II (2nd edn.). Palo Alto, CA: Consulting Psychologists Press, pp. 833–871.

Dean, J. W., Brandes, P., and Dharwadkar, R. 1998. "Organizational cynicism." *Academy of Management Review* **23**: 341–352.

Deci, E. L. and Ryan, R. M. 2002. "Self-determination research: Reflections and future directions," in E. L. Deci and R. M. Richard (eds.), *Handbook of Self-Determination Research*. Rochester, NY: University of Rochester Press, pp. 431–441.

Demarie, S. M. and Keats, B. W. 1996. "Organizational downsizing: A research framework." Paper presented at the annual conference of the Academy of Management.

DeShon, R. P. and Gillespie, J. Z. 2005. "A motivated action theory account of goal orientation." *Journal of Applied Psychology* **90**: 1096–1127.

Devine, K., Reay, T., Stainton, L., and Collins-Nakai, R. 2003. "The stress of downsizing: Comparing survivors and victims." *Human Resource Management* **42**: 109–124.

Doherty, N. and Horsted, J. 1995. "Helping survivors stay on board." *People Management* **1**: 26–31.

Driehaus, R. 2008. "DHL cuts 9,500 jobs in US, and an Ohio town takes the brunt." *New York Times*, November 11, p. A7.

Edwards, J. R. 2004. "Complementary and supplementary fit: A theoretical and empirical integration." *Journal of Applied Psychology* **89**: 822–834.

Erez, M. 2008. "Social-cultural influences on work motivation," in R. Kanfer, G. Chen, and R. D. Pritchard (eds.), *Work Motivation: Past, Present, and Future*. New York: Routledge/Taylor & Francis Group, pp. 501–538.

Fein, E. C. and Klein, H. J. 2011. "Personality predictors of behavioral self-regulation: Linking behavioral self-regulation to Five Factor Model factors, facets, and a compound trait." *International Journal of Selection and Assessment* **19**, 132–144.

Fisher, A. B. 2005. "The downside of downsizing." *New York Times*, May 23, pp. B1, B2.

Fleming, P. 2005. "'Kindergarten cop': Paternalism and resistance in a high-commitment workplace." *Journal of Management Studies* **42**: 1469–1489.

Folger, R. and Cropanzano, R. 1998. *Organizational Justice and Human Resource Management*. Thousand Oaks, CA: Sage Publications.

Freeman, S. J. 1999. "The gestalt of organizational downsizing: Downsizing strategies as packages of change." *Human Relations* **52**: 1505–1541.

Freeman, S. J. and Cameron, K. S. 1993. "Organizational downsizing: Convergence and reorientation framework." *Organization Science* **4**: 10–29.

Gelfand, M. J., Erez, M., and Aycan, Z. 2007. "Cross-cultural organizational behavior." *Annual Review of Psychology* **58**: 479–514.

Goodman, E. A., Zammuto, R. F., and Gifford, B. D. 2001. "The competing values framework: Understanding the impact of organizational culture on the quality of work life." *Organization Development Journal* **19**: 58–68.

Greenhalgh, L. 1982. "Maintaining organizational effectiveness during organizational retrenchment." *Journal of Applied Behavioral Science* **18**: 155–170.

Greenhalgh, L. and Rosenblatt, Z. 1984. "Job insecurity: Towards conceptual clarity." *Academy of Management Review* **9**: 438–448.

Greguras, G. J. and Diefendorff, J. M. 2009. "Different fits satisfy different needs: Linking person–environment fit to employee commitment and performance using self-determination theory." *Journal of Applied Psychology* **94**: 465–477.

Grunberg, L., Anderson-Connolly, R., and Greenberg, E. S. 2000. "Surviving layoffs: The effects on organizational commitment and job performance." *Work and Occupations* **27**: 7–31.

Gupta, N. and Beehr, T. A. 1979. "Job stress and employee behaviors." *Organizational Behavior and Human Performance* **23**: 373–387.

Hackman, J. and Oldham, G. R. 1976. "Motivation through the design of work: Test of a theory." *Organizational Behavior and Human Performance* **16**: 250–279.

Handy, F. and Katz, E. 1998. "The wage differential between non-profit institutions and corporations: Getting more by paying less?" *Journal of Comparative Economics* **26**: 246–261.

Harter, J. K., Schmidt, F. L., and Hayes, T. L. 2002. "Business-unit-level relationship between employee satisfaction, employee engagement, and business outcomes: A meta-analysis." *Journal of Applied Psychology* **87**: 268–279.

Herzberg, F., Mausner, B., and Snyderman, B. 1959. *The Motivation to Work* (2nd edn.). Oxford: John Wiley.

Hitt, M. A., Keats, B. W., Harback, H. F., and Nixon, R. D. 1994. "Rightsizing: Building and maintaining strategies, leadership and long-term competitiveness." *Organizational Dynamics* **23**: 18–32.

Hofstede, G. 2001. *Culture's Consequences: Comparing Values, Behaviors, Institutions, and Organizations across Nations* (2nd edn.). Thousand Oaks, CA: Sage.

Hofstede, G. and Peterson, M. F. 2000. "National values and organizational practices," in N. M. Ashkanasy, C. M. Wilderom, and M. F. Peterson (eds.), *Handbook of Organizational Culture and Climate*. Thousand Oaks, CA: Sage, pp. 401–416.

Holland, J. L. and Rayman, J. R. 1986. "The self-directed search," in W. Walsh, S. H. Osipow, W. Walsh, and S. H. Osipow (eds.), *Advances in Vocational Psychology, Vol. I: The Assessment of Interests*. Hillsdale, NJ: Lawrence Erlbaum Associates, pp. 55–82.

Hung-Wen, L. 2010. "The relationship between achievement, motivation, and psychological constructs." *The Journal of Global Business Issues* **4**: 9–17.

Ilies, R., Morgeson, F. P., and Nahrgang, J. D. 2005. "Authentic leadership and eudaemonic well-being: Understanding leader–follower outcomes." *Leadership Quarterly* **16**: 373–394.

Jacobson, D. 1987. "A personological study of the job insecurity experience." *Social Behavior* **2**: 143–155.

Jahoda, M. 1982. *Employment and Unemployment: A Social Psychological Analysis*. New York: Academic Press.

Jehn, K. A. 1997. "Affective and cognitive conflict in work groups: Increasing performance through value-based intragroup conflict," in C. W. De Dreu and E. Van de Vliert (eds.), *Using Conflict in Organizations*. Thousand Oaks, CA: Sage, pp. 87–100.

Kanfer, R. 2009. "Work motivation: Identifying use-inspired research directions." *Industrial and Organizational Psychology* **2**: 77–93.

Kanter, D. L. and Mirvis, P. H. 1989. *The Cynical Americans: Living and Working in an Age of Discontent and Disillusion*. San Francisco, CA: Jossey-Bass.

Kets de Vries, M. and Balazs, K. 1997. "The downside of downsizing." *Human Relations* **50**: 11–50.

Kettley, P. 1995. *Employee Morale During Downsizing*, Report No. 291. Brighton: Institute of Employment Studies.

Kilmann, R. H. 1981. "Toward a unique/useful concept of values for interpersonal behavior: A critical review of the literature on value." *Psychological Reports* **48**: 939–959.

Kim, H. S. 2009. "Examining the role of informational justice in the wake of downsizing from an organizational relationship management perspective." *Journal of Business Ethics* **88**: 297–312.

Kuhnert, K. W., Sims, R. R., and Lacey, M. A. 1989. "The relationship between job security and employee health." *Group and Organization Studies* **14**: 399–410.

Latham, G. P. and Pinder, C. C. 2005. "Work motivation: Theory and research at the dawn of the 21st century." *Annual Review of Psychology* **56**: 485–517.

Lee, S. and Yu, K. 2004. "Corporate culture and organizational performance." *Journal of Managerial Psychology* **19**: 340–359.

Lee, T. W. and Mitchell, T. R. 1994. "An alternative approach: The unfolding model of voluntary employee turnover." *Academy of Management Review* **19**: 51–89.

Lee, T. W., Mitchell, T. R., Sablynski, C. J., Burton, J. P., and Holton, B. C. 2004. "The effects of job embeddedness on organizational citizenship, job performance, volitional absences, and voluntary turnover." *Academy of Management Journal* **47**: 711–722.

Lee, T. W., Mitchell, T. R., Wise, L., and Fireman, S. 1996. "An unfolding model of voluntary employee turnover." *Academy of Management Journal* **39**: 5–36.

Leventhal, G. S. 1980. "What should be done with equity theory?" in K. J. Gergen, M. S. Greenberg, and R. H. Willis (eds.), *Social Exchange: Advances in Theory and Research*. New York: Plenum, pp. 27–55.

Liden, R. C. and Graen, G. 1980. "Generalizability of the vertical dyad linkage model of leadership." *Academy of Management Journal* **23**: 451–465.

Lim, V. K. G. 1996. "Job insecurity and its outcomes: Moderating effects of work-based and nonwork-based social support." *Human Relations* **49**: 171–194.

Lofquist, L. H. and Dawis, R. V. 1978. "Values as second-order needs in the theory of work adjustment." *Journal of Vocational Behavior* **1**: 12–19.

Lynch, D. J. 2008. "Hard times hit Ohio town hard: Biggest employer in town of 13,000 laying off 7,500." *USA Today*, December 16, p. B1.

Maertz, C. P., Wiley, J. J. W., LeRouge, C., and Campion, M. A. 2010. "Downsizing effects on survivors: Layoffs, offshoring, and outsourcing." *Industrial Relations* **49**: 275–285.

Martin, D. C. and Bartol, K. M. 1985. "Managing turnover strategically." *Personnel Administrator* **30**: 63–73.

McClelland, D. C., Atkinson, J. W., Clark, R. A., and Lowell, E. L. 1976. *The Achievement Motive*. Oxford: Irvington.

Meglino, B. M. and Ravlin, E. C. 1998. "Individual values in organizations: Concepts, controversies, and research." *Journal of Management* **24**: 251–289.

Miller, D. and Lee, J. 2001. "The people make the process: Commitment to employees, decision making, and performance." *Journal of Management* **27**: 163.

Minkov, M. 2007. *What Makes Us Different and Similar: A New Interpretation of World Values Survey and Other Cross-Cultural Data*. Sofia, Bulgaria: Klasika I Still.

Mirvis, P. H. and Kanter, D. L. 1992. "Beyond demography: A psychographic profile of the workforce." *Human Resource Management* **30**: 45–68.

Mitchell, T. R., Holtom, B. C., Lee, T. W., Sablynski, C. J., and Erez, M. 2001. "Why people stay: Using job embeddedness to predict voluntary turnover." *Academy of Management Journal* **44**: 1102–1121.

Mount, M. K. and Barrick, M. R. 1998. "Five reasons why the 'Big Five' article has been frequently cited." *Personnel Psychology* **51**: 849–857.

Murray, H. A. 1938. *Explorations in Personality*. Oxford: Oxford University Press.

Nolan, J. 2008. "Ohio looks for new uses for DHL hub in Wilmington." *McClatchy-Tribune Business News*, August 19.

Parker, S. K. and Ohly, S. 2008. "Designing motivating jobs: An expanded framework for linking work characteristics and motivation," in R. Kanfer, G. Chen, and R. D. Pritchard (eds.), *Work Motivation: Past, Present, and Future*. New York: Routledge/Taylor & Francis Group, pp. 233–284.

Pelley, S. 2009. "The long recession." *60 Minutes*. December 20.

Pinder, C. C. 2008. *Work Motivation in Organizational Behavior* (2nd edn.). New York: Psychology Press.

Probst, T. M. 2002. "Layoffs and tradeoffs: Production, quality, and safety demands under the threat of job loss." *Journal of Occupational Health Psychology* 7: 211–220.

Probst, T. M., Stewart, S. M., Gruys, M. L., and Tierney, B. W. 2007. "Productivity, counter-productivity, and creativity: The ups and downs of job insecurity." *Journal of Occupational and Organizational Psychology* **80**: 479–497.

Puffer, S. M. 1987. "Prosocial behavior, noncompliant behavior, and work performance among commission sales people." *Journal of Applied Psychology* **72**: 615–621.

Ritzman, R. L. and Tomaskovic-Devey, D. D. 1992. "Life chances and support for equality and equity as normative and counternormative distribution rules." *Social Forces* **70**: 745–763.

Rokeach, M. 1973. *The Nature of Human Values*. New York: Free Press.

Roskies, E. and Louis-Guerin, C. 1990. "Job insecurity in managers: Antecedents and consequences." *Journal of Organizational Behavior* **11**: 345–359.

Sahdev, K. 2004. "Revisiting the survivor syndrome: The role of leadership in implementing downsizing." *European Journal of Work and Organizational Psychology* **13**: 165–196.

Sauter, S. L., Murphy, L. R., and Hurrell, J. J. 1990. "A national strategy for the prevention of work-related disorders." *American Psychologist* **45**: 252–261.

Sheppard, B. H., Lewicki, R. J., and Minton, J. W. 1992. *Organizational Justice: The Search for Fairness in the Workplace*. New York: Lexington Books/Macmillan.

Sheridan, J. E. 1992. "Organizational culture and employee retention." *Academy of Management* **35**: 1036–1056.

Song, L., Tsui, A. S., and Law, K. S. 2009. "Unpacking employee responses to organizational exchange mechanisms: The role of social and economic exchange perceptions." *Journal of Management* **35**: 56–93.

Stiles, P., Gratton, L., Truss, C., Hope-Hailey, V., and McGovern, P. 1997. "Performance management and the psychological contract." *Human Resource Management Journal* **7**: 57–66.

Storey, J. and Sisson, K. 1993. *Managing Human Resources and Industrial Relations*. Milton Keynes: Open University Press.

Sverke, M., Hellgren, J., and Naswall, K. 2002. "No security: A review and meta-analysis of job insecurity and its consequences." *Journal of Occupational Health Psychology* **7**: 242–264.

Taras, V., Kirkman, B. D., and Steel, P. 2010. "Examining the impact of culture's consequences: A three decade, multilevel, meta-analytic review of Hofstede's cultural value dimensions." *Journal of Applied Psychology* **95**: 405–439.

Thibaut, J. W. and Walker, L. 1975. *Procedural Justice: A Psychological Analysis*. Hillsdale, NJ: Lawrence Erlbaum.

Trevor, C. O. and Nyberg, A. J. 2008. "Keeping your headcount when all about you are losing theirs: Downsizing, voluntary turnover rates, and the moderating role of HR practices." *Academy of Management Journal* **51**: 259–276.

Triandis, H. C. 1994. *Culture and Social Behavior*. New York: McGraw Hill.

Tyler, T. R., and Bies, R. 1990. "Beyond normal procedures: The interpersonal context of procedural justice," in J. S. Carroll (ed.), *Applied Social Psychology and Organizational Settings*. London: Lawrence Erlbaum, pp. 77–98.

Tziner, A. 1987. "Congruency issue retested using Fineman's achievement climate motivation." *Journal of Social Behavior and Personality* **2**: 63–78.

Tziner, A. and Falbe, C. M. 1990. "Actual and preferred climates of achievement orientation and their congruency: An investigation of their relationships to work attitudes and performance in two occupational strata." *Journal of Organizational Behavior* **11**: 159–167.

Tziner, A., Shultz, T., and Fisher, T. 2008. "Justice, leader–member–exchange, and job performance: Are their relationships mediated by organizational culture?" *Psychological Reports* **103**: 516–526.

Ulrich, D. 1998. "A mandate for human resources." *Harvard Business Review* (February/March): 124–134.

Vroom, V. 1964. *Work and Motivation*. New York: Wiley.

Wanous, J. P, Reichers, A. E., and Austin, J. T. 2000. "Cynicism about organizational change: Measurement, antecedents, and correlates." *Group and Organization Management* **25**: 132–153.

Weismal-Manor, R., Tziner, A., Berger, E., and Dikstein, E. 2010. "Two of a kind? Leader–member exchange and organizational citizenship behavior: The moderating role of leader–member similarity." *Journal of Applied Social Psychology* **40**: 167–181.

Westacott, C. 2010. "Remuneration management," in J. Stafford (ed.), *2010 Australian Master Human Resources Guide*. Sydney: CCH.

Zaccaro, S. J., Ely, K., and Nelson, J. 2008. "Leadership processes and work motivation," in R. Kanfer, G. Chen, and R. D. Pritchard (eds.), *Work Motivation: Past, Present, and Future*. New York: Routledge/Taylor & Francis Group, pp. 319–360.

# 5 | *To downsize human capital: A strategic human resource perspective on the disparate outcomes of downsizing*

GARY C. McMAHAN, ALANKRITA PANDEY, AND BRIAN MARTINSON

The process of downsizing is defined as the "planned set of organizational policies and practices aimed at reducing the extant workforce with the goal of improving firm performance" (Datta, Guthrie, Basuil, and Pandey, 2010, p. 282). It is a very complex process, far more so than research following only an economic or institutional view would suggest (McKinley, Zhao, and Rust, 2000). Whether the impetus to consider downsizing is a reaction to organizational decline or competitive pressures, the impact resulting from the design and execution of the entire process is deeply rooted within the organization and much deliberation and care must go into the proactive planning and implementation of the workforce reduction to temper or eliminate negative outcomes (Cameron, Freeman, and Mishra, 1991). Involving multiple actors and units of analysis, downsizing must be studied in ways taking into account this complexity in order to capture the full effects resulting from such a critical strategic decision.

Downsizing is an intentional process focusing on improving organizational efficiency through the reduction of employees (Cascio, 2010). The effects of downsizing on the workforce are both foreseen and unforeseen (Huber and Glick, 1993). Organizations undertake downsizing with the assumption that it preserves profitability by enhancing organizational efficiency and reducing costs (DeWitt, 1998; Freeman, 1994; Harrigan, 1980). However, the extant research shows that downsizing yields mixed results. For example, it has been found to have positive effects (Baumol, Blinder, and Wolff, 2003; Bruton, Keels, and Shook, 1996; Espahbodi, John, and Vasudevan 2000; Wayhan and Werner, 2000), negative effects (Cascio, 1993; Cascio, Young, and Morris, 1997; Caves and Kreps, 1993; Lee, 1997; Palmon, Sun, and Tang, 1997; Worrell, Davidson, and Sharma, 1991), or no effects (Cameron *et al.*, 1991) on firm performance. These disparate outcomes are in part due to the inherent complexity of downsizing.

This chapter attempts to examine organizational downsizing as a multi-theory, multi-level, and multi-disciplinary process to account for the differences in outcomes. The decision to downsize is made at the organizational level to improve the organization's financial and performance outcomes. We look at how downsizing strategies at the organization level impact human capital through employee behaviors and employee performance. We use the strategic human resource management (SHRM) model (Wright and McMahan, 1992) to examine how the disruption of human capital within the firm impacts the performance of the firm (Wright and McMahan, 1992; Delery and Shaw, 2001; Snell, Youndt, and Wright, 1996; Ulrich, 1991) through the mechanism of employee behaviors in the context of downsizing.

Additionally, the chapter includes multiple theories or theoretical models to help explain the relationships/impact that we present in Figure 5.1. Here, we attempt to provide the major models that impact downsizing within organizations. These include: the resource-based view (RBV) of the firm (Barney, 1991), human capital theory (Becker, 1964; Wright and McMahan, 2011), SHRM perspective (Wright and McMahan, 1992), systems perspective (Delery and Shaw, 2001; McMahan, Virick, and Wight, 1999; Wright and McMahan, 1992; Wright and Snell, 1991), justice theories (Greenberg, 1990; Wiesenfeld, Swann, Brockner, and Bartel, 2007), target similarity model (Lavelle, Rupp, and Brockner, 2007), and psychological contract theory (Aselage and Eisenberger, 2003; Rousseau, 1995) to examine the impact of downsizing across the organizational, unit, and individual levels of the firm.

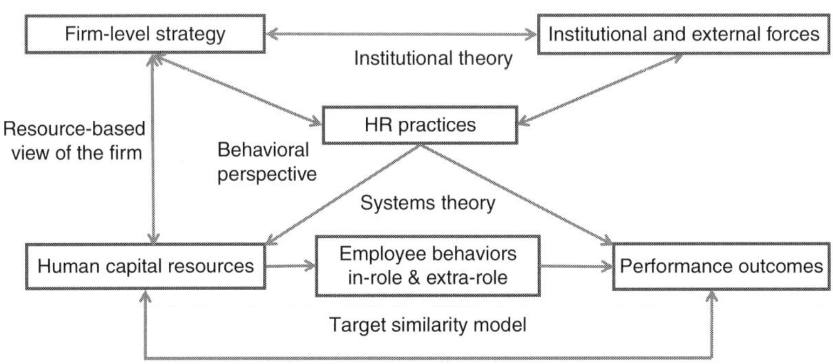


**Figure 5.1** Strategic HRM model
(Adapted from Wright and McMahan, 1992; McMahan *et al.*, 1999)

This chapter will begin with a discussion of the organization, unit, and individual outcomes of downsizing. It is important to note that organization and unit will be discussed as one level, as little research to date has been published at the unit level. Next, we discuss in some detail the impacts of downsizing on the human capital of the firm. Finally, we end the chapter with a brief discussion of future research and the conclusion.

## Organizational/unit level outcomes of downsizing

Firms downsize in response to declines in service/goods demand in order to reduce labor costs through increased capacity utilization (Cameron, Freeman, and Mishra, 1993). They may also downsize in response to structural changes when advances in technology lead to greater worker productivity. Or, they may simply be trying to stimulate greater efficiency or lower costs as a result of internal desires as opposed to external pressures (Budros, 1999). Downsizing may also be viewed as having its origin in institutional forces (Ahmadjian and Robbins, 2005; Budros, 1999; Freeman and Cameron, 1993; McKinley *et al.*, 2000) whereby firms seek to acquire legitimacy by following strategies adopted by other firms in the industry (DiMaggio and Powell, 1983). These institutional forces may have a direct impact on the strategy of the firm, which in turn affects the firm's human capital, employee behaviors, and the various outcomes as predicted through the SHRM model (Wright and McMahan, 1992; McMahan *et al.*, 1999). At the firm level, the impacts of downsizing are direct reductions in human capital and its associated impacts on firm-level performance.

The negative impacts of downsizing on performance have been observed in product quality (Mishra and Mishra, 1994), employer efficiency (Mishra and Mishra, 1994; Wagar, 1998), aspects of quality improvement and labor productivity (Mishra and Mishra, 1994; Amabile and Conti, 1999; Zatzick and Iverson, 2006; Suarez-Gonzalez, 2001; Baumol *et al.*, 2003), creativity (Amabile and Conti, 1999), innovation (Dougherty and Bowman, 1995); firm credibility (Mishra and Mishra, 1994), work environment stimulants (Amabile and Conti, 1999), and workplace performance (Gilson, Hurd, and Wagar, 2004). Additionally, downsizing was found to have a negative impact on firm reputation (Zyglidopoulos, 2005; Flanagan and O'Shaughnessy, 2005; Love and Kratz, 2009).

As we will discuss below, downsizing activities can also undermine an organization by destroying trust; creating survivor guilt and feelings of insecurity and depression; and increase managerial risk aversion (Hitt and Keats, 1992; Brockner, Davey, and Carter, 1985).

## Individual-level outcomes of downsizing

At the individual level, downsizing impacts various individuals involved in the process, from the managers who implement the downsizing, the employees who are downsized, and the employees left behind. Downsizing at this level not only results in a reduction of headcount but also has a profound impact on the emotions, attitudes, and motivations of individuals (De Meuse, Bergmann, Vanderheiden, and Roraff, 2004; Morrison and Robinson, 1997; Rousseau, 1995; Allen, Freeman, Russell, Reizenstein, and Rentz, 2001; Brockner, Sprietzer, Mishra, Pepper, and Weinberg, 2004; Luthans and Sommer, 1999; Travaglione and Cross, 2006). As shown in Figure 5.1 above, we employ the target similarity model (TSM) (Lavelle *et al.*, 2007) to explain how downsizing impacts employees' perceptions of justice, their social exchange relationships within the organization, the effects of these changes on their commitment to the organization, and, ultimately, employees' targeted extra-role behavior.

Further, individual-level downsizing has a direct impact on all employees in the organization. In downsizing nomenclature, individuals losing their positions are classified as "victims" while those who remain are known as "survivors" (Kets de Vries and Balazs, 1997). The managers who participate in the firing are often termed "executioners" (Kets de Vries and Balazs, 1997). In addition to the obvious impact of a job loss on individual employees and their families, downsizing has been found to have statistically significant negative effects on the people in an organization deciding and implementing the staff reduction. It impacts not only the victims, but also the survivors, the managers, and executives who participate in the strategy.

Kets de Vries and Balazs (1997) found that post-downsizing, management may fear the *lex talonis* – the law of retaliation; that someone would want to "get even" with them after the downsizing for having initiated the process. Thus they usually try to use euphemisms to explain the process, replacing downsizing with "rightsizing," or even calling a downsizing a reduction in force (RIF) to lessen its impact. Findings that these types of managers regress into dysfunctional behavior patterns are common. They may also become compulsive, ritualistic, abrasive, "reactive narcissists," dissociative, or hedonic, and engage in stereotypical interpersonal behaviors. In extreme scenarios, they may even get depressive – all of which impact their work most negatively.

*Victims* of the downsizing can be classified as those who are adaptable, those who completely reinvent themselves, those who become depressed, and those who become antagonistic. Depressed people may suffer from a host of problems, including insomnia as well as becoming preoccupied with negative thoughts, all of which have a significant impact on their work performance. Antagonistic people may become dysfunctional, wanting to "get even" with the organization, even indulging in harassment or sabotage (Kets de Vries and Balazs, 1997).

*Survivors* tend to react more positively to downsizing if they perceive the action to be necessary for the survival of the organization (Rousseau, 2001). A "mixed bags of emotions are often exhibited by remaining employees following a downsizing" (Doherty and Horsted, 1995, p. 26). They may feel anger, depression, fear, guilt, risk aversion, distrust, vulnerability, or powerlessness, and experience a lowering of morale or loss of motivation (Brockner, 1988; Cascio, 1993; Noer, 1993). The downsizing experience has a negative impact on employee attitudes, such as commitment (Luthans and Sommer, 1999), perceived organizational support, job satisfaction, job performance, turnover intention (minimally significant), and increased absenteeism (Travaglione and Cross, 2006). It has been found that continuance commitment remains stable (Travaglione and Cross, 2006). Burnout occurs quite regularly if there are feelings of ambiguity, characterized by emotional exhaustion, lack of energy, and feelings of emptiness. Depersonalization and a cynical, dehumanizing, and negative attitude towards people combine in a stress syndrome (Kets de Vries and Balazs, 1997). Thus, the success of downsizing is contingent upon the nurturing variables of commitment, satisfaction, perceived organizational support, and performance in a workforce (Shah, 2000). It is imperative for building and maintaining any chance of survivor trust that management is capable of "providing clear explanations of why downsizing is necessary, treating all employees with dignity, and using procedures that are fair" (Niehoff, Moorman, Blakely, and Fuller, 2001, p. 107).

Due to its disparate impacts on all employees in an organization, employee downsizing contributes to a decline in the post-downsizing work environment. Amabile and Conti (1999) found that downsizing resulted in declines in work freedom, challenge, supervisory encouragement, work group support, and resource availability. Luthans and Sommer (1999) also observed reduced support from supervisors following downsizing. In addition, Gilson *et al.* (2004), in their study of downsizing among New Zealand firms, observed that after downsizing, firms were characterized by greater workplace conflict, and this relationship was consistent across early, repeat, and late downsizers.

The following section discusses the impacts of downsizing on human capital, employee behaviors, human resource practices, and performance.

## The impacts of downsizing

We explain these effects of downsizing through an adapted strategic human resource management model as presented in Figure 5.2 below (Wright and McMahan, 1992; McMahan *et al.*, 1999; Wright and McMahan, 2011).

This strategic human resource management (SHRM) perspective of Wright and McMahan (1992) uses the RBV extensively in theory to explain the relationship between a firm's human capital and performance.[1] Wright and McMahan (1992) defined strategic human resource

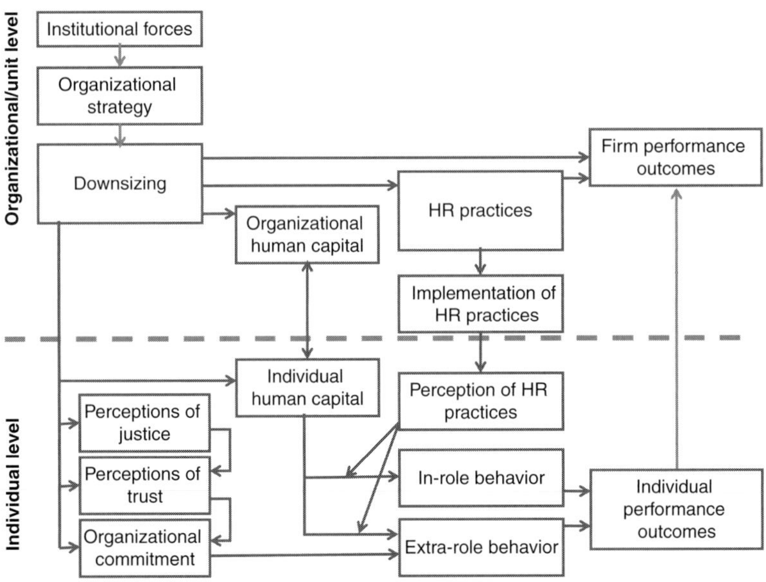


**Figure 5.2** Impacts of downsizing on performance matters

management as the "pattern of planned human resource deployments and activities intended to enable an organization to achieve its goals" (p. 298). Further the authors state that the domain of strategic HRM consisted of "the determinants of decisions about HR practices, the composition of the human capital pool, the specification of the required human resource behaviors, and the effectiveness of these decisions given various business strategies and/or competitive situations" (p. 298). SHRM examines how human capital resources influence employee behaviors, which in turn influence employee performance (Delery and Shaw, 2001; Snell *et al.*, 1996; Ulrich, 1991; Wright and McMahan, 1992). Firm performance is derived as the aggregation of individual employee performance. Capturing a stock of extraordinary talent will lead to human capital advantage for the firm (Boxall, 1998) and lead to the development of competitive advantage if these valuable and inimitable employees are properly managed (Harris, McMahan, and Wright, 2009; Lopez-Cabrales, Valle, and Herrero, 2006). This approach also takes into account the impact of HR practices implemented at the organizational level. These practices translate downwards into individual-level perceptions, which have a bearing on individual behavior and performance.

## *Impact on human capital*

The firm is an idiosyncratic collection of resources and capabilities (Penrose, 1959) comprised of physical, financial, and human capital resources. According to the resource-based view (RBV) of the firm, these strategically relevant resources can be a source of sustained competitive advantage (Barney, 1991) if they are valuable, rare, non-substitutable, and inimitable. Human capital resources (Becker, 1964) consisting of the accumulated training, experience, judgment, intelligence, and insight of individual managers and workers in a firm are valuable, rare, inimitable, and non-substitutable under certain conditions (Wright, McMahan, and McWilliams, 1994). Different jobs in an organization require various types and levels of human capital to be possessed by unique individuals who contribute in unique ways adding value to the organization. Human capital resources are usually normally distributed within a population, thus making it difficult and costly for an organization to acquire individuals with exceptional levels of knowledge, skills, and abilities or unique combinations of knowledge, skills, and abilities (KSAs), making them rare. The unique history of the firm, the causal ambiguity of a highly valued capability, and/or the social complexity that supports exceptional team productivity also contribute to making human capital resources inimitable. It is highly unlikely that one specific set of human capital resources can be completely replaced by another, making these resources non-substitutable. Although there exists the possibility of technological or process substitutes for some forms of human capital (Bamberger and Meshoulam, 2000), there are limits to the extent to which human capital can be replaced (Ployhart, Weekley, and Ramsay, 2009).

Hitt, Hoskisson, Harrison, and Summers (1994) suggest downsizing as one of the reasons for the loss of global competitiveness in US firms. The RBV would attribute this to the loss of strategic human capital through the process of downsizing. Human capital and research and development (R&D) intensity have strategic complementarities and interdependent incentives to invest in each other (Redding, 1996). Guthrie and Datta (2008) found that if R&D intensity is taken into account, downsizing has a negative effect on firm profitability. This finding can be explained in that downsizing reduces human capital that reduces the benefits that R&D intensity produces and therefore has more of a negative effect on firm profitability.

According to human capital theory, differences in human capital can lead to different levels of performance (Becker, 1964). Thus, individuals with higher levels of human capital should perform at a higher level. Research has found evidence of this relationship between human capital and performance at the individual (Harris *et al.*, 2009; Ployhart, Weekley, and Baughman, 2006; Pandey, Harris, McMahan, and Wright, 2010) and organizational levels (Hitt, Bierman, Shimizu, and Kochhar, 2001; Youndt, Subramanium, and Snell, 2004; Carmeli and Tishler, 2004a; Carmeli and Tishler, 2004b; Skaggs and Youndt, 2004; Carmeli and Schaubrocck, 2005; Lopez-Cabrales *et al.*, 2006; Hitt, Bierbam, Uhlenbruck, and Shimizu, 2006; Reed, Lubatkin, and Srinivasan, 2006; Hsu, Lin, Lawler, and Wu, 2007; Takeuchi, Lepak, Wang, and Taeuchi, 2007; Sturnman, Walsh, and Cheramie, 2008; Bruns, Holland, Shepherd, and Wiklund, 2008; Youndt *et al.*, 2004).

Human capital has both a general and a specific component (Becker, 1962; Wright and McMahan, 2011). This distinction between the two components of human capital arises as the result of "perfectly general" training and "on the job" training. General human capital refers to overall education and practical experience, while specific human capital refers to education and experience plus application limited to a particular activity or context (Becker, 1964; Gimeno, Folta, Cooper, and Woo, 1997). General human capital can easily be transferred between firms (Offstein, Gnyawali, and Cobb, 2005). It consists of knowledge, skills, and abilities that can be used across different firms or with different technologies. Specific human capital is productive only in a particular firm or with certain technologies. By definition, firm-specific knowledge is useful only within the firms providing it, whereas general knowledge is useful across other firms (Becker, 1964). This distinction has been used to explain why workers with highly specific skills are less likely to quit their jobs and are generally the last to be laid off during business downturns. According to Becker (1992), this also explains why most promotions are made from within a firm rather than through hiring externally and also why better accounting methods would include the specific human capital of employees among the principal assets of most companies. Firms that downsize workers with higher specific human capital are thus likely to lose vital knowledge, skills, and abilities that are required for sustained competitive advantage.

### *Impact on employee in-role behavior*

To be successful on the job, employees need to have high levels of human capital and exhibit the necessary work-related behaviors (Delery and Shaw, 2001; Wright *et al.*, 1994; Wright and Snell, 1991). The SHRM perspective examines how human resources are deployed to enable an organization to achieve its strategic goals of competitive advantage (Wright and McMahan, 1992, McMahan *et al.*, 1999). The potential of human capital is realized to the extent that the possessors of the human capital choose to use their human capital to exhibit the required behaviors (Wright *et al.*, 1994). Therefore, organizations must select individuals that have the human capital necessary to exhibit the required behaviors (Wright *et al.*, 1994). The role of behaviors is explained in the SHRM model (Wright and McMahan, 1992) through the systems perspective (Wright and Snell, 1991) and behavioral theory (Jackson and Schuler, 1995).

Behavior consists of what people do at work, which leads to a specific outcome (Campbell, 1990). While behavior is a multi-dimensional concept (Sonnentag, Volmer, and Spychala, 2008), and not always distinguished from individual-level performance, researchers agree that it is distinct from the outcome aspect of performance and consists of the activities that people perform while doing their jobs (Borman and Motowidlo, 1993; Campbell, McCloy, Oppler, and Sager, 1993). This behavior aspect consists of what people do at work, while the outcome aspect is the behavior which is goal oriented or what the organization hires the employee to perform (Campbell, 1990). Thus, the loss of human capital in organizations through the process of downsizing leads to a change in the behavior and thus in outcomes. Survivors of downsizings have been found to exhibit lower job involvement (Brockner, Glover, and Blonder, 1988; Allen *et al.*, 2001; Armstrong-Stassen, Wagar, and Cattaneo, 2004), decreased work effort (Brockner, Grover, Reed, and DeWitt, 1992; Brandes, Castro, James, Martinez, Matherly, and Ferris, 2008), and lower motivation to work (Brockner, Grover, O'Malley, Reed, and Glynn, 1993; Armstrong-Stassen *et al.*, 2004).

## *Impact on employee extra-role behavior*

Behavior above and beyond the call of duty is called organization citizenship behavior or OCB (Organ, 1988; Bateman and Organ, 1983; Smith, Organ, and Near, 1983). It is "individual behavior that is discretionary, not directly or explicitly recognized by the formal reward system and that in the aggregate promotes the effective functioning of the organization" (Organ, 1988). One of the three types of behaviors required for the functioning of an organization (Katz, 1964), this spontaneous activity helps the organization become a robust system as opposed to a fragile system depending only upon prescribed behavior. OCBs include helping behavior, sportsmanship, organizational loyalty, organizational compliance, individual initiative, civic virtue, and self-development. Podsakoff, Mackenzie, Paine, and Bacharach (2000) reviewed the literature on OCBs and found 30 potentially different forms of OCBs which they organized into the five major categories of: altruism, conscientiousness, civic virtue, sportsmanship, and courtesy.

Brief and Motowidlo (1986) argued that this extra-role behavior can be directed at particular parties, such as peers, supervisors, customers, or the organization. Organ (1988) noted that altruism exhibits this intended target property. The organization has been found to be the beneficiary of other pro-social behaviors (Ilies, Nahrgang, and Morgeson, 2007; LePine, Erez, and Johnson, 2002; Robinson and Morrison, 1995). Williams and Anderson (1991) distinguished between citizenship behavior directed towards the organization (OCBO) and towards individuals (OCBI).

These two behaviors were found to be different from in-role behavior. OCBI was predicted by intrinsic job cognitions, while OCBO was predicted by extrinsic job cognitions. Later research found psychological contract fulfillment to be more correlated with OCBO than OCBI (Turnley, Bolino, Lester, and Bloodgood, 2004). McNeely and Meglino (1994) found that individual directed, organization directed, and role directed behaviors were correlated but had unique antecedents. Malatesta and Byrne (1997) found evidence for supervisor directed citizenship behavior (OCBS), refining the Williams and Anderson (1991) OCBI measure, a finding later corroborated by Rupp and Cropanzano (2002). Using the logic taken by Malatesta and Byrne (1997), Lee and Allen (2002) suggest coworker directed citizenship behavior.

Lavelle *et al.* (2007) bring together the justice, social exchange, and citizenship behaviors' literature, suggesting that there are links between employee perceptions of justice, social exchange relationships, and behaviors. They suggest a multi-foci framework that employees conceptualize their work experience in a multifaceted way, differentiating between sources of justice, social exchange relationship partners, and beneficiaries of citizenship behaviors. This target similarity model (TSM) framework is empirically supported by Lavelle, McMahan, and Harris (2009) in a sample of hospital nurses. Following the logic of the systems view and the behavioral view, we can state that there is a relationship between the knowledge, skills, and abilities of registered nurses and their contextual behavior, as there is for in-role behavior.

Thus lowered perceptions of justice at multiple targets, such as supervisors, co-workers, and organizations, lead to lowered perceptions of targeted trust, lowered commitment, and therefore lower levels of extra-role behavior. Lavelle, Brockner, Konovsky, Price, Henley, Taneja, and Vinekar (2009) find evidence for the target similarity effects in the relationships between justice, social exchange, commitment, and extra-role behaviors in a study of 106 survivors of a layoff in a medical clinic. Since behavior is one of the antecedents of performance, downsizing will lead to lowered performance through its disruptions of trust, commitment, and justice. In the following section, we discuss the impacts of downsizing on the lowered perceptions of trust, commitment, and justice.

### Perceptions of justice

Perceptions of justice are impacted by the downsizing process (Sahdev, 2004). This was measured in terms of mutual trust and managerial coping strategies using survey data. Employees may also react to perceptions of whether rewards are being distributed fairly (distributive justice) and if the processes used to arrive at decisions affecting the workplace are fair (procedural justice – Thibault and Walker, 1975). If the downsizing decision is viewed as being inconsistent across individuals and time, and not conforming to moral and ethical standards (Leventhal, 1980), and if the treatment of victims of the layoff is perceived as unfair, negative reactions may be magnified. Perceptions of fairness have been positively associated with favorable employee attitudes and behaviors, including organizational commitment, organizational support, OCBs, work performance, and trust in management (e.g., Cohen-Charash and Spector, 2001; Colquitt, Conlon, Wesson, Porter, and Ng, 2001; Konovsky, 2000). When treated unfairly, employees are likely to react in unfavorable ways such as engaging in counterproductive work behaviors (e.g., damaging company property or spreading rumors), turnover, and theft (Colquitt *et al.*, 2001; Cropanzano, Byrne, Bobocel, and Rupp, 2001).

Brockner, Konovsky, Cooper-Schnieder, Folger, Martin, and Bies (1994) found that layoff severity did not have a perceptible impact on organizational trust and support when survivors perceived high procedural fairness. However, under conditions of low perceived procedural fairness, layoff severity had a significant deleterious effect on organizational trust. Mansour-Cole and Scott (1998) found that survivors perceive greater procedural fairness when they learn about impending layoffs from their managers and not from other sources. They also found that the relationship between the source of layoff information and perceived procedural fairness is contingent upon existing leader–subordinate relationships, with the association being more pronounced in relationships characterized by high mutual trust, respect, and obligation. In another study, Armstrong-Stassen (1994) observed significant differences in perceived procedural justice across different employee groups, with feelings of injustice being greater among female employees (relative to their male counterparts) and among technicians *vis-à-vis* their supervisors.

**Social exchange relationships**

Downsizing leads to a violation of psychological contract, the rebuilding of which is a considerable challenge (Hilltrop, 1995). Relationships between employers and employees are generally characterized by an exchange of socio-economic benefits, mutual trust, open-ended commitment, and a long-term focus (Blau, 1964). This social exchange theory states that employees in such relationships with their employers tend to strongly identify with the persons or entities they are engaged with (Rupp and Cropanzano, 2002). Thus high-quality social exchange relationships are likely to motivate employees to engage in behaviors that have favorable consequences for the organization over time, in part because employees tend to identify the organization's well-being with their own, and because they may feel a relational obligation to support the organization (Rhoades, Eisenberger, and Armeli, 2001; Van Dyne, Graham, and Dienesch, 1994). The quality of social exchange between people and their employers can be measured through variables such as commitment (Meyer, 1997), trust (Sitkin and Roth, 1993), and perceived support (Moorman, Deshpandé, and Zaltman, 1993). This set of mutual obligations between employees and employers is also known as the psychological contract (Rousseau, 1995). Downsizing is often perceived as a violation of the psychological contract (De Meuse *et al.*, 2004; Morrison and Robinson, 1997; Rousseau, 1995) by survivors and victims alike. Given that psychological contracts are fundamental to employees' beliefs and experiences, violations of such contracts have important consequences for employees' work attitudes and behaviors (Robinson, 1996). Surviving employees may withdraw psychologically (e.g., reduced trust and loyalty, withholding of effort, and reduced involvement) or physically (increased absences or voluntary turnover), with negative economic consequences for the firm.

**Perceptions of commitment**

Downsizing leads to lower commitment (Armstrong-Stassen, 1994; Luthans and Sommer, 1999; Allen *et al.*, 2001; Armstrong-Stassen, 1994; Chang, 2002; Spreitzer and Mishra, 2002; Brockner *et al.*, 2004; Travaglione and Cross, 2006), greater turnover intention (Armstrong-Stassen, 1994; Allen *et al.*, 2001; Brockner, Wiesenfeld, Stephan, Hurley, Grover, Reed, DeWitt, and Martin, 1997; Travaglione and Cross, 2006), and voluntary turnover (Spreitzer and Mishra, 2002; Trevor and Nyberg, 2008). Coping resources such as optimism, sense of mastery, and perceived social support, and coping strategies related to control, tend to reduce the loss of commitment and turnover intention (Armstrong-Stassen, 1994). Survivors' reactions are also mediated by how much they like fellow survivors (Brockner *et al.*, 1997). This perceived attractiveness also served to increase individual performance among a study of 597 survivors of a downsizing at a US retail store chain. Higher organizational attachment was observed if management was perceived as being more trustworthy (Spreitzer and Mishra, 2002), as was higher perceptions of distributive justice.

Downsizing also results in lower job involvement and reduced organizational commitment among survivors (Allen *et al.*, 2001; Brockner *et al.*, 2004; Luthans and Sommer, 1999; Travaglione and Cross, 2006). Studies by Armstrong-Stassen (1994) and Brockner *et al.* (2004) suggest that downsizing effects are mitigated when accompanied by high supervisor support and greater perceived control. Armstrong-Stassen's (1994) findings also suggest that job commitment following downsizing is a function of the coping strategy adopted by survivors. She suggests that control coping, defined as proactive goal setting accompanied with development of plans, results in greater commitment among survivors; and escape coping, described as denial and distancing behaviors, as having the opposite effect.

Spreitzer and Mishra (2002) and Chang (2002) indicate that the negative effects of downsizing on the attachment and commitment of survivors is mitigated by management trustworthiness and perceptions of distributive justice (fairness of outcomes from downsizing). Spreitzer and Mishra's (2002) study also highlights the role of empowerment in increasing organizational attachment among downsizing survivors. On the other hand, they observed that low procedural justice led to significant reductions in self-esteem, especially among survivors with high organizational commitment.

Downsizing increases the likelihood of voluntary turnover (Allen *et al.*, 2001; Trevor and Nyberg, 2008); however, the effects are less pronounced when employees have greater task self-esteem, are more optimistic, and/or exhibit greater organizational commitment (Armstrong-Stassen, 1994; Mone, 1994; Spreitzer and Mishra, 2002). Turnover intent is lower when employees feel a sense of powerlessness, but it increases when they believe that they have greater control of their destiny or when they perceive greater threat of job loss (Armstrong-Stassen, 1994). Turnover intent was inversely related to control coping strategies, such as active goal setting and development of plans; and positively related to escape coping, such as denial and distancing (Armstrong-Stassen, 1994). Trevor and Nyberg (2008) found that higher levels of downsizing led to greater turnover among employees, and that the relationship was mediated by organizational commitment. Downsizing also results in increased absenteeism among survivors in the post-downsizing period (Travaglione and Cross, 2006).

### *Impact on HR practices*

While the decision to downsize is strategic in nature, involving top management, the process of downsizing becomes an HR practice, since it directly influences the human resources of the organization. Downsizing has a direct impact on firm profitability, productivity, and performance (Baumol *et al.*, 2003; Bruton *et al.*, 1996; Cascio, 1993; Cascio, Young, and Morris, 1997; Caves and Krepps, 1993; Lee, 1997; Guthrie and Datta, 2008; Palmon *et al.*, 1997; Espahbodi *et al.*, 2000; Wayhan and Werner, 2000; Worrell *et al.*, 1991), thus following the universalist approach that there is a direct link between HR practices and firm performance (Delery and Doty, 1996). The impact of downsizing on firm performance is also moderated by the impact of firm attributes, such as R&D intensity, firm capital intensity, and industry growth (Guthrie and Datta, 2008), illustrating the contingency perspective of HR practices on firm performance (Delery and Doty, 1996; Guest, 1997).

Human resource practitioners and scholars find that, during downsizing, top management is generally preoccupied with short-term operational gains, thereby neglecting long-term commitments (Gandolfi, 2006, 2009). Beylerian and Kliener (2003) describe that according to an American Management Association (AMA) report, more than 70 percent of surveyed firms had downsized with no downsizing-related HR plans, policies, or programs in place for survivors to minimize the negative effects of reducing the workforce. A similar trend is observed in British firms as well, with less than 50 percent providing support for the survivors (Doherty and Horsted, 1995). Hitt *et al.* (1994) state that one of the causes for the decline in a firm's performance outcomes during downsizing is due to the neglect of the remaining human capital, thus not managing survivors could lead to the failure of downsizing strategies (Devine, Reay, Stainton, and Collins-Nakai, 2003).

Firms frequently fail to prepare to manage one of the most debilitating effects of downsizing. "Survivor sickness" (Noer, 1993) or "survivor syndrome" (Cascio, 1993), as it has been labeled, is a phenomenon associated with dysfunctional levels of reduced motivation and morale, increased stress, and even burnout among the survivors left in place after a downsizing. Kettley (1995) suggests that firms need to engage in integrating information, communication, and transparency, while providing support for survivors and victims, adjusting performance management systems, and providing training and development to successfully manage a downsizing in order to mitigate the debilitating effects of survivor syndrome (Doherty and Horsted, 1995).

There is often a redistribution of roles and responsibilities after a downsizing takes place (Allen *et al.*, 2001) making it difficult for the remaining staff to effectively manage workload issues without significant commitment from the organization to provide training and development. A sharp increase in workload, longer working hours, and fewer vacation days can exacerbate this effect leading to inefficiencies and burnout (Brockner *et al.*, 1985; Brockner, Grover, Reed, DeWitt, and O'Malley, 1987; Brockner, 1988, 1992; Mone, 1994). Furthermore, a change in the relationship between continuing employees and the organization ensues due to distrust and blame focused toward the organization (Kets De Vries and Balazs, 1997).

The role of HR practices in managing employees' experiences and perceptions through the downsizing finds support in the SHRM model (Wright and McMahan, 1992; McMahan *et al.*, 1999). Some HR practices are techniques used by the organization to help utilize the human resources more fully. For example, they can increase the value and uniqueness of knowledge through internal development. They can also influence positive and productive employee behaviors (Lopez-Cabrales *et al.*, 2006; Lepak, Liao, Chung, and Harden, 2006). There is empirical support for the superiority of high-performance work systems and their relationship to employee and organization-level performance (Arthur, 1992, 1994; Huselid, 1995; Ichniowski, Shaw, and Prennushi, 1997; MacDuffie, 1995; Patterson, West, and Wall, 2004; Way, 2002).

Certain HR practices have been found to have a statistically significant relationship with performance at the organizational level. HR practices at the organization level have a positive impact on manufacturing performance (Arthur, 1994; Huselid, 1995), productivity (Ichniowski *et al.*, 1997; Huselid, 1995; Guthrie, 2001; Wright, Gardner, Moynihan, and Allen, 2005; Birdi, Clegg, Patterson, Robinson, Stride, Wall, and Wood, 2008; Armstrong, Flood, Guthrie, Liue, MacCurtain, and Mkamwa, 2008), firm financial performance (Huselid, 1995; Wright *et al.*, 2005), innovation (Flood, Gannon, and Paauwe, 1995; Armstrong *et al.*, 2008), core task performance (Tsui, Pearce, Porter, and Tripoli, 1997), OCBs (Tsui *et al.*, 1997), retention (Guthrie, 2001), collective affective commitment (Wright *et al.*, 2005), attendance (Tsui *et al.*, 1997), quality (Wright *et al.*, 2005), negative impacts on workers' compensation claims (Wright *et al.*, 2005), shrinkage (Wright *et al.*, 2005), expenses (Wright *et al.*,

2005), and turnover (Arthur, 1994; Huselid, 1995). They have also been found to have positive statistically significant impacts at the individual level, such as intention to stay (Tsui *et al.*, 1997), trust in coworker (Tsui *et al.*, 1997), perception of fairness (Tsui *et al.*, 1997), affective commitment (Tsui *et al.*, 1997; Gong, Law, Chang, and Xin, 2009), and continuance commitment (Gong *et al.*, 2009).

Gandolfi (2001) found that training and development plays a significant role during downsizing in a study of Australian banks. However, most organizations tend to overlook such programs during downsizing for monetary reasons (Cascio, 1993; Beylerian and Kleiner, 2003; Appelbaum, Delage, Labibb, and Gault, 1997). Indeed, most firms target HR departments during cost-cutting times (Clark and Koonce, 1995), while failing to adequately focus on maintaining their surviving workforce (Lee, 1992; Cascio, 1993; Hareli and Tzafrir, 2006; Gandolfi, 2001, 2006, 2009). Survivors more often than not face increasing workloads, taking responsibilities from departing employees (Zemke, 1990; Allen, 1997; Mitchell, 1998; Dolan, Belout, and Balkin 2000; Makawatsakul and Kleiner, 2003; Gandolfi, 2006). Downsizing in other countries, notably Poland, has been found to be less harsh than it is in the United States (Redman and Keithley, 1998). Since downsizing is often undertaken to improve efficiency, it is no surprise that firms that utilize high commitment work practices are more likely to engage in downsizing (Iverson and Zatzick, 2007). However, downsizing in firms which use high commitment work practices are likely to use less harsh downsizing practices, measured by the Iverson and Zatzick (2007) index of harshness.

**Perceptions of HR practices**

HR practices implemented at the organization level have a significant impact on organizational-level outcomes. Wright and Nishii (2011) suggest that the impacts of these practices are felt at the individual level in the form of employees' perceptions. Practices at the firm level are implemented toward employees (Wright and Nishii, 2011) by managers and perceived by employees. Nishii, Lepak, and Schneider (2008) use attribution theory to explain the relationship between HR practices and employee behaviors and ultimately organizational performance. According to Nishii *et al.* (2008) perceptions by employees of practices depend on the attributions employees make about management's purpose in implementing the actual practice. This comes from social attribution theory that people can attach different meanings to social stimuli (Fiske and Taylor, 1991). Based on the way they process these stimuli, their attitudinal and behavioral responses to that information may differ. Thus employees react differently to perceptions of practices.

Walton (1985) argues that proactive HR practices will elicit employee satisfaction, which in turn will yield better organizational performance. Employee satisfaction with HRM is thus the result of employees' experiences with HRM. In other words, it is employees' perceptions of the HR practices that have been implemented and how these practices affect them that will influence organizational performance. Keenoy (1999) supports this assertion by arguing that truth (about HRM) lies outside HR departments and suggests responses from several employees must be sought to capture reality.

Since reactions to attributions depend on whether the focus of these attributions is internal or external, Nishii *et al.* (2008) build on Koys' (1988, 1991) research, addressing these two distinctions. HR practices implemented "out of a spirit of justice" or "to attract and retain employees" at their companies represent internal attributions. Those implemented to "encourage individual or organizational performance" or "to comply with government relations" are examples of external causal explanations. Internal causal attributions are related to commitment, while external are not. This assertion has a direct bearing on downsizing. If employees perceive it to be purely concerned with increased efficiency and performance, without any internal attributions impacting justice or retention, they will react differently than they would to more strategically managed downsizings. Thus the management of downsizing through integrating information, communication, and transparency (Kettley, 1995) at the organization level leads to better perceptions at the employee level and will moderate the relationships between changes in human capital and behaviors or changes in human capital and performance. Downsizings which are not accompanied by an investment in HR practices will lead to detrimental employee perceptions and will therefore have an adverse impact on the human capital outcome relationships. It has been observed that HR practices viewed as procedurally just, and job embeddedness, reduce the extent to which downsizing leads to turnover. Firms, without HR practices addressing denial and distancing, experience higher downsizing turnover (Trevor and Nyberg, 2008).

## Conclusion and future research

In this chapter, we have examined the impacts of downsizing through a strategic HRM model. Through this multi-level, multi-theory, multi-disciplinary process, we have attempted to present a full range of issues related to downsizing strategy. Downsizing originates at the organizational level, but it impacts the organization in a complex fashion, and therefore has consequences on human capital, HR practices, and employee behaviors, which aggregate into a myriad organizational/unit level disparate performance outcomes.

The strategic management of downsizing practices involve frank, frequent, and consistent communication; information about the process and progress of downsizing; the articulation of a clear vision; employee participation; and training (Appelbaum, Close, and Klasa, 1999). Since the greatest negative impact from a downsizing strategy is the simple reduction in the workforce (McElroy, Morrow, and Rude, 2001), it logically follows that unless it is accompanied by sustained improvement in communications, human resource practices, organizational design, and managerial practices in general, it will most likely yield only negative results. An organization already has a sizeable investment in employees accruing through its recruiting, selection, and training processes. Employees are generally viewed in terms of an investment to be nurtured, instead of a cost to be minimized (De Meuse, Vanderheiden, and Bergmann, 1994). Should the need arise to reduce labor costs, organizations considering significant workforce reductions might benefit more by identifying innovative ways to cut costs through attrition, general or targeted reductions of salaries, offering unpaid vacations, scheduling shortened workweeks, and supporting job sharing (De Meuse *et al.*, 1994). These actions could provide for the desired reduction in financial expenditures and increased efficiency for both the short and long term by insuring that remaining employees' attitudes toward their work, their managers, and the organization overall remain positive and they are willing to fully contribute their human capital through in-role and beyond-role behaviors directed toward the goals of the organization.

Downsizing research has very real implications for practitioners and theorists alike, as it appears to be a strategy that will remain an option. As Datta *et al.* (2010) state in their review, downsizing research needs to focus on a number of issues in order for its outcomes to be fully understood. While we are able to theorize how downsizing may play out in an organization, we have little empirical research on the entire process. Additionally, research has seemingly failed to address the ethical issues surrounding the strategy and ultimate implementation of the practice of downsizing. Finally, a greater understanding of the public policy concerns of downsizing should be included in our understanding of the societal impact of this strategy.

To better understand this phenomenon, researchers should consider the multi-level, multi-theory, and multi-disciplinary nature of this area of inquiry. Thus, the need to understand the human capital issues in an organization is a necessity. The removal of an employee, manager, or an executive extracts and disposes the knowledge, skills, and abilities that comprised the human capital of that organization member. The assessment of that reduction of human capital must be understood. The process of downsizing is much more than a reduction of force in order for executives to earn year-end bonuses or a quick way to cut costs so the unit or firm can meet its short-term goals. In some cases, these reasons go hand in hand.

*Notes*

1. (Huselid, 1995; Lado and Wilson, 1994; McMahan *et al.*, 1999; Wright, Dunford, and Snell, 2001; Wright and McMahan, 1992; Wright, McMahan, and McWilliams, 1994) and empirical research (Arthur, 1992; Combs, Liu, Hall, and Ketchen, 2006; Delery and Doty, 1996; Harris and McMahan, 2008; Huselid, 1995; MacDuffie, 1995; Wright, Smart, and McMahan, 1995).

## References

Ahmadjian, C. and Robbins, G. 2005. "A clash of capitalisms: Foreign shareholders and corporate restructuring in 1990s Japan." *American Sociological Review* 7(3): 451–471.

Allen, R. K. 1997. "Lean and mean: Workforce 2000 in America." *Journal of Workplace Learning* 9(1). Downloaded from www.emerald-library.com/brev/08609ae1.html

Allen, T. D., Freeman, D. M., Russell, J. E. A., Reizenstein, R. C., and Rentz, J. O. 2001. "Survivor reactions to organizational downsizing: Does time ease the pain?" *Journal of Occupational and Organizational Psychology* **74**: 145–164.

Amabile, T. M. and Conti, R. 1999. "Changes in the work environment for creativity during downsizing." *Academy of Management Journal* **42**(6): 630–640.

Appelbaum, S. H., Close, T., and Klasa, S. 1999. "Downsizing: An examination of some successes and more failures." *Managerial Decision* **37**(5): 424–436.

Appelbaum, S. H., Delage, C., Labibb, N., and Gault, G. 1997. "The survivor syndrome: Aftermath of downsizing." *Career Development International* **2**(6). Downloaded from www.emerald-library.com/brev/13702fd1.html

Armstrong, C., Flood, P. C., Guthrie, J. P., Liu, W., MacCurtain, S., and Mkamwa, T. 2008. "Should high performance work systems include diversity management practices?" Paper presented at the Academy of Management Proceedings, Anaheim, CA.

Armstrong-Stassen, M. 1994. "Coping with transition – a study of layoff survivors." *Journal of Organizational Behavior* **15**(7): 597–621.

Armstrong-Stassen, M., Wagar, T. H., and Cattaneo, R. J. 2004. "Work-group membership (in)stability and survivors' reactions to organizational downsizing." *Journal of Applied Social Psychology* **34**(10): 2023–2044.

Arthur, J. B. 1992. "The link between business strategy and industrial relations systems in American steel minimills." *Industrial and Labor Relations Review* **45**(3): 488–506.

Arthur, J. B. 1994. "Effects of human resource systems on manufacturing performance and turnover." *Academy of Management Journal* **37**(3): 670–687.

Aselage, J. and Eisenberger, R. 2003. "Perceived organizational support and psychological contracts: A theoretical integration." *Journal of Organizational Behavior* **24**(5): 491–509.

Bamberger, P. and Meshoulam, I. 2000. *Human Resource Management Strategy*. Thousand Oaks, CA: Sage.

Barney, J. B. 1991. "Firm resources and sustained competitive advantage." *Journal of Management* **17**(1): 99.

Bateman, T. S. and Organ, D. W. 1983. "Job satisfaction and the good soldier: The relationship between affect and employee 'citizenship'." *Academy of Management Journal* **26**: 587–595.

Baumol, W. J., Blinder, A., and Wolff, E. N. 2003. *Downsizing in America: Reality, Causes, and Consequences*. New York: Russell Sage Foundation.

Becker, G. S. 1962. "Investment in human capital: A theoretical analysis." *The Journal of Political Economy* **70**(S5): 9.

Becker, G. S. 1964. *Human Capital: A Theoretical and Empirical Analysis, with Special Reference to Education*, Vol. LXXX. New York: National Bureau of Economic Research; distributed by Columbia University Press.

Becker, G. S. 1992. "The economic way of looking at life." Gary S. Becker Nobel Prize Lecture. Downloaded from http://www.nobelprize.org/nobel_prizes/economics/laureates/1992/be ker-lecture.html

Beylerian, M. and Kleiner, B.H. 2003. "The downsized workplace." *Management Research News* **26**(2/3/4): 97–108.

Birdi, K., Clegg, C., Patterson, M., Robinson, A., Stride, C.B., Wall, T.D., and Wood, S.J. 2008. "The impact of human resource and operational management practices on company productivity: A longitudinal study." *Personnel Psychology* **61**(3): 467–501.

Blau, P.M. 1964. *Exchange and Power in Social Life*. New York: Wiley.

Borman, W.C. and Motowidlo, S.J. 1993. "Expanding the criterion domain to include elements of contextual performance," in N.S. a.W. Bormaneds (ed.), *Personnel Selection in Organizations*. New York: Jossey-Bass, pp. 71–98.

Boxall, P. 1998. "Achieving competitive advantage through human resource strategy: Towards a theory of industry dynamics." *Human Resource Management Review* **8**(3): 265–288.

Brandes, P., Castro, S.L., James, M.S.L., Martinez, A.D., Matherly, T.A., and Ferris, G.R. 2008. "The interactive effects of job insecurity and organizational cynicism on work effort following a layoff." *Journal of Leadership and Organizational Studies* **14**: 233–247.

Brief, A.P. and Motowidlo, S.J. 1986. "Prosocial organizational behaviors." *Academy of Management Review* **11**: 710–725.

Brockner, J. 1988. *Self-Esteem at Work: Research, Theory, and Practice*. Lexington, MA: Lexington Books.

Brockner, J. 1992. "The escalation of commitment to a failing course of action: Toward theoretical progress." *Academy of Management Review* **17**(1): 39–61.

Brockner, J., Davy, J., and Carter, C. 1985. "Layoffs, self-esteem, and survivor guilt: Motivational, affective, and attitudinal consequences." *Organizational Behavior and Human Decision Processes* **36**: 229–244.

Brockner, J., Grover, S.L., and Blonder, M.D. 1988. "Predictors of survivors' job involvement following layoffs: A field study." *Journal of Applied Psychology* **73**: 436–442.

Brockner, J., Grover, S., O'Malley, M.N., Reed, T., and Glynn, M.A. 1993. "Threat of future layoffs, self-esteem, and survivors' reactions: Evidence from the laboratory and the field." *Strategic Management Journal* **14**: 153–166.

Brockner, J., Grover, S., Reed, T.F., and Dewitt, R.L. 1992. "Layoffs, job insecurity, and survivors work effort – evidence of an inverted-u relationship." *Academy of Management Journal* **35**(2): 413–425.

Brockner, J., Grover, S., Reed, T., DeWitt, R., and O'Malley, M. 1987. "Survivors' reactions to layoffs: We get by with a little help from our friends." *Administrative Science Quarterly* **32**: 526–541.

Brockner, J., Konovsky, M., Cooper-Schnieder, R., Folger, R., Martin, R., and Bies, R. J. 1994. "Interactive effects of procedural justice and outcome negativity on victims and survivors of job loss." *Academy of Management Journal* 37(2): 397–409.

Brockner, J., Sprietzer, G., Mishra, A., Hockwarter, W., Pepper, L., and Weinberg, J. 2004. "Perceived control as an antidote to the negative effects of layoffs on survivors' organizational commitment and job performance." *Administrative Science Quarterly* **49**: 76–100.

Brockner, J., Wiesenfeld, B. M., Stephan, J., Hurley, R., Grover, S., Reed, T., DeWitt, R. L., and Martin, C. 1997. "The effects on layoff survivors of their fellow survivors' reactions." *Journal of Applied Social Psychology* **27**: 835–863.

Bruns, V., Holland, D. V., Shepherd, D. A., and Wiklund, J. 2008. "The role of human capital in loan officers' decision policies." *Entrepreneurship: Theory and Practice* **323**: 485–506.

Bruton, G. D., Keels, J. K., and Shook, C. L. 1996. "Downsizing the firm: Answering the strategic questions." *Academy of Management Executive* **10**: 38–43.

Budros, A. 1999. "A conceptual framework for analyzing why organizations downsize." *Organization Science* **10**: 69–84.

Cameron, K. S., Freeman, S. J., and Mishra, A. K. 1991. "Best practices in white-collar downsizing: Managing contradictions." *Academy of Management Executive* **5**: 57–73.

Cameron, K. S., Freeman, S. J., and Mishra, A. K. (eds.). 1993. *Downsizing and Redesigning Organizations*. New York: Oxford University Press.

Campbell, J. P. (ed.). 1990. *Modeling the Performance Prediction Problem in Industrial and Organizational Psychology*. Palo Alto, CA: Consulting Psychologists Press, Inc.

Campbell, J. P., McCloy, R. A., Oppler, S. H., and Sager, C. E. (eds.). 1993. *A Theory of Performance*. New York: Jossey-Bass.

Carmeli, A. and Schaubroeck, J. 2005. "How leveraging human resource capital with its competitive distinctiveness enhances the performance of commercial and public organizations." *Human Resource Management* **44**(4): 391–412.

Carmeli, A. and Tishler, A. 2004a. "The relationships between intangible organizational elements and organizational performance." *Strategic Management Journal* **25**: 1257–1278.

Carmeli, A. and Tishler, A. 2004b. "Resources, capabilities, and the performance of industrial firms: A multivariate analysis." *Managerial and Decision Economics* **25**: 299–315.

Cascio, W. F. 1993. "Downsizing: What do we know? What have we learned?" *Academy of Management Executive* **7**: 95–104.
Cascio, W. F. 2010. *Employment Downsizing and Its Alternatives: Strategies for Long-Term Success*. Alexandria, VA: Society for Human Resource Management Foundation.
Cascio, W. F., Young, C. E., and Morris, J. R. 1997. "Financial consequences of employment-change decisions in major US corporations." *Academy of Management Journal* **40**: 1175–1189.
Caves, R. and Krepps, M. 1993. "Fat: The displacement of nonproduction workers from US manufacturing industries." *Brookings Papers on Economic Activity: Microeconomics* **2**: 227–288.
Chang, E. 2002. "Distributive justice and organizational commitment revisited: Moderation by layoff in the case of Korean employees." *Human Resource Management* **41**: 261–270.
Clark, J. and Koonce, R. 1995. "Engaging organisational survivors." *Training and Development*, **29**(8): 22–30.
Cohen-Charash, Y. and Spector, P. E. 2001. "The role of justice in organizations: A meta-analysis." *Organizational Behavior and Human Decision Processes* **86**: 278–321.
Colquitt, J. A., Conlon, D. E., Wesson, M. J., Porter, C. O., and Ng, K. Y. 2001. "Justice at the millennium: A meta-analytic review of 25 years of organizational justice research." *Journal of Applied Psychology* **86**: 425–445.
Combs, J., Liu, Y., Hall, A. T., and Ketchen, D. J. 2006. "How much do high performance work practices matter? A meta-analysis of their effects on organizational performance." *Personnel Psychology* **59**: 501–528.
Cropanzano, R., Byrne, Z. S., Bobocel, D. R., and Rupp, D. R. 2001. "Moral virtues, fairness heuristics, social entities, and other denizens of organizational justice." *Journal of Vocational Behavior* **58**: 164–209.
Datta, D. K., Guthrie, J. P., Basuil, D., and Pandey, A. 2010. "Causes and effects of employee downsizing: A review and synthesis." *Journal of Management* **36**(1): 281–348.
De Meuse, K. P., Bergmann, T. J., Vanderheiden, P. A., and Roraff, C. E. 2004. "New evidence regarding organizational downsizing and a firm's financial performance: A long-term analysis." *Journal of Managerial Issues* **16**: 155–177.
De Meuse, K. P., Vanderheiden, P. A., and Bergmann, T. J. 1994. "Announced layoffs: Their effect on corporate financial performance." *Human Resource Management* **33**: 509–530.
Delery, J. E. and Doty, D. H. 1996. "Modes of theorizing in strategic human resource management: Tests of universalistic, contingency, and

configurations – performance predictions." *Academy of Management Journal* **39**(4): 802–835.

Delery, J.E. and Shaw, J.D. (eds.). 2001. *The Strategic Management of People in Work Organizations: Review, Synthesis and Extension*. Greenwich, CT: JAI Press.

Devine, K., Reay, T., Stainton, L., and Collins-Nakai, R. 2003. "Downsizing outcomes: Better a victim than a survivor." *Human Resource Management* **42**(2): 109–124.

DeWitt, R.L. 1998. "Firm, industry and strategy influences on choice of downsizing approach." *Strategic Management Journal* **19**(1): 59–79.

DiMaggio, P. and Powell, W. 1983. "The iron cage revisited: Institutional isomorphism and collective rationality in organizational fields." *American Sociological Review* **48**: 147–160.

Doherty, N. and Horsted, J. 1995. *Helping Survivors to Stay on Board*. People Management Personnel Publications Limited.

Dolan, S., Belout, A., and Balkin, D.B. 2000. "Downsizing without downgrading: Learning how firms manage their survivors." *International Journal of Manpower* **21**(1): 34–46.

Dougherty, D. and Bowman, E.H. 1995. "The effects of organizational downsizing on product innovation." *California Management Review* **17**(4): 28–44.

Espahbodi, R., John, T.A., and Vasudevan, G. 2000. "The effects of downsizing on operating performance." *Review of Quantitative Finance and Accounting* **15**: 107–126.

Fiske, S.T. and Taylor, S.E. 1991. *Social Cognition* (2nd edn.). New York: McGraw Hill.

Flanagan, D.J. and O'Shaughnessy, K.C. 2005. "The effects of layoffs on firm reputation." *Journal of Management* **31**: 445–463.

Flood, P.C., Gannon, M.J., and Paauwe, J. 1995. "Competitive advantage through strategic innovations in human resource management," in P.C. Flood, M.J. Gannon, and J. Paauwe (eds.), *Managing without Traditional Methods: International Innovations in Human Resource Management*. Wokingham: Addison-Wesley, pp. 307–326.

Freeman, S.J. 1994. "Organizational downsizing as convergence or reorientation: Implications for human resource management." *Human Resource Management* **33**: 213–238.

Freeman, S.J. and Cameron, K.S. 1993. "Organizational downsizing: A convergence and reorientation framework." *Organization Science* **4**: 10–29.

Gandolfi, F. 2001. "How and why should training and development be implemented during the process of organizational downsizing?" Doctor of Business Administration (DBA), Southern Cross University, Australia.

Gandolfi, F. 2006. *Corporate Downsizing Demystified: A Scholarly Analysis of a Business Phenomenon.* Hyderabad, India: The ICFAI University Press.

Gandolfi, F. 2009. "Training and development in an era of downsizing." *The Journal of Management Research* **9**(1): 3–14.

Gilson, C., Hurd, F., and Wagar, T. 2004. "Creating a concession climate: The case of serial downsizers." *International Journal of Human Resource Management* **15**: 1056–1068.

Gimeno, J., Folta., T. B., Cooper, A. C., and Woo, C. Y. 1997. "Survival of the fittest? Entrepreneurial human capital and the persistence of underperforming firms." *Administrative Science Quarterly* **424**: 750–783.

Gong, Y., Law, K. S., Chang, S., and Xin, K. R. 2009. "Human resources management and firm performance: The differential role of managerial affective and continuance commitment." *Journal of Applied Psychology* **94**(1): 263–275.

Greenberg, J. 1990. "Organizational justice: Yesterday, today, and tomorrow." *Journal of Management* **16**: 399–432.

Guest, D. E. 1997. "Human resource management and performance: A review and research agenda." *International Journal of Human Resource Management* **8**(3): 263–276.

Guthrie, J. P. 2001. "High-involvement work practices, turnover, and productivity: Evidence from New Zealand." *Academy of Management Journal* **44**(1): 180–190.

Guthrie, J. P. and Datta, D. K. 2008. "Dumb and dumber: The impact of downsizing on firm performance as moderated by industry conditions." *Organization Science* **19**(1): 108–123.

Hareli, S. and Tzafrir, S. 2006. "The role of causal attributions in survivors: Emotional reactions to downsizing." *Human Resource Development Review* **5**(4): 400–421.

Harrigan, K. R. 1980. "Strategy formulation in declining industries." *Academy of Management Review* **5**: 599–605.

Harris, C. M. and McMahan, G. C. 2008. "An empirical investigation of human capital and performance: NCAA men's basketball teams." Paper presented at the Annual Meeting of the Academy of Management, Anaheim, CA.

Harris, C. M., McMahan, G. C., and Wright, P. M. 2009. "Strategic human resource management 2.0: Relationships among human capital, social capital, behaviors, and performance." Paper presented at the Academy of Management Conference, Chicago, IL.

Hilltrop, J. M. 1995. "The changing psychological contract: The human resource challenge of the 1990s." *European Management Journal* **13** (3): 286–294.

Hitt, M. A., Bierman, L., Shimizu, K., and Kochhar, R. 2001. "Direct and indirect effects of human capital on strategy and performance in professional service firms: A resource-based perspective." *Academy of Management Journal* **44**: 13–28.

Hitt, M. A. Bierman, L., Uhlenbruck, K., and Shimizu, K. 2006. "The importance of resources in the internationalization of professional service firms: The good, the bad, and the ugly." *Academy of Management Journal* **49**(6): 1137–1157.

Hitt, M. A., Hoskisson, R. E., Harrison, J. S., and Summers, T. P. 1994. "Human capital and strategic competitiveness in the 1990s." *Journal of Management Development* **13**: 35–64.

Hitt, M. A. and Keats, B. W. 1992. *Strategic Leadership and Restructuring: A Reciprocal Interdependence*. Westport, CT: Quorum Books.

Hsu, C., Lin, C. Y. Y., Lawler, J., and Wu, S. H. 2007. "Toward a model of organizational human capital development: Preliminary evidence from Taiwan." *Asia Pacific Business Review* **132**: 251–275.

Huber, G. P. and Glick, W. H. 1993. *Organizational Change and Redesign*. New York: Oxford University Press.

Huselid, M. A. 1995. "The impact of human resource management practices on turnover, productivity, and corporate financial performance." *Academy of Management Journal* **38**(3): 635–672.

Ichniowski, C., Shaw, K., and Prennushi, G. 1997. "The effects of human resource practices on manufacturing performance: A study of steel finishing lines." *American Economic Review* **87**(3): 291–313.

Ilies, R., Nahrgang, J. D., and Morgeson, F. P. 2007. "Leader–member exchange and citizenship behaviors: A meta-analysis." *Journal of Applied Psychology* **92**: 269–277.

Iverson, R. D. and Zatzick, C. D. 2007. "High commitment work practices and downsizing harshness in Australian workplaces." *Industrial Relations* **46**: 456–480.

Jackson, S. E. and Schuler, R. S. 1995. "Understanding human resource management in the context of organizations and their environments." *Annual Review of Psychology* **461**: 237.

Katz, D. 1964. "The motivational basis of organizational behavior." *Behavioral Science* **9**: 131–146.

Keenoy, T. 1999. "HRM as hologram: A polemic." *Journal of Management Studies* **36**: 1–23.

Kets de Vries, M. and Balazs, K. 1997. "The downside of downsizing." *Human Relations* **50**(1): 11–50.

Kettley, P. 1995. *Employee Morale during Downsizing*. Institute of Employment Studies.

Konovsky, M. A. 2000. "Understanding procedural justice and its impact on business organizations." *Journal of Management* **26**: 489–513.

Koys, D. J. 1988. "Human resource management and a culture of respect: Effects of employees' organizational commitment." *Employee Rights and Responsibilities Journal* **1**: 57–68.

Koys, D. J. 1991. "Fairness, legal compliance, and organizational commitment." *Employee Rights and Responsibilities Journal* **4**(4): 283–291.

Lado, A. A. and Wilson, M. C. 1994. "Human resource systems and sustained competitive advantage: A competency-based perspective." *Academy of Management Review* **19**: 699–727.

Lavelle, J. J., Brockner, J., Konovsky, M. A., Price, K., Henley, A., Taneja, A., and Vinekar, V. 2009. "Commitment, procedural fairness, and organizational citizenship behavior: A multifoci analysis." *Journal of Organizational Behavior* **30**: 337–357.

Lavelle, J. J., McMahan, G. C., and Harris, C. M. 2009. "Fairness in human resource management, social exchange relationships, and citizenship behavior: Testing linkages of the target similarity model among nurses in the United States." *International Journal of Human Resource Management* **20**(12): 2419–2434.

Lavelle, J. J., Rupp, D. E., and Brockner, J. 2007. "Taking a multifoci approach to the study of justice, social exchange, and organizational citizenship behavior: The target similarity model." *Journal of Management* **3**: 841–866.

Lee, C. 1992. "After the cuts." *Training*, July 1992, 17–23.

Lee, K. and Allen, N. J. 2002. "Organizational citizenship behavior and workplace deviance: The role of affect and cognitions." *Journal of Applied Psychology* **87**(1): 131–142.

Lee, P. M. 1997. "A comparative analysis of layoff announcements and stock price reactions in the United States and Japan." *Strategic Management Journal* **18**: 879–894.

Lepak, D., Liao, H., Chung, Y., and Harden, E. 2006. "A conceptual review of human resource management systems in strategic human resource management research." *Research in Personnel and Human Resources Management* **25**: 217–271.

LePine, J. A., Erez, A., and Johnson, D. E. 2002. "The nature and dimensionality of organizational citizenship behavior: A critical review and meta-analysis." *Journal of Applied Psychology* **87**(1): 52–65.

Leventhal, G. S. 1980. *What Should Be Done with Equity Theory? New Approaches to the Study of Fairness in Social Relationships*. New York: Plenum.

Lopez-Cabrales, A., Valle, R., and Herreo, I. 2006. "The contribution of core employees to organizational capabilities and efficiencies." *Human Resource Management* **451**: 81–109.

Love, E. and Kraatz, M. 2009. "Character, conformity, or the bottom line: How and why downsizing affected corporate reputation." *Academy of Management Journal* **52**: 314–335.

Luthans, B. C. and Sommer, S. M. 1999. "The impact of downsizing on workplace attitudes: Differing reactions of managers and staff in a health care organization." *Group Organization Management* **24**: 46–70.

Macduffie, J. P. 1995. "Human resource bundles and manufacturing performance: Organizational logic and flexible production systems in the world auto industry." *Industrial and Labor Relations Review* **48**(2): 197–221.

Makawatsakul, N. and Kleiner, B. H. 2003. "The effect of downsizing on morale and attrition." *Management Research News* **26**: 52–62.

Malatesta, R. M. and Byrne, Z. S. 1997. "The impact of formal and interactional procedures on organizational outcomes." Paper presented at the 12th annual conference of the Society for Industrial and Organizational Psychology, St Louis, MO.

Mansour-Cole, D. M. and Scott, S. G. 1998. "Hearing it through the grapevine: The influence of source, leader relations, and legitimacy on survivors' fairness perceptions." *Personnel Psychology* **51**: 25–54.

McElroy, J. C., Morrow, P. C., and Rude, S. N. 2001. "Turnover and organizational performance: A comparative analysis of the effects of voluntary, involuntary, and reduction-in-force turnover." *Journal of Applied Psychology* **86**: 1294–1299.

McKinley, W., Zhao, J., and Rust, K. G. 2000. "A socio-cognitive interpretation of organizational downsizing." *Academy of Management Review* **25**: 227–243.

McMahan, G., Virick, M., and Wright, P. 1999. "Alternative theoretical perspectives for SHRM: Progress, problems, and prospects," in P. Wright, L. Dyer,J. Boudreau, and G. Milkovich (eds.), *Research in Personnel and Human Resource Management* 4(Supplement): 99–122. Greenwich, CT: JAI Press.

McNeely, B. L. and Meglino, B. M. 1994. "The role of dispositional and situational antecedents in prosocial organizational behavior: An examination of the intended beneficiaries of prosocial organizational behavior." *Journal of Applied Psychology* **76**: 845–855.

Meyer, J. P. (ed.). 1997. *Organizational Commitment*, Vol. XII. New York: Wiley.

Mishra, A. K. and Mishra, K. E. 1994. "The role of mutual trust in effective downsizing strategies." *Human Resource Management* **33**(2): 261–279.

Mitchell, G. 1998. *The Trainer's Handbook: The AMA Guide to Effective Training* (3rd edn.). New York: AMACOM American Management Association.

Mone, M. A. 1994. "Relationships between self-concepts, aspirations, emotional responses, and intent to leave a downsizing organization." *Human Resource Management* **33**(2): 281–298.

Moorman, C., Deshpandé, R., and Zaltman, G. 1993. "Factors affecting trust in market research relationships." *Journal of Marketing* **57**(1): 81–101.

Morrison, E. W. and Robinson, S. L. 1997. "When employees feel betrayed: A model of how psychological contract violation develops." *Academy of Management Review* **22**(1): 226–257.

Niehoff, B. P., Moorman, R. H., Blakely, G. L., and Fuller, J. 2001. "The influence of empowerment and job enrichment on employee loyalty in a downsizing environment." *Group and Organization Management* **26**: 93–113.

Nishii, L. H., Lepak, D. P., and Schneider, B. 2008. "Employee attributions of the "why" of HR practices: Their effects on employee attitudes and behaviors, and customer satisfaction." *Personnel Psychology* **61**: 509–545.

Noer, D. 1993. *Overcoming the Trauma of Layoffs and Revitalising Downsized Organizations*. San Francisco, CA: Jossey-Bass.

Offstein, E. H., Gnyawali, D. R., and Cobb, A. T. 2005. "A strategic human resource perspective of firm competitive behavior." *Human Resource Management Review* **15**: 305–318.

Organ, D. W. 1988. *Organizational Citizenship Behavior: The Good Soldier Syndrome*. Lexington, MA: Lexington Books.

Palmon, O., Sun, H., and Tang, A. 1997. "Layoff announcements: Stock market impact and financial performance." *Financial Management* **26**: 54–68.

Pandey, A., Harris, C. M., McMahan, G. C., and Wright, P. M. 2010. "Transforming talent into triumph: The mediating role of HR behaviors in the human capital – performance relationship." Paper presented at the Southern Management Association Conference, St. Pete Beach, FL.

Patterson, M. G., West, M. A., and Wall, T. D. 2004. "Integrated manufacturing, empowerment and company performance." *Journal of Organizational Behavior* **25**: 1–25.

Penrose, E. 1959. *The Theory of the Growth of the Firm*. New York: Oxford University Press.

Ployhart, R. E., Weekley, J. A., and Baughman, K. 2006. "The structure and function of human capital emergence: A multi-level examination of the attraction-selection-attrition model." *Academy of Management Journal* **49**(4): 661–677.

Ployhart, R. E., Weekley, J. A., and Ramsey, J. 2009. "The consequences of human resource stocks and flows: A longitudinal examination of unit service orientation and unit effectiveness." *Academy of Management Journal* **52**: 966–1015.

Podsakoff, P. M., MacKenzie, S. B., Paine, J. B., and Bachrach, D. G. 2000. "Organizational citizenship behaviors: A critical review of the theoretical and empirical literature and suggestions for future research." *Journal of Management* **26**: 513–564.

Redding, S. 1996. "The low-skill, low-quality trap: Strategic complementarities between human capital and R&D." *Economic Journal* **106**: 458–470.

Redman, T. and Keithley, D. 1998. "Downsizing goes east? Employment restructuring in post-socialist Poland." *International Journal of Human Resource Management* **9**: 274–295.

Reed, K. K., Lubatkin, M., and Srinivasan, N. 2006. "Proposing and testing an intellectual capital-based view of the firm." *Journal of Management Studies* **43**(4): 867–893.

Rhoades, L., Eisenberger, R., and Armeli, S. 2001. "Affective commitment to the organization: The contribution of perceived organizational support." *Journal of Applied Psychology* **86**: 825–836.

Robinson, S. L. 1996. "Trust and breach of the psychological contract." *Administrative Science Quarterly* **41**: 579–599.

Robinson, S. L. and Morrison, E. W. 1995. "Psychological contracts and OCB: The effect of unfulfilled obligations on civic virtue behavior." *Journal of Organizational Behavior* **16**: 289–298.

Rousseau, D. M. 1995. *Psychological Contracts in Organizations*. Thousand Oaks, CA: Sage.

Rousseau, D. M. 2001. "Schema, promise, and mutuality: The building blocks of the psychological contract." *Journal of Occupational and Organizational Psychology* **74**: 511–541

Rupp, D. E. and Cropanzano, R. 2002. "The mediating effects of social exchange relationships in predicting workplace outcomes from multifoci organizational justice." *Organizational Behavior and Human Decision Processes* **89**: 925–946.

Sahdev, K. 2004. "Revisiting the survivor syndrome: The role of leadership in implementing downsizing." *European Journal of Work and Organizational Psychology* **13**(2): 165–196.

Shah, P. P. 2000. "Network destruction: The structural implications of downsizing." *Academy of Management Journal* **43**(1): 101–112.

Sitkin, S. B. and Roth, N. L. 1993. "Explaining the limited effectiveness of legalistic 'remedies' for trust/distrust." *Organization Science* **4**: 367–392.

Skaggs, B. C. and Youndt, M. A. 2004. "Strategic positioning, human capital, and performance in service organizations: A customer interaction approach." *Strategic Management Journal* **25**: 85–99.

Smith, A., Organ, D. W., and Near, J. 1983. "Organizational citizenship behavior: Its nature and antecedents." *Journal of Applied Psychology* **68**(4): 653–663.

Snell, S. A., Youndt, M. A., and Wright, P. M. 1996. "Establishing a framework for research in strategic human resource management: Merging resource theory and organizational learning," in G. R. Ferris (ed.), *Research in Personnel and Human Resources Management* 14: 61–90.
Sonnentag, S., Volmer, J., and Spychala, A. (eds.). 2008. *Job Performance*. Sage.
Spreitzer, G. M. and Mishra, A. K. 2002. "To stay or to go: Voluntary survivor turnover following an organizational downsizing." *Journal of Organizational Behavior* **23**: 707–729.
Sturman, M. C., Walsh, K., and Cheramie, R. A. 2008. "The value of human capital specificity versus transferability." *Journal of Management* **34**: 290.
Suarez-Gonzalez, I. 2001. "Downsizing strategy: Does it really improve organizational performance?" *International Journal of Management* **18**(3): 301–307.
Takeuchi, R., Lepak, D. P., Wang, H., and Takeuchi, K. 2007. "An empirical examination of the mechanisms mediating between high-performance work systems and the performance of Japanese organizations." *Journal of Applied Psychology* **92**(4): 1069–1082.
Thibault, J. W. and Walker, L. 1975. *Procedural Justice: A Psychological Analysis*. Hillsdale, NJ: L. Erlbaum Associates.
Travaglione, A. and Cross, B. 2006. "Diminishing the social network in organizations: Does there need to be such a phenomenon as 'survivor syndrome' after downsizing?" *Strategic Change* **15**: 1–13.
Trevor, C. O. and Nyberg, A. J. 2008. "Keeping your headcount when all about you are losing theirs: Downsizing, voluntary turnover rates, and the moderating role of HR practices." *Academy of Management Journal* **51**(2): 259–276.
Tsui, A. S., Pearce, J. L., Porter, L. W., and Tripoli, A. M. 1997. "Alternative approaches to the employee–organization relationship: Does investment in employees pay off?" *Academy of Management Journal* **40**(5): 1089–1121.
Turnley, W. H., Bolino, M., Lester, S. W., and Bloodgood, J. M. 2004. "The effects of psychological contract breach on union commitment." *Journal of Occupational and Organizational Psychology* 77(4): 421–428
Ulrich, D. (ed.). 1991. *Using Human Resources for Competitive Advantage*. San Francisco, CA: Jossey-Bass.
Van Dyne, L., Graham, J. W., and Dienesch, R. M. 1994. "Organizational citizenship behavior: Construct redefinition, operationalization, and validation." *Academy of Management Journal* **37**: 765–802.
Wagar, T. H. 1998. "Exploring the consequences of workforce reduction." *Canadian Journal of Administrative Sciences* **15**(4): 300–309.
Walton, R. A. 1985. "From control to commitment in the workplace." *Harvard Business Review* **63**(2): 77–84.

Way, S. A. 2002. “High performance work systems and intermediate indicators of firm performance within the US small business sector.” *Journal of Management* **28**(6): 765–785.

Wayhan, V. B. and Werner, S. 2000. “The impact of workforce reductions on financial performance: A longitudinal perspective.” *Journal of Management* **26**: 341–363.

Wiesenfeld, B. M., Swann Jr., W. B., Brockner, J., and Bartel, C. A. 2007. “Is more fairness always preferred? Self-esteem moderates reactions to procedural justice.” *Academy of Management Journal* **50**(5): 1235–1253.

Williams, L. J. and Anderson, S. E. 1991. “Job satisfaction and organizational commitment as predictors of organizational citizenship and in-role behaviors.” *Journal of Management* **17**: 601–617.

Worrell, D. L., Davidson III, W. N., and Sharma, V. M. 1991. “Layoff announcements and stockholder wealth.” *Academy of Management Journal* **43**: 662–678.

Wright, P. and McMahan, G. 2011. “Exploring human capital: Putting human back into strategic human resource management.” *Human Resource Management Journal* **21**(2): 93–104.

Wright, P. and Nishii, L. H. 2011. *Strategic HRM and Organizational Behavior: Integrating Multiple Levels of Analysis*. Oxford: Blackwell Publishing.

Wright, P. M., Dunford, B. B., and Snell, S. A. 2001. “Human resources and the resource based view of the firm.” *Journal of Management* **27**: 701–721.

Wright, P. M., Gardner, T. M., Moynihan, L. M., and Allen, M. R. 2005. “The relationship between HR practices and firm performance: Examining causal order.” *Personnel Psychology* **58**(2): 409–447.

Wright, P. M. and McMahan, G. C. 1992. “Theoretical perspectives for strategic human resource management.” *Journal of Management* **18**(2): 295.

Wright, P. M., McMahan, G. C., and McWilliams, A. 1994. “Human resources and sustained competitive advantage: A resource-based perspective.” *International Journal of Human Resource Management* **5**(2): 301–326.

Wright, P. M., Smart, D. L., and McMahan, G. C. 1995. “Matches between human resources and strategy among NCAA basketball teams.” *Academy of Management Journal* **38**: 1052–1074.

Wright, P. M. and Snell, S. A. 1991. “Toward an integrative view of strategic human resource management.” *Human Resource Management Review* **1**(3): 203–225.

Youndt, M. A., Subramaniam, M., and Snell, S. A. 2004. “Intellectual capital profiles: An examination of investments and returns.” *Journal of Management Studies* **412**: 335–361.

Zatzick, C. D. and Iverson, R. D. 2006. "High-involvement management and workforce reduction: Competitive advantage or disadvantage?" *Academy of Management Journal* **49**: 999–1105.

Zemke, R. 1990. "The ups and downs of downsizing." *Training* (November): 27–34.

Zyglidopoulos, S. 2005. "The impact of downsizing on corporate reputation." *British Journal of Management* **16**: 253–259.

# 6 Health effect outcomes: "Survivor disease" in the context of economic change

JOHANNES SIEGRIST AND NICO DRAGANO

The process of company downsizing needs to be considered in the framework of economic change, which occurs at the macro-level (whole societies) and at the micro-level (single organizations). We will first develop a conceptual frame in which to integrate a relatively heterogeneous body of empirical evidence. A selective review of study results on the health effects of downsizing among survivors follows in the next two sections. The first section concerns the health consequences for the remaining workforce and the more distant stressful conditions related to marked changes in employment. The second section analyzes the more proximal stressful conditions of restructuring at the micro-level of single organizations, with an emphasis on workers' short-term and long-term health. Finally, some challenges for future research are identified and the policy implications of current knowledge discussed.

## Theoretical background

Probably the most important link between economic change and adverse health is the notion of threat. *Threat* arises from a sudden or recurrent interruption of habitual living and working conditions – the individual's established coping patterns are powerless to meet an undesirable challenge. Threat may fuel insecurity about one's sense of mastery or even result in loss of control, with its associated negative consequences. This then may provoke sustained activation of the body's innate stress axes and eventually trigger a variety of physical and mental disorders (Weiner, 1991; McEwen, 1998).

Threats produced by economic change manifest themselves in three areas. First, *capability* to meet the demands at work may be compromised. In times of rapid economic expansion, growing work pressure often taxes available resources to meet expected demands. Alternatively, in a recession, to be on short time or to become redundant prevents people from making adequate use of their skills. Both types of threat can be equally stressful.

A second domain of threatening experience concerns *rewards* that are expected in return for effort put forth. This becomes most evident during periods of slow economic growth or economic shocks when wages are reduced and promotion prospects blocked. Rising competition among colleagues, lack of social support, and lack of appreciation from managers, who themselves are struggling for economic survival, might further aggravate the working person's frustrations.

Third, basic threats may erode *core social position* or employment status. Again, forced downward mobility is much more prevalent during a recession than in times of growth and may intensely affect well-being. Having a job is a prerequisite for a regular income, which in turn structures a wide range of life chances and living standards. Moreover, employment characteristics determine adult socio-economic status more than any other social circumstance. In terms of psychosocial well-being, paid work provides opportunities for personal performance, learning, and achievement. Being able to meet challenging demands and to receive favorable feedback, develop skills, and be supported by colleagues are prerequisites for positive self-experience at work, and positive self-experiences lead to recurrent feelings of self-efficacy and self-esteem (Siegrist, 2009). Threats to these experiences from job insecurity may interrupt taken-for-granted routines of everyday life and evoke anxiety, anger, or helplessness and their associated psychobiological responses. These reactions also may occur in times of rapid economic expansion. Increasing job promotion opportunities and workplace restructuring may cause feelings of status inconsistency, defined as a discrepancy between a person's qualifications (for instance, low skills) and the demands of an occupational position (say, middle or upper management). Employees who experience status inconsistency are at elevated risk of stress-related disorders (Peter, Gässler, and Geyer, 2007).

To summarize, economic change provokes an increasing frequency and intensity of threats to the working person's capabilities, rewards, and employment status. Threats may occur during rapid economic growth or in times of economic crisis; they are usually more prevalent in the latter case. At the macro-level, threats from economic change can affect large populations or even the country's entire workforce (Fenwick and Tausig, 1994). Note the dramatic economic and social upheaval in Russia and other post-communist societies following the breakdown in 1989 and the harmful effects on population health (Stuckler, Basu, Suhrcke, Coutts, and McKee, 2009). Another example would be the anticipated worldwide health effects of the current financial crises (Levy and Sidel, 2009; Marmot and Bell, 2009).

At the micro-level, threats produced by economic change challenge the working person's ability to adapt to new demands and new work environments. These challenges may overtax capabilities, compromise established rewards, or even jeopardize continued employment.

This is the framework in which adverse health effects among *survivors* of economic change and economic downsizing are analyzed. At the macro-level, we assume that downsizing aggravates the health status of survivors due to wage cuts, blocked careers, loss of workplace social support, and rising competition among those who still hold jobs. All three domains of individual life are affected – capabilities, rewards, and core social position. The same holds true at the micro-level. Yet with single organizations and single work trajectories, adverse health effects due to downsizing may vary among survivors as a function of organizational consequences. For survivors who continue to be exposed to high effort, low reward, low control, and low security, negative health effects are expected to be substantial. But for survivors who somehow improve their working conditions or find better jobs, these factors in the long run may counter the negative effects of downsizing.

In the upcoming discussion of micro-level effects, we demonstrate that disease among survivors is highest where downsizing and chronic psychosocial work stress combine. Interestingly, the two theoretical models of psychosocial work stress that have been studied most widely with regard to health – the demand–control model (Karasek and Theorell, 1990) and the effort–reward imbalance model (Siegrist, 1996) – both address the stressful consequences of overtaxed capabilities, compromised rewards, and loss of control. But before describing these models and related empirical evidence, we briefly discuss the adverse health effects among survivors from a macro-perspective.

## 'Survivor disease' and macro-economic change

The empirical evidence on the impact of major macro-economic change on population health is limited, in part due to methodological difficulties. Researchers in this field are usually urged to rely on aggregated, population-level data on health and economic indicators and thus are at risk of producing ecological fallacy (Riva, Bambra, Curtis, and Gauvin, 2010). Moreover, analyzing the health impact of economic cycles requires detailed modeling of lag-time effects, which is problematic at both the conceptual and methodological levels. Despite these difficulties, some studies have produced relevant findings concerning macroeconomic change, specifically its effects on "survivor disease." Whether in the context of recession or expansion, the results suggest a complex association between time, change, and population health.

Studies in Sweden and the United States (Gerdtham and Ruhm, 2006; Riva *et al.*, 2010) found a mortality increase in times of economic expansion. This ecological association may be attributed to overall increases in work demands and related stressful experiences, an explanation that also sheds light on the elevated health risks for survivors of downsizing. But as long as these associations are not established at the individual-data level, no firm conclusions can be drawn. Moreover, these associations may vary by gender. During a recession, mortality risks were elevated in men, but not in women (Gerdtham and Johannesson, 2005). Similarly, in Russia the mortality crisis following the breakdown of communism was more severe among middle-aged men than women (Shkolnikow and Cornia, 2000). In a study of health changes during the 1990s' economic crisis in Japan, the health of working men with low socio-economic status was most severely affected (Kondo, Subramanian, Kawachi, Takeda, and Yamagata, 2008).

Given that large-scale downsizing may promote economic growth, it is important to analyze negative health effects from both perspectives, growth and recession. For instance, adverse health effects for survivors of downsizing, who subsequently experience economic growth, may arise not only from continued high work pressure, but from the relative social deprivation induced by widening income inequality (Wilkinson and Pickett, 2009). Moreover, economic growth contributes to unhealthy lifestyles – bad diet, little physical activity, increased smoking, and alcohol consumption – as demonstrated in studies analyzing the health effects of trade liberalization, the liberalization of financial markets, and economic growth (Blouin, Chopra, and van der Hoeven, 2009). Trade liberalization during economic expansion has strengthened the multinational companies that distribute tobacco and alcohol, thus contributing to an increase in unhealthy behaviors (Taylor, Chaloupka, Guindon, and Corbett., 2001; Blouin *et al.*, 2009).

As for any adverse health effects of the 2007–2008 global financial crisis, loss of income and savings and widening social inequalities were documented early on (Mackenbach, Meerding, and Kunst, 2011). Surviving an economic downsizing does not protect those who keep their jobs from subsequent financial hardship or even poverty. Importantly, the extent of disease related to economic change may be modified by national social and labor policies, that is by the characteristics of national welfare regimes (Bambra, 2010; Bambra and Eikemo, 2009). Mortality rates across economic cycles fluctuate less in countries with extended social and welfare policies (Gerdtham and Ruhm, 2006; Stuckler *et al.*, 2009).

Preliminary evidence of the moderating effect produced by labor and social policies appeared in our study of chronic psychosocial stress and depressive symptoms among older employees in 12 European countries (Dragano, Siegrist, and Wahrendorf, 2011). We hypothesized that employees exposed to chronic stress, including downsizing and restructuring, and who lived in a country with stout social protections and generous pensions were less susceptible to bad health than employees in a country whose welfare regime left the burden of coping with work adversity to the individual. This assumption was tested in the studies "Survey of Health, Ageing and Retirement in Europe" and "English Longitudinal Study on Ageing" (Börsch-Supan, Brugiavini, Jürges, Mackenbach, Siegrist, and Weber, 2005; Banks, Breeze, Lessof, and Nazroo, 2006). The sample consisted of 6,270 employed men and women aged 50–64 living in 12 European countries. Work stress was measured by a shorter version of the questionnaire assessing the effort–reward imbalance model, and depressive symptoms were measured by the CES-D (Centre for Epidemiologic Studies Depression) scale. The countries were classified by welfare regime: liberal (United Kingdom), conservative (Germany, Netherlands, Belgium, France, Austria, Switzerland), Scandinavian (Sweden, Denmark), and southern (Italy, Spain, Greece). The Scandinavian regime was found to provide the highest and the liberal regime the lowest levels of protection.

Table 6.1 presents the results of a cross-sectional analysis that calculated multivariate odds of high work stress causing depression. The reference category is defined by employees with medium or low work stress; effects are adjusted for relevant confounders (see table footnote). Although the pooled data document a twofold elevated risk of depressive symptoms among those with high work-related stress, odds vary according to type of welfare regime, with relative highest effect size in the liberal country (2.64) and relatively lowest effect size in the

**Table 6.1** ***Associations between work stress (effort–reward imbalance, low control) and depressive symptoms at baseline (9,917 employed men and women ages 50–64 in 12 European countries)***

| | Effort–reward imbalance adjusted* OR (95% CI) high versus median/low (reference) imbalance | Low control adjusted* OR (95% CI) low control versus median/high (reference) control |
|---|---|---|
| Depressive symptoms baseline (CES-D) | (*N* = 6,270) | (*N* = 6,447) |
| Pooled | 2.12. (1.83 to 2.46) | 1.81 (1.53 to 2.14) |
| Liberal | 2.64 (2.03 to 3.43) | 2.29 (1.69 to 3.11) |
| Conservative | 1.96 (1.53 to 2.50) | 1.75 (1.33 to 2.28) |
| Scandinavian | 1.69 (1.07 to 2.66) | 1.48 (0.89 to 2.45) |
| Southern | 2.14 (1.47 to 3.11) | 1.67 (1.12 to 2.50) |

*Notes:* * All models adjusted for gender, age, income, education, employment status, and work time (in case of pooled estimates in addition for welfare-state affiliation).

*Source:* Based on Dragano, Siegrist, and Wahrendorf (2011).

Scandinavian countries (1.69) (Dragano *et al.*, 2011). These findings suggest a contextual influence on the strength of associations of work stress, including job insecurity, on mental health, where weak social protection regulations magnify adversity.

To summarize: "Survivor diseases" may occur more frequently among working people who face economic recession or periods of low economic growth, but they also occur in those exposed to rapid economic expansion fueled by privatization, trade liberalization, and neoliberal policies. While threats of job loss and experienced redundancy affect survivors' health in the short run, in the long run increasing work pressure, often in combination with an unhealthy lifestyle, contributes to an increase in disease. National welfare policies to some extent may moderate the noxious effects of economic changes on population health. As the scientific evidence often is restricted to findings based on aggregate-level data, these processes need to be analyzed in more detail at the micro-, individual-data level. The next section explores this challenge.

## 'Survivor disease' and micro-economic change

Downsizing at the micro-economic level, that is in organizations or firms, usually aims to reduce personnel costs, either as a strategic decision or in response to a business downturn, and has far-reaching consequences. One impact involves occupational safety and health. Dismissing parts of the workforce directly affects the life circumstances of employees, who often experience redundancy as a critical life event. It also affects the remaining workforce (the so-called survivors), who must adjust to changing conditions, who may be faced with increased work pressure and job insecurity, and who will lose colleagues. Both groups exposed to downsizing, those who are laid off and those who survive, might experience considerable stress. In the case of job loss, adverse health effects were reported in several scientific investigations (McKee-Ryan, Song, Wanberg, and Kinicki, 2005; Voss, Nylén, Floderus, Diderichsen, and Terry, 2004; Bartley, 1994), but the strengths and limitations of current evidence will not be discussed in detail here.

With the remaining workforce, research has documented adverse effects on health as well, although this may be surprising at first glance. Remaining employed does mean continuation of membership in the organization, of job performance, or of salary. It can be interpreted as proof of performance in the past or of anticipated achievement in the future, but feelings of guilt, injustice, and imminent redundancy may weigh on the spirit. Elevated morbidity among these groups of employees has been observed in investigations since the early 1990s, resulting in the term "survivor disease" (Noer, 1998; see also Quinlan and Bohle, 2009; Quinlan, Mayhew, and Bohle, 2001; Ferrie, Westerlund, Virtanen, Vahtera, and Kivimäki., 2008; Brockner and Greenberg, 1990). A closer look at the evidence is needed, given some controversial results (Østhus and Mastekaasa, 2010; Kalimo, Taris, and Schaufeli, 2003).

This section offers a brief overview of the spectrum of health problems among survivors of downsizing. Results of empirical studies are summarized and inconsistencies discussed, followed by clarification of possible pathways underlying the reported associations. Two types of pathways are distinguished: those related to the psychological distress imposed by fear of job loss, and those emanating from adverse changes in working conditions after downsizing.

The adverse effects of downsizing are relevant in an internationalized economy with increasing competition, a globalized labor market, and rapid technological change. Downsizing will hit some companies as a shock, while others incorporate restructuring into their business routines. The European Monitoring Centre of Change reported 70,737 job losses due to internal restructuring in the European Union between October and December 2010 (Hurley, Riso, Salvatore, Miginis, and Broughton, 2011). Although prevalence of the problem is high, it is not easy to assess the consequences for occupational safety and health. This is due, in part, to the diversity of disciplines involved, the heterogeneity of search terms of interest, the broad range of research questions, and the number of scientific journals where results are published. Apart from two recent reviews (Quinlan and Bohle, 2009; Ferrie *et al.*, 2008), no meta-analysis of study results has been conducted, to our knowledge, and this may reflect the heterogeneity of designs and measurements. To reduce the heterogeneity, we restrict our overview to results from observational studies that investigated associations between health and downsizing with epidemiological methods.

Starting with studies on sickness absence among survivors and including other health outcomes, Table 6.2 summarizes evidence from several international investigations. A full systematic review of all published studies in the field goes beyond the scope of this chapter; our selection mainly illustrates the research methods as well as major trends in study results.

A majority of studies included in Table 6.2 support the assumption that organizational downsizing significantly increases the risk of ill health among survivor employees. First, sickness absence was elevated in survivors of downsizing in a number of studies (Kivimäki, Vahtera, Pentti, and Ferrie, 2000; Kivimäki, Vahtera, Ferrie, Hemingway, and Pentti, 2001; Vahtera, Kivimäki, Pentti, Linna, Virtanen, Virtanen, and Ferrie, 2004; Westerlund, Ferrie, Hagberg, Jeding, Jeding, Oxenstierna, and Theorell, 2004). In contrast, two studies report null findings or even a trend toward a reduction in sick leave under conditions of downsizing (Østhus and Mastekaasa, 2010; Theorell, Oxenstierna, Westerlund, Ferrie, Hagberg, and Alfredsson, 2003).

Investigations have studied adverse health effects using different physical or mental outcome measures. Numerous effects were shown on the remaining staff in the form to musculoskeletal disorders (Kivimäki *et al.*, 2001), disability pensions (Vahtera, Kivimäki, Forma, Wikström, Halmeenmäki, Linna and Pentti, 2005), physiological stress reactions (Hertting and Theorell, 2002), medical symptoms (Dragano, Verde, and

**Table 6.2** ***Associations between downsizing and health – examples from international studies***

| Authors and country | Study design | Downsizing* | Health outcome | Main results** |
|---|---|---|---|---|
| Kivimäki *et al.*, 2000 Finland | cohort study with 764 municipal employees | reduction of staff ≥8% from 1991–93 at the respective workplace | sick leave in a 4.9-year follow-up after downsizing (linkage with OSH registry) | + survivors of layoffs had a 2.2 fold higher rate of sick leave than the control group |
| Vahtera *et al.*, 2004 Finland | cohort study with 22,430 municipal employees | reduction of staff ≥8% from 1991–93 at the respective workplace | sickness absence and mortality (register-based) in a 7.5-year follow-up period | + survivors of layoffs had a 2.0 fold higher cardiovascular mortality compared to the control group; sickness spells increased after downsizing |
| Westerlund *et al.*, 2004 Sweden | cohort study with 24,036 employees | accumulated reduction of staff ≥8% from 1990–96 at the respective workplace | long-term sick leave and hospital admission in a 3-year follow-up period after downsizing (record linkage) | + long-term sick leave was more common in participants who experienced downsizing |

| | | | | |
|---|---|---|---|---|
| Østhus and Mastekaasa, 2010 Norway | register-based cohort study with 1,651,387 employees from 19,918 organizations with more than 25 employees | (a) 1-year reduction of staff by ≥8% in the organization; (b) management survey reporting downsizing | sick leave in the year following downsizing (linkage with Norwegian sickness absence register) | 0 (–) trend toward slight decrease in sick leave in organizations with downsizing compared to stable organizations |
| Theorell *et al.*, 2003 Sweden | cohort study with 5,720 employees from 40 companies | 1-year reduction of staff by ≥8% in the organization | long-term sick leave (>15 days) in the year following downsizing (linkage with health insurance register) | 0 (–) no effect in men, slight decrease in sick leave in women working in companies with downsizing |
| Kivimäki *et al.*, 2001 Finland | cohort study with 764 municipal employees | reduction of staff ≥8% from 1991–93 at the respective workplace | musculoskeletal problems (self-reported and sickness absence records) in a 3-year follow-up period | + survivors of layoffs had a 2.6 fold higher disease rate than the control group |
| Kivimäki *et al.*, 2007 Finland | cohort study with 26,682 municipal employees | reduction of staff ≥8% from 1991–93 at the respective workplace | use of psychotropic drugs in a 7-year follow-up period (linkage with insurance data) | + survivors of layoffs had a 1.5 fold higher prescription rate than the control group |
| Vahtera *et al.*, 2005 Finland | cohort study with 19,273 municipal employees | reduction of staff ≥8% from 1991–93 at the respective workplace | medically certified full-disability pension in a 5-year follow-up period (linkage with registry) | + survivors of layoffs had a 1.8 fold risk of becoming a disability pension case compared to the control group |

**Table 6.2** (*cont.*)

| Authors and country | Study design | Downsizing* | Health outcome | Main results** |
|---|---|---|---|---|
| Hertting and Theorell, 2002 Sweden | pre-post comparison with 31 women working in a hospital that underwent downsizing | hospital reduced personnel by one fifth (no control group) | blood samples, 1-year change in relevant parameters, e.g. cortisol levels, apoliporoteins A/B | + negative physiological changes were observed after downsizing |
| Moore *et al.*, 2004 US | cohort study with 1,244 white- and blue-collar workers from a large company that underwent downsizing | participants were asked if they had experience with layoffs in their departments | Self-reported depression and medical symptoms after 5 years | + significantly more depression and health symptoms in persons who experienced downsizing |
| Nordang *et al.*, 2010 Norway | quasi-experimental study with 46 nurses, pre-post comparison | downsizing in the hospital took place between the 1. and the 3. wave of the study | changes in burnout status (Bergen Burnout Inventory) and job satisfaction between waves (30-month) | + burnout measures increased after downsizing, and job satisfaction decreased |
| Parker *et al.*, 1997 UK | pre-post comparison with 139 male employees from a chemical factory | company underwent an extensive strategic downsizing during the study period | 4-year change in self-reported, job-related mental well-being | 0 no change in mental well-being despite downsizing |

| | | | | |
|---|---|---|---|---|
| Pepper *et al.*, 2003 US | cross-sectional survey with 5,889 employees from 5 sites of the US Department of Energy | process data about downsizing rate at the different sites during a period of massive layoffs | self-reported medical symptoms and conditions, mental health outcomes | + higher levels of impaired health in employees who experienced downsizing |
| Dragano *et al.*, 2005 Germany | cross-sectional survey with 22,559 employees | self-reports about a reduction of staff 2 years prior to the survey | self-reported medical symptoms and work stress | + persons reporting downsizing had more symptoms and higher stress |
| Armstrong-Stassen, 2001 Canada | pre-post comparison with 187 federal government employees | department underwent an extensive downsizing during the study period | 1-year change in self-reported medical symptoms and burnout (Maslach Burnout) | 0 (+) non-significant increase in symptoms and burnout during a period of downsizing |

*Notes:* * in all studies with control groups, controls were defined as persons who did not experience downsizing and had stable employment.
** meaning of symbols: 0 no association, – lower disease rates in survivors, + higher disease rates in survivors.

Siegrist, 2005; Moore, Grunberg, and Greenberg, 2004; Pepper, Messinger, Weinberg, and Campbell, 2003), and burnout (Armstrong-Stassen, 2001; Nordang, Hall-Lord, and Farup, 2010). In the widely cited Finnish Ten-Town Study of public employees, Vahtera *et al.* (2004) reported 40 percent excess risk of all-cause mortality and an almost 100 percent excess risk of cardiovascular mortality of survivors of downsizing compared to employees in more stable organizations. The same research team found elevated rates of prescription of psychotropic drugs among employees in downsizing situations, particularly anxiolytic drugs among men (Kivimäki, Honkonen, Wahlbeck, Elovainio, Pentti, and Klaukka, 2007). This finding is exciting from a methodological perspective, as an unbiased external outcome based on national register data was used. It is in line with previous studies that reported an increase in symptoms of depression and burnout following major layoffs. These results should be viewed with caution, however, as it is not clear whether a selection bias contributed to these elevated risks or if the restructuring randomly targeted different employee groups.

Another question concerns the long-term job prospects for survivors of downsizing and whether short-term adversity can be compensated for in the longer run. A large register-based study of Finnish men and women concluded that those survivors who kept their positions in the downsized company exhibited no more mortality risk than employees who were never exposed to restructuring (Martikainen, Mäki, and Jäntti, 2008). This finding is remarkable because it includes a large sample of occupations and summarizes data over an eight-year observation. Thus, it is vital to analyze occupational trajectories over a longer time period where job stability may compensate for the stress of temporal shocks produced by downsizing and may even reduce mortality risk (Martikainen *et al.*, 2008).

It seems important to define unambiguous outcomes in this area of research. As sickness absence data often contain medical and non-medical reasons for absenteeism, it may not be surprising that the evidence of associations between downsizing and sickness absence is mixed. In a register-based study in Norway, covering a large section of the workforce from 2000 to 2003, no support was found for increased sickness absence among survivors of downsizing (Østhus and Mastekaasa, 2010). This finding could in part be explained by the fact that "presenteeism" might mask existing associations between downsizing and sick leave. This term describes the behavior of employees who remain at work despite having health problems, for fear of negative consequences if they stayed at home.

At the methodological level, the predominant study design is the cohort with register linkage. Although this design is reliable and allows an examination of causal relationships, other study designs are needed to supplement the findings from cohort studies (or pre-post comparisons without control groups). Longitudinal studies covering changes within one part of the organization (such as privatization by outsourcing from a public company), while leaving other parts of the same organization unchanged, provide a potentially more vigorous test of the hypothesis of health-adverse effects of restructuring. At least this is the case if no selection effect of employees has occurred.

In an attempt to meet these criteria, a recent report from the British Whitehall II Study found a 60 percent elevated risk of work disability over about eight years among civil servants who had been transferred to an executive agency in the early 1990s ($N = 1.263$; 27%) compared to those who remained in the civil service ($N = 3.419$; 73%). This elevated risk was evident after adjustment for several main confounders, including preexisting health, and it was stronger for men than for women (Virtanen, Kivimäki, Singh-Manoux, Gimeno, Shipley, Vahtera, Akbaraly, Marmot, and Ferrie, 2010). In interpreting this finding, it is not clear whether there is a direct causal link between a major organizational change, such as transfer into an executive agency, and work disability. There are still missing links. In these studies, it is always important to monitor contextual effects, such as differences in employment contracts or financial incentives in case of early retirement. A final concern relates to the small number of large-scale studies. It must be pointed out that many of the described results rely on a small set of studies from Scandinavian countries. It would be crucial to broaden the database to studies from other countries in order to ensure the generalizability of the findings.

Despite these limitations, evidence clearly indicates that downsizing in the surviving workforce is a major concern for occupational health. Given this relevance, it is crucial that we understand the mechanisms underlying the reported associations of downsizing with health.

Two such mechanisms are distinguished. First, feelings of job instability and threatened job security may be seen in survivors, creating prospects of an uncertain future. As one consequence, negative psychological reactions may occur, with potential negative effects on mental and physiological well-being. Second, a reduction in personnel often increases the workload for the surviving employees. Increased work pressure, changes in work organization, and, eventually, overtime work are then likely to produce recurrent reactions, with cumulative long-term chronic psychosocial stress. These two mechanisms are discussed next.

## *Health effects of job insecurity*

A meta-analysis of associations between job insecurity and mental health outcomes included 37 study samples with a total of 14,888 participants (Sverke, Hellgren, and Naswall, 2002). Overall, an average correlation between job insecurity and mental health of $r = -0.24$ was found, thus pointing to a relatively modest effect size. In this review, the quality of study designs varied widely. Prospective cohort studies provide the relatively highest level of evidence in this field, and several such studies supported the result. Employees with chronic job insecurity over a two-and-a-half-year period had significantly higher psychological morbidity compared to those with a secure job baseline and follow-up (Ferrie, Shipley, Stansfeld, and Marmot, 2002). In another study, high job insecurity was associated with increased risk of depression, independent of, but magnified by, the co-occurrence of chronic work-related stress as defined by the demand–control model (Strazdins, D'Souza, Lim, Broom, and Rodgers, 2004). However, there are also exceptions to this trend (for review, see Ferrie *et al.*, 2008).

It has been pointed out that job instability matters most if it is considered a threat. Indeed, a Dutch study found a high incidence of psychological maladies among employees who declared their self-reported job insecurity, but no effect was observed among those who did not think they were at risk of job loss (Swaen, Bültmann, Kant, and van Amelsvoort, 2004). This latter assumption was confirmed in an earlier longitudinal study of blue-collar workers where a marker of physical health, an atherogenic lipid profile, was analyzed (Siegrist, Matschinger, Cremer, and Seidel, 1988). In small homogeneous subgroups of workers suffering from chronic occupational stress over a two-year period, a clinically relevant indicator of atherogenic risk – the ratio of low-density lipoprotein (LDL) to high-density lipoprotein (HDL) – was higher in the group defined by co-occurrence of objective occupational instability and perceived job insecurity. While the influence of nutrition habits could not be ruled out in this study, additional findings support recurrent excessive activation of the sympathetic nervous system elicited by work-related stress that significantly changes lipid metabolism.

In summary, however, no strong evidence has been uncovered linking job insecurity with physical health (Ferrie *et al.*, 2008). Only the well-known Nurses' Health Study found a significant effect of job insecurity on short-term non-fatal myocardial infarction in women (Lee, Colditz, Berkman, and Kawachi, 2004).

Finally, several studies indicate reduced self-rated health as an outcome of job insecurity (Bethge, Radoschewski, and Müller-Fahrnow, 2008; Lau and Knardahl, 2008; Rugulies, Aust, Burr, and Bültmann, 2008). A recent investigation deserves special mention for its analysis of job insecurity and self-rated health in 16 European countries (László, Pikhart, Kopp, Bobak, Pajak, Malyutina, Salavecz, and Marmot, 2010). Although based on a cross-sectional design, the study supports the notion of significant effect in nine out of 16 countries. In the pooled data analysis, the odds ratio of poor health by job insecurity was 1.39, and this association was not reduced by adjustment of main socio-demographic and socio-economic factors.

The study of temporary employment may shed additional light on the association of job insecurity with health. However, workforce motivations vary widely, and this may be one reason for inconsistent findings (Siegrist, Benach, McKnight, and Goldblatt, 2009). Scarcity of perspective studies is another reason. Two longitudinal investigations found no effect of temporary employment on health (Bardasi and Francesconi, 2004; Liukkonen, Virtanen, Kivimäki, Pentti, and Vahtera, 2004), whereas two reports from Finland identified some health-adverse effects. Virtanen, Kivimäki, Elovainio, Vahtera, and Ferrie (2003) observed elevated odds ratios of chronic disease and poor self-rated health among employees with atypical contracts indicating precarious employment, but these effects were not present among fixed-term employees. In a large representative sample, Kivimäki, Vahtera, Virtanen, Elovainio, Pentti, and Ferrie (2003) identified a moderately increased risk of all-cause mortality among male and female temporary employees compared with permanent employees.

We conclude from empirical evidence that job insecurity is associated with a modest increased risk of poor mental health and, to some extent, poor physical health. These effects are likely to be much stronger if the job insecurity combines with an adverse psychosocial work environment. Specifically, a synergistic effect of work stress and downsizing on health is expected.

## *Health effects of restructuring in combination with chronic psychosocial stress*

Although an adverse psychosocial work environment has become an important concern of research and policy, conceptual clarification and valid measurement are major challenges to science. Occupational demands, threats, and conflicts act as psychosocial stressors if coping efforts cannot be easily applied. These conditions cannot be identified by direct physical or biological measurement. Rather, *theoretical concepts* are needed to delineate particularly stressful job characteristics so that they can be identified at a level of generalization that allows for their use in a range of occupations. These concepts can be translated into measures with the help of social science research methods (standardized questionnaires, observation techniques, etc.) that meet the criteria of reliability and data validity. A variety of concepts that encapsulate adverse psychosocial work environments have been developed in occupational health psychology and sociology, social epidemiology, and the organizational sciences (for reviews, see Antoniou and Cooper, 2005; Cartwright and Cooper, 2009).

Two such concepts – the *demand–control* model (Karasek and Theorell, 1990) and the *effort–reward imbalance* model (Siegrist, 1996) – have attracted attention in international research. The demand–control model posits that stress at work results from a distinct job task profile defined by the psychological demands on the working person and the control available to perform required tasks. Jobs defined by high demands and low control limit the individual's autonomy while generating continued pressure (high job strain). In addition to high demand and low control at work, a third dimension, social support at work, was added to the original formulation of this theoretical model. According to this formulation, the highest stress is expected in jobs that are characterized by high demands, low control, and low social support at work or social isolation (iso-strain jobs) (Johnson and Hall, 1988).

The model of *effort–reward imbalance* involves stressful features of the work contract. It builds on the notion of social reciprocity, a fundamental principle of all types of transactions that are characterized by some form of utility. Social reciprocity lies at the core of the work contract, which defines distinct obligations in exchange for rewards – money, esteem, career opportunities (promotion, job security). Contractual reciprocity operates through norms of return expectancy, where effort spent by employees is reciprocated by equitable rewards from employers. The effort–reward imbalance model asserts that lack of reciprocity occurs frequently under specific conditions. Failed reciprocity, in terms of high cost and low gain, generates strong negative emotions and associated stress with adverse long-term health consequences, comparable in strength and impact to those postulated in the demand–control model. High-cost, low-gain work conditions occur frequently if the workers have no alternative choice in the labor market, but there are also psychological reasons for maintaining strong effort, particularly among "overcommitted" persons. Overcommitment represents a pattern of excessive coping, and may be triggered by informal social pressure, perhaps in a highly competitive environment. These two models complement each other by focusing on "toxic" components of job task profiles and employment contracts, respectively. Low control and low reward are assumed to be equally stressful in the context of work that requires high effort. They both elicit negative emotions and enhanced stress responses with adverse long-term consequences (Kivimäki, Virtanen, Elovainio, Kouvonen, Väänänen, and Vahtera, 2006; Siegrist, 2009; Stansfeld and Candy, 2006).

It is of considerable interest to know whether employees who are simultaneously exposed to downsizing and stressful work exhibit health risks beyond those produced by each exposure separately. A large cross-sectional study with a representative sample of 0.1 percent of the German working population ($n = 22{,}559$ participants) gives a preliminary answer. In the study, the prevalence of having experienced a marked downsizing during the last two years was assessed, together with information on chronic work stress, measured by the effort–reward imbalance model (Dragano, Verde, and Siegrist, 2005). Separate and combined effects of these two exposures on the risk of suffering from cumulative physical and mental symptoms were analyzed, separately for men and women, and adjusting for major potential confounders. As demonstrated in Figure 6.1, a clear gradient of risk exists according to whether downsizing alone, work stress alone, or the two exposures combined are considered. Highest risks of cumulative symptom load are observed in those men and women who are simultaneously exposed to downsizing and chronic work stress. A further statistical test revealed a significant respective interaction term.

Despite the relevance of this synergy effect, it is difficult to interpret possible mediating processes. For instance, downsizing reduces the probability of stable social support at work, a condition that buffers the adverse effects of stress on health. Moreover, guilt and anger among survivors might act as additional stressors, thus increasing their susceptibility to

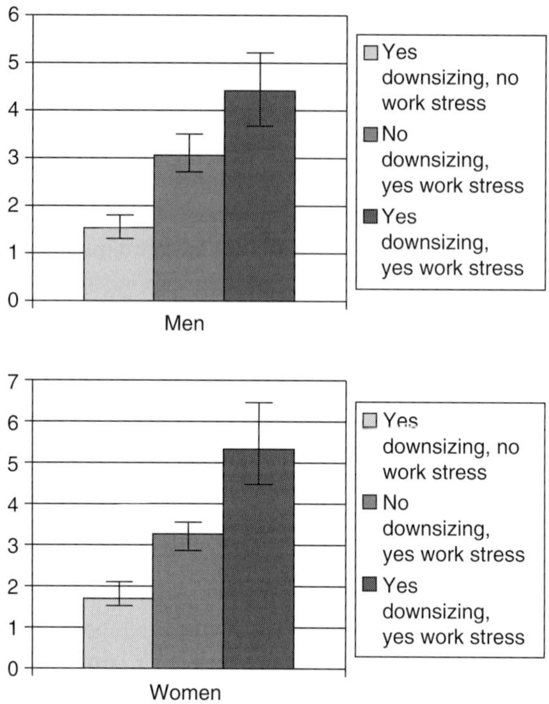


**Figure 6.1** Combined exposure to downsizing and work stress (effort–reward imbalance) in relation to symptom load. Multivariate logistic regression, odds ratios and 95% confidence intervals (*N* = 12,240 men and 10,319 women; 0.1% cross-sectional sample of the German working population).

impaired health (Noer, 1998). Another explanation points to the loss of trust in management and to increased feelings of organizational injustice that follow downsizing, specifically in employees deprived of anticipatory coping.

In summary, extensive empirical research at the micro-economic level shows adverse effects on surviving employees' health following downsizing or restructuring. However, the evidence is not consistent, and such effects were assessed under conditions of recession as well as expansion. The inconsistency may be due to methodological weaknesses of single studies, to the use of ambiguous health measures, or to the paucity of longitudinal studies. Furthermore, the review demonstrates that most pervasive health effects are observed when downsizing is followed by exposure to chronic psychosocial adversity. Taken together, this evidence, supplemented by studies on the macro-economic effects on health, justifies the development of policies aimed at mitigating survivor disease. At the same time, the research needs to be further improved. The final section of this chapter deals briefly with these two aspects.

## Challenges to research and implications for practice and policy

In our view, future studies dealing with economic change and population health should attempt to overcome several shared shortcomings. First, most studies lack an explicit theoretical background from which to derive specific hypotheses. This prevents the production of a cumulative and consistent body of systematic knowledge. Lack of a theoretical foundation and differentiation limits the interpretation of the research findings, with the risk of replicated or falsified hypotheses. In many studies, downsizing is assumed to affect all workers at the company in similar ways. Yet this is highly unlikely from a stress-theoretical perspective. Taking the approach outlined above, we maintain that there are substantial differences in how capabilities, rewards, and employment opportunities are affected (Parker, Chmiel, and Wall, 1997). It is probable that persons who are the main breadwinners or whose social identity is linked to their job are more vulnerable to threats of restructuring, and the same holds true for those in lower socio-economic positions, because they have fewer resources to cope with adversity. These limited specifications and limited generalizations are further aggravated by a lack of comparability of measures when studying organizational and employment-related characteristics, or when assessing health-related outcomes.

A second shortcoming concerns the paucity of longitudinal studies that analyze employment trajectories of workers who have been downsized. We need to know more about the timing of adverse health effects following exposure to economic change. Some effects may occur rather soon, such as deteriorating health or onset of depression. Other effects may take longer to appear. For instance, a major pathway through which chronic psychosocial work stress increases the risk of heart disease is the acceleration of athero-thrombotic lesions in coronary vessels (Xu, Zhao, Guo, Guo, and Gao, 2010); however, this usually takes years to result in clinically overt disease. For preventive reasons, it is important to know what types of health risks are expected within what time window following exposure to economic change.

Scant data are available on the immediate impact of downsizing on employee well-being. How do survivors cope? Some studies mention feelings of guilt, but careful monitoring of adaptive processes is largely missing. Again, in order to combat major negative consequences by implementing work-site health promotion programs, more detailed information is warranted. We have argued that recovery from downsizing may mitigate the adverse effects on survivor disease once more favorable working conditions are achieved. We also pointed out that negative work trajectories may be experienced where the acute stress of downsizing among survivors translates into chronic psychosocial stress, thus aggravating the risk of ill health. In a recent study, our group demonstrated that chronic psychosocial stress at work assessed in late midlife exerts long-term effects on mental and physical health in retirement, after a mean nine-year period of follow-up (Wahrendorf, personal communication).

A third shortcoming relates to insufficient exploration of the role of national labor and social policies as well as corporate policies that may impact the frequency and intensity of work-related stress. Internationally comparative investigations are needed that combine individual-level employment and health data with aggregate-level data on the national welfare system and on macro-economic developments using multi-level statistical approaches. As mentioned above, a few promising studies have been done, but more countries studied and longer observation time would draw robust conclusions from this pioneering line of research.

Summing up, we maintain that future research will face substantial theoretical and methodological challenges, but at the same time will be able to build on an impressive body of already available knowledge. It is hoped that scientific progress will reinforce these investments in healthy work at different policy levels.

We may therefore ask what are the *practical consequences and policy implications* of the evidence discussed in this chapter. One measure concerns the rise in awareness and the communication of evidence on the long-term economic and human costs of downsizing among decision-making managers, employers, and shareholders. The productivity-enhancing effects of downsizing seem to have been exaggerated, as only a minority of firms reported improved profits (Kieselbach, 2009). At the same time, the negative effects on survivors – poor health, increased absenteeism, turnover intentions, wavering work commitment – were largely neglected. Therefore, a strong case must be made for investments in health-promoting organizations. These organizations provide stability, security, equitable employment conditions, and transparent information flow across the organizational hierarchy. They reinforce productivity while reducing the costs of absenteeism, sickness, and disability. Clearly, such investments are more likely where organizations depend on better-qualified employees and are interested in their long-term engagement.

In addressing the human costs of downsizing, it is difficult to motivate firms that favor short-term contracts or hire temporary, unskilled, or semi-skilled workers. Efforts are needed on a global scale to ensure labor rights and to guarantee decent work standards. This responsibility needs reinforcement from national policies and legal frameworks, and several initiatives have appeared. The European Employment Strategy in the year 2000 defined clear ways to promote decent work; recent policies substantiate these approaches, including the "European Framework Agreement on Stress," the "Framework Agreement on Harassment and Violence at Work," and "Towards Common Principles of Flexicurity" (Kieselbach, 2009). This latter initiative calls for less segmented labor markets and fewer precarious jobs, and it emphasizes the need for better management of, and adjustment to, economic shocks by lessening employee concerns about outsourcing and relocation. Official policies need to be supplemented by bottom-up initiatives, such as the recent movement labeled corporate social responsibility (CSR), which has become the norm in several European and other countries. CSR provides "framework agreements" within and beyond single firms that declare the employers' social responsibility in terms of specific duties and commitments.

We must not overlook the role of occupational health services (OHS). Broad variety can be found in the legal safeguards and the amount and quality of activities offered by OHS, even within a relatively homogeneous network of countries such as the European Union. Most OHS endeavors focus on surveillance of legal norms and the prevention of accidents and occupational diseases, while largely ignoring the promotion of health at work and the prevention of work stress-related disease. Therefore, the role of occupational health professionals in monitoring the risks associated with job insecurity and restructuring and in implementing support programs has been marginal. We do see an exception in the Netherlands, where trained professionals deal with crisis intervention in organizations exposed to economic shocks or major restructuring.

The lessons learned here include the need for a sensitive information strategy toward employees in an environment where restructuring is likely, a selection process of remaining personnel that is based on explicit and consistently applied criteria, and the involvement of employee representatives in critical decision-making. Tensions are obvious under these conditions, and external coaching for conflicting partners can help. More training for those at risk of being laid off as well as for surviving employees will strengthen coping resources and increase reemployment options. More medical and psychological screening, consulting, and support services will minimize the adverse effects of stressful transition processes.

In conclusion, in these times of widespread restructuring, downsizing, merging, and outsourcing, the adverse health effects, not only on those who are laid off but on those who survive, deserve special attention. Despite several open questions requiring more research, a solid basis of scientific knowledge has identified considerable excess job morbidity and mortality attributable to the stressful consequences of restructuring. Although impairing the health and well-being of working populations may not be altogether avoidable, powerful policy measures are now available at both the macro- and micro-levels to mitigate the effects. Still, efforts are needed to implement these measures more vigorously and more widely in order to improve health at work in a globalized economy.

## References


Antoniou, A. G and Cooper, C. L. (eds.). 2005. *Research Companion to Organizational Health Psychology*. Cheltenham: Edward Elgar.

Armstrong-Stassen, M. 2001. "Reactions of older employees to organizational downsizing: The role of gender, job level, and time." *Journal of Gerontology* **56**: 234–243.

Bambra, C. 2010. "Yesterday once more? Unemployment and health in the 21st century." *Journal of Epidemiology and Community Health* **64**: 213–215.

Bambra, C. and Eikemo, T. A. 2009. "Welfare regimes, unemployment and health: A comparative study of the relationship between unemployment and self-reported health in 23 European countries." *Journal of Epidemiology and Community Health* **63**: 92–98.

Banks, J., Breeze, E., Lessof, C., and Nazroo, J. 2006. *Retirement, Health and Relationships of Older Population in England: The 2004 English Longitudinal Study of Ageing (Wave 2)*. London: Institute for Fiscal Studies.

Bardasi, E. and Francesconi, M. 2004. "The impact of atypical employment on individual well-being: Evidence from a panel of British workers." *Social Science and Medicine* **58**: 1671–1688.

Bartley, M. 1994. "Unemployment and ill health: Understanding the relationship." *Journal of Epidemiology and Community Health* **48**: 333–337.

Bethge, M., Radoschewski, F. M., and Müller-Fahrnow, W. 2008. "Arbeitsplatzunsicherheit als Risiko für gesundheitliche Beeinträchtigungen bei deutschen Erwerbstätigen: eine Kohortenstudie." *Gesundheitswesen* **70**: 381–386.

Blouin, C., Chopra, M., and van der Hoeven, R. 2009. "Trade and social determinants of health." *Lancet* **373**: 502–507.

Börsch-Supan, A., Brugiavini, A., Jürges, H., Mackenbach, J., Siegrist J., and Weber, G. 2005. *Health, Ageing and Retirement in Europe: First Results from the Survey of Health, Ageing and Retirement in Europe*. Mannheim: Mannheim Research Institute for the Economics of Ageing.

Brockner, J. and Greenberg, J. 1990. "The impact of layoffs on survivors: An organizational justice perspective," in J. S. Carroll (ed.), *Applied Social Psychology and Organizational Settings*. Hillsdale: Lawrence Erlbaum Associates, pp. 45–75.

Cartwright, S. and Cooper, C. C. (eds.). 2009. *The Oxford Handbook of Organizational Well-Being*. Oxford: Oxford University Press.

Dragano, N., Siegrist, J., and Wahrendorf, M. 2011. "Welfare regimes, labour policies and unhealthy psychosocial working conditions: A comparative study with 9,917 older employees from 12 European countries." *Journal of Epidemiology and Community Health* **65**: 793–799.

Dragano, N., Verde, P. E., and Siegrist, J. 2005. "Organisational downsizing and work stress: Testing synergistic health effects in employed men and women." *Journal of Epidemiology and Community Health* **59**: 694–699.

Fenwick, R. and Tausig, M. 1994. "The macroeconomic context of job stress." *Journal of Health and Social Behavior* **35**: 266–282.

Ferrie, J. E, Shipley, M. J., Stansfeld, S. A., and Marmot, M. G. 2002. "Effects of chronic job insecurity and change in job security on self-reported health, minor psychiatric morbidity, psychological measures and health-related behaviors in British civil servants: The Whitehall II study." *Journal of Epidemiology and Community Health* **56**: 450–454.

Ferrie, J. E., Westerlund, H., Virtanen, M., Vahtera, J., and Kivimäki, M. 2008. "Flexible markets and employee health." *Scandinavian Journal of Work, Environment and Health* **6**(Supplement): 98–110.

Gerdtham, U. G. and Johannesson, M. 2005. "Business cycles and mortality: Results from Swedish microdata." *Social Science and Medicine* **60**: 205–218.

Gerdtham, U. G. and Ruhm, C. J. 2006. "Deaths rise in good economic times: Evidence from the OECD." *Economics and Human Biology* **4**: 298–316.

Hertting, A. and Theorell, T. 2002. "Physiological changes associated with downsizing of personnel and reorganisation in the health care sector." *Psychotherapy and Psychosomatics* **71**: 117–122.

Hurley, J., Riso, S., Salvatore, L., Miginis, M., and Broughton, A. 2011. *European Restructuring Monitor Quarterly*, Issue 4, European Foundation for the Improvement of Living and Working Conditions, Dublin.

Johnson, J. V. and Hall, E. M. 1988. "Job strain, workplace social support and cardiovascular disease: A cross- sectional study of a random sample of the Swedish working population." *American Journal of Public Health* 78: 1336–1342.

Kalimo, R., Taris, T. W., and Schaufeli, W. B. 2003. "The effects of past and anticipated future downsizing on survivor well-being: An equity perspective." *Journal of Occupational Health Psychology* **8**: 91–109.

Karasek, R. A. and Theorell, T. 1990. *Healthy Work*. New York: Basic Books.

Kieselbach, K. (ed.). 2009."Health in restructuring: Innovative approaches and policy recommendations (HIRES)." Unpublished report, University of Bremen.

Kivimäki, M., Honkonen, T., Wahlbeck, K., Elovainio, M., Pentti, J., and Klaukka, T. *et al.* 2007. "Organisational downsizing and increased use of psychotropic drugs among employees who remain in employment." *Journal of Epidemiology and Community Health* **61**: 154–158.

Kivimäki, M., Vahtera, J., Ferrie, J. E., Hemingway, H., and Pentti, J. 2001. "Organisational downsizing and musculoskeletal problems in employees: A prospective study." *Occupational and Environmental Medicine* 58: 811–817.

Kivimäki, M., Vahtera, J., Pentti, J., and Ferrie, J. E. 2000. "Factors underlying the effect of organisational downsizing on health of employees: A longitudinal cohort study." *British Medical Journal* **320**: 971–975.

Kivimäki, M., Vahtera, J., Virtanen, M., Elovainio, M., Pentti, J., and Ferrie, J. E. 2003. "Temporary employment and risk of overall and cause-specific mortality." *American Journal of Epidemiology* **158**: 663–668.

Kivimäki, M., Virtanen, M., Elovainio, M., Kouvonen, A., Väänänen, A., and Vahtera, J. 2006. "Work stress in the etiology of coronary heart disease: A meta-analysis." *Scandinavian Journal of Work, Environment and Health* **32**: 431–442.

Kondo, N., Subramanian, S. V., Kawachi, I., Takeda, Y., and Yamagata, Z. 2008. "Economic recession and health inequalities in Japan: Analysis with a national sample, 1986–2001." *Journal of Epidemiology and Community Health* **62**: 869–875.

László, K. D., Pikhart, H., Kopp, M., Bobak, M., Pajak, A., Malyutina, S., Salavecz, G., and Marmot, M. 2010. "Job insecurity and health: A study of 16 European countries." *Social Science and Medicine* **70**: 867–874.

Lau, B. and Knardahl, S. 2008. "Perceived job insecurity, job predictability, personality and health." *Journal of Occupational and Environmental Medicine* **50**: 172–181.

Lee, S., Colditz, G. A., Berkman, L. F., and Kawachi, I. 2004. "Prospective study of job insecurity and coronary heart disease in US women." *Ann Epidemiol* **14**: 24–30.

Levy, B. S. and Sidel, V. W. 2009. "The economic crises and public health." *Social Medicine* **4**: 82–87.

Liukkonen, V., Virtanen, P., Kivimäki, M., Pentti, J., and Vahtera, J. 2004. "Social capital in working life and the health of employees." *Social Science and Medicine* **59**: 2447–2458.

Mackenbach, J. P., Meerding, W. J., and Kunst, A. E. 2011. "Economic costs of health inequalities in the European Union." *Journal of Epidemiology and Community Health* **65**: 412–419.

Marmot, M. and Bell, R. 2009. "How will the financial crisis affect health?" *British Medical Journal* **338**: b1314.

Martikainen, P., Mäki, N., and Jäntti, M. 2008. "The effects of workplace downsizing on cause-specific mortality: A register-based follow-up study of Finnish men and women remaining in employment." *Journal of Epidemiology and Community Health* **62**: 1008–1013.

McEwen, B. 1998. "Protective and damaging effects of stress mediators." *New England Journal of Medicine* **338**: 171–179.

McKee-Ryan, F., Song, Z., Wanberg, C. R., and Kinicki, A. J. 2005. "Psychological and physical well-being during unemployment: A meta-analytic study." *Journal of Applied Psychology* **90**: 53–76.

Moore, S., Grunberg, L., and Greenberg, E. 2004. "Repeated downsizing contact: The effects of similar and dissimilar layoff experiences on work and well-being outcomes." *Journal of Occupational Health Psychology* **9**: 247–257.

Noer, D. 1998. "Layoff survivor sickness: What it is and what to do about it," in M. K. Gowing, J. D. Kraft, and J. C. Quick (eds.), *The New Organizational Reality: Downsizing, Restructuring, and Revitalization*. Washington, DC: American Psychological Association, pp. 207–220.

Nordang, K., Hall-Lord, M. L., and Farup, P. G. 2010. "Burnout in health-care professionals during reorganizations and downsizing: A cohort study in nurses." *BMC Nursing* **9**: 8.

Østhus, S. and Mastekaasa, A. 2010. "The impact of downsizing on remaining workers' sickness absence." *Social Science andMedicine* **71**: 1455–1462.

Parker, S. K., Chmiel, N., and Wall, T. D. 1997. "Work characteristics and employee well-being within a context of strategic downsizing." *Journal of Occupational Health Psychology* **2**: 289–303.

Pepper, L., Messinger, M., Weinberg, J., and Campbell, R. 2003. "Downsizing and health at the United States Department of Energy." *American Journal of Industrial Medicine* **44**: 481–491.

Peter, R., Gässler, H., and Geyer, S. 2007. "Social status, status inconsistency, and risk of ischemic heart disease – a prospective study among members of a statutory health insurance company." *Journal of Epidemiology and Community Health* **61**: 605–611.

Quinlan, M. and Bohle, P. 2009. "Overstretched and unreciprocated commitment: Reviewing research on the occupational health and safety effects of downsizing and job insecurity." *International Journal of Health Services* **39**: 1–44.

Quinlan, M., Mayhew, C., and Bohle, P. 2001. "The global expansion of precarious employment, work disorganization and consequences for occupational health: A review of recent research." *International Journal of Health Services* **31**: 335–414.

Riva, M., Bambra, C., Curtis, S., and Gauvin, L. 2010. "Collective resources or local social inequalities? Examining the social determinants of mental health in rural areas." *European Journal of Public Health* **21**: 197–203.

Rugulies, R., Aust, B., Burr, H., and Bültmann, U. 2008. "Job insecurity, chances on the labour market and decline in self-rated health in a representative sample of the Danish workforce." *Journal of Epidemiology and Community Health* **62**: 245–250.

Shkolnikow, V. M. and Cornia, G. A. 2000. "Population crisis and rising mortality in transitional Russia," in G. A. Cornia and R. Paniccia (eds.), *The Mortality Crisis in Transitional Economies*. Oxford: Oxford University Press, pp. 253–279.

Siegrist, J. 1996. "Adverse health effects of high-effort/low-reward conditions." *Journal of Occupational Health Psychology* **1**: 27–41.

Siegrist, J. 2009. "Job control and reward: Effects on well-being," in S. Cartwright and C. L. Cooper (eds.), *The Oxford Handbook of Organizational Well-Being*. Oxford: Oxford University Press, pp. 109–132.

Siegrist, J., Benach, J., McKnight, A., and Goldblatt, P. 2009. "Employment arrangements, work conditions and health inequalities." Report for the Strategic Review of health inequalities post-2010 in England, Marmot Review. www.ucl.ac.uk/gheg/armotreview/consultation/Employment_arrangements_work_conditions_report

Siegrist, J., Matschinger, H., Cremer, P., and Seidel, D. 1988. "Atherogenic risk in men suffering from occupational stress." *Atherosclerosis* **69**: 211–218.

Stansfeld, S. and Candy, B. 2006. "Psychosocial work environment and mental health – a meta-analytic review." *Scandinavian Journal of Work, Environment and Health* **32**: 443–462.

Strazdins, L., D'Souza, R. M., Lim, L. L., Broom, D. H., and Rodgers, B. 2004. "Job strain, job insecurity and health: Rethinking the relationship." *Journal of Occupational Health Psychology* **9**: 296–305.

Stuckler, D., Basu, S., Suhrcke, M., Coutts, A., and McKee, M. 2009. "The public health effect of economic crises and alternative policy responses in Europe: An empirical analysis." *Lancet* **374** (9686): 315–323.

Sverke, M., Hellgren, J., and Naswall, K. 2002. "No security: A meta-analysis and review of job insecurity and its consequences." *Journal of Occupational Health Psychology* 7: 242–264.

Swaen, G.M., Bültmann, U., Kant, I., and van Amelsvoort, L.G. 2004. "Effects of job insecurity from a workplace closure threat on fatigue and psychological distress." *Journal of Occupational and Environmental Medicine* **46**: 443–449.

Taylor, A., Chaloupka, F.J., Guindon, E., and Corbett, M. 2001. "The impact of trade liberalisation on tobacco consumption," in P. Jha and F. Chaloupka (eds.), *Tobacco Control in Developing Countries*. Oxford: Oxford University Press.

Theorell, T., Oxenstierna, G., Westerlund, H., Ferrie, J., Hagberg, J., and Alfredsson, L. 2003. "Downsizing of staff is associated with lowered medically certified sick leave in female employees." *Occupational and Environmental Medicine* **60**(9): E9.

Vahtera, J., Kivimäki, M., Forma, P., Wikström, J., Halmeenmäki, T., Linna, A., and Pentti, J. 2005. "Organisational downsizing as a predictor of disability pension: The 10-town prospective cohort study." *Journal of Epidemiology and Community Health* **59**: 238–242.

Vahtera, J., Kivimäki, M., Pentti, J., Linna, A., Virtanen, M., Virtanen, P., and Ferrie, J.E. 2004. "Organisational downsizing, sickness absence and mortality: 10-town prospective cohort study." *British Medical Journal* **328**: 555–560.

Virtanen, M., Kivimäki, M., Elovainio, M., Vahtera, J., and Ferrie, J. E. 2003. "From insecure to secure employment: Changes in work, health, health-related behaviours, and sickness absence." *Occupational and Environmental Medicine* **60**: 948–953.

Virtanen, M., Kivimäki, M., Singh-Manoux, A., Gimeno, D., Shipley, M.J., Vahtera, J., Akbaraly, T.N., Marmot, M.G., and Ferrie, J.E. 2010. "Work disability following major organisational change: The Whitehall II study." *Journal of Epidemiology and Community Health* **64**: 461–464.

Voss, M., Nylén, L., Floderus, B., Diderichsen, F., and Terry, P.D. 2004. "Unemployment and early cause-specific mortality: A study based on the Swedish twin registry." *American Journal of Public Health* **94**: 2155–2161.

Weiner, H. 1991. *Perturbing the Organism: The Biology of Stressful Experience*. Chicago: University of Chicago Press.

Westerlund, H., Ferrie, J .E., Hagberg, J., Jeding, J., Jeding, K., Oxenstierna, G., and Theorell, T. 2004. "Workplace expansion, long-term sickness absence and hospital admission." *Lancet* **363**: 1193–1197.
Wilkinson, R. and Pickett, K. 2009. *The Spirit Level*. London: Penguin.
Xu, W., Zhao, Y., Guo, L., Guo, Y., and Gao, W. 2010. "The association between effort–reward imbalance and coronary atherosclerosis in a Chinese sample." *American Journal of Industrial Medicine* **53**: 655–661.

# PART III

# *Organizational outcomes*

# 7 Employee downsizing and organizational performance: What do we know?

DEEPAK K. DATTA, DYNAH A. BASUIL, AND ELENA A. RADEVA

## Employee downsizing – the phenomenon

Globalization and rapidly changing industry conditions over the past couple of decades have dramatically increased the competitive pressures faced by most corporations. To stay ahead in this more competitive environment, firms are being forced to constantly reevaluate their current strategy. Often this entails a reexamination of existing cost structures and the exploration of efficiency enhancing options. In this context, it should come as no surprise that employee downsizing has become an integral part of organizational life in corporate America. While downsizing is not a new phenomenon, it was only during the major economic downturn in the early 1980s that we started to see high levels of employee reductions for reasons other than job performance. Prior to that, such reductions were often temporary, with employees laid off during downturns being recalled when business conditions improved. More recently, firms have often engaged in employee downsizing of a more permanent nature. Radical restructurings undertaken in response to increased, often foreign, competition and the desire on the part of firms to drastically reduce payroll costs have often meant plant closures and permanent layoffs. Indeed, employee downsizing has emerged as an important weapon in the arsenal of many managers seeking enhanced efficiency and improved firm performance. As Datta, Guthrie, Basuil, and Pandey (2010, p. 282) suggest, "given its magnitude and impact, employee downsizing can legitimately be viewed as one of the most far reaching and significant management issues of the current era." Very importantly, what used to be a primarily US practice has now become a global phenomenon with large-scale layoffs becoming commonplace in European and Asian corporations.

The downsizing frenzy over the past couple of decades has undoubtedly come at a significant cost. Millions of American workers have been

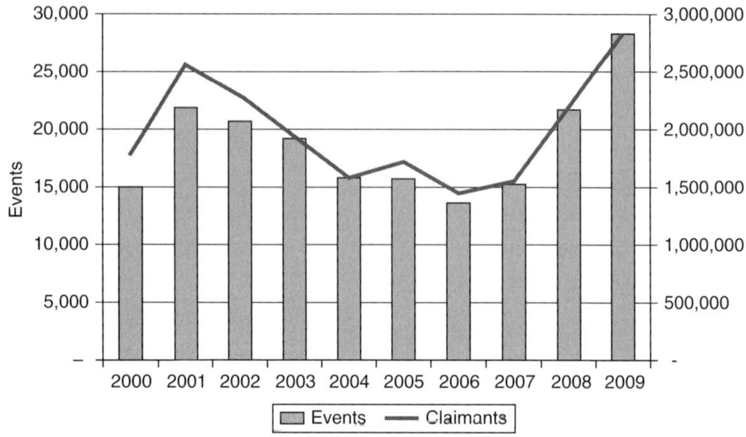


**Figure 7.1** Number of mass layoff events in the US and associated mass layoff claimants (2000–2009)

laid off (or "downsized") and the recent recession following the financial crisis brought with it unprecedented levels of downsizing activity. Data compiled by the Bureau of Labor Statistics indicate that the number of mass layoff events in 2009 alone exceeded 28,000, entailing a loss of over 2.7 million jobs. The number of mass layoff events along with the number of jobs lost during the first decade of the twenty-first century are provided in Figure 7.1.

While several arguments have been used to justify employee downsizing, the most common relates to the streamlining of existing operations and the improvement of organizational performance via the reduction of organizational slack. Downsizings can be reactive or proactive. In the former, it is generally triggered by performance declines. However, an increasing number of organizations have taken a more proactive approach to downsizing, with healthy firms often reducing headcount to rid themselves of what they perceive as being "organizational fat." However, the key question, which every organization contemplating downsizing needs to ask itself, is whether employee reductions will actually achieve the desired outcomes. In other words, "Will employee downsizing contribute to improved performance and enhanced shareholder value?" To address this question, we examine the body of extant research that has specifically focused on the performance effects of employee downsizing. In addition to synthesizing the existing literature, we seek to identify areas of consensus and divergence, examine possible reasons for divergent findings, and suggest potential areas for future research.

## Employee downsizing – benefits and costs

Datta *et al.* (2010) define employee downsizing as "a planned set of organizational policies and practices aimed at workforce reduction with the goal of improving firm performance" (p. 282). Much of the extant literature on downsizing has focused on the performance implications of downsizing. Employee reductions are often seen as a way of arresting performance declines via efficiency and productivity improvements. As previously mentioned, downsizing has generally been associated with changing environmental and industry conditions. Demand declines stemming from a weakening economy pose significant challenges from the standpoint of incumbent firms who often resort to employee layoffs in an effort to reduce costs to remain profitable. Employee downsizing can also stem from structural changes occurring within an industry, with technological advances contributing to increased substitution of labor for capital. The enhanced labor productivity emanating from such technology often manifests itself in the form of redundancies and employee layoffs (Cameron, Freeman, and Mishra, 1993). In addition, the structural changes brought about by globalization in several industries (e.g., steel) have forced incumbent firms to engage in employee reductions to remain competitive (Budros, 1999). In fact, much of the downsizing witnessed in recent years can be attributed to rapid technological changes, greater foreign competition, and increased reliance on outsourcing and offshoring by US firms. Downsizing is also common in the context of certain corporate strategies. For example, in the aftermath of mergers and acquisitions, acquiring firms generally seek cost savings via the consolidation of activities and functions. That often means significant layoffs among employees seen as being redundant in the combined organization (O'Shaughnessy and Flanagan, 1998).

In sum, downsizing is typically motivated by a desire to reduce labor expenses in order to stem eroding profitability and/or to increase future profitability. As Kets de Vries and Balazs (1997, p. 12) suggest, in increasingly competitive markets, "downsizing has turned into one of the inevitable outcomes of living in a global world where continual adjustments to products, services, and the price of labor are needed to remain competitive." Whether downsizing brings about the intended outcomes, however, depends on whether the benefits override potential revenue losses resulting from such downsizing. As Cascio (2002) notes, managers often seek to reduce costs via downsizing rather than emphasize revenue enhancements because they see costs as being more controllable than revenues. While employee downsizing might produce short-term savings in the form of reduced payroll and related expenses, it should be noted that job eliminations often result in large direct and indirect costs that can paralyze long-term revenue-generating streams. Direct costs are more visible and include costs associated with severance pay, remuneration for early retirement programs, and outplacement services. Indirect costs, on the other hand, arise from the psychological and emotional effects of downsizing. Employees (including survivors) often view downsizing as a violation of the implicit psychological contract that governs their relationships with the firm (De Meuse, Bergmann, Vanderheiden, and Roraff, 2004; Morrison and Robinson, 1997; Rousseau and Tijoriwala, 1998). Given that such contracts are fundamental to employees' beliefs and experiences, violations have important consequences for employees' work attitudes and behaviors (Robinson, 1996). Surviving employees may withdraw psychologically (e.g., reduced trust and loyalty, withholding of effort, and reduced job involvement) or physically (increased absences or voluntary turnover), with negative economic consequences for the firm (Allen, Freeman, Russell, Reizenstein, and Rentz, 2001; Brockner, Sprietzer, Mishra, Hochwarter, Pepper, and Weinberg, 2004; Luthans and Sommer, 1999; Travaglione and Cross, 2006). This reduced loyalty and lower commitment can translate into diminished productivity and increased turnover among the firm's most valued employees (Mowday, Porter, and Steers, 1982).

In sum, while lower headcount may result in immediate cost savings, the intermediate and long-term costs (both direct and indirect) associated with downsizing can easily wipe out much of the purported benefits. In the following section, we examine the empirical evidence on whether downsizing does indeed result in improved performance.

## Does employee downsizing pay? The empirical evidence

We identified a total of 41 studies on the performance effects of downsizing. These studies have been organized around the framework presented in Figure 7.2. As indicated in the framework, Stream I studies

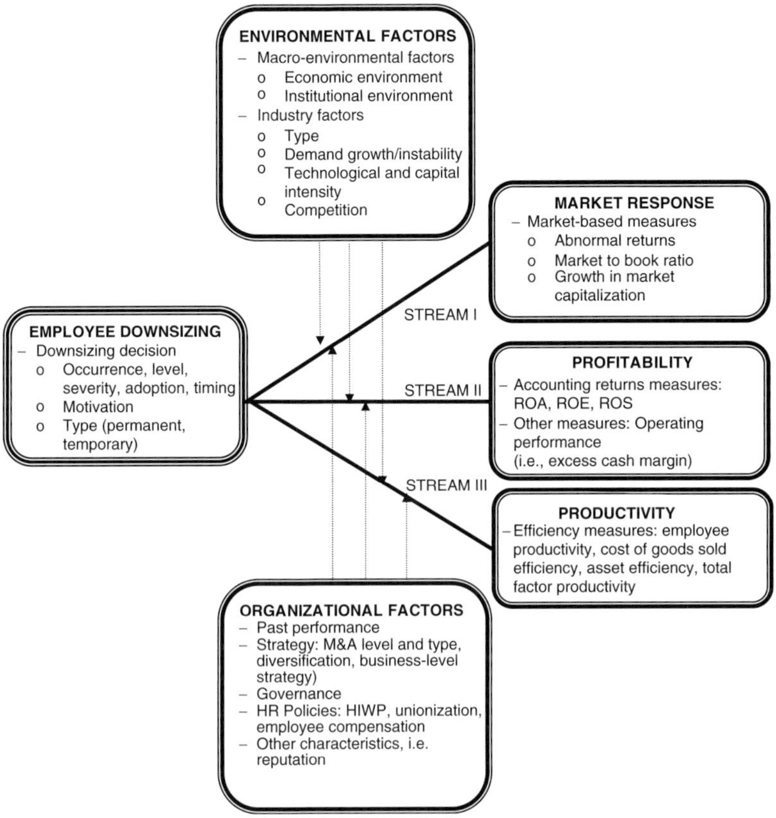


**Figure 7.2** The performance outcomes of employee downsizing

involve the assessment of downsizing-related performance in the context of stock price movements and shareholder wealth effects. These studies have typically examined stock market reactions over relatively short event windows surrounding the downsizing announcement date using the event study methodology. In addition, a few studies belonging to this stream have examined the impact of downsizing on the firm market-to-book ratio. Stream II research relates to examination of the effects of downsizing on firm profitability, with profitability being assessed primarily as return on assets (ROA), return on equity (ROE), or return on sales (ROS). Finally, Stream III consists of studies that have examined performance in the context of changes in employee productivity.

Table 7.1 lists the studies in the three streams. It also identifies the sample used by the researchers to assess the effects of employee layoffs.

### *Stream I: Employee downsizing and market returns*

Of the 20 studies that have used market measures in studying the effects of employee downsizing, most (17 studies) have used the event study methodology to assess the shareholder wealth effects associated with downsizing announcements reported in the *Wall Street Journal* and/or the *New York Times*. These studies have used the said methodology to assess the cumulative abnormal returns (CARs) or cumulative prediction errors (CPEs) over different windows surrounding the announcement date. However, a couple of studies (Chen, Mehrotra, Sivakumar, and Yu, 2001; Hillier, Marshall, McColgan, and Werema, 2007) have explored the long-term wealth effects associated with downsizing by computing buy-and-hold abnormal returns (BHARs) in the three-year period following the announcement date.

The findings of studies on the wealth effects of downsizing generally indicate that the announcement of a downsizing event has either a neutral or a negative impact on firm shareholder value. For example Cagle, Sen, and Pawlukiewicz's (2009) study of employee downsizing in US financial firms found no significant wealth effects in the three-day (–1, +1) window surrounding the announcement date. Likewise, no significant results were observed by Brookman, Chang, and Rennie (2007) in their study of 484 layoff announcements between 1993 and 2003 by firms in both the manufacturing and the service sectors. The study by Goins and Gruca (2008) of downsizing in the oil and gas industry also found no significant wealth effects associated with downsizing for the (–1, 0) and the (–5, +5) windows.

Most studies belonging to this stream suggest that downsizing results in negative wealth effects and shareholder value destruction. Studies by Iqbal and Shetty (1995), Chen *et al.* (2001), Hallock (1998), Franz, Crawford, and Dwyer (1998), and Hillier *et al.* (2007) have all found significant negative wealth effects in the period around the downsizing announcement date (that is, the (–1, +1) and the (–1, 0) windows). In addition, research by Lee (1997), Hallock (1998), and Franz *et al.* (1998) indicates that negative wealth effects are also prevalent in the slightly longer (–5, +5), (–10, +10), and the (–20, +20) windows surrounding the announcement date. In the aforementioned studies,

Table 7.1 *Studies examining the performance implications of downsizing*

| Study | Sample | Market response | Profitability | Productivity |
|---|---|---|---|---|
| Worrell *et al.* (1991) | 194 layoff announcements (1979–87) identified in the *Wall Street Journal* | CARs (−5,+5), (−1, +1) | | |
| Linn and Rozeff (1993) | 246 temporary and 137 permanent layoff announcements (1978–85) reported in the *Wall Street Journal* | CARs (−1,0), (1,60) | | |
| De Meuse *et al.* (1994) | 17 *Fortune* 100 firms with layoff announcements in 1989 | MKBK | Profit margin/sales, ROA, ROE | Asset turnover |
| Mishra and Mishra (1994) | Workforce reduction at 91 business units of 43 North American automotive firms (1990–91) | | | Labor productivity improvements |
| Iqbal and Shetty (1995) | 75 firms announcing layoffs (1986–89) identified from *Wall Street Journal* | CARs (−1,+1) | | |
| Chatrath *et al.* (1995) | 231 layoff announcements (1981–92) reported in the *Wall Street Journal* | CARs (−10,+10), (0,+1) | | |
| Madura *et al.* (1995) | 48 bank layoffs between 1984–92 reported in *Wall Street Journal* | CARs 0, −1, (−5, −2), (+1,+5) | | |
| Bruton *et al.* (1996) | 100 *Fortune* 500 companies that reduced workforce by at least 3% (1985–87) | | ROA | |
| Kang and Shivdasani (1997) | 92 Japanese firms that experienced significant performance declines (1986–90) | | Change in operating performance (operating income to assets) | |
| Cascio *et al.* (1997) | 722 employee downsizing occurrences in 537 companies (1980–94) | | ROA change between year prior to downsizing and 0, 1, 2 years | |

**Table 7.1** (*cont.*)

| Study | Sample | Market response | Profitability | Productivity |
|---|---|---|---|---|
| Palmon *et al.* (1997) | 140 layoff announcements (1982–90) reported in the *Wall Street Journal* and the *New York Times* | CARs (−1,0), (−1, +1), (−1,+10) | ROA, ROE | |
| Lee (1997) | 300 US layoff announcements and 73 in Japanese firms (1980–94) reported in the *Wall Street Journal*, the Asian *Wall Street Journal*, Nihon KeizaiShinbun | CARs (−2,+2) | | |
| Elayan, Swales, Maris, and Scott (1998) | 646 layoff announcements (1979–91) identified using the *Wall Street Journal* and the National Newspaper Index | CARs (−1,0) | | |
| Franz *et al.* (1998) | 351 involuntary layoff announcements (1978–92) reported in *Wall Street Journal* | CARs (−90,−2), (−1,0), (−5,+5) | | |
| Hallock (1998) | 550 US firms with layoff announcements (1987–95) reported in *Wall Street Journal* | CARs (−1,+1), (−5, +5), (−10,+10), (−20,+20) | | |
| Wagar (1998) | 1907 Canadian establishments with 55% reporting reductions in their workforce over a 2-year period in the 1990s | | | Employer efficiency |
| Espahbodi *et al.* (2000) | 118 firms that announced employee downsizing (1989–93) in the *Wall Street Journal* or *New York Times* | | ROA, ROE, current ratio | Asset turnover, changes in labor costs/sales |

| | | | | |
|---|---|---|---|---|
| Wayhan and Werner (2000) | 225 large US firms (1991–92) that announced a workforce reduction initiative of at least 3% | Growth in market capitalization | | |
| Chen *et al.* (2001) | 349 layoff announcements (1990–95) reported in the *Wall Street Journal* | CARs (–1,0) | ROA, ROS | Sales/employee |
| Suárez-González (2001) | 297 large Spanish firms (141 downsizers and 156 non-downsizers) | | ROS | Labor productivity |
| McElroy *et al.* (2001) | 31 subunits of a national financial services company | | Profitability | |
| Chalos and Chen (2002) | Employee downsizing in 365 *Fortune* 500 firms (1993–95) identified using *Wall Street Journal* | CARs (–1,0,+1) | ROA change | Sales productivity, cost of goods sold efficiency |
| Cascio and Young (2003) | 657 employment change occurrences (1982–2000) | Stock returns in years 0,1, and 2 | ROA in years 0,1, and 2 | |
| Baumol *et al.* (2003) | 267 establishments in 20 manufacturing industries (1967–97) | | Profitability, market value | Productivity growth, unit labor costs |
| Chadwick, Hunter, and Walston (2004) | Downsizing at 114 acute care major hospitals (1996–97) | | Operating performance (excess cash margin) | |
| De Meuse *et al.* (2004) | Layoff announcements by 78 *Fortune* 100 firms (1989–96) reported in Work Place Trends and the *Wall Street Journal* | MKBK | ROS, ROA, ROE | Asset efficiency (sales/assets) |
| Nixon *et al.* (2004) | 364 downsizing announcements by US firms (1990–98) identified using *Wall Street Journal* and Lexis-Nexis | CARs (–1,+1) | | |

**Table 7.1** (*cont.*)

| Study | Sample | Market response | Profitability | Productivity |
|---|---|---|---|---|
| Love and Nohria (2005) | Downsizing in *Fortune* 100 firms (1977–93) identified using *Wall Street Journal* and *New York Times* and several wire services | | ROA market, ROA Book | |
| Perry and Shivdasani (2005) | 94 non-financial firms in the US that downsized in 1993 after financial decline (at least 33% drop in pretax income) | | ROA change | |
| Carswell (2005) | 155 companies in New Zealand (1997–99) | | ROA, ROE, profitability | Sales/employee |
| Yu and Park (2006) | 258 publicly traded firms in Korea (1997–99) with 63% involved in downsizing | | ROA change | |
| Zatzick and Iverson (2006) | 3,080 Canadian workplaces (1999–2001) and 2,970 workplaces in 2002 | | | Employee productivity |
| Brookman *et al.* (2007) | Layoff announcements by 484 firms (1993–2003) reported in the *Wall Street Journal* | CARs (–5,0), (–1,0) | | |
| Said *et al.* (2007) | 140 downsizers and 99 stable employers in the US and Canadian manufacturing sector (1990–96) | | | Employee productivity |
| Hillier *et al.* (2007) | 322 layoff announcements by UK firms (1990–2000) | | ROA change | Sales/employee, value added/ employee |
| Guthrie and Datta (2008) | 144 non-diversified US firms (1998–2000) | | ROA | |

| | | | | |
|---|---|---|---|---|
| Goins and Gruca (2008) | 57 companies with layoff announcements (downsizing 1% or more) in the US oil and gas industry (1989–96) | CARs (–1,0), (–5, +5) | | |
| Cagle *et al.* (2009) | 79 financial institutions (1994–2003), layoff announcements reported in *Wall Street Journal* | CARs (–1,0), (–1, +1), (–10,–2), (+2,+10) | | |
| Atanassov and Kim (2009) | 25,698 industrial companies from 41 countries (1993–2004) identified from Worldscope | | Change in operating performance (Operating Income and Sales to Assets) | |
| Dong and Xu (2008) | 2,300 firms in China (1998–2002) | | Change in profitability | Change in total-factor productivity |
| Bullon and Bueno (2010) | 709 downsizing announcements from Spanish companies (1995–2001) | | ROA, ROA change, profitability | |

cumulative abnormal returns ranged from –0.3 percent to –1.78 percent. However, Worrell, Davidson, and Sharma (1991) observed that while shareholder returns were negative in the shorter events windows of (–1, +1) and (–5, +5), they were not so for the (–90, +90) window. Likewise, Madura, Aigbe, and Kenneth (1995) observed significant negative wealth effects among downsizing firms on the announcement date; however, cumulative abnormal returns in the pre- (–5, –2) and post-announcement (+1, +5) windows were not significant.

A closer examination of the nature of downsizing and the circumstances surrounding downsizing events provides evidence of a number of contingent factors that influence market responses to downsizing announcements. For one, wealth effects associated with employee downsizing appear to be different in firms that are in sound financial health *vis-à-vis* those that are in financial distress. In the former, market reactions are either negative or insignificant. In contrast, when downsizing involves distressed firms, market response tends to be more favorable. Studies by Madura *et al.* (1995), Iqbal and Shetty (1995), and Franz *et al.* (1998) support this observation. Based on a sample of banks that downsized, Madura *et al.* (1995) found that while, on average, there were shareholder wealth gains when low market value firms were involved, no significant effects were observed in the context of firms with high market value. Likewise, Iqbal and Shetty (1995) observed that while financially healthy firms experienced downsizing-related losses in market value over the two-day window surrounding the announcement date, poorly performing firms did not. In another study, Franz *et al.* (1998) categorized their sample of downsizing firms into healthy, marginal, and distressed firms, and found that, while all three experienced significant negative wealth effects in the period immediately surrounding the announcement date (event window –1, 0), marginal and distressed (but not healthy) firms were associated with positive wealth effects in the post-announcement (+1, +90) period.

A firm's strategic intent also appears to affect market responses to downsizing announcements, with proactive downsizing aimed at restructuring firms, refocusing their revenues, or raising their efficiency, being perceived more positively by the market. Palmon, Sun, and Tang (1997), for example, observed that proactive downsizing led to significant positive wealth effects over the three-day (–1, +1) and two-day (–1, 0) event windows. In addition, our review highlights that layoffs that represent an *ex post* reaction to unforeseen declines in demand or increases in cost structure are more likely to be perceived negatively by the market. This was evident in the study by Franz *et al.* (1998). In it, the authors found that firms that downsized to reduce costs experienced significant losses in shareholder value during the two-day and the 11-day periods surrounding the announcement date. Similarly, Chen *et al.* (2001) observed significant declines in shareholder wealth following the announcement of downsizing targeted at controlling costs or responding to demand declines.

Other factors influencing shareholder wealth in the context of downsizing include the nature of layoffs (permanent versus temporary) and the size of such layoffs. Studies indicate that when layoffs are viewed as being permanent, they elicit a less favorable market response than those seen as being temporary (Hallock, 1998; Lee, 1997; Worrell *et al.*, 1991). The level of downsizing has also been shown to affect market responses. Hillier *et al.* (2007) found that firms involved in major employee reductions (higher than the mean level among firms in their sample) experienced greater loss in market value in the three-day window surrounding the announcement day. Likewise, Worrell *et al.* (1991) found that when downsizing involved employee reductions in excess of 4.5 percent, the loss in shareholder value in the 11-day window surrounding the announcement date was significantly greater than for medium (reductions between 1 percent and 4.5 percent) and small (less than 1 percent) employment downsizing. These findings were corroborated by Nixon, Hitt, Lee, and Jeong (2004). They found a significant negative relationship between the level of downsizing and the three-day CARs observed around the announcement date.

Interestingly, research indicates a temporal effect associated with market responses to downsizing announcements. The study by Chatrath, Ramchander, and Song (1995) found that downsizings during 1981–1983 resulted in higher negative wealth effects than those in the 1984–1990 period. In addition, they also observed significant positive wealth effects for downsizings that occurred during 1991–1992. Similarly, Lee (1997) observed that early downsizers (that is, firms that were among the first to downsize in their industry) suffered greater shareholder losses than those who downsized later. In addition, the study by Hillier *et al.* (2007) found that among "repeat" downsizers, the first downsizing event is generally associated with a more pronounced negative impact on shareholder wealth than subsequent events. A similar pattern was observed in an earlier study by Linn and Rozeff (1993). They found that while the first announcement of layoffs of permanent salaried and hourly employees resulted in significant negative wealth effects, the effects were not significant in subsequent downsizing announcements.

While the studies reviewed so far have focused on short-term wealth effects associated with employee downsizing, we also identified two studies that have examined the long-term effects of such downsizing. Using the long-horizon event study methodology, Chen *et al.* (2001) examined wealth effects (known as the buy-and-hold abnormal returns or BHAR) in the three years following the downsizing event. BHAR returns can be viewed as "the average multiyear return from a strategy of investing in all firms that complete an event and selling at the end of a pre-specified holding period versus a comparable strategy using otherwise similar non-event firms" (Mitchell and Stafford, 2000, p. 296). They found that while downsizing firms experienced no significant gains or losses in the first two years, there were significant positive gains in the third year following downsizing. However, in a more recent study on long-term effects of downsizing, Hillier *et al.* (2007) failed to find any significant impact on shareholder value in any of the three years following downsizing.

While research related to market responses to downsizing has primarily examined the wealth effects associated with downsizing announcements, we were able to identify three studies that have examined the effects of downsizing on changes in market value of the firm. In a study of downsizing at 17 large *Fortune* 100 firms in 1989, De Meuse, Vanderheiden, and Bergmann (1994) found that downsizing firms, when compared to control firms, had a lower market-to-book ratio in the two years following downsizing. In a later study, De Meuse *et al.* (2004) used a larger sample of 78 downsizing events among *Fortune* 100 firms between 1989 and 1996. They too found that firms that downsized had significantly lower market to book values than stable employers in the year of downsizing and also in the two subsequent years. This drop was more pronounced in firms with high levels of downsizing (reduction of more than 10 percent of their workforce). Downsizing has also been associated with changes in market capitalization with Wayhan and Werner (2000) finding that firms that downsized exhibited improved market capitalization (when compared to control firms) in the year following downsizing. However, the difference was not significant in subsequent years.

In sum, Stream I research suggests that rather than increased shareholder value, employee downsizing results in the firm experiencing value losses. This loss in shareholder value is magnified when layoffs are permanent and the level of downsizing is greater. And while research on long-term shareholder wealth effects of downsizing has been sparse, the limited evidence suggests that firms that engage in layoffs do not experience significant improvements in long-run market value versus those that do not. However, there are certain conditions under which market reactions to downsizing tend to be more favorable – for example, when downsizing is undertaken by poorly performing firms or by firms engaged in strategic, proactive downsizing. An interesting finding relates the temporal effects surrounding the relationships between downsizing and shareholder returns, with the negative effects being more pronounced in the context of early downsizing among repeat downsizers. While it might be interpreted as either firms benefiting from learning in their subsequent downsizings, it might also be reflective of financial markets' greater acceptance or increased tolerance of the practice of downsizing.

One of the limitations of Stream I research is that, barring a few exceptions, studies have primarily focused on examining only the direct effects of downsizing. It is quite likely that the wealth effects associated with downsizing are contingent on the context within which downsizing occurs. For example, market assessment of value of downsizing may be a function of the primary industry within which the firm operates. As the study by Guthrie and Datta (2008) suggests, downsizing undertaken in industries characterized by rapid growth might have a more deleterious effect than downsizing undertaken in an industry with relatively slow growth. Likewise, downsizing by a firm that emphasizes R&D investments might send a stronger negative signal to the market, resulting in lower (possibly, negative) wealth effects than one by a firm that seeks to be a cost leader. In the latter case, downsizing might even be viewed as appropriate in the context of the strategy it seeks to pursue.

## *Stream II: Employee downsizing and firm profitability*

The body of research belonging to this stream relates to the performance effects of downsizing on subsequent firm profitability. It involves a total of 22 studies that have examined downsizing-related performance effects using accounting-based measures such as return on assets (ROA), return on equity (ROE), and/or return on sales (ROS). Compared to the event studies belonging to Stream I, studies here have generally examined the performance implications of downsizing from a longer-term perspective – typically one, two, or three years after the occurrence of the downsizing event. In other words, while the event studies do not account for the effectiveness of the downsizing implementation process, the findings of studies belonging to this stream necessarily incorporate not just the downsizing event, but also the effectiveness of the implementation process.

Consistent with research on the wealth effects of downsizing, studies belonging to this stream also suggest that from a firm's perspective the financial benefits related to employment downsizing are relatively elusive. The findings, however, are more mixed. A number of studies (e.g., Cascio, Young, and Morris, 1997; Guthrie and Datta, 2008; De Meuse *et al.*, 1994, 2004; Hillier *et al.*, 2007; Kang and Shivdasani, 1997) indicate that downsized firms do not experience profitability improvements in the post-downsizing phase. The study by Cascio *et al.* (1997), for example, demonstrates that firms which engaged in layoffs experienced reduced profitability (change in ROA) in the post-layoff period. Likewise, De Meuse *et al.* (1994) found that, when compared to firms that did not downsize, those that did had lower ROA, ROE, and ROS in the first and the second years following downsizing. In addition, in their study of employee reductions in the financial services sector, McElroy, Morrow, and Rude (2001) observed that such reductions were accompanied by significant negative performance consequences in the two years following downsizing. A more recent study by Guthrie and Datta (2008) also observed a significant negative association between workforce downsizing and post-downsizing firm performance.

Studies on the performance effects of downsizing in non-US countries reveal similar findings. For example, Carswell (2005), in a study of employee reductions by New Zealand firms between 1997 and 1999, found that firms that had downsized were characterized by lower levels of profitability in the period following the downsizing. Similar results were observed in two studies on the effects of downsizing in the Spanish context. Suárez-González (2001) found that firms that downsized during the period 1989–94 had, on average, significantly lower return on sales (ROS) than control firms that did not engage in such downsizing. More recently, Bullon and Bueno (2010) in their of study of Spanish firms that downsized between 1995 and 2001 found that employee layoffs led to negative changes in ROA in the year following the downsizing.

A more limited set of studies have, however, observed positive profitability effects associated with downsizing. For example, Baumol, Blinder, and Wolff (2003) found that, at both the establishment and the firm level, downsizing had a positive impact on profitability. Likewise, in their study of downsizing by Korean firms during the period 1997–99, Yu and Park (2006) found a positive association between downsizing and ROA changes between the pre- and the post-downsizing periods. Similarly, Chen *et al.* (2001), using a sample of 349 downsizing events between 1990 and 1995 found that relative to non-layoff firms, those with layoffs showed greater improvements in both ROA and ratio of operating margins to sales over the three-year post-layoff period. Sometimes, the benefits of employee reductions are experienced only two or three years after the downsizing event. This was borne out in the study by Kang and Shivdasani (1997) who found that, while there were no significant changes in operating performance in the first and second years following layoffs, firms experienced improved performance in their third year. The findings of Espahbodi, John, and Vasudevan (2000) were somewhat similar. They found that, when compared to control firms, downsized firms exhibited improved industry-adjusted ROE, but only in the third and fourth years after downsizing.

In addition to the above studies that indicate significant positive or negative profitability effects associated with downsizing, a few studies have found no significant relationship between downsizing and firm profitability. Kang and Shivdasani (1997) and Perry and Shivdasani (2005), for example, observed no significant industry adjusted profitability gains in the first two years following layoffs. In another study based on downsizing at *Fortune* 500 companies, Bruton, Keels, and Shook (1996) found that the level of downsizing had no impact on post-downsizing ROA. Finally, Espahbodi *et al.*'s (2000) study of downsizing at 118 firms between 1989 and 1993 found no significant profitability changes in the two years following downsizing. In addition to the direct effects, studies provide some evidence that the effect of downsizing on firm profitability is contingent on environmental, organizational, and process factors. In a recent study, Guthrie and Datta (2008) examined the moderating role of industry in the context of downsizing performance and found that the negative relationship between downsizing and performance was magnified in industries characterized by high R&D intensity, low capital intensity, and high growth. Firms in such industries exhibited more pronounced ROA declines in the three years following downsizing. However, industry demand instability did not make a difference. In addition, a few studies have focused on the contingency effects of organizational and process factors. Perry and Shivdasani (2005) examined the effects of board composition on the relationships between downsizing and ROA change and found that firms with a greater proportion of outsiders on their boards exhibited improved profitability in the two years following downsizing. In contrast, those with inside boards had negative (but, non-significant) changes in ROA over the same period. The motivation underlying downsizing also appears to play an important moderating role in influencing profitability outcomes associated with downsizing. Palmon *et al.* (1997), for example, found that while downsizing undertaken with the objective of efficiency enhancement was associated with increased ROA, ROE, and profit margins; those undertaken in response to demand declines did not. Likewise, Chalos and Chen (2002) found that firms that engaged in strategic downsizing to refocus their revenues had higher ROA in the post-downsizing period than firms which downsized in response to rising costs. In addition, research by Love and Nohria (2005) indicates that proactive downsizers with greater absorbed slack exhibited greater profitability improvements than those with lower levels of slack. They also found that broadly scoped downsizings, involving structural/process changes and changes in the strategic domain of the firm, were associated with superior post-downsizing performance than narrowly scoped downsizings. Finally, De Meuse *et al.* (2004) in their study examined whether the level and frequency of downsizing influences subsequent performance. They found no difference in the post-downsizing profitability levels between low and high downsizers or between low and high frequency downsizers. In addition, the study by Carswell (2005) suggests that the employee downsizing process makes a difference. They found that firms engaged in downsizing experienced superior performance when affected employees perceived the downsizing process as being "just" and when firms provided outplacement help to downsized employees.

In summary, while findings have been equivocal, a majority of Stream II studies indicate that firms do not experience improved profitability following the downsizing event; however, firms that proactively downsize and where employees perceive the process as being "fair" do better. And, while industry characteristics such as R&D and capital intensity and growth appear to moderate the effects of downsizing on firm profitability, the paucity of research in this area makes it difficult to arrive at definite conclusions.

## *Stream III: Employee downsizing and productivity*

Stream III research addresses the effects of employment downsizing on firm productivity (e.g., sales per employee, labor costs per employee, asset efficiency, and assets per employee). Table 7.1 identifies the 14 studies that fall into this category. Contrasted with the findings of studies belonging to Streams I and II, those belonging to this stream provide a more positive picture. For example, research by Chen *et al.* (2001) and Hillier *et al.* (2007) found that downsizing led to improved productivity in relation to their control groups. Additionally, Suárez-González (2001) found that while the firms that downsized had significantly lower productivity when compared to the control group (non-downsizers) prior to downsizing, their productivity in the post-downsizing period improved to equal that of the control group. Chalos and Chen (2002) also found that firms that engaged in revenue refocusing or cost-cutting enhanced their sales productivity (but not their cost-of-goods sold efficiency). Finally, De Meuse *et al.* (1994, 2004) found that downsizers, compared to control firms, improved their asset efficiency only in the year that downsizing was undertaken but not before or after the downsizing. Moderating factors, such as the magnitude and the frequency of downsizing, had no effect on the relationship between downsizing and asset efficiency.

Other studies, including those by Mishra and Mishra (1994), Wagar (1998), Carswell (2005), Zatzick and Iverson (2006), Yu and Park (2006), and Dong and Xu (2008) indicate either a negative or a non-significant relationship between downsizing and post-downsizing productivity. For example, Mishra and Mishra (1994) found that downsizing had a negative effect on both machine efficiency and labor productivity. Likewise, Wagar (1998) found that while there was a negative relationship between layoffs and productivity, it was, however, attenuated when firms implemented high involvement work practices (HIWP) during the downsizing event. Likewise, Zatzick and Iverson (2006) found that while downsizing, in general, resulted in productivity declines, firms that invested in HIWP prior to downsizing were able to minimize such declines in the post-downsizing period. Finally, in a study of downsizing at US and Canadian firms, Said, Le Louarn, and Tremblay (2007) failed to find any significant changes in productivity levels following downsizing among sample firms.

In sum, while the studies in Streams I and II generally suggest a deleterious effect for downsizing on shareholder value and firm profitability, those in Stream III provide a somewhat more positive picture. Again, the downsizing process appears to make a significant difference, with the adoption of high involvement work practices during and after downsizing mitigating the negative effects of downsizing on employee productivity.

## Conclusions and directions for future research

Employment downsizing is generally undertaken with the explicit goal of improving organizational performance. Our review of the literature on performance outcomes associated with employment downsizing indicates equivocal findings. Indeed, more often than not, the outcomes are not consonant with performance expectations. With a relatively high percentage of studies associating employment downsizing with negative performance outcomes, one can conceivably conclude that firms that downsize "rather than becoming lean and mean, often end up lean and lame" (Henkoff, 1994, p. 58). Our review of the literature also lends credence to Pfeffer's (1998) argument that diminished employment security is not conducive to superior performance in today's competitive environment. It also begs the question, "Why is employee downsizing so pervasive when it often fails to produce the desired results?"

A possible explanation lies in the phenomenon of mimetic isomorphism and interorganizational imitation (Dacin, 1997; DiMaggio and Powell, 1983; Westphal, Gulati, and Shortell, 1997). Studies have highlighted the important role of mimetic behavior in several strategic decisions, including acquisitions (Haunschild, 1993), market entry (Haveman, 1993), changes in organizational structure (Burns and Wholey, 1993), and top management hiring (Williamson and Cable, 2003). Mimetic isomorphism may lead to negative performance consequences as was demonstrated in Westphal *et al.*'s (1997) study and, more recently, in Barreto and Baden-Fuller's (2006) study of market expansion by Portuguese firms. Employment downsizing can be viewed as being driven by the desire on the part of managers to enhance the legitimacy of their firms with external stakeholders and, thereby, improve their ability to attract the resources needed to survive and thrive in a competitive environment. Alternatively, the findings might suggest that downsizing decisions are affected by managerial hubris – with managers being motivated to undertake downsizing based on a strong belief (bordering on overconfidence) that employee reductions will invariably result in improved returns by reducing costs without a corresponding reduction in post-downsizing revenues. In other words, managers' propensity to overestimate the benefits that can be extracted from employee downsizing leads them to pursue the downsizing path even when such benefits are likely to be negated by the direct and indirect costs associated with employee reductions.

The mixed findings suggest that while, on average, downsizing does not create value or enhance profitability, it might do so under certain circumstances. In other words, downsizing is neither "right" nor "wrong" – the appropriateness of downsizing depends on the context. Unfortunately, research on what these contextual factors might be is rather limited. Relatively few studies have examined the moderating effects that might explain the equivocal findings identified in our review. Improved insights along with a better understanding of the performance implications of downsizing should come from greater use of models examining both moderating and mediating effects in future research. For example, it can be argued that attrition involving employees who are less critical about the attainment of firm competitive advantage may not have the kind of adverse impact on organizational performance as layoffs involving "strategic" employees (those directly involved in activities that relate to firm core competencies). Future work on downsizing performance that makes the distinction between "strategic" and "non-strategic" employee groups should provide interesting insights.

The divergent findings that we observed in our review might also be related to studies relying, almost exclusively, on linear models. The relationships between downsizing and firm performance may not be necessarily linear; yet research on the exploration of non-linear effects is virtually non-existent. It can be argued that too low or too high a level of downsizing is likely to be suboptimal from the standpoint of firm performance. In other words, the relationship may be curvilinear. Another limitation of extant research is that most studies have focused on the direct relationship between downsizing and organizational performance. They are generally based on the assumption that downsizing impacts performance via employee-related effects. However, researchers have failed to specifically assess such effects on the performance implications of downsizing. Extensive research (e.g., Armstrong-Stassen and Schlosser, 2008; Brockner and Greenberg, 1990; Brockner and Wiesenfeld, 1993; Greenhalgh and Rosenblatt, 1984; Travaglione and Cross, 2006) on the behavioral outcomes of downsizing using multiple theoretical perspectives (e.g., those related to equity, organizational justice, job insecurity, job redesign, uncertainty, and organizational stress) suggests that downsizing manifests itself in the form of significant negative survivor reactions during the implementation process. Unfortunately, very few studies have examined the mediating role of behavioral outcomes in explaining downsizing performance (especially, profitability and firm value). Research which informs managers on how the implementation processes can be improved by taking into consideration key behavioral issues surrounding employee reductions will undoubtedly be an important contribution to the literature on downsizing.

To facilitate an improved understanding of the downsizing phenomenon and its performance implications, we suggest that such effects be assessed at multiple levels. Studies that combine outcomes at both the individual and the organizational levels through the use of hierarchical linear modeling (HLM) techniques to accommodate multi-level measures and designs should provide interesting insights. In addition, future research can benefit from greater use of structural equation modeling (SEM) that allows downsizing attributes to be included both as exogenous and endogenous variables. In addition, there is need for research on how downsizing processes impact outcomes. Extant research has generally treated the implementation process as a "black box." Yet, as the study by Carswell (2005) suggests, how employment downsizing is implemented and whether affected parties perceive the process as being "fair" has much to do with whether downsizing goals are met. The negative performance outcomes associated with employment downsizing may not solely reflect problems with downsizing decisions *per se*, but may be a function of the conditions under which downsizing is initiated or the approach used in its implementation. In other words, negative outcomes may result from a failure on the part of the firm to meet the organizational requirements of effective employee downsizing, suggesting the need to delve deeper into more complex relationships in examining downsizing performance.

A couple of studies in Stream II (Espahbodi *et al.*, 2000; Kang and Shivdasani, 1997) on the effects of downsizing on firm profitability observed an interesting phenomenon. They found that while firms experienced weak profitability in the period immediately following downsizing, performance improved in the longer term (third or fourth years after downsizing). It would be interesting to further explore the causes behind this phenomenon. To do so, researchers can fruitfully employ longitudinal designs wherein they record the characteristics of the downsizing events and also of the implementation process via regularly scheduled observations over an extended period. The findings of such research should have important implications from the standpoint of managers involved in downsizing. They need to be aware that employee downsizing represents more than just reductions in headcount with cost-related benefits. Indeed, as our review indicates, in the short term the benefits are often more than offset by the problems (structural and otherwise) that are associated with the implementation of a downsizing. Overall, when managing a layoff, managers need to be cognizant of the various procedural factors that might jeopardize downsizing success. Future research that emphasizes the identification of key issues in the various stages of the implementation process using appropriate longitudinal data should be particularly valuable in informing managers on how best to manage the downsizing process.

Given evidence that downsizing is often detrimental to firm performance, perhaps now is the right time to consider the implication of such findings from the perspective of public policy. Apart from the WARN (Worker Adjustment and Retraining Notification Act), which requires employers with more than 100 employees to give 60 days or more advance notice in plant closings and mass layoffs, there is no legislation which regulates US firms that are contemplating layoffs. In Europe, where public policy on downsizing dictates mandatory severance packages in many countries, firms are often required to consult with work councils (elected work representatives) and inform special government agencies of their intent to downsize. In the case of Germany, a social plan covering the compensation for laid-off workers acceptable to both the firm and work council must first be crafted. Such consultations with workers and governmental agencies may prove beneficial as it might result in firms more actively examining alternatives to downsizing. Additionally, the government can utilize its resources and provide benefits to firms that maintain stable employment levels that may hopefully discourage firms from using layoffs as their first recourse. The findings of this review also have important implications for managerial practice. With a majority of studies indicating that downsizing does not, on average, result in expected benefits, managers need to pay greater attention to the circumstances under which downsizing might be appropriate. In some instances, downsizing may be averted via alternative actions. For example, if downsizing is being considered in the context of a temporary economic downturn, such actions can include the freezing of salaries, temporary cuts in benefits, elimination of overtime, and the implementation of reduced hours and furloughs.

In conclusion, while employment downsizing has become a ubiquitous feature of organizational life, we do not have a definite answer to the question on whether such downsizing results in desired organizational outcomes. As our review indicates, there has been considerable research on the performance implications of employment downsizing; however, the findings have been characterized by considerable ambiguity. The equivocal findings, in turn, suggest the need for additional research aimed at obtaining a better understanding of when and how downsizing creates value. We believe that future research aimed at addressing some of the issues identified above, using relevant methodologies, will provide some of the insights that we need to better comprehend the complex relationship between employee downsizing and organizational performance.

## References

Allen, T. D., Freeman, D. M., Russell, J. E., Reizenstein, R. C., and Rentz, J. 2001. "Survivor reactions to organizational downsizing: Does time ease the pain?" *Journal of Occupational and Organizational Psychology* **74**(2): 145–164.

Armstrong-Stassen, M. and Schlosser, F. K. 2008. "Taking a positive approach to organizational downsizing." *Canadian Journal of Administrative Sciences* **25**: 93–106.

Atanassov, J. and Kim, H. 2009. "Labor and corporate governance: International evidence from restructuring decisions." *The Journal of Finance* **64**(1): 341–374.

Barreto, I. and Baden-Fuller, C. 2006. "To conform or to perform? Mimetic behaviour, legitimacy-based groups and performance consequences." *Journal of Management Studies* **43**(7): 1559–1581.

Baumol, W. J., Blinder, A., and Wolff, E. N. 2003. *Downsizing in America: Reality, Causes, and Consequences*. New York: Russell Sage Foundation.

Brockner, J. and Greenberg, J. 1990. "The impact of layoffs on survivors: An organizational justice perspective," in J. Carroll (ed.), *Advances in Applied Social Psychology Business Settings*. Hillsdale, NJ: Lawrence Erlbaum Associates.

Brockner, J. and Wiesenfeld, B. M. 1993. "Living on the edge (of social and organizational psychology): The effects of layoffs on those who remain," in J. K. Murnighan (ed.), *Social Psychology in Organizations: Advances in Theory and Research*. Englewood Cliffs: Prentice Hall, pp. 119–140.

Brockner, J., Sprietzer, G., Mishra, A., Hochwarter, W., Pepper, L., and Weinberg, J. 2004. "Perceived control as an antidote to the negative effects of layoffs on survivors' organizational commitment and job performance." *Administrative Science Quarterly* **49**: 76–100.

Brookman, J. T., Chang, S., and Rennie, C. G. 2007. "CEO cash and stock-based compensation changes, layoff decisions, and shareholder value." *Financial Review* **42**: 99–119.

Bruton, G. D., Keels, J. K., and Shook, C. L. 1996. "Downsizing the firm: Answering the strategic questions." *Academy of Management Executive* **10**: 38–43.

Budros, A. 1999. "A conceptual framework for analyzing why organizations downsize." *Organization Science* **10**: 69–84.

Bullon, F. and Bueno, M. J. 2010. "Downsizing implementation and financial performance." *Management Decision* **48**(8): 1181–1197.

Bureau of Labor Statistics, Mass Layoffs, http://data.bls.gov/pdq/SurveyOutputServlet?data_tool=latest_numbers&series_id=MLSMS00N-N0119005 and http://data.bls.gov/pdq/SurveyOutputServlet?data_tool=latest_numbers&series_id=MLSMS00N0119003. Accessed on 02/03/2011.

Burns, L. R. and Wholey, D. R. 1993. "Adoption and abandonment of matrix management programs: Effects of organizational characteristics and interorganizational networks." *Academy of Management Journal* **36**: 106–138.

Cagle, J., Sen, A., and Pawlukiewicz, J. 2009. "Inter-industry differences in layoff announcement effects for financial institutions." *Journal of Economics and Finance* **33**(1): 100–110.

Cameron, K. S., Freeman, S. J., and Mishra, A. K. 1993. "Downsizing and redesigning organizations," in G. P. Huber and W. H. Glick (eds.), *Organizational Change and Redesign*. New York: Oxford University Press, pp. 19–65.

Carswell, P. J. 2005. "The financial impact of organisational downsizing practices," *The New Zealand Experience* **22**: 41–63.

Cascio, W. F. 2002. *Managing Human Resources, Productivity, Quality of Work Life, Profits* (6th edn.). New York: McGraw-Hill.

Cascio, W. F. and Young, C. E. 2003. "Financial consequences of employment-change decisions in major US corporations, 1982–2000," in K. P. De Meuse and M. L. Marks (eds.), *Resizing the Organization: Managing Layoffs, Divestitures, and Closings*. San Francisco, CA: Jossey-Bass.

Cascio, W. F., Young, C. E., and Morris, J. R. 1997. "Financial consequences of employment-change decisions in major US corporations." *Academy of Management Journal* **40**: 1175–1189.

Chadwick, C., Hunter, L. W., and Walston, S. L. 2004. "Effects of downsizing practices on the performance of hospitals." *Strategic Management Journal* **25**: 405–427.

Chalos, P. and Chen, C. J. P. 2002. "Employee downsizing strategies: Market reaction and post announcement financial performance." *Journal of Business Finance and Accounting* **29**(5/6): 847–870.

Chatrath, A., Ramchander, S., and Song, F. 1995. "Are market perceptions of corporate layoffs changing?" *Economics Letters* **47**(3–4): 335–342.

Chen, P., Mehrotra, V., Sivakumar, R., and Yu, W. W. 2001. "Layoffs, shareholders' wealth, and corporate performance." *Journal of Empirical Finance* **8**: 171–199.

Dacin, M. T. 1997. "Isomorphism in context: The power and prescription of institutional norms." *Academy of Management Journal* **40**(1): 46–81.

Datta, D. K., Guthrie, J. P., Basuil, D., and Pandey, A. 2010. "Causes and effects of employee downsizing: A review and synthesis." *Journal of Management* **36**: 281–348.

De Meuse, K. P., Bergmann, T. J., Vanderheiden, P. A., and Roraff, C. E. 2004. "New evidence regarding organizational downsizing and a firm's financial performance: A long-term analysis." *Journal of Managerial Issues* **16**(2): 155–177.

De Meuse, K. P., Vanderheiden, P. A., and Bergmann, T. J. 1994. "Announced layoffs: Their effect on corporate financial performance." *Human Resource Management* **33**(4): 509–530.

DiMaggio, P. and Powell, W. 1983. "The iron cage revisited: Institutional isomorphism and collective rationality in organizational fields." *American Sociological Review* **48**(2): 147–160.

Dong, X. and Xu, L. 2008. "The impact of China's millennium labour restructuring program on firm performance and employee earnings." *Economics of Transition* **16**(2): 223–245.

Elayan, F. A., Swales, G. S., Maris, B. A., and Scott, J. R. 1998. "Market reactions, characteristics, and the effectiveness of corporate layoffs." *Journal of Business Finance and Accounting* **25**(3–4): 329–351.

Espahbodi, R., John, T. A., and Vasudevan, G. 2000. "The effects of downsizing on operating performance." *Review of Quantitative Finance and Accounting* **15**: 107–126.

Franz, D. R., Crawford, D., and Dwyer, D. J. 1998. "Downsizing corporate performance, and shareholder wealth." *Mid-American Journal of Business* **13**(1): 11–19.

Goins, S. and Gruca, T. S. 2008. "Understanding competitive and contagion effects of layoff announcements." *Corporate Reputation Review* **11**(1): 12–34.

Greenhalgh, L. and Rosenblatt, Z. 1984. "Job insecurity: Toward conceptual clarity." *Academy of Management Review* **9**: 438–448.

Guthrie, J. P. and Datta, D. K. 2008. "Dumb and dumber: The impact of downsizing on firm performance as moderated by industry conditions." *Organization Science* **19**(1): 108–123.

Hallock, K. F. 1998. "Layoffs, top executive pay, and firm performance." *American Economic Review* **88**(4): 711–723.

Haunschild, P. R. 1993. "Interorganizational imitation: The impact of interlocks on corporate acquisition activity." *Administrative Science Quarterly* **38**: 564–592.

Haveman, H. A. 1993. "Following the leader: Mimetic isomorphism and entry into new markets." *Administrative Science Quarterly* **38**: 593–627.

Henkoff, R. 1994. "Getting beyond downsizing." *Fortune* **129**(1): 58–64.

Hillier, D., Marshall, A. P., McColgan, P., and Werema, S. 2007. "Employee layoffs, shareholder wealth and firm performance: Evidence from the UK." *Journal of Business Finance and Accounting* **34**(3 and 4): 467–494.

Iqbal, Z. and Shetty, S. 1995. "Layoffs, stock price, and financial condition of the firm." *Journal of Applied Business Research* **11**(2): 67–72.

Kang, J. K. and Shivdasani, A. 1997. "Corporate restructuring during performance declines in Japan." *Journal of Financial Economics* **46**: 29–65.

Kets de Vries M. and Balazs, K. 1997. "The downside of downsizing." *Human Relations* **50**: 11–50.

Lee, P. M. 1997. "A comparative analysis of layoff announcements and stock price reactions in the United States and Japan." *Strategic Management Journal* **18**: 879–894.

Linn, J. and Rozeff, M. S. 1993. "Capital market behavior and operational announcements of layoffs, operation closings, and pay cuts." *Review of Quantitative Finance and Accounting* **3**(1): 29–45.

Love, E. G. and Nohria, N. 2005. "Reducing slack: The performance consequences of downsizing by large industrial firms, 1977–93." *Strategic Management Journal* **26**: 1087–1108.

Luthans, B. C. and Sommer, S. M. 1999. "The impact of downsizing on workplace attitudes: Differing reactions of managers and staff in a health care organization." *Group Organization Management* **24**: 46–70.

Madura, J., Aigbe, A., and Kenneth, B. 1995. "Intra-industry effects of bank layoff announcements." *Review of Financial Economics* **4**: 187–195.

McElroy, J. C., Morrow, P. C., and Rude, S. N. 2001. "Turnover and organizational performance: A comparative analysis of the effects of voluntary, involuntary, and reduction-in-force turnover." *Journal of Applied Psychology* **86**: 1294–1299.

Mishra, A. K. and Mishra, K. E. 1994. "The role of mutual trust in effective downsizing strategies." *Human Resource Management* **33**(2): 261–279.

Mitchell, M. and Stafford, E. 2000. "Managerial decisions and long-term stock-price performance." *Journal of Business* **73**(3): 287–329.

Morrison, E. W. and Robinson, S. L. 1997. "When employees feel betrayed: A model of how psychological contract violation develops." *Academy of Management Review* **22**(1): 226–257.

Mowday, R., Porter, L., and Steers, R. 1982. "Employee–organization linkages," in P. Warr (ed.), *Organizational and Occupational Psychology*. New York: Academic Press, pp. 219–229.

Nixon, R. D., Hitt, M. A., Lee, H., and Jeong, E. 2004. "Market reactions to announcements of corporate downsizing actions and implementation strategies." *Strategic Management Journal* **25**: 1121–1129.

O'Shaughnessy, K. C. and Flanagan, D. J. 1998. "Determinants of layoff announcements following M&As: An empirical investigation." *Strategic Management Journal* **19**: 989–999.

Palmon, O., Sun, H., and Tang, A. 1997. "Layoff announcements: Stock market impact and financial performance." *Financial Management* **26**: 54–68.

Perry, T. and Shivdasani, A. 2005. "Do boards affect performance? Evidence from corporate restructuring." *Journal of Business* **78**(4): 1403–1431.

Pfeffer, J. 1998. *The Human Equation: Building Profits by Putting People First*. Boston, MA: Harvard Business School Press.

Robinson, S. L. 1996. "Trust and breach of the psychological contract." *Administrative Science Quarterly* **41**: 574–599.

Rousseau, D. M. and Tijoriwala, S. A. 1998. "Assessing psychological contracts: Issues, alternatives and measures." *Journal of Organizational Behavior* **19**: 679–695.

Said, T., Le Louarn, J., and Tremblay, M. 2007. "The performance effects of major workforce reductions: Longitudinal evidence from North America." *International Journal of Human Resource Management* **18**(12): 2075–2094.

Suárez-González, I. 2001. "Downsizing strategy: Does it really improve organizational performance?" *International Journal of Management* **18**(3): 301–307.

Travaglione, A. and Cross, B. 2006. "Diminishing the social network in organizations: Does there need to be such a phenomenon as 'survivor syndrome' after downsizing?" *Strategic Change* **15**: 1–13.

Wagar, T. 1998. "Exploring the consequences of workforce reduction." *Canadian Journal of Administrative Sciences* **15**(4): 300–309.

Wayhan, V. B. and Werner, S. 2000. "The impact of workforce reductions on financial performance: A longitudinal perspective." *Journal of Management* **26**: 341–363.

Westphal, J., Gulati, R., and Shortell, S. 1997. "Customization or conformity? An institutional and network perspective on the content and consequences of TQM adoption." *Administrative Science Quarterly* **42**: 366–392.

Williamson, I. O. and Cable, D. M. 2003. "Predicting early career research productivity: The case of management faculty." *Journal of Organizational Behavior* **24**: 25–44.

Worrell, D. L., Davidson III, W. N., and Sharma. V. M. 1991. "Layoff announcements and stockholder wealth." *Academy of Management Journal* **43**: 662–678.

Yu, G. and Park J. 2006. "The effect of downsizing on the financial performance and employee productivity of Korean firms." *International Journal of Manpower* **27**(3): 230–250.

Zatzick, C. D. and Iverson, R. D. 2006. "High-involvement management and workforce reduction: Competitive advantage or disadvantage?" *Academy of Management Journal* **49**(5): 999–1015.

# 8 *Executive perceptions: Probing the institutionalization of organizational downsizing*

WILLIAM McKINLEY AND JASMIN CHIA-JUNG LIN

## Introduction

Organizational downsizing surrounds us. There was a significant surge in organizational downsizing in public sector organizations in the late 1970s and early 1980s (Bozeman and Slusher, 1979; Glassberg, 1978; Levine, 1978). In the late 1980s and the 1990s, organizational downsizing also became prominent in the private sector (Freeman and Cameron, 1993). By one estimate (Kozlowski, Chao, Smith, and Hedlund, 1993), 66 percent of firms with more than 500 employees intentionally reduced their workforces during the latter half of the 1980s. During that entire decade, several million manufacturing jobs were lost through downsizing (Kozlowski *et al.*, 1993). According to Littler and Innes (2004), the pace of private sector downsizing in the 1990s was similar, with 68 percent of organizations represented in a 1992 British Institute of Management Survey reporting a delayering or restructuring exercise in the previous five years.

More recently, organizational downsizing has undergone another renaissance in the public sector, with deficit-ridden state and municipal governments in the United States laying off teachers, furloughing workers, and taking other workforce reduction measures in an attempt to shrink the size and cost of government (e.g., Medina, 2011; Otterman, 2011). In Europe, the bursting of the housing and banking bubbles have produced implosions in economies, such as those of Ireland and Spain, and these implosions have led to higher interest rates on government debt, austerity policies, and intense bond market pressure for downsizing of government work forces.

Given the prevalence of downsizing in the private and public sectors over the last four decades, considerable academic attention has been focused on this phenomenon. In the scholarly literature, organizational downsizing is usually defined as an intentional reduction of an organization's workforce with the goal of improving the organization's effectiveness (Freeman and Cameron, 1993; McKinley, Zhao, and Rust, 2000). As an intentional strategy, organizational downsizing is distinguished from organizational decline, which is normally conceptualized as an unintended erosion of organizational resources that is not planned or desired by the organization's managers (Cameron, Kim, and Whetten, 1987; Freeman and Cameron, 1993; McKinley *et al.*, 2000). Scholarly recognition of the difference between organizational downsizing and organizational decline has led to the bifurcation of the management literatures on these two topics (see McKinley, 1993; Mone, McKinley, and Barker, 1998 for reviews of the organizational decline literature).

In the organizational downsizing literature, most of the scholarly effort has been devoted to understanding the consequences of organizational downsizing. Perhaps the most developed stream in this domain is a series of studies focusing on the effects of downsizing on the financial performance of the organizations that engage in it. Though managers generally downsize with the expectation that reduction in their organizations' workforces will reduce costs and increase profitability (McKinley *et al.*, 2000), there is little evidence that these outcomes are reliably achieved. A portion of the existing research suggests that downsizing has little discernible effect on accounting measures of financial performance (e.g., Cascio, Young, and Morris, 1997; Mentzer, 1996; Wayhan and Werner, 2000), while other work concludes that downsizing reduces return on investment or return on assets in those firms that practice it (Chadwick, Hunter, and Walston, 2004; Krishnan, Hitt, and Park, 2007; Guthrie and Datta, 2008; Gandolfi, 2008).

These negative effects are paralleled by the uniformly negative effects that layoff announcements have on the market-adjusted stock prices of firms (Capelle-Blancard and Couderc, 2007). Studies by Worrell, Davidson, and Sharma (1991), Lee (1997), and Nixon, Hitt, Lee, and Jeong (2004), among others, have showed that layoff announcements are followed by reductions in shareholder wealth, though this effect seems to be moderated by the framing of the layoff announcement (Worrell *et al.*, 1991). Thus the overall conclusion from the shareholder wealth studies is that layoff announcements constitute a negative signal to investors, causing them to infer that the announcing firm is in trouble and its equity should be divested. Such negative signals are also implied by recent studies that show a negative influence of downsizing on the reputation of corporations (Flanagan and O'Shaugnessy, 2005; Love and Kraatz, 2009).

A second distinct stream of work in the "consequences of downsizing" literature focuses on the effects of organizational downsizing on organizational structure. Early work in this stream (Freeman and Hannan, 1975; Littler and Innes, 1999; McKinley, 1992, Mentzer and Near, 1992; Sutton and D'Aunno, 1989) concluded that reduction in workforce size does not necessarily reverse the influence of growing size (Blau, 1970) on the structure of organizations. Therefore downsizing is not automatically a route to a leaner, less complex organizational structure. Later research (Amabile and Conti, 1999; Dougherty and Bowman, 1995; Fisher and White, 2000; Shah, 2000) has stressed the destructive impact of organizational downsizing on the networks that support learning and innovation in organizations. By removing workers who constitute important nodes in these networks, downsizing can undercut an organization's capacity to adjust to environmental change by producing new products and services. Though theory and empirical research have not yet focused on the issue, it is possible that these consequences mediate the negative effects of downsizing on financial performance.

On a more micro-level of analysis, several streams in the "consequences of downsizing" literature have investigated the influence of downsizing on various participants in the workforce reduction process: "victims," survivors, and layoff agents. Victims are those employees who lose their jobs as the result of a downsizing, and existing research (e.g., Leana and Feldman, 1992; Leana and Ivancevich, 1987; Pugh, Skarlicki, and Passell, 2003) emphasizes the stress that job loss creates for those subject to it. Parallel investigations of the impact of downsizing on survivors, those who remain in the organization after a downsizing episode, show similar psychological consequences, including guilt, job insecurity, and mistrust of management (Brockner, 1988; Brockner, Davy, and Carter, 1985; Brockner, Grover, O'Malley, Reed, and Glynn, 1993). These outcomes are apparently moderated by the perceived justice of the downsizing and the degree to which acquaintances who are victims receive assistance (Brockner, Grover, Reed, DeWitt, and O'Malley, 1987), as well as by survivor optimism (Armstrong-Stassen and Schlosser, 2008). However, there seems to be little doubt that being a survivor of a downsizing is stressful.

Finally, a growing stream of work (Clair and Dufresne, 2004; Grunberg, Moore, and Greenberg, 2006; Kets de Vries and Balazs,

1997) has begun to investigate the consequences that participation in organizational downsizing has for layoff agents. Layoff agents are those employees who participate in planning layoffs, deciding which workers will lose their jobs, and delivering the bad news to victims. Interestingly, the field research conducted by those scholars cited above suggests that the layoff agency role is as debilitating for its occupants as the victim role or the survivor role. Experimental work by Folger and Skarlicki (1998) tends to confirm that conclusion by indicating that managers have a tendency to distance themselves from victims as bad news is being delivered. Seeking to integrate the existing research on layoff agency, Parker and McKinley (2008) proposed a theory of layoff agency that focused on the cognitive dissonance created by the layoff agency role. Parker and McKinley (2008) postulated that the layoff agency–cognitive dissonance relationship will be moderated by a number of variables at the industry, organizational, and cognitive levels of analysis, such as the layoff agent's past experience with layoffs and the layoff agent's belief in certain business ideologies.

Considerably less effort has been devoted to understanding the causes of organizational downsizing than has been allocated to research on the consequences of downsizing. Even so, a significant body of material has accumulated in this domain as well. For example, Budros (1997, 1999, 2001, 2002, 2004) has published several comprehensive theoretical models and empirical studies that identify variables that influence the incidence and magnitude of downsizing. For example, Budros's (1997) empirical study concluded that declining market share, low productivity, low shareholder value, and large organizational size were all determinants of downsizing events. Budros (2001) expanded his investigation of downsizing events to include early retirement programs in universities, and he reported that dependence on government funding and funding decline at the university level were both predictors of early retirement programs. Budros (2002) distinguished between voluntary and involuntary downsizing programs, comparing the factors that influenced the probability of each of these types of programs. In work that paralleled Budros's studies, Filotachev, Buck, and Zhukov (2000) analyzed downsizing in privatized firms in Russia, Ukraine, and Belarus, singling out industry decline and non-management shareholding as stimuli for firm downsizing, and managerial ownership of equity as a barrier to downsizing.

Because of the negative consequences of downsizing for financial performance listed above, and the disruptive impact that downsizing apparently has on internal social networks, on victims, and on survivors, several theorists have surmised that organizational downsizing is not a rational process, and have attempted to explain the phenomenon with theory that deviates from assumptions of managerial rationality. The most commonly invoked framework is neo-institutional theory (DiMaggio and Powell, 1983; Meyer and Rowan, 1977). For example, McKinley, Sanchez, and Schick (1995) argued that downsizing has diffused through the mimetic, coercive, and normative isomorphic processes that DiMaggio and Powell (1983) described. McKinley *et al.* (1995) labeled these isomorphic processes "cloning," "constraining," and "learning." McKinley *et al.* (2000) offered a socio-cognitive model of organizational downsizing, in which they attempted to trace the historical evolution in the schematic representations of downsizing held by managers, and the effects of that evolution on the institutionalization of downsizing. Ahmadjian and Robinson (2001) also took a neo-institutional perspective, conceptualizing downsizing in Japanese firms as an indicator of the de-institutionalization of the practice of lifetime employment. Ahmadjian and Robinson (2001) explored the causes of this de-institutionalization, as represented by the deconstructive practice of downsizing. Alakent and Lee (2010) reported a similar analysis for Korean firms, arguing, like Ahmadjian and Robinson, that financial constraints have led to downsizing, while large organizational size, organizational age, social embeddedness, and other correlates of prominence and high reputation have retarded acquiescence to downsizing. Finally, Lamertz and Baum (1998) traced the evolution in explanatory media accounts about downsizing in Canadian newspapers, suggesting that these accounts reveal an increasingly taken-for-granted status for downsizing over time.

Although the neo-institutional and socio-cognitive approaches to explaining downsizing are promising, we cannot necessarily assume that downsizing is irrational when viewed from the perspective of the executive, because executives almost certainly are not privy to the academic research detailing the negative consequences of downsizing. Executives are probably much more heavily influenced by viewpoints espoused by Wall Street security analysts and by consultants, which communicate the message that downsizing is financially effective, and that protecting the interests of employees simply hurts the bottom line

(Cappelli, Bassi, Katz, Knoke, Osterman, and Useem, 1997). For better or worse, organizational downsizing does not appear to be an "evidence-based" (Pfeffer and Sutton, 2006) management enterprise. This suggests that if we wish to understand the spread of organizational downsizing, we must examine the perspective of the executive, and focus on executive perceptions of the downsizing phenomenon.

Perceptions of organizational downsizing have been studied before; for example, Sronce and McKinley (2006) measured perceptions of downsizing along four distinct dimensions. Those dimensions were the degree to which downsizing is perceived as financially effective, the degree to which downsizing is perceived as inevitable, the degree to which downsizing is perceived as liberating for layoff victims (Noer, 1993), and the degree to which downsizing is perceived as a breach of the implicit contract between employer and employee (Rousseau, 1995; Edwards, Rust, McKinley, and Moon, 2003). Also, Skarlicki, Ellard, and Kelln (1998) studied third-party perceptions of a layoff, concentrating on the degree to which the layoff was perceived as procedurally just. However, the perceptions studied by researchers such as Sronce and McKinley (2006) and Skarlicki *et al.* (1998) were investigated as dependent variables, and no study, to our knowledge, has used perceptions of downsizing as independent variables that might explain the incidence and the institutionalization of the phenomenon.

In this chapter, we seek to fill that gap. We assume that executive perceptions of downsizing are an important stimulus for organizational downsizing activity and the institutionalization of downsizing, and we attempt to develop a theoretical model that articulates those causal relationships. In particular, we focus on two perceptual dimensions studied by Sronce and McKinley (2006): the perception that downsizing is financially effective and the perception that downsizing is inevitable. We believe that these perceptions will vary across groups of executives in different populations or organizational fields (DiMaggio and Powell, 1983; Hannan and Freeman, 1977), and we argue that this variance is an important determinant of the level of downsizing activity in an organizational population or field. Also, the effects of executive perceptions of downsizing on the level of downsizing activity will be moderated by executive power and past executive experience with planning and executing downsizing. The high incidence of downsizing that is driven by executive perceptions that downsizing is financially effective and executive perceptions that downsizing is inevitable then institutionalizes downsizing, fostering the impression that it is legitimate and natural. This leads to the paradox that a practice that is instigated, at least in part, by subjective cognitions of executives comes eventually to be seen by observers as an objectified entity beyond the control of those executives (Berger and Luckmann, 1967).

In developing our model, we also argue that the institutionalization of downsizing has feedback effects on the perceptions of executives, reinforcing the perceptions of financial effectiveness and the perceptions of inevitability that stimulate high levels of downsizing in the first place. In this way, we portray the institutionalization of organizational downsizing as a self-reinforcing process that is dependent on a continuing stream of executive perceptions, organizational downsizing activity, and objectification of the practice represented by the activity.

This model contributes to current efforts to understand the spread of organizational downsizing in the absence of documented positive effects of downsizing for organizational performance and for the employees and managers who are affected by the practice. The model generates novel insights by locating the causal impetus for downsizing activity and the institutionalization of downsizing in the cognitions of the executives who have authority over decisions about downsizing. However, we make no claim that these cognitions are the only drivers of the organizational downsizing process. Still, an effort to understand organizational downsizing from the point of view of the executive is arguably long overdue. At each stage in the description of our model, we state propositions that summarize the theoretical logic we are presenting, so that those propositions can be a guide for future empirical research. At the end of the chapter, in the discussion section, we focus on implications of our model for future empirical research, and describe some tentative approaches that might be used to test the propositions. We also devote some space to implications for future management practice, which are important given the key role played by executives in the implementation of intentional workforce reduction.

## Theoretical framework

### *Perceptions of downsizing and downsizing activity*

As noted above, Sronce and McKinley (2006) measured perceptions of organizational downsizing along several dimensions, but the two most relevant for our theoretical model here are the perception that organizational downsizing is financially effective and the perception that organizational downsizing is inevitable. Sronce and McKinley (2006) pointed out that observer perceptions that downsizing is financially effective may be stimulated by the business press and also by certain managerial ideologies (see also McKinley, Mone, and Barker, 1998). Sronce and McKinley (2006) also theorized that layoff agency will stimulate perceptions that downsizing is financially effective, because layoff agents will attempt to compensate for the cognitive dissonance promoted by participation in the layoff process by adopting this positive perception of downsizing. Sronce and McKinley (2006) also showed that layoff agency and managerial ideologies were stimuli for the perception that downsizing is inevitable. Moving beyond Sronce and McKinley (2006), however, in this chapter we are less concerned about the origins of perceptions of downsizing than with their causal effects when they are present in powerful executives with authority to order workforce reductions.

Sronce and McKinley (2006) measured variation in perceptions of downsizing's financial effectiveness through items designed to elicit subjects' degree of belief that organizational downsizing improves companies' financial performance, that organizational downsizing helps the balance sheet, and that organizational downsizing restores companies to financial health. Here we argue that if executives perceive downsizing as financially effective, their motivation to engage in the practice will increase, because financial effectiveness is a desired outcome for most organizations, especially profit-making firms (McKinley *et al.*, 2000). The motivation to downsize will often be translated into a decision to downsize, increasing downsizing activity in the industries or populations to which the executives holding perceptions that downsizing is financially effective belong. When executives perceive that downsizing is financially effective, their expectations of positive financial returns or efficiency following a downsizing are enhanced, and they are more likely to engage in downsizing in pursuit of such outcomes. Irrespective of the actual outcomes of downsizing, which may follow a downsizing episode by a considerable interval and may not be easily monitored by executives, executives' *ex ante* beliefs in the effectiveness of the practice will lead those executives to engage in downsizing activity. This leads to the first of the propositions in our theoretical framework:

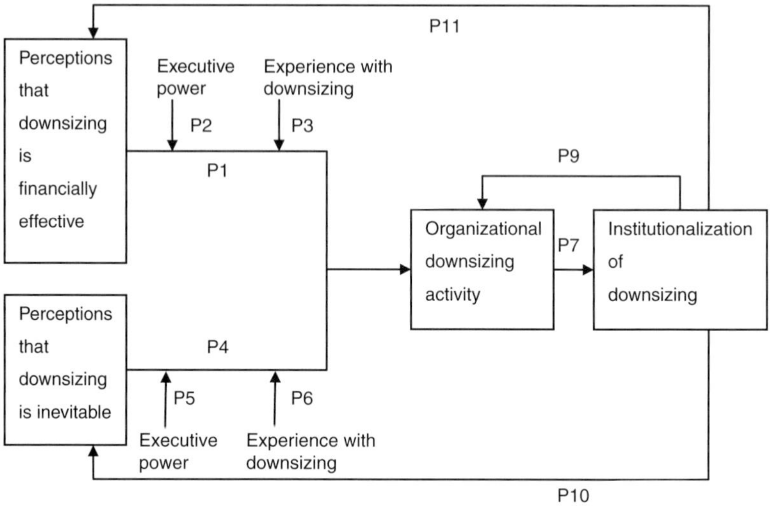


**Figure 8.1** Executive perceptions, downsizing activity, and the institutionalization of downsizing

*Proposition 1: The stronger executive perceptions that downsizing is financially effective, the greater the subsequent downsizing activity.*

"Downsizing activity," as we use the term, can refer either to the frequency of downsizing programs in a population or industry, or the average size of the workforce reductions being implemented in that industry over a particular period of time. The causal effect predicted by our first proposition is represented by the arrow labeled P1 at the top left-hand side of Figure 8.1.

While executive perceptions that downsizing is financially effective are likely to stimulate organizational downsizing activity, the capacity of executives to translate their beliefs and motivations about downsizing into action will depend on their power. The construct of power has been extensively studied in the organization studies literature (e.g., Pfeffer and Salancik, 1974, 1978; Salancik and Pfeffer, 1974), and power can be usefully conceptualized as the obverse of dependence (Emerson, 1962; Blau, 1964). Thus executives have power to the extent that they are dependent on few other persons for critical resources or for resolution of strategic problems (Hickson, Hinings, Lee, Schneck, and Pennings, 1971), and also to the extent that many others are dependent on them for such resources and resolutions. If an executive has power, it is more likely that the vision of downsizing's financial effectiveness can be promoted to other executives in the top management team (Hambrick and Mason, 1984). Statements from executives about the financial benefits of downsizing are more likely to be plausible to the extent that the executives have power, since power is an important determinant of the construction of knowledge (Calas and Smircich, 1999; see also Donaldson, 2003). Thus the combination of executive power with a strong belief in the financial effectiveness of downsizing should be a particularly potent stimulus for subsequent downsizing activity, as expressed in Proposition 2:

*Proposition 2: Executive perceptions that downsizing is financially effective will have a stronger positive effect on subsequent downsizing activity when executive power is high than when executive power is low.*

This moderating effect is captured by the vertical arrow labeled P2 at the top left-hand side of Figure 8.1.

While executive power frees executives from constraints that might otherwise be imposed by their external networks, constraints imposed by the executives' internal psychology are another matter. In particular, executives who believe that downsizing is financially effective may still be hesitant to engage in the practice even if they have the power to persuade other members of the top management team that it is the right thing to do. This hesitation may stem from residual concerns about negative outcomes for the employees who would be victims of the downsizing and the employees who would be survivors of the process. An executive may see downsizing as a "necessary evil" (Molinsky and Margolis, 2005) – necessary because it will improve financial returns or efficiency, but evil because there is the possibility of disrupting the lives of those whose jobs will be lost and those who must carry on after the downsizing. If the "evil" component of this equation is salient in the executive's cognitions, the executive may hesitate to authorize a downsizing program even if the executive has the power to implement it.

We argue that such hesitation to downsize will be stronger the less experience the executive has with past downsizing programs (Parker and McKinley, 2008). If the executive has conducted few (or no) previous downsizings, the cognitive dissonance (Festinger, 1957) inherent in the juxtaposition of perceived organizational benefit with potential employee damage will loom large. On the other hand, if the executive has conducted downsizings before, downsizing programs will have become more routine, and it is more likely that she will have discovered ways to insulate herself psychologically from the negative consequences that any decision made may have for downsizing victims, survivors, and middle management layoff agents (Folger and Skarlicki, 1998). In Molinsky and Margolis's (2005) terms, the executive will have become a more competent practitioner of the "necessary evil" of downsizing. Because of this competence, psychological barriers to implementing downsizing will be lowered. This is consistent with Parker and McKinley's (2008) argument that layoff agent experience reduces the effect that layoff agency has on the layoff agent's cognitive dissonance. We summarize our logic in a third proposition:

*Proposition 3: Executive perceptions that downsizing is financially effective will have a stronger positive effect on subsequent downsizing activity when executives have long experience with downsizing than when their experience is short.*

The moderating effect postulated in Proposition 3 is represented by the vertical arrow labeled P3 at the upper left-hand side of Figure 8.1.

Sronce and McKinley (2006) also measured a second perceptual attribute – the degree to which downsizing is perceived as inevitable. McKinley *et al.* (2000) pointed out that downsizing is portrayed as inevitable in many business press articles and statements from top managers (Lamertz and Baum, 1998; Palmer, Kabanoff, and Dunford, 1997). Executives exposed to such material may come to believe in the inevitability of downsizing also. Sronce and McKinley (2006) measured the perceived inevitability of downsizing with items such as "organizational downsizing is a natural law of capitalism," "organizational downsizing is an inevitable fact of corporate life," and "organizational downsizing is an expected part of the business cycle." When grouped with the items measuring perceptions of downsizing's financial effectiveness and the items measuring perception of downsizing along other dimensions, the items measuring the perceived inevitability of downsizing clustered on their own factor (Sronce and McKinley, 2006). This supports the conclusion that perceived inevitability is an independent dimension from perceived financial effectiveness, perceived liberation potential (Noer, 1993; Sronce and McKinley, 2006), and perceived contract breach (Rousseau, 1995; Sronce and McKinley, 2006).

If executives believe that organizational downsizing is inevitable, it is likely that they will feel increased pressure to downsize, because they will be motivated to "get the jump" on competitors who will soon be engaging in the same action. If downsizing is seen as inevitable, acquiring whatever advantages it may bestow on one's organization requires moving quickly, before those advantages are eroded by competitors moving forward with their own downsizing programs. Thus, a perception that downsizing is inevitable should be a strong motivator to downsize, and it seems unlikely that executives will be deterred by the possibility that choices motivated by their perceptions of inevitability actually counter the objective facticity of inevitability. That kind of logical nuance is unlikely to be salient in the cognitions of executives, because they are focused on the more pressing nuance of organizational survival. Based on this logic, we can predict:

*Proposition 4: The stronger executive perceptions that downsizing is inevitable, the greater the subsequent downsizing activity.*

The relationship summarized in this proposition is represented by the arrow labeled P4 in the lower left-hand corner of Figure 8.1.

While the perception that downsizing is inevitable may increase pressure on executives to engage in downsizing, we believe that this relationship will be subject to the same moderating effects as the relationship between executive perceptions of downsizing's financial effectiveness and subsequent downsizing activity. That is, executives with higher power and more experience with past downsizing will have more social and psychological discretion to actually implement downsizing when their beliefs that it is inevitable are strong. Focusing first on power, a high-powered executive will be able to provide a more compelling account to others of the inevitability that is salient in her own cognitions, and will be able to more readily convince others that this inevitability should be followed by immediate downsizing. This persuasion process will enlist other members of the top management team to the downsizing cause, smoothing the path to collective decisions that result in the implementation of one or more downsizing events. This reasoning supports a fifth proposition:

*Proposition 5: Executive perceptions that downsizing is inevitable will have a stronger positive effect on subsequent downsizing activity when executive power is high than when executive power is low.*

Figure 8.1 represents this moderating effect by the vertical arrow labeled P5 in the lower left-hand corner of the figure.

Executives who perceive that downsizing is inevitable and also have experience with past downsizings should feel freer to get ahead of the competition and move quickly to anticipate the inevitability than their colleagues who have less experience with downsizing. The routines established in past downsizing episodes will lower barriers to enactment of the inevitability that the executive senses (McKinley *et al.*, 2000). Those routines clarify the executive's path forward and buffer the executive from dominance by the "evil" component of the "necessary evil" (Molinsky and Margolis, 2005) of downsizing. A belief that downsizing is inevitable is thus more readily transformed into future reality through actual downsizing programs if the executive has past experience with downsizing. Put another way, the executive's past history of enactment of downsizing facilitates the transformation of a cognition of inevitability into the object of that cognition. This suggests an additional proposition:

*Proposition 6: Executive perceptions that downsizing is inevitable will have a stronger positive effect on subsequent downsizing activity when executives have long experience with downsizing than when their experience is short.*

The vertical arrow in Figure 8.1 labeled P6 (bottom left-hand corner) represents this moderating effect.

In summary, we have argued that executive perceptions that downsizing is financially effective and executive perceptions that downsizing is inevitable will be important stimuli for the enactment of downsizing programs. These cognitions are not the only drivers of downsizing, but our focus on them helps explain downsizing from the executive's point of view. The positive effects of these two cognitions on subsequent downsizing activity are moderated by the power of the executives experiencing the cognitions and the degree of experience with past downsizing that those executives have. Looked at as a process that unfolds over time, executive power and memories of past downsizing programs ease the transformation of cognition into downsizing action in the executives' organizations, and that action adds to the reservoir of memories and routines that support perception-induced downsizing in the future.

## *Downsizing activity and the institutionalization of downsizing*

As noted in the introduction, the institutionalization of organizational downsizing has been explored by theorists and empirical researchers intent on finding an explanation for the diffusion of downsizing that is not dependent on assumptions about the objective rationality of managers. This work has drawn on neo-institutional theory (DiMaggio and Powell, 1983; Meyer and Rowan, 1977; Powell and DiMaggio, 1991; Scott, 1995), which points to the existence of "institutional myths," or normative prescriptions, that define how organizations should be structured. Organizations conform to these myths in exchange for legitimacy, and the conformity increases the ability of the organizations to acquire resources and therefore to survive (Baum and Oliver, 1991, 1992; DiMaggio and Powell, 1983). The literature advocating an institutional explanation of organizational downsizing (Budros, 1999; Lamertz and Baum, 1998; McKinley *et al.*, 1995; Mentzer, 2005) takes the position that downsizing has become an institutional myth. In other words, downsizing is understood as a rational way to manage organizations, and it has become a normative prescription to downsize even in the absence of financial performance problems in organizations (McKinley *et al.*, 1995; Tyler and Wilkinson, 2007). According to the neo-institutional explanation, conformity to the institutionalized myth of downsizing accounts for the rapid dispersion of downsizing across organizational populations in the public and private sectors (McKinley *et al.*, 1995).

To say that downsizing is institutionalized is not to explain how this institutionalization came about, and the downsizing literature is just beginning to grapple with this problem. McKinley *et al.* (2000) suggested that the institutionalization of downsizing emerged from an evolution and consolidation of schemas about downsizing, followed by the externalization of the cognitive product as an objectified social reality. In this section of the chapter, we take a somewhat different approach, arguing that the institutionalization of downsizing depends fundamentally on the mediating role that observable downsizing activity plays in the relationship between executive cognitions about downsizing and the institutionalization process. In other words, executive cognitions about downsizing cannot consolidate directly into an institutionalized template without the presence of visible downsizing activity. The downsizing activity that is impelled, in part, by executive cognitions, is an essential cause of the externalization of downsizing as a taken-for-granted reality. While it might appear that executive perceptions about organizational downsizing, especially the perception of inevitability, would be easily objectified into an institutional "law" (Meyer and Rowan, 1977), we maintain that the process is more complex than that.

We believe that there are at least two reasons why observable organizational downsizing activity promotes the institutionalization of downsizing (see the right-hand side of Figure 8.1). First, high levels of downsizing activity legitimize the practice of downsizing, making it appear to be a normatively sanctioned phenomenon. If many organizations in a population or an organizational field are observed to be downsizing, the practice acquires legitimacy simply because of its frequency, which carries the implication of normative acceptability. This logic echoes the argument of density dependence theory in population ecology (Hannan and Carroll, 1992), which maintains that increases in the number of organizations in a population legitimate the organizational form represented by that population. The result of this density-induced legitimacy (Hannan and Carroll, 1992) is increasing organizational birth rates and declining organizational death rates, at least until high enough levels of density are reached that competition begins to overwhelm the advantages of legitimation. By this "density induces legitimacy" reasoning, higher levels of organizational downsizing activity do not just represent a greater quantitative incidence of activity, but also an increase in the legitimacy of the practice being represented by the activity.

The second reason that high levels of observed downsizing activity institutionalize the practice of downsizing is that extensive downsizing makes the practice seem like the product of forces that are beyond the control of any individual human agent. This objectification process is not the same thing as legitimacy, and it would operate even if legitimacy were not increasing (as might be true, for example, in an expanding population of massage parlors). Instead, objectification casts the practice in question as a natural law, like the force of gravity or the law of supply and demand. This is part of the reification that Berger and Luckmann (1967) drew attention to, in which human social action is externalized into social institutions by the very humans producing it. In the same way, we suggest that high levels of downsizing activity lead to the reification of the practice of downsizing. Downsizing seemingly becomes an external reality that cannot be resisted (McKinley *et al.*, 2000), and managerial awareness of discretion over the choice to downsize begins to disappear. Thus, extensive downsizing activity "constructs" downsizing as a social fact, part of the ongoing constraint of the objective world that surrounds us.

Summarizing the arguments in the preceding paragraphs, we can state the following proposition:

*Proposition 7: The greater the downsizing activity in an organizational population or field, the greater the institutionalization of downsizing in that population or field.*

The arrow marked P7 on the right-hand side of Figure 8.1 represents this relationship.

Combining Proposition 7 with the earlier propositions about the role that executive perceptions play in stimulating organizational downsizing activity, we can derive another proposition:

*Proposition 8: The level of downsizing activity in a population or field mediates the effects of executive perceptions about downsizing on the institutionalization of downsizing.*

This proposition suggests a causal process in which specific perceptions of downsizing, especially those held by powerful executives with experience in past downsizing work, lead to elevated levels of downsizing activity in an environmental domain, and those levels in turn stimulate the institutionalization of the practice of downsizing.

## *Feedback effects*

Taking the argument one step further, we maintain that the institutionalization of the practice of downsizing feeds back to influence both the level of subsequent downsizing activity and the strength of subsequent executive perceptions about downsizing's financial effectiveness and inevitability. Taking the feedback effect on downsizing activity first, the institutionalization of the practice of downsizing makes it more acceptable to engage in concrete downsizing actions, because such actions can be justified as phenomena that are beyond the discretion of any individual decision-maker (McKinley *et al.*, 2000). This is, of course, a paradox: an action implemented by an agent (downsizing) is justified as a part of immutable forces over which the agent has no control. Nevertheless, given the human tendency to evade discretion over outcomes that have unpleasant consequences for some parties ("necessary evils": Molinsky and Margolis, 2005), it seems unlikely that this paradox will be salient to the downsizing executive. The institutionalization of downsizing also makes it more difficult for dissenters in an organization to argue against the practice, because in protesting a legitimate and objectified practice, the dissenter is cast as a deviant who does not understand the nature of reality. Thus the institutionalization of the practice of downsizing promotes additional downsizing activity, which further solidifies the institutionalization that gave rise to it. Put somewhat differently, the institutional rule that downsizing is proper and rational practice stimulates future downsizing, which in turn supports the objectivity of the institutional rule. We express this self-reinforcing loop (Masuch, 1985) in the following proposition:

*Proposition 9: The institutionalization of downsizing in a population or field feeds back to promote additional downsizing activity, which sustains the institutionalization of the practice.*

The feedback link labeled P9 on the right-hand side of Figure 8.1 represents the first part of this loop, while the arrow labeled P7 represents the second part.

Turning now to feedback effects of the institutionalization of downsizing on subsequent executive perceptions, it seems plausible that the institutionalization of downsizing would have a causal effect on subsequent executive perceptions of the inevitability of downsizing. Indeed, this is just one manifestation of the phenomenon that Berger and Luckmann (1967) termed "internalization": the apprehension of an aspect of socially constructed reality as a subjective, meaningful cognition by the individual who is subject to that reality. Institutionalization of downsizing as a practice is likely comprehended by individual executives as a cognition of inevitability – executives likely have no cognitions about "institutions" or "institutionalization," since these are terms that are part of academic discourse, but the executives arguably do have cognitions about inevitability. This reasoning suggests an additional proposition focusing on feedback effects:

*Proposition 10: The institutionalization of downsizing in a population or field feeds back to promote executive perceptions that downsizing is inevitable.*

This proposition is represented by the arrow labeled P10 at the bottom of Figure 8.1.

Finally, in an environmental domain where the practice of downsizing has become institutionalized, executive perceptions that downsizing is financially effective are also likely to be encouraged. The executive assimilating the social reality of taken-for-granted downsizing may explain that taken-for-grantedness, at least in part, by the financial efficacy of the practice. In other words, the institutionalization of downsizing will foster explanatory accounts by executives that lead to the emergence (or strengthening) of a perception that downsizing is financially effective. The financial effectiveness of downsizing will appear to have stimulated widespread acceptance and use of the practice, a state of affairs that in reality is the product of cognitions and activity that may have little to do with objective effectiveness. To express this accounts-based reasoning, we can formulate a final proposition:

*Proposition 11: The institutionalization of downsizing in a population or field feeds back to promote executive perceptions that downsizing is financially effective.*

This feedback effect is captured by the arrow labeled P11 at the top of Figure 8.1.

## Discussion

In this chapter, we have developed a theory that describes the causal linkages between executive perceptions about downsizing, concrete downsizing activity, and the institutionalization of the practice of downsizing. Variance in executive perceptions about the financial effectiveness and inevitability of downsizing is related to the level of downsizing activity, and these relationships are particularly strong when the executives at issue are powerful and experienced at past downsizing action. In turn, downsizing activity is a stimulus for the institutionalization of downsizing as an objectified practice. As a practice that takes on the appearance of a law-like phenomenon (McKinley *et al.*, 1995; Tyler and Wilkinson, 2007), the institutional rule of downsizing has feedback effects on subsequent downsizing activity and on the executive cognitions that we took as the beginning of the causal process examined here. Thus executive cognitions, downsizing activity, and the institutionalization of downsizing continually reinforce one another, and our choice of executive cognitions as the starting point was clearly arbitrary. Such a choice was necessary for sequential presentation of the theory and for the specification of propositions about specific parts of the theory, but it is important to keep in mind the iterative nature of the process we are describing. Executive cognitions, downsizing activity, and the institutionalization of the practice of downsizing create a mutually supportive nexus of causation that resembles the iterative action-structure dynamic described by Giddens (1984), the enactment process depicted by Weick

(1979), and the relationship between strategic cognition and strategic alignment analyzed by Porac, Thomas, Wilson, Paton, and Kanfer (1995).

It is also important to emphasize that the institutionalization of downsizing, as conceptualized here, is not intentional. The executives who are the agents of the process do not intend to reify or naturalize the practice of downsizing – it happens as a byproduct of their efforts to attain other goals. As noted already, it seems unlikely that executives have cognitions about "institutions" or "institutionalization," because these are abstract terms that are familiar to social scientists, but arguably not to managers. Executives are trying to improve the performance of their organizations, act in normatively prescribed ways, or reduce their own uncertainty (McKinley *et al.*, 1995, 2000; Mentzer, 2005), not create new institutions. Thus we are skeptical of the constructs of "institutional entrepreneurship" and "institutional work" that have gained such popularity in the contemporary organization studies literature (see Lawrence and Suddaby, 2006; Lawrence, Suddaby, and Leca, 2009; and Aldrich, 2011 for a critical perspective). Those constructs assume that entrepreneurs approach the transformation of social institutions as a conscious goal (Lawrence, 1999), a possibility that seems unlikely in the everyday world of practice. Instead, we would argue that the advent of institutionalized downsizing, as is true for most other institutional change, is an unanticipated consequence of purposive social action directed at mundane objectives (Merton, 1936).

The causal processes depicted in Figure 8.1 may seem so tightly coupled and so mutually reinforcing that no event could ever interrupt the iterative action of executive perceptions, downsizing activity, and the institutionalizing of downsizing practice. This raises the question: might the institutionalization of downsizing ever evolve to the point that downsizing becomes an objectified norm that dominates late-stage capitalism permanently? That possibility is certainly implicit in papers such as Tyler and Wilkinson's (2007) discussion of "the tyranny of corporate slenderness," but it may oversimplify the case. One can imagine events that might interrupt the self-reinforcing loops we have presented in Figure 8.1. For example, exposure of executives to academic research that suggests downsizing is not financially effective (e.g., Chadwick *et al.*, 2004; Krishnan *et al.*, 2007; Guthrie and Datta, 2008) might create enough disruption to slow down, or even halt, the flow of causation that connects executive perceptions to institutionalized downsizing. As we have already argued, such exposure is unlikely, but we use it here as an example of an occurrence that might deconstruct the self-reinforcing loops we are discussing. And of course, perceptions of downsizing's effectiveness and inevitability will vary across executives in different populations or fields, so the migration of executives into new environmental domains might conceivably alter cognitive templates enough to disrupt the causal processes in Figure 8.1. Finally, legislation that would limit corporate downsizing to certain circumstances or require that financial performance problems exceed certain thresholds before corporate downsizing programs could be implemented might have a similar disruptive effect. Without such events, however, we can expect the iterative causal processes hypothesized in Figure 8.1 and captured by the propositions in this chapter to exhibit some permanence. The cognitive order produced by the institutionalization of downsizing also provides strong reinforcement for it (McKinley *et al.*, 2000). As long as downsizing is normatively accepted as a proper response to problems of low organizational performance or to aspirations for higher performance, that normative state of affairs will narrow the range of solutions that executives contemplate when facing those situations. This narrowing reduces the executives' uncertainty and creates a satisfying sense of order (McKinley *et al.*, 2000; Miller, 1993). The overall conclusion is that in deciding what to do next, executives do not necessarily want more options, and this applies to decisions about downsizing as well as other kinds of executive decisions.

## *Implications for empirical research*

The theoretical model presented in this chapter suggests priorities for future empirical research on downsizing. First, we need to gain a better empirical grasp of how executive perceptions of downsizing affect executive decision-making and resulting downsizing activity. Also, more attention is required to the moderating effects of executive attributes, such as their power and their past experience with downsizing, on the executive perceptions–downsizing activity relationship. Do subjective cognitions about downsizing really impel executives to implement downsizing programs, as we have suggested in this chapter? How much do executives actually trust their own perceptions, and to what extent do they seek objective evidence to confirm (or deny) those perceptions before making decisions to downsize? We have few empirical answers to such questions, and they might be explored either through experimental studies or through intensive field research. For example, if executive subjects were primed by scenario studies with varying perceptions of the effectiveness and the inevitability of downsizing, and then asked to make decisions about downsizing in organizations portrayed in the scenarios, one might be able to test the first set of propositions in this chapter. In accompanying field studies, naturally occurring variance in perceptions of downsizing could be combined with measures of executive power (e.g., Salancik and Pfeffer, 1974; Finkelstein, 1992) and measures of executive experience with downsizing to test the moderating effects proposed in Propositions 2, 3, 5, and 6. Such work would give us a preliminary indication of the validity of the relationships represented on the left-hand side of Figure 8.1.

Second, our theoretical model suggests much closer empirical attention to the relationship between downsizing activity and the institutionalization of the practice of downsizing. This raises tricky issues of operationalization, because the measurement of institutionalization is not well developed in the organization studies literature. Most empirical studies of institutionalization infer institutionalization from proxy measures such as the diffusion of a practice (e.g., Tolbert and Zucker, 1983; Suchman, 1995) or the homogeneity of organizational attributes in a population or field (DiMaggio and Powell, 1983). Effective testing of our propositions about the effect of downsizing activity on the institutionalization of downsizing, and the mediating role played by downsizing activity in the executive perceptions–institutionalization relationship, would require more direct measures of institutionalization. One might devise such measures by surveying participants in a population or field (employees of key corporations, of customers and suppliers to those corporations, and of regulatory agencies) to assess the degree of legitimacy and objectivity attributed to downsizing practice in that domain. One could then compile a measure of institutionalization from the responses, and regress the measure on lagged measures of the level of downsizing activity in the population or field. Such measures might include the number of layoff announcements in a given time period or the average percentages by which workforces in the organizations in the field have been reduced. A positive regression coefficient for the activity–institutionalization relationship would offer preliminary validation for Proposition 7. Standard tests for mediation (Baron and Kenny, 1986) could then be used to examine whether downsizing activity mediates the causal relationship between lagged executive perceptions of downsizing and the institutionalization of downsizing (Proposition 8).

Third, the theoretical model presented in this chapter suggests more holistic studies of downsizing that would devote attention to the iterative relationships between executive perceptions of downsizing, the downsizing activity that is stimulated by those perceptions, and the institutionalization of downsizing practice encouraged by the activity. This could include tests of the feedback effects diagrammed in Figure 8.1 and captured in Propositions 9–11. If one could obtain plausible measures of the degree to which downsizing is institutionalized in a population or field, one could then evaluate whether changes in the degree of institutionalization over time in that population or field feed back to influence subsequent executive cognitions about downsizing or subsequent downsizing activity. Or one could opt for a cross-industry approach, examining an array of industries that vary in the degree to which downsizing is institutionalized in order to see whether that variance is related to cross-industry variance in executive cognitions or downsizing activity measured at a later point in time. Such studies, while admittedly difficult, would advance our knowledge about the long-term influence of the institutionalization of downsizing on the cognitions and activities that give rise to it, as well as illuminating the continuing supportive role played by those cognitions and activities in ongoing institutionalization.

## *Implications for practice*

One of the most important practical implications that flows from this chapter is simply the realization that organizational downsizing is probably not evidence-based, at least not as currently conducted by executives in late-capitalist societies. This point bears elaboration here. If executives were aware of the research indicating negative effects of downsizing on financial performance (Chadwick *et al.*, 2004; Guthrie and Datta, 2008; Krishnan *et al.*, 2007), and the work reporting negative influences of downsizing on corporate reputation and innovative capability (Amabile and Conti, 1999; Dougherty and Bowman, 1995; Flanagan and O'Shaugnessy, 2005; Love and Kraatz, 2009), they might be less prone to downsize than the statistics cited in the introductory paragraph of this chapter suggest. The fact that downsizing has become so commonplace implies that executives are not responding to such evidence, and this reinforces our conclusion that the subjective views of executives, which may be based on other factors than academic studies, are an important neglected explanatory factor in downsizing.

Given this situation, if executives were to examine their own perceptions of downsizing more consciously, those executives might become more reflective about the process of downsizing as they engage in it. Put in a different way, our theoretical model invites executives to "problematize" (Alvesson and Sandberg, 2011; Locke and Golden-Biddle, 1997) any assumptions about the effectiveness or the inevitability of downsizing. Such problematizing might be productive, because this chapter leads to the conclusion that executive perceptions have important consequences for downsizing "victims," survivors, and mid-level layoff agents impacted by downsizing programs. Is downsizing really a financially effective tool for dealing with performance problems or improving an organization's performance? Is downsizing really an inevitable byproduct of the capitalist system in which we find ourselves? Executives holding strong preconceptions about these issues should be nudged to scrutinize them, lest the preconceptions become solidified through the unintended institutionalization process that they lead the executives to enact.

## Conclusion

Considerable effort has been devoted to understanding the causes of organizational downsizing (e.g., Budros, 1997, 1999, 2002, 2004; Filatotchev *et al.*, 2000; Mentzer, 1996; O'Shaughnessy and Flanagan, 1998), but most of this work has concentrated on macro variables. Little research attention has been devoted to the cognitions of the executives who make the decisions to downsize, in particular their perceptions of attributes such as downsizing's financial effectiveness or downsizing's inevitability. This chapter has tried to rectify this imbalance by presenting a cognition-driven theory about the role played by executive perceptions in the genesis of downsizing activity, and the part played by that activity in the solidification of downsizing as an institutionalized practice. We have also discussed feedback effects of institutionalization on future executive cognitions about downsizing and future levels of downsizing activity. We hope that this chapter will provide an impetus for a research program that will attempt to document the iterative causal relationships presented in Figure 8.1, so that the genesis and diffusion of organizational downsizing in populations and organizational fields will be better understood. Such a research program would pay dividends for academics and also potentially for practitioners, holding out the hope that downsizing might one day be guided by more objective decision-making criteria than those that apparently predominate today.

## References

Ahmadjian, C. L. and Robinson, P. 2001. "Safety in numbers: Downsizing and the deinstitutionalization of permanent employment in Japan." *Administrative Science Quarterly* **46**: 622–654.

Alakent, E. and Lee, S.-H. 2010. "Do institutionalized traditions matter during crisis? Employee downsizing in Korean manufacturing organizations." *Journal of Management Studies* **47**: 509–532.

Aldrich, H. E. 2011. "Heroes, villains, and fools: Institutional entrepreneurship, NOT institutional entrepreneurs." *Entrepreneurship Research Journal* **1**(2): Article 2.

Alvesson, M. and Sandberg, J. 2011. "Generating research questions through problematization." *Academy of Management Review* **36**: 247–271.

Amabile, T. M. and Conti, R. 1999. "Changes in the work environment for creativity during downsizing." *Academy of Management Journal* **42**: 630–640.

Armstrong-Stassen, M. and Schlosser, F. 2008. "Taking a positive approach to organizational downsizing." *Canadian Journal of Administrative Sciences* **25**: 93–106.

Baron, R. M. and Kenny, D. A. 1986. "The moderator-mediator variable distinction in social psychological research: Conceptual, strategic, and statistical considerations." *Journal of Personality and Social Psychology* **51**: 1173–1182.

Baum, J. A. C. and Oliver, C. 1991. "Institutional linkages and organizational mortality." *Administrative Science Quarterly* **36**: 187–218.

Baum, J. A. C. and Oliver, C. 1992. "Institutional embeddedness and the dynamics of organizational populations." *American Sociological Review* **57**: 540–559.

Berger, P. L. and Luckmann, T. 1967. *The Social Construction of Reality: A Treatise in the Sociology of Knowledge*. New York: Doubleday.

Blau, P. M. 1964. *Exchange and Power in Social Life*. New York: Wiley.

Blau, P. M. 1970. "A formal theory of differentiation in organizations." *American Sociological Review* **35**: 201–218.

Bozeman, B. and Slusher, E. A. 1979. "Scarcity and environmental stress in public organizations: A conjectural essay." *Administration and Society* **11**: 335–355.

Brockner, J. 1988. "The effects of work layoffs on survivors: Research, theory, and practice." *Research in Organizational Behavior* **10**: 213–255.

Brockner, J., Davy, J., and Carter, C. 1985. "Layoffs, self-esteem, and survivor guilt: Motivational, affective, and attitudinal consequences." *Organizational Behavior and Human Decision Processes* **36**: 229–244.

Brockner, J., Grover, S., O'Malley, M. N., Reed, T., and Glynn, A. 1993. "Threat of future layoffs, self-esteem and survivors' reactions: Evidence from the laboratory and the field." *Strategic Management Journal* **14**: 153–166.

Brockner, J., Grover, S., Reed, T., Dewitt, R., and O'Malley, M. 1987. "Survivors' reactions to layoffs: We get by with a little help for our friends." *Administrative Science Quarterly* **32**(4): 526–542.

Budros, A. 1997. "The new capitalism and organizational rationality: The adoption of downsizing programs, 1979–1994." *Social Forces* **76**(1): 229–249.

Budros, A. 1999. "A conceptual framework for analyzing why organizations downsize." *Organization Science* **10**(1): 69–82.

Budros, A. 2001. "An institutional theory of organizational retrenchment: Adoption of early faculty retirement programs among Ontario universities." *Canadian Journal of Administrative Sciences* **18**(3): 221–236.

Budros, A. 2002. "The mean and lean firm and downsizing: Causes of involuntary and voluntary downsizing strategies." *Sociological Forum* **17**(2): 307–342.

Budros, A. 2004. "Causes of early and later organizational adoption: The case of corporate downsizing." *Sociological Inquiry* **74**(3): 355–380.

Calas, M. B. and Smircich, L. 1999. "Past postmodernism? Reflections and tentative directions." *Academy of Management Review* **24**: 649–671.

Cameron, K. S., Kim, M. U., and Whetten, D. A. 1987. "Organizational effects of decline and turbulence." *Administrative Science Quarterly*, **32**: 222–240.

Capelle-Blancard, G. and Couderc, N. 2007. "How do shareholders respond to downsizing? A meta-analysis." Unpublished manuscript, Universite Paris X Nanterre.

Cappelli, P., Bassi, L., Katz, H., Knoke, D., Osterman, P., and Useem, M. 1997. *Change at Work*. New York: Oxford University Press.

Cascio, W. F., Young, C. E., and Morris, J. R. 1997. "Financial consequences of employment-change decisions in major US corporations." *Academy of Management Journal* **40**(5): 1175–1189.

Chadwick, C., Hunter, L. W., and Walston, S. L. 2004. "Effects of downsizing practices on the performance of hospitals." *Strategic Management Journal* **25**: 405–427.

Clair, J. A. and Dufresne, R. L. 2004. "Playing the grim reaper: How employees experience carrying out a downsizing." *Human Relations* **57**(12): 1597–1625.

DiMaggio, P. J. and Powell, W. W. 1983. "The iron cage revisited: Institutional isomorphism and collective rationality in organizational fields." *American Sociological Review* **48**(2): 147–160.

Donaldson, L. 2003. "A critique of postmodernism in organizational studies." *Research in the Sociology of Organizations* **21**: 169–202.

Dougherty, D. and Bowman, E. H. 1995. "The effects of organizational downsizing on product innovation." *California Management Review* 37(4): 28–44.

Edwards, J. C., Rust, K. G., McKinley, W., and Moon, G. 2003. "Business ideologies and perceived breach of contract during downsizing: The role of the ideology of employee self-reliance." *Journal of Organizational Behavior* **24**(1): 1–23.

Emerson, R. M. 1962. "Power-dependence relations." *American Sociological Review* **27**: 31–41.

Festinger, L. 1957. *A Theory of Cognitive Dissonance*. Stanford, CA: Stanford University Press.

Filatotchev, I., Buck, T., and Zhukov, V. 2000. "Downsizing in privatized firms in Russia, Ukraine, and Belarus." *Academy of Management Journal* **43**: 286–304.

Finkelstein, S. 1992. "Power in top management teams: Dimensions, measurement, and validation." *Academy of Management Journal* **35**: 505–538.

Fisher, S. R. and White, M. A. 2000. "Downsizing in a learning organization: Are there hidden costs?" *Academy of Management Review* **25**(1): 244–251.

Flanagan, D. J. and O'Shaughnessy, K. C. 2005. "The effect of layoffs on firm reputation." *Journal of Management* **31**: 445–463.

Folger, R. and Skarlicki, D. P. 1998. "When tough times make tough bosses: Managerial distancing as a function of layoff blame." *Academy of Management Journal* **41**(1): 79–87.

Freeman, S. J. and Cameron, K. S. 1993. "Organizational downsizing: A convergence and reorientation framework." *Organization Science* **4**(1): 10–29.

Freeman, J. and Hannan, M. T. 1975. "Growth and decline processes in organizations." *American Sociological Review* **40**: 215–228.

Gandolfi, F. 2008. "Learning from the past – downsizing lessons for managers." *Journal of Management Research* **8**(1): 3–17.

Giddens, A. 1984. *The Constitution of Society: Outline of the Theory of Structuration*. Berkeley, CA: University of California Press.

Glassberg, A. 1978. "Organizational responses to municipal budget decreases." *Public Administration Review* **38**: 325–332.

Grunberg, L., Moore, S., and Greenberg, E. S. 2006. "Managers' reactions to implementing layoffs: Relationship to health problems and withdrawal behaviors." *Human Resource Management* **45**(2): 159–178.

Guthrie, J. P. and Datta, D. K. 2008. "Dumb and dumber: The impact of downsizing on firm performance as moderated by industry conditions." *Organization Science* **19**: 108–123.

Hambrick, D. and Mason, P. 1984. "Upper echelons: The organization as a reflection of its top managers." *Academy of Management Journal* **15**: 514–535.

Hannan, M. T. and Carroll, G. R. 1992. *Dynamics of Organizational Populations*. New York: Oxford University Press.

Hannan, M. T. and Freeman, J. 1977. "The population ecology of organizations." *American Journal of Sociology* **82**: 929–964.

Hickson, D. J., Hinings, C. R., Lee, C. A., Schneck, R. E., and Pennings, J. M. 1971. "A strategic contingencies' theory of intraorganizational power." *Administrative Science Quarterly* **16**: 216–229.

Kets de Vries, M. F. R. and Balazs, K. 1997. "The downside of downsizing." *Human Relations* **50**(1): 11–50.

Kozlowski, S. W. J., Chao, G. T., Smith, E. M., and Hedlund, J. 1993. "Organizational downsizing: Strategies, interventions, and research implications," in C. L. Cooper and I. T. Robertson (eds.), *International Review of Industrial and Organizational Psychology*, Vol. VIII. New York: Wiley, pp. 263–332.

Krishnan, H. A., Hitt, M. A., and Park, D. 2007. "Acquisition premiums, subsequent workforce reductions and post-acquisition performance." *Journal of Management Studies* **44**: 709–732.

Lamertz, K. and Baum, J. A. C. 1998. "The legitimacy of organizational downsizing in Canada: An analysis of explanatory media accounts." *Canadian Journal of Administrative Sciences* **15**: 93–107.

Lawrence, T. B. 1999. "Institutional strategy." *Journal of Management* **25**: 161–188.

Lawrence, T. B. and Suddaby, R. 2006. "Institutions and institutional work," in S. Clegg, C. Hardy, T. Lawrence, and W. R. Nord (eds.), *Handbook of Organization Studies* (2nd edn.). Thousand Oaks, CA: Sage, pp. 215–254.

Lawrence, T. B., Suddaby, R., and Leca, B. (eds.). 2009. *Institutional Work: Actors and Agency in Institutional Studies of Organizations*. Cambridge: Cambridge University Press.

Leana, C. R. and Feldman, D. C. 1992. *Coping with Job Loss*. New York: Lexington Books.

Leana, C. R. and Ivancevich, J. M. 1987. "Involuntary job loss: Institutional interventions and a research agenda." *Academy of Management Review* **12**(2): 301–312.

Lee, P. M. 1997. "A comparative analysis of layoff announcements and stock price reactions in the United States and Japan." *Strategic Management Journal* **18**: 879–894.

Levine, C.H. 1978. "Organizational decline and cutback management." *Public Administration Review* **38**: 316–325.

Littler, C.R. and Innes, P. 1999. "How firms contract – a longitudinal study of the effects of downsizing on firm employment structures." Paper presented at the annual meeting of the Academy of Management, Chicago.

Littler, C.R. and Innes, P. 2004. "The paradox of managerial downsizing." *Organization Studies* **25**: 1159–1184.

Locke, K. and Golden-Biddle, K. 1997. "Constructing opportunities for contribution: Structuring intertextual coherence and 'problematizing' in organizational studies." *Academy of Management Journal* **40**: 1023–1062.

Love, E.G. and Kraatz, M. 2009. "Character, conformity, or the bottom line? How and why downsizing affected corporate reputation." *Academy of Management Journal* **52**: 314–335.

Masuch, M. 1985. "Vicious circles in organizations." *Administrative Science Quarterly* **30**: 14–33.

McKinley, W. 1992. "Decreasing organizational size: To untangle or not to untangle?" *Academy of Management Review* **17**(1): 112–123.

McKinley, W. 1993. "Organizational decline and adaptation: Theoretical controversies." *Organization Science* **4**(1): 1–9.

McKinley, W., Mone, M.A., and Barker III, V.L. 1998. "Some ideological foundations of organizational downsizing." *Journal of Management Inquiry* 7(3): 198–212.

McKinley, W., Sanchez, C.M., and Schick, A.G. 1995. "Organizational downsizing: Constraining, cloning, learning." *Academy of Management Executive* **9**(3): 32–42.

McKinley, W., Zhao, J., and Rust, K.G. 2000. "A sociocognitive interpretation of organizational downsizing." *Academy of Management Review* **25**(1): 227–243.

Medina, J. 2011. "Short on funds, but long on pink slips." *The New York Times*, March 24.

Mentzer, M.S. 1996. "Corporate downsizing and profitability in Canada." *Canadian Journal of Administrative Sciences* **13**: 237–250.

Mentzer, M.S. 2005. "Toward a psychological and cultural model of downsizing." *Journal of Organizational Behavior* **26**: 993–997.

Mentzer, M.S. and Near, J.P. 1992. "Administrative cuts amidst decline in American railroads." *Organization Studies* **13**(3): 357–373.

Merton, R.K. 1936. "The unanticipated consequences of purposive social action." *American Sociological Review* **1**: 894–904.

Meyer, J. and Rowan, B. 1977. "Institutionalized organizations: Formal structure as myth and ceremony." *American Journal of Sociology* **83**(2): 340–363.

Miller, D. M. 1993. "The architecture of simplicity." *Academy of Management Review* **18**: 116–138.

Molinsky, A. and Margolis, J. 2005. "Necessary evils and interpersonal sensitivity in organizations." *Academy of Management Review* **30**(2): 245–268.

Mone, M. A., McKinley, W., and Barker III, V. L. 1998. "Organizational decline and innovation: A contingency framework." *Academy of Management Review* **23**(1): 115–132.

Nixon, R. B., Hitt, M. A., Lee, H.-K., and Jeong, E. 2004. "Market reactions to announcements of corporate downsizing actions and implementation strategies." *Strategic Management Journal* **25**: 1121–1129.

Noer, D. 1993. *Healing the Wounds: Overcoming the Trauma of Layoffs and Revitalizing Downsized Organizations*. San Francisco, CA: Jossey-Bass.

O'Shaughnessy, K. C. and Flanagan, D. J. 1998. "Determinants of layoff announcements following M&As: An empirical investigation." *Strategic Management Journal* **19**: 989–999.

Otterman, S. 2011. "Doubts on mayor's forecast of 4,600 teacher layoffs." *The New York Times*, March 17.

Palmer, I., Kabanoff, B., and Dunford, R. 1997. "Managerial accounts of downsizing." *Journal of Organizational Behavior* **18**: 623–629.

Parker, T. and McKinley, W. 2008. "Layoff agency: A theoretical framework." *Journal of Leadership and Organizational Studies* **15**(1): 46–58.

Pfeffer, J. and Salancik, G. R. 1974. "Organizational decision making as a political process: The case of a university budget." *Administrative Science Quarterly* **19**: 135–151.

Pfeffer, J. and Salancik, G. R. 1978. *The External Control of Organizations: A Resource Dependence Perspective*. New York: Harper & Row.

Pfeffer, J. and Sutton, R. I. 2006. "Evidence-based management." *Harvard Business Review* (January): 1–13.

Porac, J. F., Thomas, H., Wilson, F., Paton, D., and Kanfer, A. 1995. "Rivalry and the industry model of Scottish knitwear producers." *Administrative Science Quarterly* **40**: 203–227.

Powell, W. W. and DiMaggio, P. J. (eds.). 1991. *The New Institutionalism in Organizational Analysis*. Chicago: University of Chicago Press.

Pugh, S. D., Skarlicki, D. P., and Passell, B. S. 2003. "After the fall: Layoff victims' trust and cynicism in re-employment." *Journal of Occupational and Organizational Psychology* **76**(2): 201–212.

Rousseau, D. M. 1995. *Psychological Contracts in Organizations: Understanding Written and Unwritten Agreements*. Thousand Oaks, CA: Sage Publications.

Salancik, G. R. and Pfeffer, J. 1974. "The bases and use of power in organizational decision making: The case of a university." *Administrative Science Quarterly* **19**: 453–473.

Scott, W. R. 1995. *Institutions and Organizations*. Thousand Oaks, CA: Sage.

Shah, P. P. 2000. "Network destruction: The structural implications of downsizing." *Academy of Management Journal* **43**(1): 101–112.

Skarlicki, D. P., Ellard, J. H., and Kelln, B. R. C. 1998. "Third-party perceptions of a layoff: Procedural, derogation, and retributive aspects of justice." *Journal of Applied Psychology* **83**: 119–127.

Sronce, R. and McKinley, W. 2006. "Perceptions of organizational downsizing." *Journal of Leadership and Organizational Studies* **12**(4): 89–108.

Suchman, M. C. 1995. "Localism and globalism in institutional analysis: The emergence of contractual norms in venture finance," in W. R. Scott and S. Christensen (eds.), *The Institutional Construction of Organizations: International and Longitudinal Studies*. Thousand Oaks, CA: Sage, pp. 39–63.

Sutton, R. I. and D'Aunno, T. 1989. "Decreasing organizational size: Untangling the effects of money and people." *Academy of Management Review* **14**(2): 194–212.

Tolbert, P. S. and Zucker, L. G. 1983. "Institutional sources of change in the formal structure of organizations: The diffusion of civil service reform, 1880–1935." *Administrative Science Quarterly* **28**: 22–39.

Tyler, M. and Wilkinson, A. 2007. "The tyranny of corporate slenderness: 'Corporate anorexia' as a metaphor for our age." *Work, Employment and Society* **21**: 537–549.

Wayhan, V. B. and Werner, S. 2000. "The impact of workforce reductions on financial performance: A longitudinal perspective." *Journal of Management* **26**(2): 341–363.

Weick, K. E. 1979. *The Social Psychology of Organizing* (2nd edn.). New York: McGraw-Hill.

Worrell, D. L., Davidson III, W. N., and Sharma, V. M. 1991. "Layoff announcements and stockholder wealth." *Academy of Management Journal* **34**(3): 662–678.

# 9 *Reducing costs and enhancing efficiency or damaging the company: Downsizing in today's global economy*

KENNETH P. DE MEUSE AND GUANGRONG DAI

We have all seen the headlines: "The Worst Recession since the 1930s," "More Foreclosures, More Bankruptcies, and More Layoffs." Although the recent economic decline in the global economy has spawned many attention-grabbing news stories of job loss, organizational downsizing in reality has been implemented in large numbers for the past 25 years. It has been estimated that roughly 2,000 employees were downsized in American corporations *each business day* throughout the 1990s (De Meuse and Marks, 2003). According to the US Department of Labor (2011), this number rose to more than 4,000 employees each business day between 2000 and 2007. And certainly, layoffs have increased markedly during the past few of years of economic difficulty – not only in America but around the globe.

Nearly two decades ago, we delivered a presentation at Cornell University entitled, "Is lean and mean really better than fat and happy?" (De Meuse, Vanderheiden, and Bergmann, 1993). The research tracked the financial performance of corporations that downsized during a five-year period relative to those firms that did not. Although the findings were not a ringing endorsement of large-scale layoffs, they point out an interesting observation. Given the length of time organizations have been implementing downsizing and the frequency in which they occur, one would expect companies to be highly effective at it. And yet, this does not appear to be the case. Numerous studies have reported that downsizing can lead to several adverse organizational outcomes, such as decreased employee morale and commitment, increased employee stress and involuntary turnover, and reductions in employee creativity and innovation (see Datta, Guthrie, Basuil, and Pandey, 2010; De Meuse, Marks, and Dai, 2011). In addition, several studies have found that an organization's financial performance frequently does not improve in the near term (Cascio, 1998; Cascio and Young, 2003; De Meuse, Bergmann, Vanderheiden, and Roraff, 2004; De Meuse, Vanderheiden, and Bergmann, 1994). Cascio and Young (2003) concluded that "managers must be very cautious in implementing a strategy that can impose such traumatic costs on employees, both on those who leave as well as on those who stay" (p. 153).

Most likely, there are many possible reasons why downsizing fails to produce the desired results in some cases. One of the key factors may be the manner in which it is implemented (Brockner, 2006). One of the most intriguing aspects of talent management is the planful, meticulous approach organizations use when *selecting* employees, but often the harried, haphazard process they employ when *de-selecting* (that is, downsizing) them. For example, McCune, Beatty, and Montagno (1988) reported that 94 percent of human resource managers had less than two months to conduct staff reductions. Further, it appears that corporate executives frequently do not possess an overall strategy on when to downsize, how much to downsize, and how quickly to downsize.

The purpose of this chapter is to systematically review the extant literature on downsizing with an eye to ascertaining whether it works or not. That is, do companies that downsize perform more effectively following downsizing or perform better than companies that do not? Special attention will be devoted to investigate the impact of downsizing on individuals and organizations. In addition, we will present the findings of a recent longitudinal examination of downsizing among *Fortune* 1000 American corporations to glean the extent to which downsizing might have impacted the financial performance of these organizations. Finally, we will discuss some fundamental questions for future researchers, as well as share some key observations regarding the proper implementation of downsizing to minimize negative outcomes and increase the likelihood of financial success. Overall, it is hoped that this chapter will enlighten our understanding of the effects of downsizing on various individual and organizational outcomes.

## Review of the theoretical and empirical literature on downsizing

Corporate executives have continually shaped their organizations through the hiring and firing of employees since the beginning of organizations. What makes downsizing different is that employees are terminated regardless of their performance or a company's seasonal work cycles. Employees are terminated due to outsourcing work, relocating production facilities overseas, discontinuing product lines, selling business units, reengineering internal operations, or simply cutting costs due to financial difficulty. Downsizing became a popular business strategy in US corporations beginning in the late 1980s and since has been widely implemented throughout Asia, Europe, and the world (Datta *et al.*, 2010; De Meuse, Lester, Kickul, and Oh, 2006; Dewettinck and Buyens, 2002).

There has been much discussion on the negative impact of downsizing on employees, customers, suppliers, local communities, and the organizations themselves. Journalists and business scholars have expressed strong views. For example, books such as *The Disposable American* (Uchitelle, 2006) and *The Human Equation* (Pfeffer, 1998) have condemned the insensitive attitude of executives toward employees. Until recently, little scientific attention has been given to measuring the systematic effect that downsizing has on employee performance and organizational outcomes or directed to understanding its theoretical underpinnings. Despite its pervasiveness, the number of academic journal articles devoted to downsizing remains relatively limited and the literature is fragmented. Scholars in a variety of disciplines have explored the topic, ranging from economics, business strategy, management, psychology, finance, and human resources. In general, researchers appear much more interested in studying the dynamics of "selecting" new employees rather than "de-selecting" current ones. There are two primary theoretical approaches which can help explain the impact of downsizing on individuals and organizations. One approach is referred to as *psychological contract* theory; the other is *economic theory*.

### *Psychological contract theory*

*Psychological contract theory* centers on the individual and posits that a mutual relationship based on trust and predictability evolves between employees and employers. According to this informal code, employees are expected to do a "fair day's work" and in return receive "a fair day's pay" (De Meuse and Tornow, 1990; Rousseau, 1995). Downsizing is a violation of this trust and the organization's responsibility to provide a positive work environment and secure employment. Consequently, it can lead to a number of adverse effects, as employees react to such a unilateral breach.

The psychological contract literature suggests that employees that survive a downsizing may reduce their organizational contributions (e.g., motivation, engagement, loyalty) and/or avoid executing tasks which will benefit organizational goals (e.g., performing at a high level or initiating organizational citizenship behaviors). In rare cases, employees might engage in theft, sabotage, or other counterproductive behaviors (Buono, 2003). Overall, the research evidence is strong. Downsizing can lead to many adverse individual and organizational outcomes. For example, Brockner and his associates observed that the so-called "lucky" employees who survive a layoff often experience guilt because they continue to have a job while their fellow coworkers and friends do not (Brockner, 1989; Brockner, Wiesenfeld, and Martin, 1995). This survivor syndrome leads to feelings of sadness, anger, and fear, which can translate into anti-organizational sentiments, such as distrust in management, little company loyalty, and decreased job satisfaction. In turn, those attitudes may lead to lower job performance and increases in absence and turnover. Thus, individual outcomes associated with downsizing can have a direct effect on organizational performance and financial success (see Table 9.1). Exactly how organizations can mitigate or prevent these dysfunctional behaviors is unclear. It appears that several factors likely play a role (e.g., how the downsizing is implemented, the size of the layoff, the motive for the downsizing). We will explore these issues a little later in the chapter.

## *Economic theory*

A second theoretical approach examines the impact of downsizing from an economic or macro-perspective. *Economic theory* is based on the assumption that organizations engage in downsizing to reduce costs, gain efficiency, and ultimately increase a company's financial performance by making it more competitive in today's global marketplace (Cameron, 1994; McKinley, Zhao, and Rust, 2000). More specifically, economic theory states that downsizing will have a positive impact on financial outcomes because it enables organizations to eliminate redundancies, streamline operations, and cut labor costs. The early research testing this theory was based largely on employee and management *perceptions* of downsizing efficacy. For example, one study reported that employees in 30 automotive plants that had downsized *perceived* a decline in product quality and quantity, as well as a loss in employee morale (Cameron, Freeman, and Mishra, 1991). Another study conducted a national survey and found that managers in 75 percent of the companies that downsized *believed* performance did not improve ("Pink-slip productivity," 1992).

Table 9.1 *Negative employee and organizational outcomes associated with organizational downsizing*

| Employee and organizational outcomes | Select references |
|---|---|
| *Employee outcomes* | |
| Lower self-esteem, loss of identity, and depression (terminated employees) | Kivimaki *et al.* (2000); Noer (1993) |
| "Survivor syndrome" (employees who remain with company) | Brockner (1989) |
| Increased employee workloads | Amabile and Conti (1999) |
| Increased work-related and life stress | Bardwick (2008); Kets de Vries and Balazs (1997) |
| Decreased job satisfaction, morale, loyalty, and trust in management | Feldheim (2007); Spreitzer and Mishra (2002) |
| Increased tardiness, absence, and turnover | Allen, Freeman, Russell, Reizenstein, and Reitz (2001) |
| Fewer organizational citizenship behaviors | Chadwick, Hunter, and Walston (2004) |
| Increased potential for counter-productive behaviors (e.g., sabotage, theft) | Buono (2003); Chen and Spector (1992) |
| Additional mental and physical health problems | Vahtera, Kivimaki, and Pentti (1997) |
| *Organizational outcomes* | |
| Depletion of employee experience and skills base | Littler and Innes (2003) |
| Loss of teamwork | DeRue, Hollenbeck, Johnson, Ilgen, and Jundt (2008) |
| Increase in work-related accidents and injuries | Probst and Brubaker (2001) |
| Additional health care costs | De Meuse and Marks (2003) |
| Strained relations with labor union(s) | Leana and Feldman (1992) |
| Unwanted turnover among surviving employees | Trevor and Nyberg (2008); Spreitzer and Mishra (2002) |
| Lower employee creativity and innovation | Amabile and Conti (1999); Mellahi and Wilkinson (2010) |
| Lower customer service and satisfaction | Guterman (2009); Lewin, Biemans, and Ulaga (2010) |
| Reduced financial performance | De Meuse *et al.* (2004); Guthrie and Datta (2008) |
| Lower status in local community | Feldman (2003) |

Two independent series of ongoing research studies have directly investigated the financial performance of organizations implementing downsizing. In the late 1990s, Wayne Cascio identified 311 firms in the Standard and Poor's 500 which had downsized between 1981 and 1990 (Cascio, 1998). He measured five indices of financial performance: (a) profit margin, (b) return on assets, (c) cost of goods sold, (d) expenses to sales ratio, and (e) stock price. Financial performance averages were calculated for three years prior to the downsizing and three years after it. The results revealed that none of those five financial indices was significantly affected by the downsizing. Cascio concluded "downsizing per se did not appear to lead to improved company financial performance, nor did it have a detrimental effect on company financial performance" (1998, p. 69). Subsequently, Cascio and Young (2003) investigated the Standard and Poor's 500 companies again, but this time from 1982 to 2000. They also altered their research design, examining companies that either had downsized or upsized their workforce, downsized or upsized their assets, or remained relatively stable regarding their workforce and assets. They observed that *both* workforce and asset downsizers registered *lower* financial performance than either stable employers or upsizers in (a) the year prior to the layoff, (b) the year of the layoff, and (c) the two years following the layoff. During the entire 18-year period, the researchers found companies that downsized did not perform significantly higher than stable ones.

Ken De Meuse and his colleagues also examined the organizational impact of downsizing by tracking various indices of financial success across time (De Meuse *et al.*, 1994; Vanderheiden, De Meuse, and Bergmann, 1999). After controlling for industry, they found that *Fortune* 100 companies that downsized did not differ financially from those which did not – one and two years *before* the layoffs were implemented. Beginning in the year of the downsizing, differences in financial performance appeared and continued to increase in magnitude *each* of the subsequent two years. Their findings revealed companies that downsized had substantially lower profit margins, returns on assets, returns on equity, and market-to-book ratios for the year of the downsizing (as they hypothesized), during the next year, as well as two years later. Overall, the researchers discovered that downsizing had no apparent effect on either increasing financial performance or stemming the downward spiral of financial loss.

In 2004, De Meuse *et al.* published a follow-up study investigating the financial success of these *Fortune* 100 companies over a 12-year period – two years before the downsizing, the year of it, and the following nine years. They observed that the downsized companies reported significantly lower performance (relative to the non-downsized ones) during the initial few years. However, these companies then improved to a similar level financially as the non-downsized ones. Interestingly, Mellahi and Wilkinson (2010) likewise found that an organization's innovation (that is, the number of patents granted) significantly decreased following downsizing, but only during the initial two years before returning to pre-downsizing levels. De Meuse *et al.* (2004) concluded organizations that downsized should not expect a fast turnaround in financial health. Rather, they declared that there likely is an initial "healing period" when financial results fall before companies rebound. It also should be noted that these researchers observed that the performance of the group of downsizing companies never outperformed the non-downsizing set of companies throughout the entire nine-year post-downsizing period.

Despite the above evidence of the financial difficulties associated with downsizing (see also Guthrie and Datta, 2008; Sheaffer, Carmeli, Steiner-Revivo, and Zionit, 2009), a few studies report some support for economic theory. For example, Hammer (1996) reported that downsizing can lead to enhanced teamwork, because employees become cross-trained and multi-skilled. Communication and decision-making also may become more effective as tiers of management are eliminated and bureaucratic policies are removed (Appelbaum and Donia, 2000; McClelland and Wilmot, 1990). Thus, it is contended that efficiency should increase and organizations should become more strategically flexible and agile. In addition, a major benefit of downsizing is the purported savings in labor costs due to the employees who are terminated. In reality, however, labor costs actually can increase as companies are forced to rehire former employees as temps and consultants (frequently at higher salaries). Moreover, the financial enticements and severance packages given to downsized workers can reduce any labor savings obtained through a leaner workforce.

## *Summary*

Clearly, the literature examining the impact of downsizing on individuals and organizations favors the psychological contract theory. There appears to be more disadvantages than advantages to laying off large numbers of employees. Nevertheless, an argument that has been frequently raised is that companies would be in far worse shape financially or perhaps out of business if not for the downsizing. It is difficult to counter this assertion directly. Obviously, one readily can point out that many organizations experiencing financial difficulties do not resort to downsizing and yet survive. Cascio, Young, and Morris (1997) conducted an intriguing study, tracking industry-adjusted profitability of companies that had downsized versus stable employers. They observed that the companies that had downsized did not show significantly higher profitability than those that did not. Hence, downsizing appeared to have no appreciable positive effect on hastening the turnaround in profitability relative to other organizations within the industry (Cascio *et al.*, 1997). There is evidence to suggest that the organizational trauma created by the mass exodus of employees may take several years to overcome. Although at times corporate executives will have little choice but to downsize, such a step should be made cautiously and prudently with a realistic expectation that the return to profitability will take time. Further, many factors likely will affect how quickly an organization recovers. We address many of these issues in the next section.

## Factors influencing the effectiveness of downsizing

Research suggests there are several factors that can mitigate the effectiveness of a downsizing strategy. Aspects such as what is driving the layoff, how deep is the workforce cut, how often are employees subjected to layoffs, and how the downsizing is implemented all appear to play a role. We examine these issues below.

### *Motive for the downsizing*

Executives generally implement large-scale layoffs for one of two reasons. In some cases, the organization is in severe financial trouble and costs need to be reduced immediately. Downsizing tends to be reactionary and operational. In other cases, downsizing occurs primarily to enhance efficiency or to eliminate staff redundancy (e.g., in the case of an acquisition). In these instances, downsizing is proactive and strategic. Companies that downsize to reduce costs quickly tend to focus simply on lowering the employee head count. This approach usually results in much employee stress, increased workloads, and a number of unintended labor problems (Cameron, 1994; Mishra, Mishra, and Spreitzer, 2009). On the other hand, organizations that downsize to increase process efficiency typically focus on eliminating unnecessary levels of management, consolidating duplicative departments, streamlining operations, and concentrating on core product lines. Research suggests that the latter motive is more likely to be successful (Hoskisson, Johnson, and Douglas, 1994), although some research has found improved profitability – albeit transient – following reactive downsizing as well (Sheaffer *et al.*, 2009).

### *Size of the layoff*

A key strategic question executives must answer is: "Should we conduct one massive reduction-in-force and then be finished, or should we cut as few employees as possible initially and then layoff only as many as necessary in subsequent layoffs?" The preponderance of evidence suggests that large-scale layoffs lead to worse results than smaller ones. Cody, Hegeman, and Shanks (1987) observed that downsizings of 30–50 percent of the workforce resulted in a significant decline in employee morale and commitment and a substantial increase in employee stress. Vahtera, Kivimaki, and Pentti (1997) also reported that employee stress was 2.3 times higher when companies implemented a major layoff relative to a small one. More recently, Trevor and Nyberg (2008) observed that larger layoffs generally produced more voluntary turnover. De Meuse and his colleagues found that "for every 1% increase in the size of announced layoff, there is a corresponding 0.29% decline in profit margin" (1994, p. 517). Further, De Meuse *et al.* (2004) observed that companies downsizing 10 percent or more of their workforce performed significantly worse financially than those laying off less than 10 percent. Although the precise percentage of workforce reduction that will trigger poor performance is unknown, it seems safe to conclude that large-scale layoffs create high anxiety, increased workloads, and significant job security concerns among employees. Consequently, executives can expect that the company's performance will be affected more severely by large downsizing efforts than small ones.

## *Frequency of layoffs*

If small layoffs cause less trauma, perhaps it would be prudent for organizations to implement a series of small staff reductions rather than one massive one? Indeed, De Meuse *et al.* (2004) found that the financial performance of companies conducting one or two layoffs was virtually no different than companies implementing three or more. Cascio and Young (2003) also found no difference in financial performance related to frequency of downsizing. Although there are few studies that have investigated frequency of layoffs, present research findings suggest organizations would be better served conducting a series of small layoffs rather than one large one. Such an approach enables executives to avoid being put in to a compromising situation delaying future layoffs, because they promised there would be no more downsizing. Evidence indicates that once an organization begins to employ downsizing as a business strategy, it continues to use it when faced with environmental uncertainty (De Meuse *et al.*, 1994).

## *Downsizing implementation practices*

The amount of time an organization has to plan and implement a downsizing often is very limited (McCune *et al.*, 1988). When under time pressure, executives may select employees to downsize in an arbitrary manner or use crude decision rules such as salary level, years of service, or general perceptions of overall performance. Therefore, frequently the wrong employees get terminated, morale problems arise as workers perceive layoff decisions to be based on politics or cronyism, and accusations of illegal layoff practices are raised. Studies indicate that the procedures used to identify, notify, and support employees are important – both for the *victims* (terminated employees) as well as the *survivors* (employees who remain with the company). For example, Brockner (2006) found that when victims perceived downsizing practices were fair, few employees filed wrongful termination claims. Further, theft and turnover among survivors were low. Trevor and Nyberg (2008) also reported that when surviving employees perceived the organization to be fair and just in layoffs, it was associated with lower voluntary turnover rates. Wiley (2008) observed that when senior-level managers treated employees with dignity and respect, engagement scores actually increased following downsizing. In sum, the research findings suggest the following six practices should be implemented when downsizing: (a) clear, open, and honest communication with employees throughout the downsizing process; (b) procedural fairness in selecting employees to be terminated and sufficient notification to all those affected; (c) adequate severance pay and extended benefits; (d) outplacement services; (e) counseling for *both* victims and survivors; and (f) all employees treated with respect and dignity throughout the termination process (De Meuse and Marks, 2003; Mishra *et al.*, 2009; Norman, Avolio, and Luthans, 2010).

## A longitudinal investigation of the impact of downsizing

In the current study, we examined the effect of downsizing on several financial outcomes in *Fortune* 1000 companies across a five-year period – 2003–2007. We selected this period to avoid the confounding influence of the economy. The United States entered a mild recession after the "dot-com" bubble burst in early 2000. The 9/11 attack on the World Trade Center further strained the weak economy into an outright contraction. The stock market crash of 2000–2002 caused a loss of $5 trillion in the market values of companies from March 2000 to October 2002 (Gaither and Chmielewski, 2006). Beginning in 2003, the US economy experienced a period of sustained growth. This trend is reflected in the stock market. The Dow Industrial Average peaked at 14,198 on October 11, 2007, an all time high. In December of 2007, the US economy entered into another recession according to the National Bureau of Economic Research. To illustrate this point, about 19 percent of the *Fortune* 1000 companies reduced headcount by at least 5 percent in 2007. This number increased to 25 percent in 2008 and 37 percent in 2009.

### *Sample*

Companies were included in the sample if they were in the *Fortune* 1000 list during *all* five years of our investigation. In total, 731 companies met this criterion. The year of 2003 served as the baseline year. Based on the extent of change in employment size from 2003 to 2004, companies were categorized into two groups: (a) downsizing companies or (b) a comparison group of non-downsizing companies. A common approach scholars have used to operationalize downsizing is to identify companies experiencing greater than a 5 percent employment reduction from the previous year (cf. Cascio and Young, 2003; Sheaffer *et al.*, 2009). Among the 731 companies in our sample, 123 (17 percent) reduced headcount by at least 5 percent from 2003 to 2004. The financial performance of these two groups of companies was then compared during the year of downsizing (referred to as the "concurrent year) and during *each* of the three subsequent years.

## *Dependent variables*

As previously indicated, organizations frequently reduce headcount to cut costs and improve margins. The business environment is full of uncertainty. When executives are under pressure to improve their companies' profitability, some of them decide to downsize to reduce costs. In line with this management philosophy, *return on assets* (ROA) and *profit margin* are appropriate outcome variables to examine. If everything is held equal, when companies reduce the cost of their workforce, they may experience an improvement in ROA and profit margin (at least for a short period of time after they downsize). In this study, ROA is defined as the ratio of profits to assets. Similarly, profit margin is defined as the ratio of profits to revenues. A company's profitability also is reflected in *earnings per share*. The earnings per share ratio is useful information for investors when reviewing the financial performance of publicly traded companies. Thus, in addition to ROA and profit margin, we examined the potential impact of downsizing on earnings per share.

There are additional reasons for companies to reduce the size of their workforce. According to the efficiency assumption, companies can streamline their internal processes by cutting structural redundancies (Bruton, Keels, and Shook, 1996). In theory, such an approach enhances communication, accelerates decision-making, and enables quicker response times to customers. If downsizing really streamlines a company's processes, eventually it will lead to improved competitiveness in the marketplace. Consequently, downsized companies will not only improve their profitability, but increase their sales following downsizing. In this study, we therefore compared the two groups of companies on *revenue growth*. Revenue growth is calculated as the percentage of change in revenue over the previous year. A positive percentage suggests that the company increased its revenue.

Finally, we compared the two types of companies on *market capitalization*. Market capitalization denotes an organization's worth if it were put up for sale. It is the value of a company computed by multiplying the price per share times the number of shares. If downsizing enhances a company's competitiveness, it ultimately should be reflected in a financial measure from the shareholders' point of view. Market capitalization represents the extent of confidence investors have in a company's future performance after a strategic decision. Because market capitalization is related to company size, we examined the influence of downsizing on the change of market capitalization instead of the actual market capitalization. It is calculated as the percentage of change in market capitalization over the previous year. A positive number indicates that investors have confidence in a company and are willing to invest more money in it.

All the above employment and financial data were obtained from the *Fortune Magazine* online services. Before analyzing the data, we examined the distribution of the variables for outliers. Performance numbers that were three standard deviations from the mean were viewed as outliers and were deleted. On average, this occurred less than 3 percent of the time for any specific performance variable.

## *Results*

Before contrasting the financial performance means of the two groups of companies, a repeated measures analysis was conducted. If the between-subjects variable (downsized versus not downsized) had a significant impact, it suggested there were significant differences between the two sets of companies across the years. T-tests then were conducted to compare the two company groups for specific years. Financial performance in 2003 served as the baseline. The year of 2004 is the "Concurrent Year" when the downsizing occurred. The years of 2005, 2006, and 2007 are "Year 1," "Year 2," and "Year 3" following the downsizing. Therefore, this study was able to examine the influence of downsizing across several years.

### Return on assets

Repeated measures analysis indicated that downsizing had a significant impact on ROA ($F(1, 680) = 9.46, p < 0.01$). Table 9.2 presents the results of the T-tests. As one would expect, downsized companies were outperformed by companies without downsizing during the base year ($p = 0.07$). This difference continued and increased during the concurrent year ($p < 0.01$), as well as in year 1 ($p < 0.01$) and in year 2 ($p < 0.01$). By the third

Table 9.2 ***Return on assets for the downsized and comparison companies, 2003–2007***

| | Downsized | | Comparison | | |
|---|---|---|---|---|---|
| Year | *Mean* | *Std* | *Mean* | *Std* | *p* |
| Base | 3.00 | 18.40 | 4.72 | 6.28 | 0.07 |
| Concurrent | 3.50 | 4.93 | 5.53 | 4.57 | 0.00 |
| Year 1 | 4.03 | 6.30 | 5.98 | 5.28 | 0.00 |
| Year 2 | 4.08 | 5.76 | 6.14 | 5.43 | 0.00 |
| Year 3 | 5.15 | 5.56 | 5.67 | 5.79 | 0.38 |

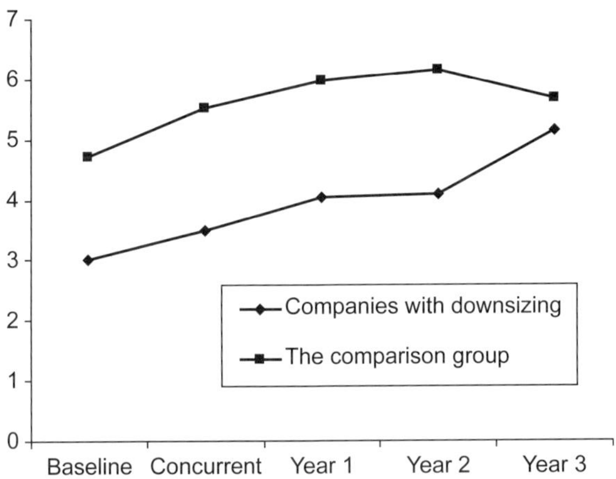


**Figure 9.1** Longitudinal trend for return on assets

year, downsized companies continued to be outperformed by the comparison companies, although the difference was not statistically significant ($p = 0.38$). Figure 9.1 illustrates the performance trends across the five years. As can be seen, both types of companies improved their performance in terms of return on assets. However, by the third year, the downsized companies were able to reduce the gap against their counterparts.

**Profit margin**

The repeated measures analysis indicated that downsizing had a significant effect on profit margin ($F$ (1, 696) = 11.43, $p < 0.01$). Subsequently, independent T-tests were conducted to compare the mean profit margins

Table 9.3 *Profit margin for the downsized and comparison companies, 2003–2007*

| | Downsized | | Comparison | | |
|---|---|---|---|---|---|
| Year | *Mean* | *Std* | *Mean* | *Std* | *p* |
| Base | 3.10 | 18.20 | 6.08 | 8.87 | 0.01 |
| Concurrent | 4.22 | 7.92 | 7.04 | 6.56 | 0.00 |
| Year 1 | 5.09 | 7.69 | 7.33 | 6.77 | 0.00 |
| Year 2 | 5.32 | 7.14 | 7.49 | 7.24 | 0.00 |
| Year 3 | 6.23 | 6.93 | 6.64 | 7.11 | 0.56 |

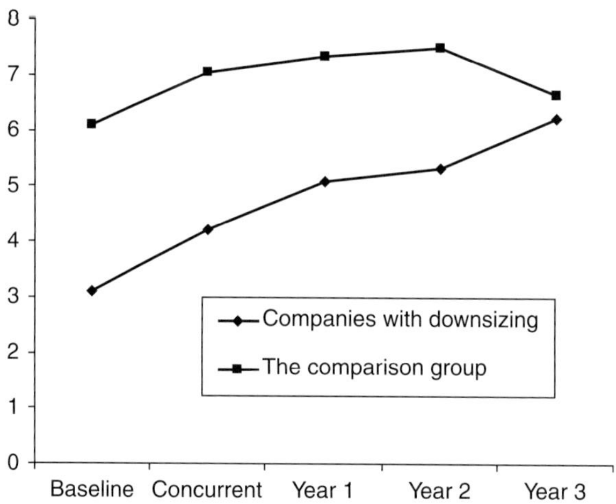


**Figure 9.2** Longitudinal trend for profit margin

for these two types of companies across each of the five years (see Table 9.3). Similar to what we observed for ROA, downsized companies were outperformed by the comparison companies on the base year ($p < 0.01$), the concurrent year ($p < 0.01$), year 1 ($p < 0.01$), and year 2 ($p < 0.01$). Again, by the third year, the downsized companies continued to be outperformed by the comparison group in terms of profit margin, but the difference was not statistically significant ($p = 0.56$). Figure 9.2 depicts the performance trends across the five years. As can be seen, both groups of companies improved their profit margins over time. By the third year after downsizing, the downsized companies were able to reduce the gap relative to the comparison companies.

Table 9.4 *Earnings per share for the downsized and comparison companies, 2003–2007*

| | Downsized | | Comparison | | |
|---|---|---|---|---|---|
| Year | *Mean* | *Std* | *Mean* | *Std* | *p* |
| Base | 1.22 | 4.94 | 1.90 | 3.83 | 0.10 |
| Concurrent | 1.44 | 3.42 | 2.52 | 6.92 | 0.10 |
| Year 1 | 1.99 | 4.13 | 2.34 | 13.29 | 0.78 |
| Year 2 | 2.07 | 3.29 | 3.09 | 10.00 | 0.28 |
| Year 3 | 2.39 | 2.95 | 2.61 | 7.91 | 0.77 |

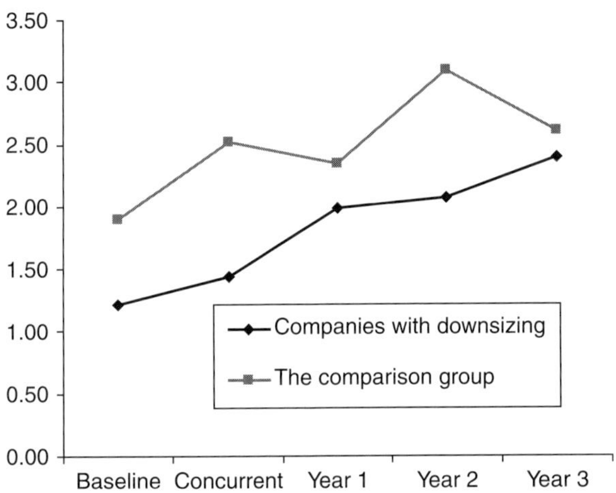


**Figure 9.3** Longitudinal trend for earnings per share

### Earnings per share

Repeated measures analysis suggested that downsizing had no significant impact on this performance outcome ($F\,(1{,}648) = 1.38, p = 0.24$). In other words, there was not a significant difference between downsized companies and the contrasting companies across the five years. Independent T-tests confirmed this result (see Table 9.4). None of the comparisons was statistically significant ($ps > 0.05$). Figure 9.3 shows the trend in earnings per share across the five years. Although the downsized companies improved this financial outcome continuously, the comparison group of companies always slightly outperformed them.

Table 9.5 ***Revenue growth for the downsized and comparison companies, 2004–2007***

| | Downsized | | Comparison | | |
|---|---|---|---|---|---|
| Year | *Mean* | *Std* | *Mean* | *Std* | *p* |
| Concurrent | 5.72 | 13.97 | 14.08 | 12.96 | 0.00 |
| Year 1 | 5.09 | 14.13 | 13.04 | 12.15 | 0.00 |
| Year 2 | 7.08 | 10.72 | 9.54 | 11.52 | 0.03 |
| Year 3 | 4.61 | 12.56 | 6.46 | 11.63 | 0.12 |

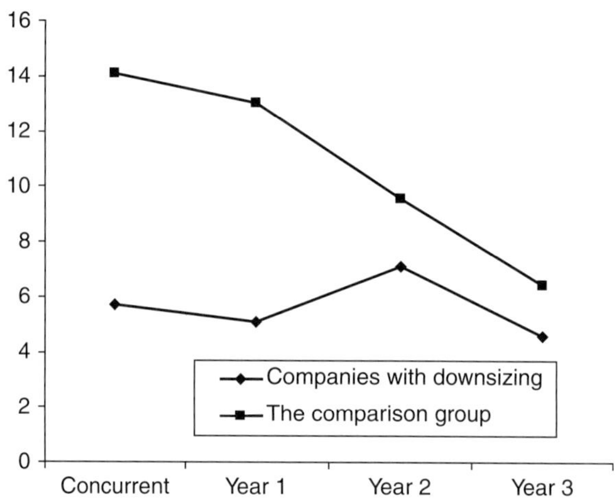


**Figure 9.4** Longitudinal trend for revenue growth

**Revenue growth**

The revenue growth of a specific year was calculated as the percentage of change in revenue over the previous year. Since it is a ratio, the two groups of companies could not be compared on the base year. Repeated measures analysis indicated that downsizing had a significant impact on revenue growth ($F$ (1, 689) = 37.21, $p < 0.01$). Table 9.5 presents the results of T-tests. Downsized companies were significantly outperformed by the comparison companies in the concurrent year ($p < 0.01$). The significant difference was continued in year 1 ($p < 0.01$) as well as year 2 ($p < 0.05$). By the third year, downsizing companies continued to be outperformed by the comparison companies, although again the difference was not statistically significant ($p = 0.12$). Figure 9.4 depicts the

Table 9.6 *Change in market capitalization for the downsized and comparison companies, 2004–2007*

| | Downsized | | Comparison | | |
|---|---|---|---|---|---|
| Year | *Mean* | *Std* | *Mean* | *Std* | *p* |
| Concurrent | 13.59 | 39.08 | 17.95 | 34.91 | 0.24 |
| Year 1 | 11.05 | 34.39 | 15.15 | 32.71 | 0.23 |
| Year 2 | 20.64 | 36.13 | 14.67 | 33.61 | 0.10 |
| Year 3 | –14.75 | 31.60 | –15.95 | 31.93 | 0.73 |

longitudinal trend in revenue growth after the downsizing. It can be observed that the line for the downsized companies was always below the one for the comparison companies. Although downsized companies were able to increase their revenues in each of the years following downsizing, their growth rates were lower than the ones for the comparison group. Similar to what we have seen with the other performance variables, the difference became insignificant by year 3.

**Change in market capitalization**

In this study, change in market capitalization for a given year was calculated as a ratio of change over the previous year. Therefore, the two types of companies could not be compared on the base year. Repeated measures analysis demonstrated that the downsizing had no significant effect on this performance measure ($F$ (1, 625) = 0.15, $p$ = 0.70). That is, the fluctuation in the market generally cannot be attributed to the downsizing. Independent T-tests confirmed this result (see Table 9.6). The two groups of companies were not statistically different in the change in market capitalization for the concurrent year or each of the three years after downsizing. Figure 9.5 illustrates the change in market capitalization across the four years. As can be seen, the downsized companies were slightly outperformed by the comparison companies in the concurrent year and the year after the downsizing, but were above the comparison companies in years 2 and 3 (although none of the differences was statistically significant). One observation is particularly noteworthy. Market capitalization shrank in 2007 for both types of companies, perhaps reflecting the beginning of the economic recession.

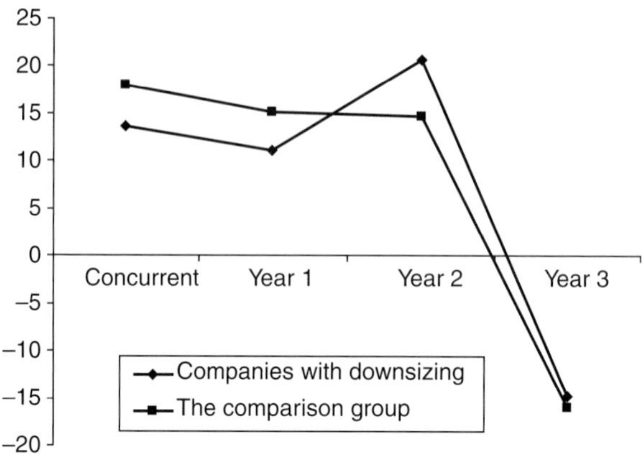


**Figure 9.5** Trend in the change of market capitalization

### *Summary*

Using the *Fortune* 1000 data, we investigated the impact of downsizing on several financial outcomes. We tracked the financial performance for five years – the year before the downsizing (2003), the year of the downsizing (2004), and each of the following three years (2005–2007). In general, we observed that the downsized companies enjoyed continuous improvement after the downsizing, but the comparison group of companies grew at even higher financial rates. Throughout the years investigated in this study, downsized companies were outperformed by the comparison companies on most of the performance indicators. It appeared that the downsizing did *not* help companies enhance their competitiveness in the short term. However, by the third year following downsizing, downsized companies were able to reduce the financial gap with the comparison companies. It likely will take longer for downsized companies to eventually outperform the other companies, although we do not have data to determine this possibility.

There is evidence showing that the stock market has an immediate and dramatic reaction to the announcement of a firm's downsizing (Kashefi and McKee, 2002). In terms of market capitalization, our findings suggest investors did not differentiate between downsized and non-downsized companies in the near-term. Or, perhaps, they simply did not expect quick benefits due to downsizing. For example, during the year of the downsizing (that is, the concurrent year) as well as the first year after it, we found investors had slightly more confidence in the comparison group of companies (see Figure 9.5). Beginning in year 2, the downsized companies surpassed the comparison group and it continued the subsequent year. This pattern of change in market capitalization is consistent with revenue growth. For return on assets, profit margin, and earnings per share, noticeable improvement began during year 3. Overall, our findings indicate that it probably takes several years for companies to actualize the benefits of downsizing.

## Discussion

In this chapter, we reviewed the theoretical and empirical literature on the individual and organizational outcomes associated with downsizing, as well as discussed various factors that influence the efficacy of downsizing. In addition, we presented the results of a longitudinal study examining the effects of downsizing on the financial performance of *Fortune* 1000 companies in the United States between the years 2003 and 2007. Overall, the scientific literature strongly suggests that downsizing frequently causes many adverse consequences for both employees and organizations (Brockner, 1989; Feldman, 2003; Trevor and Nyberg, 2008). Our current study and research in general clearly reveals that the strategic benefits of downsizing most likely take several years to materialize, contrary to the expectation of executives who demand immediate financial results (Cascio and Young, 2003; De Meuse *et al.*, 2004). Given the increased frequency of this practice by companies in today's global economy, it is somewhat surprising to *not* locate more scientific support for it. Much of the literature on downsizing is multi-disciplinary, atheoretical, and fragmented. Further research needs to be conducted to enhance our understanding of the general nature of downsizing, its systematic effects, and to provide guidance to executives on how to implement it more effectively. To conclude this chapter, we will discuss some theoretical and practical implications.

### *Theoretical implications*

#### Combine the psychological and economic approaches

A number of empirical studies in a diversity of disciplines have been conducted to investigate the impact of downsizing on individuals and organizations during the past 20 years. However, to date, the two lines of research – *psychological contract theory* at the individual level and *economic theory* at the organizational level – have been performed in relative isolation. The current literature does not provide solid answers as to how the psychological and behavioral impact of downsizing on employees is related to the financial outcomes of downsizing (De Meuse *et al.*, 2011). As Datta *et al.* (2010) contended, research focusing on organizational-level outcomes often reflects "black box" studies that assume layoffs influence organizations through cumulative effects on individual employees. Unfortunately, these studies do not measure individual-specific variables. An integrated approach which addresses downsizing at multiple levels would enable scholars to discover how downsizing affects financial outcomes through intermediate employee attitudes and behaviors.

**Conduct "controlled" field studies**

The majority of the outcome studies have been post hoc and retrospective. In other words, scholars typically have identified companies that implemented large-scale layoffs and then compared their performance against other companies over a period of time. The validity and generalizability of the findings are limited for several methodological reasons. Naturally, the up and down nature of a company's financial performance is related to the economy. Without attempting to control for this confounding economic influence, findings can be inconsistent and potentially misleading. In addition, various empirical studies treat downsizing as a universal concept. Yet in practice, organizations downsize their workforces in several different ways. The relationship between downsizing and organizational outcomes likely will vary from situation to situation. Mishra *et al.* (2009), Trevor and Nyberg (2008), and others have observed that the motive for implementing layoffs, the size of the layoff, as well as how employees are selected to be terminated all directly affect its success. Field studies with carefully crafted methodological designs will enable scholars to examine how the variation in the downsizing implementation parameters may influence the effectiveness of downsizing.

**Monitor post-downsizing organizational interventions**

As the findings of our study presented in this chapter as well as the results observed by other researchers demonstrate, it takes several years for organizations to realize the benefits of the downsizing (Cascio and Young, 2003; De Meuse *et al.*, 2004; Mellahi and Wilkinson, 2010). Because of this time gap, events happening during the post-downsizing period can have a substantial influence on the effectiveness of the downsizing. Such events as an up-turn in the global economy or the acquisition of another company can greatly affect an organization's performance following layoffs. Further, other circumstances more directly related to the downsizing itself may affect the speed of the turnaround of a firm's performance. For example, how the layoffs are communicated, the procedures used to select employees to be terminated, and the role of the immediate supervisor managing the surviving employees can all expedite the turnaround. Yet, most downsizing research does not systematically address these issues.

Organizational transitions often do not have an identifiable or abrupt ending (Marks, 2003). Existing research tracking organizational outcomes generally has devoted little attention to other organizational interventions after the downsizing to measure their impact on employee attitudes and behaviors. One particular area worthy of study is employee engagement. During the recent economic recession, business corporations in North America laid off millions of workers. Survey studies have found that employee engagement, especially the engagement level of high potential employees, has dropped substantially in the United States during the same period (Corporate Leadership Council, 2009). Companies that can reengage their employees following downsizing will position themselves much better than other companies since employee engagement has been found to have a direct relationship with important performance outcomes (Harter, Schmidt, and Hayes, 2002; Schneider, 2006).

### Consider a stage model to integrate downsizing research

A close examination of the downsizing literature reveals there is no overarching theoretical framework to integrate downsizing research. Recently, Datta *et al.* (2010) proposed a model to connect different types of research on downsizing. However, this model does not adequately describe the dynamic, evolving nature of the layoff process. In reality, downsizing is a type of organizational transition that involves several stages. For a downsizing to deliver strategic benefits, at least four stages can be identified: (a) a pre-downsizing period, (b) the planning phase, (c) implementation, and (d) a post-downsizing period.

Downsizing involves a sequence of organizational decisions and actions which can be categorized naturally into the above four periods. Many factors likely impact the ultimate efficacy of downsizing. Such a stage model can help scholars organize their research and hopefully lead to the development of an integrated theory of downsizing. In the next section, we discuss the practical implications of downsizing using a stage model approach.

## *Practical implications*

### Pre-downsizing

This stage addresses the strategic necessity for downsizing. Mass layoff decisions should never be implemented quickly, capriciously, or non-strategically. Some authors assert that mimicry plays a role in the adoption of downsizing by companies (cf. Budros, 2000). Executives observe other companies have reaped dramatic benefits through downsizing by redesigning their business processes. Consequently, they perceive their companies can do the same thing. Such a cloning response to their rivals seldom produces positive results, however. It is a symptom of an erroneous strategy endorsed by flawed management (Rigby, 2002).

Before jumping onto the "downsizing bandwagon," executives must carefully weigh the trauma such a strategy will cause the organization and its stakeholders. Although layoffs in some situations are required, the systematic elimination of employees carries with it strong symbolism. If previous messages from top leadership assert that employees are the company's greatest asset, downsizing can temporarily destroy management credibility and damage an organization's culture. A number of firms on the *Fortune Magazine*'s recent list of "100 Best Companies to Work For" have never had a layoff (Moskowitz, Levering, and Tkaczyk, 2011). As Judith Bardwick eloquently noted, "treating people right pays off in real, hard numbers" (2008, p. 60). Executives always should consider alternative measures before cutting headcount. Hiring and wage freezes, abolishing or postponing bonuses, suspending overtime, employee furloughs, shortened workweeks, the elimination of temporary and contract workers, scaling back on outsourcing, temporary wage cuts, reducing business travel, and lowering company contributions to benefit plans are some approaches which might prevent widespread layoffs (Cascio, 2009). Large corporations usually have multiple business units. The units may be in different financial condition. Rather than simply laying off employees in one business unit and hiring them in another, perhaps the organization can provide training and transfer employees to the growing businesses.

The pros and cons of downsizing need to be analyzed within the context of the long-term organizational objectives and talent management strategies. Most importantly, business leaders should strategically rethink if and how they downsize. Downsizing is not simply "doing more with less." It is about creating flexibility, innovation, and responsiveness. It is about enhancing communication and decision-making. Rather than focusing on being smaller, leaner, and more efficient *today*, the goal of downsizing should be on becoming more competitive in the marketplace *tomorrow*.

**Planning**

Once an organization decides to reduce the workforce, executives must carefully plan the downsizing. Things to be considered include the timeframe, the scope, de-selection criteria, communication vehicles and sequencing, severance packages, outplacement activities, counseling programs, and supervisory training to ensure proper messaging and support. The design of the de-selection criteria is especially critical at this stage (Connell, 2001). As diligently and cautiously as employees are brought into the organization, they should be ushered out. The quest for urgency should not hamper an organization's efforts to meticulously identify which employees should be terminated. It is vital for organizations to retain the knowledge and skills that will contribute to its long-term competitiveness. In general, organizations should avoid the temptation of across-the-board job cuts. Although such a strategy gives the illusion of fairness, because it standardizes the treatment of employees, across-the-board cuts ignore the relative importance of different job functions to a company's future success (Cascio, 2009). For example, innovation is a strategic imperative for high-tech companies. By proportionately downsizing this slice of the workforce, it damages the company's creative capability and ultimately its competitiveness in the industry (Guthrie and Datta, 2008; Probst *et al.*, 2007). Therefore, companies that consider innovation as their core organizational competency may want to preserve those elements of the workforce (e.g., research and development, intellectual property design) as much as possible.

For organizations that have never downsized, it is especially crucial to craft a comprehensive communication plan. Those companies may have espoused a corporate culture – either implicitly or explicitly – against laying off employees. Downsizing likely will be viewed as a violation of this company value. It is important that management be transparent from the very beginning. Senior leadership should describe the situation the company is facing, explain the rationale for the downsizing decision, and allow employees to raise concerns. The preliminary objective of the communication at this point is to prepare employees as well as other stakeholders for the upcoming organizational transition (Marks and De Meuse, 2005).

**Implementation**

The manner in which organizations execute layoffs has a significant influence on its effectiveness. Bossidy and Charan (2002) assert that 90 percent of strategic change is execution. A major issue in this stage is the perceived fairness of downsizing. Studies have indicated that the negative effects of downsizing on employees' job attitudes are mitigated by the perceptions of fairness (cf. Brockner, 2006). Perceptions of fairness are related largely to the criteria established for termination decisions and their communication to employees (e.g., openness, candor, and honesty). Naturally, perceptions also are related to the implementation process itself. Immediate managers play a pivotal role during any organizational change and particularly in downsizing, in terms of messaging, supporting, and maintaining productivity (Larkin and Larkin, 1996). Ironically, managers likewise may be experiencing many of the same concerns and emotions as their direct reports. It is prudent for organizations to provide training to help them handle this situation. In addition, it is critical to treat laid-off employees with respect and sensitivity. Explain the business reasons for the layoff. Acknowledge their prior contributions. Listen and empathize; avoid arguing. Offer outplacement assistance, such as serving as a reference, providing temporary office support, and assisting in job-hunting and networking. If at all possible, make counseling available to help affected employees and their families cope with their emotions (see Noer, 1993).

It also is critical to remember the "survivors," those employees who still have jobs. Survivors frequently can become as angry, frustrated, and anxious as those individuals who are terminated. Besides, survivors are the ones who will continue to work at the firms. Their behavior and performance directly influence the success of the downsizing (Bardwick, 2008). Organizations should address (at least) the following four psychological issues:

1. *Sensemaking*. Surviving employees want to understand why the layoffs happened. Top management needs to communicate the rationale behind the downsizing decision through methods such as town hall meetings, video-conferencing, intranet newsletters, and departmental get-togethers. Make sure a good dose of listening occurs, so employees can vent and openly share their concerns.
2. *Job security concerns*. Employees will worry whether there will be further job cuts. Be honest and transparent about the possibility of future downsizing, but also attempt to provide some degree of certainty. Explain how layoff decisions were made. If some job functions or business units were spared from cuts, make it clear why this was the case. An engaged workforce is more likely to be productive and less likely to turnover.
3. *Impact on jobs (and careers)*. Now, the company is "doing more with less." Process engineering and organizational redesign is often necessary following downsizing. Managers should explain how the workforce reductions will impact the surviving employees' jobs, and involve them as much as possible in the redesign process. They should also discuss how the restructuring can open doors for new career opportunities.
4. *Visioning a new future*. Employees will need to have confidence in the future of the company, so they have a reason to stay. Top management must communicate clearly the vision of the company and the business plans to achieve this success. It is imperative to build an optimistic and winning culture even when the company is experiencing a difficult time (Marks and De Meuse, 2005).

**Post-downsizing**

Organizations must recognize they will not achieve their strategic goals simply by cutting headcount (Boroughs, 1992). Executives need to monitor the impact of downsizing and take the necessary post-downsizing actions to ensure the organization is becoming more competitive. Ideally, downsizing is viewed as only one part of an entire set of strategies designed to improve the company's performance. When cutting the workforce, executives should reexamine the organizational structure and operational processes to minimize interruption. Frequently, downsizing has the most direct impact on the human resources function. For example, absence and tardiness might increase. Health care costs may escalate. The talent supply chain may become broken as some employees unexpectedly leave. Organizations should revisit their succession plans and talent management practices to ensure a sufficient talent supply satisfies future leadership requirements. Organizations also should assess the level of employee engagement periodically, taking the necessary steps to reengage the workforce. It is particularly critical to develop talent in strategic roles. Finally, it is important for organizations to assess the culture to prevent a downward spiral (Kanter, 2003). A financial turnaround is often predicated upon a psychological turnaround. Most successful downsizings pay very close attention to employee morale, commitment, and performance as the company moves toward renewal. As Rosabeth Moss Kanter pointed out, "In every case [of turnaround], executives restored their people's confidence in themselves and in one another . . . In short, each had to lead a psychological turnaround" (2003, p. 59).

## Conclusion

Organizational downsizing requires strategic analysis, thoughtful planning, and careful execution. And even when this occurs, executives should not expect financial miracles to occur immediately. Chances are the company did not get into the financial hardship overnight. It will not get out of it overnight either. Research has demonstrated that it likely will take two to three years for organizations to be able to truly see the benefits of downsizing. Consequently, the actions companies take during this prolonged recovering period will have a significant impact on the outcomes achieved.

In many ways, downsizing is similar to any other organizational transformation (e.g., corporate merger or acquisition, installation of new technology) or personal change (e.g., weight loss, smoking, or drug cessation). As we know, most of those change attempts fail. These failures are more due to a lack of motivation, willingness, and discipline than due to a lack of information and know how. Most likely, the same holds true for downsizing to work in this global economy. It is hoped that the knowledge conveyed in this chapter will inspire both scholars and practitioners to redirect their efforts to implementing downsizing efforts more successfully.

## References


Allen, T. D., Freeman, D. M., Russell, J. E. A., Reizenstein, R. C., and Rentz, J. O. 2001. "Survivor reactions to organizational downsizing: Does time ease the pain?" *Journal of Occupational and Organizational Psychology* **74**: 145–164.

Amabile, T. M. and Conti, R. 1999. "Changes in the work environment for creativity during downsizing." *Academy of Management Journal* **42**: 630–640.

Appelbaum, S. H. and Donia, M. 2000. "The realistic downsizing preview: A management intervention in the prevention of survivor syndrome (Part 1)." *Career Development International* **5**: 333–350.

Bardwick, J. M. 2008. *One Foot Out the Door: How to Combat the Psychological Recession that's Alienating Employees and Hurting American Business*. New York: AMACOM.

Boroughs, D. L. 1992. "Amputating assets." May 4, *US News and World Report*, pp. 50–51.

Bossidy, L. and Charan, R. 2002. *Execution: The Discipline of Getting Things Done*. New York: Crown Business.

Brockner, J. 1989. "The effects of work layoffs on survivors: Research, theory, and practice," in B. M. Staw and L. L. Cummings (eds.), *Research in Organizational Behavior*, Vol. X. Greenwich, CT: JAI Press, pp. 213–256.

Brockner, J. 2006. "Why it's so hard to be fair." *Harvard Business Review* **84** (3): 122–129.

Brockner, J., Wiesenfeld, B. M., and Martin, C. L. 1995. "Decision frame, procedural justice and survivors' reactions to job layoffs." *Organizational Behavior and Human Decision Processes* **63**: 59–69.

Bruton, G. D., Keels, J. K., and Shook, C. L. 1996. "Downsizing the firm: Answering the strategic questions." *Academy of Management Executive* **10**: 38–45.

Budros, A. 2000. "Organizational types and organizational innovation: Downsizing among industrial, financial and utility firms." *Sociological Forum* **17**: 307–342.

Buono, A. F. 2003. "The hidden costs and benefits of organizational resizing activities," in K. P. De Meuse and M. L. Marks (eds.), *Resizing the Organization: Managing Layoffs, Divestitures, and Closings*. San Francisco, CA: Jossey-Bass, pp. 306–346.

Cameron, K. S. 1994. "Strategies for successful organizational downsizing." *Human Resource Management* **33**: 477–500.

Cameron, K. S., Freeman, S. J., and Mishra, A. K. 1991. "Best practices in white-collar downsizing: Managing contradictions." *Academy of Management Executive* **5**: 57–73.

Cascio, W.F. 1998. "Learning from outcomes: Financial experiences of 311 firms that have downsized," in M.K. Gowing, J.D. Kraft, and J.C. Quick (eds.), *The New Organizational Reality: Downsizing, Restructuring, and Revitalization*. Washington, DC: American Psychological Association, pp. 55–70.

Cascio, W.F. 2009. *Employment Downsizing and Its Alternatives: Strategies for Long-Term Success*. Alexandria, VA: Society for Human Resource Management.

Cascio, W.F. and Young, C.E. 2003. "Financial consequences of employment-change decisions in major US corporations: 1982–2000," in K.P. De Meuse and M.L. Marks (eds.), *Resizing the Organization: Managing Layoffs, Divestitures and Closings*. San Francisco, CA: Jossey-Bass, pp. 131–156.

Cascio, W.F., Young, C.E., and Morris, J.R. 1997. "Financial consequences of employment-change decisions in major US corporations." *Academy of Management Journal* **40**: 1175–1189.

Chadwick, C., Hunter, L.W., and Walston, S.L. 2004. "Effects of downsizing practices on the performance of hospitals." *Strategic Management Journal* **25**: 405–427.

Chen, P.Y. and Spector, P.E. 1992. "Relationships of work stressors with aggression, withdrawal, theft, and substance use: An exploratory study." *Journal of Occupational and Organizational Psychology* **65**: 177–184.

Cody, A.M., Hegeman, G.B., and Shanks, D.C. 1987. "How to reduce the size of the organization but increase effectiveness." *Journal of Business Strategy* **8**: 66–70.

Connell, D.S. 2001. "RIF a la carte: Using reported cases to develop effective reduction-in-force criteria." *Employee Relations Law Journal* **27**(3): 7–47.

Corporate Leadership Council. 2009. "The employee engagement crisis." Retrieved from http://hr.executiveboard.com/Improving_Employee_Performance.html

Datta, D.K., Guthrie, J.P., Basuil, D., and Pandey, A. 2010. "Causes and effects of employee downsizing: A review and synthesis." *Journal of Management* **36**: 281–348.

De Meuse, K.P., Bergmann, T.J., Vanderheiden, P.A., and Roraff, C.E. 2004. "New evidence regarding organizational downsizing and a firm's financial performance: A long-term analysis." *Journal of Managerial Issues* **16**: 155–177.

De Meuse, K.P., Lester, S.W., Kickul, J., and Oh, S.H. 2006. "Downsizing and upsizing in Japan: Its frequency, magnitude, and effects on financial performance." Paper presented at the Academy of Management Annual Meeting, August, Atlanta.

De Meuse, K. P. and Marks, M. L. 2003. *Resizing the Organization: Managing Layoffs, Divestitures, and Closings*. San Francisco, CA: Jossey-Bass.

De Meuse, K. P., Marks, M. L., and Dai, G. 2011. "Organizational downsizing, mergers and acquisitions, and strategic alliances: Using theory and research to enhance practice," in S. Zedeck (ed.), *APA Handbook of Industrial and Organizational Psychology*, Vol. III. Washington, DC: American Psychological Association, pp. 729–768.

De Meuse, K. P. and Tornow, W. W. 1990. "The tie that binds – has become very, very frayed!" *Human Resource Planning* **12**: 203–213.

De Meuse, K. P., Vanderheiden, P. A., and Bergmann, T. J. 1993. "Is lean and mean really better than fat and happy?" Paper presented at the Human Resource Planning Society Research Symposium, Cornell University, New York.

De Meuse, K. P., Vanderheiden, P. A., and Bergmann, T. J. 1994. "Announced layoffs: Their effect on corporate financial performance." *Human Resource Management Journal* **33**: 509–530.

DeRue, D. S., Hollenbeck, J. R., Johnson, M. D., Ilgen, D. R., and Jundt, D. K. 2008. "How different team downsizing approaches influence team-level adaptation and performance." *Academy of Management Journal* **51**: 182–196.

Dewettinck, K. and Buyens, D. 2002. "Downsizing: Employee threat or opportunity? An empirical study on external and internal reorientation practices in Belgian companies." *Employee Relations* **24**: 389–402.

Feldheim, M. A. 2007. "Public sector downsizing and employee trust." *International Journal of Public Administration* **30**: 249–271.

Feldman, D. C. 2003. "The impact of layoffs on family, friendship, and community networks," in K. P. De Meuse and M. L. Marks (eds.), *Resizing the Organization: Managing Layoffs, Divestitures, and Closings*. San Francisco, CA: Jossey-Bass, pp. 188–219.

Gaither, C. and Chmielewski, D. C. 2006. "Fears of dot-com crash, Version 2.0." *Los Angeles Times*, July 16. Retrieved from http://articles.latimes.com/2006/jul/16/ business/fi-overheat16.

Guterman, J. 2009. "Don't let layoffs ruin customer service." *Harvard Business Publishing*, 3–5.

Guthrie, J. P. and Datta, D. K. 2008. "Dumb and dumber: The impact of downsizing on firm performance as moderated by industry conditions." *Organization Science* **19**: 108–123.

Hammer, M. 1996. *Beyond Reengineering*. London: HarperCollins.

Harter, J. K., Schmidt, F. L., and Hayes, T. L. 2002. "Business-unit level relationship between employee satisfaction, employee engagement, and business outcomes: A meta-analysis." *Journal of Applied Psychology* **87**: 268–279.

Hoskisson, R. E., Johnson, R. A., and Douglas, D. M. 1994. "Corporate divestiture intensity in restructuring firms: Effects of governance, strategy, and performance." *Academy of Management Journal* **37**: 1207–1251.

Kanter, R. 2003. "Leadership and the psychology of turnaround." *Harvard Business Review* **81**(6): 58–67.

Kashefi, J. and McKee, G. J. 2002. "Stock prices' reactions to layoff announcement." *Journal of Business and Management* 8(2): 99–107.

Kets de Vries, M. F. R. and Balazs, K. 1997. "The downside of downsizing." *Human Relations* **50**: 11–50.

Kivimaki, M., Vahtera, J., Pentti, J., and Ferrie, J. E. 2000. "Factors underlying the effect of organizational downsizing on health of employees: A longitudinal cohort study." *British Medical Journal* **320**: 971–975.

Larkin, T. J. and Larkin, S. 1996. "Reaching and changing front-line employees." *Harvard Business Review* **74**(3): 95–104.

Leana, C. R. and Feldman, D. C. 1992. *Coping with Job Loss: How Individuals, Organizations, and Communities Respond to Layoffs*. New York: Lexington Books.

Lewin, J. E., Biemans, W., and Ulaga, W. 2010. "Firm downsizing and satisfaction among United States and European customers." *Journal of Business Research* **63**: 697–706.

Littler, C. R. and Innes, P. 2003. "Downsizing and de-knowledging the firm." *Work, Employment, and Society* **17**(1): 73–100.

Marks, M. L. 2003. "Revitalization after resizing," in K. P. De Meuse and M. L. Marks (eds.), *Resizing the Organization: Managing Layoffs, Divestitures, and Closings*. San Francisco: Jossey-Bass, pp. 275–305.

Marks, M. L. and De Meuse, K. P. 2005. "Resizing the organization: Maximizing the gain while minimizing the pain of layoffs, divestitures, and closings." *Organizational Dynamics* **34**(1): 19–35.

McClelland, V. and Wilmot, D. 1990. "Lateral communication as seen through the eyes of employees." *Communication World* 7(12): 32–35.

McCune, J. T., Beatty, R. W., and Montagno, R. V. 1988. "Downsizing: Practices in manufacturing firms." *Human Resource Management* **27**: 145–161.

McKinley, W., Zhao, J., and Rust, K. G. 2000. "A sociocognitive interpretation of organizational downsizing." *Academy of Management Review* **25**: 227–243.

Mellahi, K. and Wilkinson, A. 2010. "A study of the association between level of slack reduction following downsizing and innovation output." *Journal of Management Studies* **47**: 483–508.

Mishra, A. K., Mishra, K. E., and Spreitzer, M. 2009. "Downsizing the company without downsizing morale." *Sloan Management Review* **50**(3): 39–44.

Moskowitz, M., Levering, R., and Tkaczyk, C. 2011. "100 best companies to work for." *Fortune* **163**(2): 91–101.

Noer, D. M. 1993. *Healing the Wounds: Overcoming the Trauma of Layoffs and Revitalizing Downsized Organizations*. San Francisco, CA: Jossey-Bass.

Norman, S. M., Avolio, B. J., and Luthans, F. 2010. "The impact of positivity and transparency on trust in leaders and their perceived effectiveness." *The Leadership Quarterly* **21**: 350–364.

Pfeffer, J. 1998. *The Human Equation: Building Profits by Putting People First*. Boston, MA: Harvard Business School Press.

Pink-slip productivity. 1992. *The Economist*, March, p. 79.

Probst, T. M. and Brubaker, T. L. 2001. "The effects of job insecurity on employee safety outcomes: Cross-sectional and longitudinal explorations." *Journal of Occupational Health Psychology* **6**(2): 139–159.

Probst, T. M., Stewart, S. M., Gruys, M. L., and Tierney, B. W. 2007. "Productivity, counterproductivity and creativity: The ups and downs of job insecurity." *Journal of Occupational and Organizational Psychology* **80**: 479–497.

Rigby, D. 2002. "Look before you lay off: Downsizing in a downturn can do more harm than good." *Harvard Business Review* **80**(4): 20–21.

Rousseau, D. M. 1995. *Psychological Contracts in Organizations: Understanding Written and Unwritten Agreements*. Thousand Oaks, CA: Sage.

Schneider, B. 2006. "Customer satisfaction." *Leadership Excellence* **23**(8): 13.

Sheaffer, Z., Carmeli, A., Steiner-Revivo, M., and Zionit, S. 2009. "Downsizing strategies and organizational performance: A longitudinal study." *Management Decision* **47**: 950–974.

Spreitzer, G. M. and Mishra, A. K. 2002. "To stay or go: Voluntary survivor turnover following an organizational downsizing." *Journal of Organizational Behavior* **23**: 707–729.

Trevor, C. O. and Nyberg, A. J. 2008. "Keeping your headcount when all about you are losing theirs: Downsizing, voluntary turnover rates, and the moderating role of HR practices." *Journal of Management Journal* **51**: 259–276.

Uchitelle, L. 2006. *The Disposable American: Layoffs and Their Consequences*. New York: Knopf.

United States Department of Labor. 2011. "Extended mass layoffs – fourth quarter 2010, annual totals – 2010." Press release, February 11. Retrieved from http://www.bls.gov/news.release/pdf/mslo.pdf.

Vahtera, J., Kivimaki, M., and Pentti, J. 1997. "Effect of organizational downsizing on health of employees." *Lancet* **350**: 1124–1128.

Vanderheiden, P. A., De Meuse, K. P., and Bergmann, T. J. 1999. "And the beat goes on: Corporate downsizing in the twenty-first century." *Human Resource Management* **38**: 261–268.

Wiley, J. E. 2008. "Going beyond the basics: The effects of mergers and acquisitions on employee retention and engagement." Symposium presented at the Society for Industrial and Organizational Psychology Conference, Multiple Perspectives on Retaining and Engaging Employees suring Organizational Transitions, M. L. Marks (Chair), San Francisco.

PART IV

# *Post-downsizing implications*

# 10 The stress outcomes of downsizing

M. BLAKE HARGROVE, CARY L. COOPER, AND JAMES CAMPBELL QUICK

## Introduction

Too many managers and scholars alike may overlook post-downsizing. There are important considerations in the aftermath of a downsizing event, some of which very much need to be anticipated as the downsizing process begins. These considerations include:

- effects on the organization,
- outcome goals (e.g., surviving versus revitalizing), and
- effects on individuals.

A key question here is: what are the impacts a downsizing climate has on people and their relationship to work? The primary concern of this chapter is the human side of the business and the effects of downsizing on individuals. There are five groups of individuals that are impacted by the downsizing process. These are:

- employees and managers who are downsized and lose their positions as a result (primary casualties);
- employees who survive the downsizing and remain within the organization (secondary casualties but survivors);
- managers who orchestrate and execute the downsizing event (secondary casualties but survivors);
- spouses, family members, and loved ones who have personal, intimate relationships with those who are let go in the downsizing process as well as those employees and managers who remain (secondary casualties);
- external spectators, care givers, and community members who are witness to the downsizing event and may either have direct or indirect contact with any or all of the above-mentioned groups (tertiary casualties).

Downsizing is a traumatic and stressful event that poses the threat of loss to those in any way involved with the process (Quick, Quick,

Nelson, and Hurrell, 1997). While downsizing is inevitably stressful, the ultimate outcomes may or may not be distressful.

We explore how downsizing causes stress for primarily the first three groups of individuals noted above. We examine in some details the research evidence concerning the perceptual, attitudinal, and behavioral outcomes of downsizing. Finally, we consider environmental or contextual factors, individual moderators of the process, and most importantly the management actions that can facilitate the most positive outcomes while mitigating or guarding against adverse consequences of downsizing.

## Downsizing as a source of individual stress

In their comprehensive review of the downsizing literature, Datta, Guthrie, Basuil, and Pandey (2010) define downsizing as "a planned set of organizational policies and practices aimed at workforce reduction with the goal of improving firm performance" (p. 281). At the heart of this definition is *workforce reduction* – real people losing their jobs. When downsizing occurs some individuals *get fired*, other individuals *witness the firings but keep their jobs*, and some *managers do the firing*. This experience has the potential to be traumatizing for all those exposed (Gandolfi, 2008; Moore, Grunberg, and Greenberg, 2004). In this section, we will define each of the affected groups of individuals and describe how downsizing may serve as a source of stress for these individuals.

### *Primary casualties – victims*

Victims are those individuals who are terminated during an organizational downsizing action; they are those who lose their jobs. Understandably, victims have received more public attention than have any other group of individuals affected by downsizing. The stress caused by downsizing can be severe. For example, McKee-Ryan, Song, Wanberg, and Kinicki (2005) found that some victims of layoffs experience Post Traumatic Stress Disorder. It is well understood that victims experience stress due to economic factors, for example loss of employment, loss of income, and loss of benefits. In addition, stress can result from socio-emotional sources such as loss of social relationships (Shah, 2000), psychological contract breach (Pugh, Skarlicki, and Pasell, 2003), and perceived injustice

(Brockner, Konovsky, Cooper-Schneider, Folger, Martin, and Bies, 1994; McKee-Ryan *et al.*, 2005).

Stress from job loss has been specifically linked to lingering effects among victims. Pugh *et al.* (2003) found that the psychological contract breach experienced by some victims of downsizing affected their trust toward future employers and caused the cynicism with which they viewed their subsequent jobs. This finding suggests that the socio-emotional impact of downsizing is not limited to the short term. Some longitudinal evidence supports this finding; McKee-Ryan *et al.* (2005) studied the impact of layoff fairness on subsequent employment outcomes. This study provides evidence that victims who perceived greater degrees of unfairness had more difficulty coping and returning to pre-downsizing equilibrium.

## *Secondary casualties – survivors*

The second group of individuals affected by downsizing are the survivors. Survivors are those individuals within an organization that witness the layoff and are affected by the layoff but retain their jobs. In other words, survivors are those employees who are left after the cut. Downsizings exposes survivors to stressors due to both organizational and socio-emotional factors. Some evidence indicates that this stress may be equal or even exceed that suffered by victims (Devine, Reay, Stainton, and Collins-Nikai, 2003). One study in the *British Medical Journal* found a positive correlation between exposure to downsizing and illness-absenteeism, cardiovascular disease, and death among downsizing survivors (Vahtera, 2004).

For victims, downsizing results in job loss; for survivors, downsizing often results in job change and organizational restructuring. Survivors are often asked to do more and assume additional responsibilities following a layoff (*Journal of Accountancy*, 2009; Virick, Lillu, and Casper, 2007). Some of these survivors may experience task overload (Gillespie, Walsh, Winefields, Dua, and Stough, 2001) or burnout (*Journal of Accountancy*, 2009) may be the result. In addition to being asked to do more work, survivors are sometimes asked to change how they do their jobs, where they do their jobs, or even which jobs they do. The changes to organizational structure, which often occur in parallel to downsizing, may result in significant stress to those who remain.

As with victims, survivors are also affected by socio-emotional factors which can be significant sources of stress. Most obvious, perhaps, is their sympathy for the victims. Most workers care about their peers and teammates. When coworkers lose their jobs, the survivors who care are affected sympathetically by the loss (Brockner, Grover, Reed, DeWitt, and O'Malley, 1987). Other socio-emotional factors affecting survivors include perceptions of injustice (Bies, Martins, and Brockner, 1993; Brennan and Skarlicki, 2004; Brockner *et al.*, 1994; Brockner, Wiesenfeld, and Martin, 1995; Hamilton, 2000; Kim, 2009; Lavelle, Brockner, Konovsky, Price, Henley, and Taneja, 2009), breach of trust (Hopkins and Weathington, 2006; A.K. Mishra and Mishra, 1994; Mishra and Spreitzer, 1998), job insecurity (Brockner, Grover, O'Malley, Reed, and Glynn, 1993; Brockner, Grover, Reed, and Dewitt, 1992; Probst, Stewart, and Gruys, 2007; Sora, Caballer, Peiro, and de Witte, 2009; ), and changes in social network (Shah, 2000). Working with numerous colleagues, Joel Brockner has published at least a dozen articles containing the term "survivor" in the abstract. Brockner and his colleagues have focused especially on the impact of downsizing on social exchange constructs (Bies *et al.*, 1993; Brockner *et al.*, 1994; Brockner *et al.*, 1995; Lavelle *et al.*, 2009). These social exchange consequences will be the focus of the outcomes section of this chapter.

### *Secondary casualties – agent-survivors*

Those managers who implement and execute the organizational downsizing action are a special case of survivors. We refer to them as agent-survivors. Like survivors, they are exposed to the economic and socio-emotional stressors typified by those who witness downsizing.

In addition, agent-survivors are subject to additional stressors resulting from their "stuck in the middle" status (Dewitt, Trevino, and Mollica, 2003). As agents of the organization, agent-survivors experience unique stressors associated with carrying out organizational imperatives (Dewitt *et al.*, 2003; Folger and Skarlicki, 1998; Wiesenfeld, Brockner, and Thibault, 2000). Some of these additional stressors include anticipation of negative reactions and anticipation of harm (Folger and Skarlicki, 1998): Folger and Skarlicki's empirical findings indicate that some agent-survivors engage in counterproductive management behaviors such as distancing in an attempt to minimize the impact of negative reactions and retribution. Similarly, Wiesenfeld *et al.* (2000) found evidence that agent-survivors engaged in self-protective behaviors related to downsizing in cases in which the agent-survivors felt threatened by their agency role. Interestingly, these authors also found a link between agent-survivors' self-esteem and the perceived fairness of the downsizing activity. We have just focused on the various groups of individuals affected by downsizing, now we turn to the individual outcomes of the downsizing process.

## Individual outcomes

When organizations downsize, victims, supervisors, and agent-supervisors are exposed to significant stress as a result of organizational-level and individual-level change. The perceptions of individuals and groups of the processes through which downsizing occurs (that is, of how it is done) have important impacts on a range of individual outcomes of these processes.

Lavelle, Rupp, and Brockner (2007) presented a theoretical framework, the target similarity model (TSM), which synthesized much of the social exchange theory of the previous decade. This framework has two dimensions. The horizontal dimension contains the social exchange mechanisms; on the left are perceptions of justice, which flow to attitudes, which flow to citizenship behavior. Attitudes, including trust and commitment, mediate the relationship between sources of justice and citizenship behavior. On the vertical dimension are the sources of justice and the targets of social exchange and behavior. The sources/targets contemplated by this framework are the organization as a whole, the supervisor, and the work group.

In this chapter, we utilize the TSM as a conceptual framework for our discussion of the individual outcomes resulting from the stress of downsizing. Following the horizontal logic of the TSM, we argue that perceptions form attitudes which, in turn, predict behavior. We accept the theoretical arguments made by Lavelle *et al.* (2007) with regard to the mediating role of the attitudes of trust and commitment.

### *Individual perceptions*

During downsizing, individuals learn of the event through a variety of sensory inputs. Perceptions, by definition, involve subjective appreciations of a given set of sensory information at the individual level. Though perceptions come into being within, and are significantly affected by, the social context, individuals ultimately become aware and form their own understanding of a set of sensory information individually. When a downsizing action occurs, the first set of individual outcomes of importance is these individual perceptions. The manner in which the downsizing information is perceived will impact the degree to which the downsizing event induces stress. Distress is most likely to occur under conditions in which highly negative perceptions are formed (Dewe, O'Driscoll, and Cooper, 2010).

Perceptions that seem to be most relevant as individual outcomes resulting from downsizing are those concerning fairness and support. Depending upon what information is conveyed and how that information is conveyed, individuals will form perceptions regarding the fairness of a downsizing event. Similarly, individuals will perceive varying levels of support from their organizations and supervisors depending upon their individual processing of sensory information received. As the following sections will discuss, these perceptions initiate a sequence of attitude formation and behavior that is crucial to the understanding of the consequences of downsizing. Perceptions of justice and support are not independent. Theory and empirical evidence suggest that perceptions of justice are antecedents of perceptions of support (Lavelle *et al.*, 2007).

**Categories of organizational justice**

Within the social exchange framework suggested by Lavelle *et al.* (2007), perceptions of justice are the antecedents of subsequent individual attitudes and behaviors. The conceptualization of organizational justice in this chapter relies on the four-factor model proposed by Colquitt (2001) and his colleagues, Colquitt, Conlon, Wesson, Porter, and Ng, 2001, Greenberg and Colquitt, 2005) in his construct validation study. This four-factor model relies in part on an extensive meta-analytic review of the organizational justice literature (Colquitt *et al.*, 2001). This research stream provides evidence that organizational justice is best understood in terms of four dimensions. Basing the items of each justice dimension carefully on the seminal work of previous researchers, Colquitt (2001) adapted measures for each of the factors. For distributive justice (DJ), Colquitt measures the degree to which the outcomes are fair and appropriate based upon effort, contribution, and performance. For procedural justice (PJ), the degree to which the processes leading to the outcomes are fair and appropriate is measured. PJ is based upon employee input and influence, consistency across those affected, absence of bias, decisions made using accurate information, adherence to ethical norms, and the possibility of appeal. Colquitt's third factor, interpersonal justice (IpJ) is a measurement of the degree to which individual treatment is polite, dignified, and proper. The final dimension in the four-factor model, informational justice (InfoJ), is measured as the degree to which the information conveyed to individuals is perceived as candid, thorough, reasonable, timely, and tailored to individuals' needs. Perceptions of organizational justice are key to understanding subsequent attitudes and behaviors (Lavelle *et al.*, 2007).

**Distributive justice (DJ)**

One crucial outcome of any downsizing action is how those affected perceive the DJ of the action. Specifically DJ in the context of downsizing means whether or not the downsizing decisions accurately reflect the individual perceptions of the effort, contributions, and performance of those affected. In other words, did management fire the "right" people. In theory, if management is perceived to have downsized stronger performers and retained weaker employees, the action will be perceived as unfair.

Theory and empirical findings suggest that perceptions of DJ will have less effect on the attitudinal and behavioral outcomes than the other dimensions. DJ is often linked with the economic and organizational factors more than the socio-emotional factors (Greenberg and Colquitt, 2005). Early empirical work in downsizing provided evidence that survivors react to downsizing most negatively when they perceive victims to be inadequately compensated (Brockner *et al.*, 1987). Thus, perceptions of DJ will often involve the more objective issues in a downsizing event: who is fired, who keeps their jobs, what do the victims get, what changes are in store for the survivors.

Hopkins and Weathington (2006) found a strong correlation between DJ and trust and also identified positive relationships between DJ and affective commitment and organizational satisfaction. A quasi-experimental panel study among survivors and victims of downsizing in the Russian army officer corps found that survivors viewed the outcomes as more than just victims (Hamilton, 2000). Additionally, victims with higher perceived DJ saw overall outcomes as less negative than those with perceived low levels of DJ (Hamilton, 2000).

**Procedural justice (PJ)**

A substantial body of research indicates that organizational constituents are willing to tolerate negative distributive outcomes when processes are perceived as fair (Folger and Konovsky 1989; McFarlin and Sweeney, 1992; Konovsky and Pugh, 1994). Perceptions of PJ have been linked with perceived support (Moorman, Blakely, and Niehoff, 1998), trust (Folger and Konovksy, 1989), affective commitment (McFarlin and Sweeney, 1992), and citizenship behavior (Konovsky and Pugh, 1994). When the distributive outcome is downsizing, victims, survivors, and agent-survivors are all sensitive to perceptions of PJ. Within the context of downsizing, perceived PJ is the degree to which individuals believe the processes resulting in the downsizing decision are fair. Following Colquitt's (2001) theoretical definition of PJ, this implies that individuals would be sensitive to at least six procedural factors during a downsizing event.

First, individuals would wish to perceive that they had an opportunity to influence the process by being given voice or input prior to the decision being made. This finding was supported within a downsizing context among a sample of German workers experiencing layoff (Pfeifer, 2007). Second, individuals would expect that the downsizing actions were applied consistently across those individuals affected. In other words, processes which ensure that intended distributive outcomes are consistently applied are more desirable than haphazard or random processes. Third, individuals expect downsizing decisions to be free of bias. If individuals perceive that some individuals or groups are receiving preferential or detrimental treatment, an adverse perception of PJ would follow. Fourth, individuals expect downsizing decisions to be made based upon accurate information. Individuals perceive greater degrees of PJ during a downsizing action when they have confidence that the organization has based layoff decisions on current and valid data. Fifth, individuals expect organizations to adhere to organizational ethical norms during a downsizing event. Downsizing activities must not just be legal; in order to be perceived as procedurally just, the downsizing activities must be congruent with the stated and enacted ethical norms within the organization. Sixth, and finally, individuals expect there to be an appeals process in place during a downsizing event. Individuals are more likely to perceive high levels of PJ if they believe there is a system in place to redress mistakes and/or amend unjust outcomes.

Among agent-survivors some evidence suggests that procedural unfairness leads to a less favorable sense of self (Wiesenfeld, Brockner, and Thibault, 2000). In addition, this study found that sense of self mediated the relationship between agent-survivors' perceptions of PJ and positive managerial behaviors. Thus, perceptions of PJ appear to be predictive of more positive agent-survivor behavior (Wiesenfeld *et al.*, 2000). Other research concerning PJ in the downsizing context provided evidence that PJ has a moderate positive relationship with affective commitment and organizational satisfaction (Hopkins and Weathington, 2006). Other empirical evidence found a strong relationship between perceived PJ and perceived outcome negativity among victims and survivors of downsizing (Brockner *et al.*, 1994). This relationship was demonstrated among those who perceived both high and low levels of PJ. In other words, this finding suggests that under the high PJ condition there are few negative reactions to a downsizing event.

**Interpersonal justice (IpJ)**

Not surprisingly, individuals are sensitive not only to the message delivered, but to the interpersonal characteristics of the message. Colquitt's (2001) scale measures IpJ as the degree to which individual treatment is polite, dignified, and proper. In a downsizing action, affected individuals will perceive unfairness if they believe the downsizing is accomplished without sufficient interpersonal care. Victims will perceive downsizing as unjust if they feel their treatment is impolite, undignified, or improper. Similarly, survivors who witness inappropriate interpersonal treatment are less likely to perceive a downsizing action as just. Consistent with their dual role, agent-survivors are simultaneously sensitive to the interpersonal nature of their own behavior and the behavior they witness in other organizational actors. When this behavior is rude or inappropriate, agent-survivors are likely to perceive it as unjust.

In the previously mentioned study of Russian army officers, evidence was presented that treating downsizing victims with respect was a humane and low-cost method of reducing negative perceptions of outcome (Hamilton, 2000). Hamilton suggests that perceived respect aids victims in coping with a stressful change by reshaping their overall perception of the event.

A study among 190 managers in 99 firms, taken from a broad range of industries, suggests that the ability to show empathetic concern positively relates to manager's sense of interpersonal fairness (Patient and Skarlicki, 2010). Though being empathetic required managers to take more time and effort, the finding suggests that managers were willing to subordinate their narrow self-interest in order to be more empathetic. Patient and Skarlicki's study suggests that one important coping strategy for agent-survivors is delivering the bad news in a more empathetic manner (2010). This positive coping behavior stands in contrast to the distancing behavior described by Folger and Skarlicki (1998).

#### Informational justice (InfoJ)

As with other forms of fairness, a growing body of evidence suggests that individuals affected by downsizing are sensitive to perceptions of InfoJ. According to Colquitt's (2001) scale validation study, individuals are sensitive to the degree to which the information conveyed to individuals is perceived as candid, thorough, reasonable, timely, and tailored to individuals' needs. Within the context of downsizing, victims and survivors perceive information that fails to possess the above qualities as insufficient and inadequate and may be more likely to perceive unfairness. Pompa (1992) makes ethical arguments against withholding layoff information based on consequentialist and deontological grounds. With regard to individuals, Pompa argues that harm occurs to individuals who are not candidly and timely informed because they are poorly prepared to respond to the economic and psychological stressors of downsizing. Similarly, agent-survivors who are charged with conveying the information may perceive downsizing actions as more unjust if they are asked to deliver low-quality information. In a sample of survivors of downsizing in South Korea, findings suggest higher levels of InfoJ decreased intention to turnover (Kim, 2009). The same study found that employees perceiving high InfoJ were more likely to have communal relationships than exchange-based relationships. Other empirical research links low levels of InfoJ with higher levels of counterproductive retaliatory behaviors (Skarlicki, Barclay, and Pugh, 2008).

#### Perceived support

Like perceptions of justice, perceptions of support depend upon the individual processing of sensory information. Also like perceptions of justice, perceptions of support will vary depending upon the quality of this information set. Consistent with the TSM proposed by Lavelle *et al.* (2007), support is perceived at different levels within the organization. Within the context of downsizing, this means that individuals may form perceptions of support at the organizational (POS) and supervisory (PSS) level. These perceptions may be congruent or conflicting depending upon the circumstances. At both source levels, research indicates that low levels of perceived support are associated with numerous negative social exchange outcomes ultimately affecting individual behaviors (Lavelle *et al.*, 2007).

Victims and survivors of downsizing are most likely to perceive organizational support under conditions in which the organization has adequately prepared for the predictable consequences of a downsizing event (Cascio, 2010). If the organization has failed to provide adequate systems of support for victims and survivors, these individuals will understandably perceive a lack of support. Perceptions of DJ and PJ are closely theoretically related to POS (Moorman *et al.*, 1998); if survivors and victims perceive that the downsizing actions produce unfair outcomes or the processes leading to the outcomes are unjust, they will not perceive adequate organizational support. Research indicates that organizations that fail to provide adequate pay, continuation of benefits, and to give warning will not be perceived favorably (Cascio, 2010). Theoretically, POS should be most directly tied to perceptions of DJ and PJ in as much as they share many of the same antecedents. Another inquiry into the impact of POS in a downsizing context was accomplished by Lee and Peccei (2007). In this study, POS was positively related to affective commitment among survivors and predicted lower turnover intent.

For agent-survivors, POS depends both on what systems the organization has in place for the victims and survivors and how well agents are supported in the performance of their duties. In a study of Canadian government managers experiencing downsizing, findings suggest that in conditions of higher perceived organizational support, coping measures were less constrained (Armstrong-Stassen, 2006). In other words, positive behavioral outcomes were more likely to occur in downsizing organizations in which there was a higher degree of POS.

PSS depends upon victim and survivor perceptions of the behavior of the supervisors involved in the downsizing action. PSS is theoretically associated with the perceptions of IpJ and InfoJ based upon the behavior of supervisors; this may be tied to the greater degree of discretion which supervisors possess with regard to matters of interactional justice (Scott, Paddock, and Colquitt, 2009). Theoretically, PSS depends upon both the quality of the information provided by supervisors and the interpersonally sensitive manner in which the information is conveyed. PSS is an important theoretical antecedent of subsequent attitudes and behaviors targeted at supervisors (Lavelle *et al.*, 2007).

## *Individual attitudes*

Consistent with the social exchange theory, individual attitudes follow from individual perceptions (Lavelle *et al.*, 2007). Thus, the second level of individual outcomes associated with downsizing stress are attitudinal outcomes. When a downsizing event occurs, information regarding the downsizing will be transmitted to and then perceived by those individuals affected. Following this perceptive process, individual attitudes are formed. Attitudes such as trust, commitment, and satisfaction are in turn well understood predictors of behavior.

Following the phased-logic of Lavelle *et al.* (2007), we classify attitudes as primary or secondary. A primary attitude is formed based upon perceptions and predicts subsequent attitudes. The attitude of most relevance in the context of downsizing stress is trust. Trust often takes long periods of time to establish, yet can be broken in an instant. Depending upon how a downsizing action is perceived, changes in trust can occur. Breaches in trust are associated with individual distress (van Dijke and de Cremer, 2008). Secondary attitudes are formed subsequent to both perceptions and primary attitudes. For example, empirical evidence supports the contention that trust is predictive of commitment (Spreitzer and Mishra, 2002). Attitudes such as commitment and job satisfaction are directly dependent in part upon trust (Lavelle *et al.*, 2007).

### Primary attitude – trust

Individuals vary with regard to the degree of trust they bestow upon their organizations and managers. Downsizing events may impact levels of trust in individuals. This impact need not be negative. Though trust among victims is unlikely to increase during a downsizing event, it need not be destroyed. In theory, a properly managed downsizing event could even be an opportunity to increase trust among survivors and agent-survivors. Mishra and Spreitzer (1998) argue that trust facilitates constructive responses and positive coping to downsizing actions. Empirical evidence supports the contention that trust mediates the relationship both between perceptions of justice and job satisfaction and between perceptions of justice and intent to turnover (Hopkins and Weathington, 2006).

Of course, the more common result of a downsizing event is a decrease in trust. Empirical research in downsizing suggests that decreases in trust are associated with psychological contract breach (Pugh *et al.*, 2003). In addition, this research suggests that breaches of trust increase the negative emotional experiences associated with layoff. As mentioned before, some of these negative emotional experiences linger in the long-term as victims pursue other employment opportunities.

**Secondary attitudes – satisfaction and commitment**

Satisfaction is a well-studied and well-understood construct within the organizational and behavioral sciences. Because victims of downsizing lose their jobs, their continuing satisfaction in their work at the downsizing organizations is not likely to be relevant. For survivors and survivor-agents, however, satisfaction is an important theoretical consideration. Empirical research supports the contention that satisfaction is dependent upon procedural justice and predictive of affective commitment (Hopkins and Weathington, 2006, Mansour-Cole and Scott, 1998). In a study among European layoff survivors, researchers found that perceptions of job insecurity resulting from downsizing activities predicted lower satisfaction (Sora *et al.*, 2009).

Individual commitment is an important attitudinal outcome of downsizing. Meyer and Allen (1991) present a three-factor model of organizational commitment: affective, continuance, and normative. Affective commitment is the degree to which individuals feel committed. Continuance commitment is the degree to which individuals remain committed due to the perceived costs of disaffiliation. Normative commitment is the degree to which an individual remains committed to an organization out of a sense of duty or obligation. For victims of downsizing, continuance commitment is no longer a factor; whatever the costs are, they are going to suffer them. Affective commitment and normative commitment are relevant among victims. Depending upon their experience with the event, victims might feel differently and might infer different levels of obligation about an organization or manager.

For survivors and agent-survivors, commitment is a crucial outcome. In general, downsizing has been associated with lower levels of organizational commitment (Brockner *et al.* 2004). Large bodies of research link organizational commitment to improved performance and reduced turnover (Colquitt *et al.*, 2011). Research indicates that survivors might feel differently toward organizations and managers following downsizing (Lee and Peccei, 2007). Other empirical findings suggest the effects of downsizing on commitment. In the previously mentioned study of European employees experiencing downsizing, increased levels of job insecurity was predictive of decreased affective commitment (Sora *et al.*, 2009).

Organizations are not helpless with regard to the effects of downsizing on affective commitment. In a study of surviving mid-level managers and supervisors in transit systems undergoing restructuring and downsizing, evidence was found that organizations can employ strategies to mitigate the impact of downsizing on affective commitment (Ugboro, 2006). Organizational efforts to redesign jobs, increase task autonomy, and increase employee empowerment were positively related to commitment, despite the downsizing environment. Similarly, Brockner *et al.* (2004) found evidence among layoff survivors that affective commitment can be increased by a higher degree of perceived control. These findings suggest that efforts to empower survivors during a downsizing event are effective managerial tools to improve individual commitment.

## *Individual behaviors*

Behavioral outcomes are always of principal interest to business practitioners. While perceptions and attitudes are the internal psychological processes which impact individual performance, behaviors are the external consequences which are critical to firm performance. Within the social exchange model, behaviors follow from perceptions and attitudes (Lavelle *et al.*, 2007; Nelson and Quick, 2008). Individual behaviors can be characterized as positive or negative. Positive behaviors include improved job performance and citizenship behaviors. Negative behaviors include poor job performance, increased turnover, and deviant behaviors.

### Job performance

Job performance is perhaps the single most important outcome variable in organizational behavior; developing, maintaining, and improving job performance may rightfully be understood as the *raison d'être* of the discipline. Thus, during any downsizing action, future job performance must be one of the principal considerations. Because their role is being eliminated by design, future job performance is an irrelevant outcome for victims of downsizing. For survivors and agent-survivors, however, job performance outcomes are pivotal.

Research has indicated that downsizing has an adverse impact on individual job performance (Data *et al.*, 2010). In a longitudinal study of the effect of job security on job performance, survivor job performance decreased significantly immediately following a downsizing and remained lower than the initial level for three years (Armstrong-Stassen,

2002). Other research suggests a more complicated relationship. Brockner *et al.* (1992) produced empirical findings that the relationship between job insecurity and work effort is curvilinear. In this study, work effort was highest in conditions of moderate job insecurity; under conditions of very low job insecurity and very high job insecurity, work effort was lower. This study also found that economic need moderated the relationship between job insecurity and performance.

**Turnover and intent to turnover**

Termination of employees is one of the purposes of downsizing. When undertaking downsizing activities, organizations seek to control which employees they retain and which they dismiss. Losing valued employees through voluntary turnover is generally undesirable. Thus, retaining survivors and agent-survivors is an important consideration for organizations undertaking downsizing.

Several studies have explored the impact of downsizing on individual intent to turnover and turnover. In a sample of union employees at a plant undergoing downsizing, evidence was found that increased organizational commitment decreased voluntary turnover. Commitment was, in turn, predicted by trust, organizational justice, and employee empowerment (Spreitzer and Mishra, 2002). Similar results were found in a study of Canadian nurses. In this study, nurses reported an increase in turnover intention as a result of decreased satisfaction associated with downsizing (Armstrong-Stassen and Cameron, 2003). The relationship between downsizing and job performance is not all bad news. Trevor and Nyberg (2008) found that HR practices during downsizing can reduce voluntary turnover rates. The researchers found that voluntary turnover rates were improved promoting job development and employee social embeddedness.

**Citizenship behaviors**

Citizenship behaviors, positive discretionary behaviors above and beyond those mandated by an employee's role, are associated with a large variety of positive organizational outcomes (Organ, Podsakoff, and MacKenzie, 2006). Citizenship behaviors may be directed at organizations, supervisors, or coworkers (Lavelle *et al.*, 2007). As with job performance and turnover, future citizenship behavior is an important outcome for the survivors and agent-survivors who remain after a downsizing event. Little empirical research, however, has been conducted regarding citizenship behaviors during layoffs. One study to attempt to explore citizenship behaviors produced results consistent with social exchange and target similarity logic. In a sample of layoff survivors in the medical field, evidence that targeted citizenship behaviors during a layoff are predictive of targeted citizenship behaviors (Lavelle *et al.*, 2009). The study provided evidence that organizational commitment is related to organizational citizenship behavior but not to citizenship behavior directed at coworkers; additionally, the study found that commitment to coworkers was related to citizenship behavior directed at coworkers but not to organizational citizenship behavior (Lavelle *et al.*, 2009).

**Negative behaviors**

Individual negative behavior occurs on a wide spectrum within the organizational context; these behaviors have been studied as counterproductive work behavior, workplace deviance, and workplace violence (Fox and Spector, 2004). Some behaviors are negative because they adversely affect organizational performance financially. Others are negative because they have the potential to physically or psychologically harm those that work within an organization. Some negative behaviors are relatively petty and may be presumed to have only a minor adverse effect. Other behaviors are more significant and can cause a loss of productivity and damage to the social structure of the organization and psycho-emotional health of workers (Fox and Spector, 2009). Still more serious behaviors such as fraud, theft, and harassment rise to the level of criminal acts and can have lasting or permanent effects on organizations and people. Finally, negative behaviors in the workplace can culminate in violence or even murder. Just as organizations should uniformly seek to promote and maximize positive behavioral outcomes, organizations should strive to mitigate, minimize, or eliminate negative behavioral outcomes.

Within the context of downsizing, negative behavioral outcomes are an often-feared and sometimes-realized reality. Negative behaviors are a consideration for all those individuals affected by downsizing. As with positive behavioral outcomes, organizations are concerned with the continuing and future likelihood of negative behavior among survivors and agent-survivors. During those periods immediately following the downsizing activity, organizations may be chiefly concerned with the potential negative behavioral outcomes among victims.

Some research in downsizing has focused on workplace violence and other serious forms of negative behavior. Much of this research has focused on victims of downsizing. In a study of 2,800 Scandinavian health and welfare employees, organizational downsizing was linked to violent behavior (Viitasara, Sverke, and Menckel, 2003). In extreme cases, laid-off employees may come back to work and kill. Weide and Abbott (1994) report that layoffs and terminations are one of the reported explanations for murder in the workplace.

Less research has been directed at less serious forms of negative behavior associated with downsizing. One study that has made this attempt made a surprising finding that job insecurity predicted lower levels of counter-productive work behaviors, such as petty theft and intentionally reduced work effort (Probst, Stewart, Gruys, and Tierney, 2007). This finding may be related to the curvilinear relationship identified by Brockner *et al.* (1992). Another empirical finding suggests that layoff survivors' perceptions of managerial integrity moderated the relationship between perceived informational justice and retaliation behaviors (Skarlicki *et al.*, 2008).

## Moderators of individual outcomes

As with most psychological and behavioral constructs within the field of organizational behavior, individual outcomes related to downsizing stress are moderated by both environmental and individual factors. Environmental factors provide the overall context in which outcomes occur. Context is always an important consideration when exploring outcomes. Similarly, individual variation contributes substantially to the variety of outcomes that might be expected to result from any significant stimulus. Simply put, different individuals placed in the same environment and exposed to identical stimuli can still be expected to perceive the stimuli differently, form different attitudes, and respond with a variety of behaviors.

### *Environmental moderators*

Environmental moderators of the individual outcomes resulting from downsizing are not a well-studied field. There are a number of environmental factors that are worthy of exploration. One opportunity involves overall economic and employment outlook. The timing of a downsizing activity in relation to the overall economic conditions should theoretically moderate individual outcomes (Lin, Lee, and Peterson, 2006; Stjernberg and Tillberg, 1998). For a victim of downsizing during a recession or period of high unemployment, the consequences and thus the stress associated with the layoff might be substantially more severe. For survivors and agent-survivors, continuance commitment might increase and intent to turnover might decrease during tough economic periods. In periods of significant economic growth or boom on the other hand, the effects of downsizing stress might be minimized. Victims may not be overly concerned with losing one job if they believe they can easily acquire another. Because the effects of downsizing on victims are minimized during economic good times, logic argues that the degree of negative stress impact on the survivors and agent-survivors caused by witnessing would be similarly reduced.

Another environmental moderator may involve governmental intervention and policy. Conventional wisdom has argued that the availability of a governmental social safety net and reemployment programs may reduce the negative outcomes of downsizing stress (Gandolfi, 2008). A contrary empirical finding, however, calls this conventional thinking into question. Bennett, Martin, Bies, and Brockner (1995) found no significant relationship between government assistance, or corporate assistance, and coping strategies among layoff victims.

Industry-specific factors can theoretically moderate stress outcomes for individuals affected by outcomes. Without regard to overall economic conditions, certain industries experience periods of growth and decline. For example, steel manufacturing and textile manufacturing have gone from being important industries to becoming virtually extinct in the United States over the past 40 years. In declining industries, downsizing would be theoretically associated with increased levels of negative stress because employees would be aware of the necessity of retraining and career transition. If changing jobs is stressful, changing careers is presumably more so. Finally, another variable which has potential as an environmental moderator is national culture. Probst and Lawler (2006) provided empirical evidence that Chinese workers (collectivists) react more negatively than American workers (individualists) to job insecurity.

### *Individual moderators*

Individual variance significantly affects outcomes related to downsizing stress. Because individual variance occurs on such a wide range of dimensions, empirical research has only begun to explore the many theoretical possibilities concerning individual moderators of downsizing-related stress. In the Russian officers' study, the author found that tenure was significantly related to outcome negativity and increased distress (Hamilton, 2000). Results of some research suggest that gender may influence coping responses to downsizing stress. Harris, Heller, and Braddock (1988) investigated the potential effect of gender on coping mechanisms for downsizing-related stress. Their findings suggest that women report more psychological health problems than men and that men receive more support from spouses but less support from friends and relatives than women. Women reported a greater range of physical and behavioral responses to stress; for example, women reported more alcohol use and feelings of shame related to the loss of emotional control in the work setting (Maki, Moore, Grunberg, and Greenberg, 2005). The findings, especially those regarding alcohol as a coping mechanism, should be accepted cautiously, given the relatively small sample size.

Armstrong-Stassen (1994) found evidence among unionized telecommunications employees exposed to layoffs that optimistic predispositions and sense of control are positively related to control coping. This finding suggests that certain personality traits can predict positive coping mechanisms. Brockner *et al.* (1993) found that survivors low in self-esteem were more likely to feel worried and that these feelings of anxiety translated into more motivation to work than their high self-esteem counterparts. Another study provided evidence that individual self-discipline moderated the relationship between perceived interactional justice and citizenship behavior among survivors (Brennan and Skarlicki, 2004). In this study, self-discipline moderated the relationship such that there was only a positive correlation between perceptions of interactional justice and OCB among those employees who were low on self-discipline. Another empirical finding among managers within an organization undergoing downsizing found that those agent-survivors who were optimistic and had a high tolerance for ambiguity were less negatively affected than those who lacked those resources (Armstrong-Stassen, 1998). Taken together, these empirical findings support the proposition that experiential and personality factors moderate individual outcomes to stress resulting from downsizing.

In addition to those individual moderators explored above, there are many other theoretical possibilities worthy of exploration. One such possibility is human capital. An individual's knowledge, skills, and abilities (KSA) should impact the level of stress experienced via downsizing.

Some sets of KSAs might help in coping with stress, while other less advantageous sets might exacerbate an already stressful situation. Other individual moderators worthy of consideration include personality, general intelligence, and emotional intelligence. Although this is not an exhaustive list, it seems clear that a wide range of individual differences could result in modifying the effects caused by downsizing on any given individual.

## Managerial interventions as moderators of outcomes

Although environmental and individual moderators have the theoretical potential to affect the outcomes of downsizing-related stress, they have little practical significance. With regard to environmental factors, discreet organizations have minimal impact on the overall environment in which downsizing occurs. Similarly, organizations hire people to perform work not on the basis of how they will respond to downsizing. Thus, individual moderators are incidental inasmuch as they occur without intentional organizational input.

Downsizing is generally undertaken as an attempt to improve firm performance by eliminating excess or redundant employees (Datta *et al.*, 2010). It is not undertaken to avoid individual outcomes, rather downsizing is undertaken despite the potential negative individual outcomes. Much research has focused on how organizations reach the strategic decision to downsize and how to properly implement downsizing decisions.[1] The final focus of this chapter concerns those actions which managers may undertake to maximize positive outcomes and minimize negative outcomes associated with stress induced by downsizing. Management interventions can improve individual coping in the face of stressful stimuli (Quick *et al.*, 1997). Managers have opportunities to moderate stress and outcomes related to stress in three distinct stages in the downsizing process: preparation stage prior to downsizing, implementation stage when downsizing action occurs, and the follow-through and completion stage during the period following the downsizing action.

### *Intervention while preparing to downsize*

Preparing for downsizing is a proactive process that might be considered primary prevention because it aims to prevent counterproductive stress by goal-setting, planning, and managing the process in the most positive, constructive way possible (Quick *et al.*, 1997). In this preparation stage, there are three key considerations for managers to address to maximize the positive outcomes and mitigate the adverse, destructive outcomes. These are ethical considerations to ensure fairness for all concerned decision criteria to use throughout the process with an eye to justice concerns, and the planning and training aspects of the downsizing process.

**Ethical considerations**

If managers do not act with integrity, whatever they say may be inadequate (Skarlicki *et al.*, 2008). As with any important managerial action, ethical considerations should be evaluated from the beginning. Because downsizing decisions present predictable ethical dilemmas, managers have a professional obligation to consider the ethical ramifications of their actions as part of the preparation process (Eby and Buch, 1998). As with all business ethics decisions, the first obligation of management is to determine the legality of their downsizing action; legality being the necessary but not sufficient condition of ethical business behavior (Clarkson, Miller, Jentz, and Cross, 2006). Legal considerations involve complex questions and likely necessitate seeking competent legal advice. Employers who risk downsizing without carefully following the law risk potential damage through litigation and public relations (Camardella, 2002).

Once legality has been established, purely ethical considerations can be addressed. One such consideration is the obligation of the powerful over the relatively powerless. Those who make the decisions for downsizing need to consider what duties they owe to those who may be downsized (Hollander, 1995). Another is the conflict between the managerial duties to the organization in comparison to the duties owed to employees (Lamsa and Takala, 2000). In this era of globalization, ethical challenges arise as norms vary from nation to nation and culture to culture (McMahon, 2000).

Although no one ethical approach can be considered universally authoritative, Bright, Cameron, and Caza (2006) suggest that practicing virtue ethics may reduce the negative impact of downsizing by buffering the shocks associated with job loss and organizational change. These authors present empirical findings that forgiveness reduced the negative impact of downsizing and that employees were more likely to forgive when top managers expressed some form of responsibility. Stjernberg and Tillberg (1998) concur that taking responsibility is a key managerial obligation.

These findings taken together suggest that the old axiom that "good ethics is good business" may be supported in the case of downsizing.

**Decision criteria and justice concerns**

As previously discussed in the sections on distributive justice and procedural justice, employees are sensitive to decision criteria, decision and implementation processes, and the resulting outcomes. When preparing for downsizing action, managers should be careful that the decision-making criteria carefully match the organizational needs with elements of distributive justice. It is important that managers lay off and keep the "right" people. According to principles of procedural justice, employees should be given appropriate influence in the decision-making process, and procedures to appeal downsizing decisions should be established. These criteria need to be congruent with the legal, ethical, policy, and cultural norms under which the organization operates.

**Planning and training**

As with any important organizational action, crucial parts of preparation are planning an action carefully and training those who will be responsible for implementation (LaMarsh, 2009; Lin *et al.*, 2006). With regard to planning, important variables must be identified, alternatives must be developed, and evaluations of alternatives must be carefully selected (Lin *et al.*, 2006). Once action alternatives are selected, each step of the implementation should be carefully planned. Plans are never wholly adequate and inevitably fall short in the face of unexpected future developments. However, prudent managers accept this imperfect state and produce the best plans they can. These plans address all known variables and include the contingency plans that should be developed to deal with foreseeable conditions which may arise.

Complex organizational action requires preparation of the persons responsible for acting. Even small investments in training can yield large returns in performance. Managers responsible for downsizing should be trained in all relevant aspects of the process. Research is especially clear that method of delivery matters (Greenberg and Colquitt, 2005; LaMarsh, 2009; Stjernberg and Tillberg, 1998). Managers should be trained regarding their duties before, during, and after the layoff. Critical managerial priorities, such as emotional tone and communication methods, should be identified and managers should be specifically trained in these priorities (LaMarsh, 2009).

## *Intervention during downsizing*

Implementation is always critical. How managers do things is often as important as what they do. Given the social exchange consequences of procedural and interactional justice, it is especially important that managers implement downsizing actions in the "right" way. Managers should carefully follow the downsizing plan, adapting it as appropriate to their situation. During implementation, managers should be mindful of the managerial priorities about which they have been trained.

### Leadership

The actions of senior leaders in a downsizing process send powerful messages throughout the organization, either for good or for ill. Take for example the actions of the commanding general of the US Air Force's largest depot, the San Antonio Air Logistics Center, which was identified in 1995 for a major realignment and then closure action. This major downsizing and then closure action put the well-being of thousands of federal civil servants at risk as was the mission of maintaining the flying capability of the US Air Force. The commanding general took three key actions. First, he made clear that the mission of the depot was to continue to support the combat effectiveness of the US Air Force while taking good care of all personnel in the organization. Second, he worked with the Air Force Office of the Surgeon General to recruit a full-time organizational clinical psychologist to oversee the mental health of the depot's managers and employees. Third, he assigned this chief psychological officer with responsibility to coordinate all offices related to human resource support, such as the civilian personnel office, the chaplains, the occupational physicians, and the security police (Klunder, 2008).

In this organizational downsizing and closure case, the chief executive officer created a supportive leadership structure to address the range of individual needs that would emerge from the organizational trauma. The chief psychological officer engaged in preventive stress management actions that identified the most high risk individual early in the downsizing process and delivered essential services to ensure their health and performance through the process (Klunder, 2008). The positive outcomes included no fatalities and over US$33,000,000 in cost avoidance through preventive interventions for conflict resolutions.

**Informational justice concerns**

Research indicates that perceived informational justice on the part of those affected by downsizing is a key predictor of outcomes. Therefore, just management requires that leaders be as open, thorough, and clear as possible with regard to communicating downsizing information (Greenberg and Colquitt, 2005). If information can be released, it should be released in a timely fashion and should provide employees with as much time as reasonably possible to deal with the effects of the downsizing action (Pompa, 1992). Managers who ignore employees' desires for good information risk causing breaches in perceived support, commitment, and increasing risks of negative behavior. Organizational secrecy should always be balanced with employees' reasonable right to information (Pompa, 1992).

**Interpersonal justice concerns – caring for employees**

Perhaps the single most important managerial action to reduce the negative effects of downsizing involves interpersonal justice. Managers who treat their employees with compassion, respect, dignity, and empathy greatly reduce potential negative outcomes (Folger and Skarlicki, 1998; Hamilton, 2000; Patient and Skarlicki, 2010). It should be noted that being nice does not cost more than being rude or indifferent; interpersonal justice can be practiced at virtually no cost to managers or to their organizations. Simply put, being nice does not cost more than being rude or indifferent. Good management and good ethics dictate that managers should treat employees as emotionally sensitive human beings (Freeman, 2009; Molinksy and Margolis, 2006); this argues against the emotionally distant approach observed by Folger and Skarlicki (1998). Managers who treat their employees well can expect two principal benefits. First, managers will feel better about themselves (Wiesenfeld *et al.*, 2000). Second, managers will induce fewer negative outcomes from those impacted by downsizing via social exchange pathways; therefore, managers can expect better performance, lower turnover, more citizenship behavior, and less negative behavior.

## *Intervention after downsizing*

Once the downsizing is accomplished, managers are not done. Research indicates that the effects of downsizing can continue for years (Armstrong-Stassen, 2002). The completion of the downsizing action initiates a new stage of managerial intervention. In this stage, managers should concentrate on following through with the downsizing plan and continuing to support their remaining employees as needed. Maintaining control is one of the principal functions of managers. During the follow through and support stage, conscientious managers keep their eye on the ball and avoid the potentially serious consequences of underestimating the effects of downsizing stress on survivors.

**Attentiveness and responsiveness**

After downsizing, managers need to maintain an awareness of the delicate condition of some of the survivors working within their organizations. Being aware of the situation is predicate to taking appropriate intervention actions. Coping with significant stress takes time (Quick *et al.*, 1997). It is unrealistic to expect employees to "bounce back" from the significant stress which downsizing can induce. As managers patiently await the return of normalcy, they should be vigilant with regard to the changed and evolving conditions under their supervision. Simply put, managers need to pay attention. Some functional factors which the research indicate require special vigilance are work overload (Virick *et al.*, 2007) and burnout (*Journal of Accountancy*, 2009). In addition, managers must pay attention to the socio-emotional needs of their surviving employees. Disruptions in social networks, problems resulting from violations of trust (Pugh *et al.*, 2003), and apparent changes in attitudes all may require managerial intervention. Finally, managers should maintain awareness of the psychological and physical health needs of their employees (Quick *et al.*, 1997) as well as monitoring for possible warning signs of violent behavior (Viitasara *et al.*, 2003).

Managers who identify potential opportunities for intervention or become aware of particular risks need to respond in a timely and appropriate manner. Pretending problems do not exist or delaying action are rarely appropriate responses to problems in the workplace. Many problems grow larger, rather than go away. On the other hand, managers need to balance responsiveness against the dangers of over-management. Judgment is required to determine whether or not a situation needs intervention. In some cases, the best response is no response. However, choosing not to respond is very different than avoiding a duty to respond.

**Continuing to care**

Just as maintaining a high level of interactional justice was crucial during implementation, caring for surviving employees is of paramount importance during the post-downsizing stage. As survivors cope with the changes to the organization, it is important that managers continue to treat employees with compassion, respect, dignity, and empathy in order to restore equilibrium in the organization. For the same reasons that caring and interactional justice are important during execution, managers must continue to treat their employees well after downsizing.

**Understanding social exchange**

It has been the thesis of this chapter that many of the outcomes related to stress induced by downsizing are related to the social exchange process. It is therefore crucial for managers to understand this process and behave accordingly. Perceptions of justice matter. Perceptions of DJ and especially PJ, IpJ, and InfoJ are crucial in the formation of attitudes. Similarly, attitudes, once formed, depend upon perceptions of support (Lavelle *et al.*, 2007). Attitudes once formed are the important psychological states that predict positive and negative behaviors. Trust, satisfaction, and commitment all predict behaviors upon which organizational performance depend. Trust, even after a crisis, can be rebuilt; managers must strive to rebuild damaged trust relationships. Affective commitment to the organization and organizational commitment are encouraged by actions which communicate support and by managerial behavior that is predictably fair (Lavelle *et al.*, 2007).

## Conclusion

Loss-related events have always been associated with stressful outcomes, for the individual as well as families, communities, and organizations. Downsizing is one of these loss-related events, particularly for those who have a long association with a particular organization or industry. We have tried to highlight what impact downsizing can have on the individual, what some of the moderating factors are in terms of individual outcomes, and what can be done to minimize the negative consequences of this. We have focused on social exchange theory, emphasizing the important role of perceptions of justice in the process. We have discussed this not only in the context of those who have been downsized, but also in respect of the survivors as well. We can minimize the negative effect of this on individuals, but no matter what we do, the impact of downsizing will have some negative outcomes on people and the organization.

Most significant organizational change can be managed, and its counterproductive effects minimized, but it will still have some consequences in the near and medium term. This is aptly highlighted by Machiavelli in his book *The Prince*: "It should be borne in mind that there is nothing more difficult to arrange, more doubtful of success, and more dangerous to carry through than initiating change ... The innovator makes enemies of all those who prospered under the old order, and only lukewarm support is forthcoming from those who would prosper under the new." Our challenge in organizational behavior is to bring what science we have to bear on moderating any potentially adverse outcomes of downsizing, which, given the current economic climate, will be part of the business landscape.

*Note*

1. A comprehensive review of the practical and theoretical considerations regarding downsizing decisions is beyond the scope of this chapter. See Datta *et al.* (2010) for comprehensive discussion and literature review.

## References

Armstrong-Stassen, M. 1994. "Coping with transition: A study of layoff survivors." *Journal of Organizational Behavior* **15**(4): 597–621.

Armstrong-Stassen, M. 1998. "Downsizing the federal government: A longitudinal study of managers' reactions." *Canadian Journal of Administrative Sciences* **15**(4): 310–322.

Armstrong-Stassen, M. 2002. "Designated redundant but escaping layoff: A special group of lay-off survivors." *Journal of Occupational and Organizational Psychology* **75**(1): 1–13.

Armstrong-Stassen, M. 2006. "Determinants of how managers cope with organisational downsizing." *Applied Psychology: An International Review* **55**(1): 1–26.

Armstrong-Stassen, M. and Cameron, S. J. 2003. "Nurses' job satisfaction and turnover intentions over a six-year period of hospital downsizing and amalgamation." *International Journal of Public Administration* **26**(14): 1607–1620.

Bennett, N., Martin, C. L., Bies, R. J., and Brockner, J. 1995. "Coping with a layoff: A longitudinal study of victims." *Journal of Management* **21**(6): 1025–1041.

Bies, R. J., Martin, C. L., and Brockner, J. 1993. "Just laid off, but still a 'good citizen?' only if the proess is fair." *Employee Responsibilities and Rights Journal* **6**(3): 227–238.

Brennan, A. and Skarlicki, D. P. 2004. "Personality and perceived justice as predictors of survivors' reactions following downsizing." *Journal of Applied Social Psychology* **34**(6): 1306–1328.

Bright, D. S., Cameron, K. S., and Caza, A. 2006. "The amplifying and buffering effects of virtuousness in downsizing organizations." *Journal of Business Ethics* **64**(3): 249–269.

Brockner, J., Grover, S., O'Malley, M. N., Reed, T. F., and Glynn, M. A. 1993. "Threat of future layoffs, self-esteem, and survivors' reactions: Evidence from the laboratory and the field." *Strategic Management Journal* **14**(Summer): 153–166.

Brockner, J., Grover, S., Reed, T. F., and DeWitt, R. L. 1992. "Layoffs, job insecurity, and survivors' work effort: Evidence of an inverted-U relationship." *Academy of Management Journal* **35**(2): 413–425.

Brockner, J., Grover, S., Reed, T., DeWitt, R., and O'Malley, M. 1987. "Survivors' reactions to layoffs: We get by with a little help for our friends." *Administrative Science Quarterly* **32**(4): 526–541.

Brockner, J., Konovsky, M., Cooper-Schneider, R., Folger, R., Martin, C., and Bies, R. J. 1994. "Interactive effects of procedural justice and outcome negativity on victims and survivors of job loss." *Academy of Management Journal* **37**(2): 397–409.

Brockner, J., Spreitzer, G., Mishra, A., Hochwarter, W., Pepper, L., and Weinberg, J. 2004. "Perceived control as an antidote to the negative effects of layoffs on survivors' organizational commitment and job performance." *Administrative Science Quarterly* **49**(1): 76–100.

Brockner, J., Wiesenfeld, B. M., and Martin, C. L. 1995. "Decision frame, procedural justice, and survivors' reactions to job layoffs." *Organizational Behavior and Human Decision Processes* **63**(1): 59–68.

Camardella, M. J. 2002. "Legal considerations of a workforce reduction." *Employment Relations Today* **29**(3): 101–106.

Cascio, W. F. 2010. *Employment Downsizing and Its Alternatives: Strategies for Long-Term Success*. Alexandria, VA: Society for Human Resource Management Foundation.

Clarkson, K. W., Miller, R. L., Jentz, G. A., and Cross, F. B. 2006. *West's Business Law Text and Cases: Legal, Ethical, International, and E-Commerce Environment* (10th edn.). Mason, OH: Thomson.

Colquitt, J. A. 2001. "On the dimensionality of organizational justice: A construct validation of a measure." *Journal of Applied Psychology* **86**: 356–400.

Colquitt, J. A., Conlon, D. E., Wesson, M. J., Porter, C. O., and Ng, K. Y. 2001. "Justice at the millennium: A meta-analytic review of 25 years of organizational justice research." *Journal of Applied Psychology* **86**: 425–445.

Colquitt, J. A., LePine, J. A., and Wesson, M. J. 2011. *Organizational Behavior: Improving Performance and Commitment in the Workplace* (2nd edn.). Burr Ridge, IL: McGraw-Hill Irwin.

Datta, D. K., Guthrie, J. P., Basuil, D., and Pandey, A. 2010. "A review and synthesis." *Journal of Management* **36**(1): 281–348.

Devine, K., Reay, T., Stainton, L., and Collins-Nakai, R. 2003. "Downsizing outcomes: Better a victim than a survivor?" *Human Resource Management* **42**(2): 109–124.

Dewe, P., O'Driscoll, M., and Cooper, C. L. 2010. *Coping with Work Stress: A Review and Critique*. Oxford: Wiley-Blackwell.

DeWitt, R., Trevino, L., and Mollica, K. A. 2003. "Stuck in the middle: A control-based model of managers' reactions to their subordinates' layoffs." *Journal of Managerial Issues* **15**(1): 32.

Eby, L. T. and Buch, K. 1998. "The impact of adopting an ethical approach to employee dismissal during corporate restructuring." *Journal of Business Ethics* **17**(12): 1253–1264.

Folger, R. and Konovsky, M. A. 1989. "Effects of procedural and distributive justice on reactions to pay raise decisions." *Academy of Management Journal* **32**(1): 115–130.

Folger, R. and Skarlicki, D. P. 1998. "When tough times make tough bosses: Managerial distancing as a function of layoff blame." *Academy of Management Journal* **41**(1): 79–87.

Fox, S. and Spector, P. E. (eds.). 2004. *Counterproductive Work Behavior: Investigations of Actors and Targets*. Washington, DC: APA.

Freeman, K. W. 2009. "The right way to close an operation." *Harvard Business Review* 87(5): 45–51.

Gandolfi, F. 2008. "Reflecting on downsizing: What have managers learned?" *SAM Advanced Management Journal* 73(2): 46–55.

Greenberg. J. and Colquitt, J. A. (eds.). 2005. *Handbook of Organizational Justice*. Mahwah, NJ: Lawrence Erlbaum.

Gillespie, N. A., Walsh, M. M., Winefield, A. H., Dua, J. J., and Stough, C. C. 2001. "Occupational stress in universities: Staff perceptions of the causes, consequences and moderators of stress." *Work and Stress* **15**(1): 53–72.

Hamilton, V. 2000. "(In)Justice in waiting: Russian officers' organizational commitment and mental distress during downsizing." *Journal of Applied Social Psychology* **30**(10): 1995–2027.

Harris, M. M., Heller, T., and Braddock, D. 1988. "Sex differences in psychological well-being during a facility closure." *Journal of Management* **14**(3): 391–402.

Hollander, E. P. 1995. "Ethical challenges in the leader-follower relationship." *Business Ethics Quarterly* **5**(1): 55–65.

Hopkins, S. M. and Weathington, B. L. 2006. "The relationship between justice perceptions, trust, and employee attitudes in a downsized organization." *Journal of Psychology* **140**(5): 477–498.

*Journal of Accountancy*. 2009. "Layoff survivors' relief turning to stress." *Journal of Accountancy* **208**(2): 13.

Kim, H. 2009. "Examining the role of informational justice in the wake of downsizing from an organizational relationship management perspective." *Journal of Business Ethics* **88**(2): 297–312.

Klunder, C. S. 2008. "Preventive stress management at work: The case of the San Antonio Air Logistics Center, Air Force Materiel Command (AFMC)." Managing and Leading, SPIM Conference and Institutes, San Antonio, February 29.

Konovsky, M. A. and Pugh, S. D. 1994. "Citizenship behavior and social exchange." *Academy of Management Journal* **37**: 656–669.

LaMarsh, J. 2009. "How companies reduce the downside of downsizing." *Global Business and Organizational Excellence* **29**(1): 7–16.

Lamsa, A. M. and Takala, T. 2000. "Downsizing and ethics of personnel dismissal." *Journal of Business Ethics* **23**(4): 389–399.

Lavelle, J. J., Brockner, J., Konovsky, M. A., Price, K. H., Henley, A. B., Taneja, A. *et al.* 2009. "Commitment, procedural fairness, and organizational citizenship behavior: A multifoci analysis." *Journal of Organizational Behavior* **30**(3): 337–357.

Lavelle, J. J., Rupp, D. E., and Brockner, J. 2007. "Taking a multifocal approach to the study of justice, social exchange, and citizenship behavior: The target similarity model." *Journal of Management* **33**(6): 841–866.

Lee, J. and Peccei, R. 2007. "Perceived organizational support and affective commitment: The mediating role of organization-based self-esteem in the context of job insecurity." *Journal of Organizational Behavior* **28**(6): 661–685.

Lin, B., Lee, Z., and Peterson, R. 2006. "An analytical approach for making management decisions concerning corporate restructuring." *Managerial and Decision Economics* **27**(8): 655–666.

Maki, N., Moore, S., Grunberg, L., and Greenberg, E. 2005. "The responses of male and female managers to workplace stress and downsizing." *North American Journal of Psychology* **7**(2): 295–312.

Mansour-Cole D. M. and Scott, S. G. 1998. "Hearing it through the grapevine: The influence of source, leader relations, and legitimacy on survivors' fairness perceptions." *Personal Psychology* **51**: 25–54.

McKee-Ryan, F., Song, Z., Wanberg, C. R., and Kinicki, A. J. 2005. "Psychological and physical well-being during unemployment: A meta-analytic study." *Journal of Applied Psychology* **90**: 53–76.

McFarlin, D. B. and Sweeney, P. D. 1992. "Distributive and procedural justice as predictors of satisfaction wtih personal and organizational outcomes." *Academy of Management Journal* **35**(3): 626–637.

McMahon, T. F. 2000. "Lifeboat ethics in business." *Business Ethics Quarterly* **10**(1): 269–276.

Meyer, J. P. and Allen, N. J. 1991. "A three-component conceptualization of organizational commitment: Some methodological considerations." *Human Resource Management Review* **1**: 61–98.

Mishra, A. K. and Mishra, K. E. 1994. "The role of mutual trust in effective downsizing strategies." *Human Resource Management* **33**(2): 261–279.

Mishra, A. K. and Spreitzer, G. M. 1998. "Explaining how survivors respond to downsizing: The roles of trust, empowerment, justice, and work redesign." *Academy of Management Review* **23**(3): 567–588.

Molinsky, A. and Margolis, J. 2006. "The emotional tightrope of downsizing: Hidden challenges for leaders and their organizations." *Organizational Dynamics* **35**(2): 145–159.

Moore, S., Grunberg, L., and Greenberg, E. 2004. "Repeated downsizing contact: The effects of similar and dissimilar layoff experiences on work and well-being outcomes." *Journal of Occupational Health Psychology* **9**(3): 247–257.

Moorman, R. H., Blakely, G. L., and Niehoff, B. P. 1998. "Does perceived organizational support mediate the relationship between procedural justice and organizational citizenship behavior?" *Academy of Management Journal* **41**(3): 351–357.

Nelson, D. L. and Quick, J. C. 2008. *Organizational Behavior: Science the Real World and You* (6th edn.). Mason, OH: South-Western Cengage Learning.

Organ, D. W., Podsakoff, P. M., and MacKenzie, S. B. 2006. *Organizational Citizenship Behavior: Its Nature, Antecedents, and Consequences.* Beverly Hills, CA: Sage.

Patient, D. L. and Skarlicki, D. P. 2010. "Increasing interpersonal and informational justice when communicating negative news: The role of the manager's empathetic concern and moral development." *Journal of Management* **36**(2): 555–578.

Pfeifer, C. 2007. "The perceived fairness of layoffs in Germany: Participation, compensation, or avoidance?" *Journal of Business Ethics* **74**(1): 25–36.

Pompa, V. 1992. "Managerial secrecy: An ethical examination." *Journal of Business Ethics* **11**(2): 147–156.

Probst, T. M. and Lawler, J. 2006. "Cultural values as moderators of employee reactions to job insecurity: The role of individualism and collectivism." *Applied Psychology: An International Review* **55**(2): 234–254.

Probst, T. M., Stewart, S. M., Gruys, M. L., and Tierney, B. W. 2007. "Productivity, counterproductivity and creativity: The ups and downs of job insecurity." *Journal of Occupational and Organizational Psychology* **80**(3): 479–497.

Pugh, S., Skarlicki, D. P., and Passell, B. S. 2003. "After the fall: Layoff victims' trust and cynicism in re-employment." *Journal of Occupational and Organizational Psychology* **76**(2): 201.

Quick, J. C., Quick, J. D., Nelson, D. L., and Hurrell, J. J. 1997. *Preventive Stress Management in Organizations*. Washington, DC: American Psychological Association.

Scott, B. A., Paddock, E., and Colquitt, J. A. 2009. "An Actor-Focused Model of Justice Rule Adherence and Violation: The Role of Managerial Motives and Discretion." *Journal of Applied Psychology* **94**(3): 756–769.

Shah, P. P. 2000. "Network destruction: The structural implications of downsizing." *Academy of Management Journal* **43**(1): 101–112.

Skarlicki, D. P., Barclay, L. J., and Douglas Pugh, S. S. 2008. "When explanations for layoffs are not enough: Employer's integrity as a moderator of the relationship between informational justice and retaliation." *Journal of Occupational and Organizational Psychology* **81**(1): 123–146.

Sora, B., Caballer, A., Peiro, J. M., and de Witte, H. 2009. "Job insecurity climate's influence on employees' job attitudes: Evidence from two European countries." *European Journal of Work and Organizational Psychology* **18**(2): 125–147.

Spreitzer, G. M. and Mishra, A. K. 2002. "To stay or to go: Voluntary survivor turnover following an organizational downsizing." *Journal of Organizational Behavior* **23**(6): 707.

Tillberg, T. S. 1998. "When structure and meaning break down: Taking responsibility in downsizing." *European Journal of Work and Organizational Psychology* **7**(3): 355–371.

Trevor, C. O., and Nyberg, A. J. 2008. "Keeping your headcount when all about you are losing theirs: Downsizing, voluntary turnover rates, and the moderating role of HR practices." *Academy of Management Journal* **51**(2): 259–276.

Ugboro, I. O. 2006. "Organizational commitment, job redesign, employee empowerment and intent to quit among survivors of restructuring and downsizing." *Journal of Behavioral and Applied Management* 7(3): 232–257.

Vahtera, J. 2004. "Organisational downsizing, sickness absence, and mortality: 10-town prospective cohort study." *British Medical Journal* **328**: 555.

van Dijke, M. and de Cremer, D. 2008. "How leader prototypicality affects followers' status: The role of procedural fairness." *European Journal of Work and Organizational Psychology* **17**: 226–250.

Viitasara, E., Sverke, M., and Menckel, E. 2003. "Multiple risk factors for violence to seven occupational groups in the Swedish caring sector." *Relations Industrielles/Industrial Relations* **58**(2): 202–231.

Virick, M., Lilly, J. D., and Casper, W. J. 2007. "Doing more with less: An analysis of work life balance among layoff survivors." *Career Development International* **12**(5): 463–480.

Weide, S. and Abbott, G. E. 1994. "Murder at work: Managing the crisis." *Employment Relations Today* **21**(2): 139–151.

Wiesenfeld, B. M., Brockner, J., and Thibault, V. 2000. "Procedural fairness, managers' self-esteeem, and managerial behaviors following a layoff." *Organizational Behavior and Human Decision Processes* **83**: 1–32.

# 11 *Good downsizing*

ROCKI-LEE DEWITT*

Downsizing, broadly conceptualized here as an intentional selective reduction in a firm's physical and/or human capital (DeWitt, 1998), is most commonly equated with layoffs, one choice in a broad range of intentional workforce reduction alternatives (Cascio, 1993; Greenhalgh, Lawrence, and Sutton, 1988). Because of downsizing's often detrimental effect on those let go (Leanna and Feldman, 1992; Newman, 1988; Uchitelle, 2006), it is difficult to promote the idea that downsizing might be considered great. But research suggests that downsizing can be good.

Insights into what makes downsizing good can be found in studies of the relationship between downsizing and a firm's financial performance. First, downsizing does not happen without a reason. Erosion in corporate performance, either experienced or expected, precedes use of workforce reductions (Datta, Guthrie, Basuil, and Pandey, 2010; Wayhan and Werner, 2000). Second, poorly executed downsizing, including large employment cuts and across the board cuts, triggers negative market reactions (Nixon, Hitt, Lee, and Jeong, 2004; Worrell, Davidson, and Sharma, 1991). Thirdly, short-run financial improvements are evidenced when employment cuts are part of corporate refocusing (Nixon *et al.*, 2004; Wayhan and Werner, 2000) or asset restructuring (Cascio, Young, and Morris, 1997). Additionally, where short-run financial erosion occurs, longer-run financial recuperation may follow (De Meuse, Bergmann, Vanderheiden, and Roraff, 2004). But, many of these studies focus on market reactions to very large, diversified, publicly traded company announcements. As it is hard to discern what a firm did other than at the most coarse of levels, questions remain regarding how "good downsizing" is obtained. What are investors reacting to? Is it the change in the relative weight of the business units within the portfolio or the change in the size of the corporate staff? Is it change in the way business units are positioned within their market? Or, perhaps more appropriately, is it the relative effectiveness of the change; how does the change being undertaken by a particular firm compare to the changes being undertaken across the firm's competitive context? Answers to these questions, though important, are not this chapter's focus.

Rather, this chapter builds upon the research that examines the relationship between the attitudes and behavioral intentions of those whose commercial relationships are either directly or indirectly affected by a firm's downsizing activity. "Good" downsizing positively affects the attitudes and behavioral intentions of those who remain through their perceptions of the treatment of those who were let go and their perceptions of their own treatment (Brockner and Greenberg, 1990; Brockner, Grover, Reed, DeWitt, and O'Malley, 1987; Datta *et al.*, 2010; Lewin, Biemans, and Ulaga, 2010; Lewin and Johnston, 2008). Clear, consistent communication about the reasons for the cuts and explanations about the firm's future, in combination with perceived adequacy of the severance provisions for those involuntarily let go, enhance the perceptions of the remaining exchange partners (employees, suppliers, buyers) that they have viable commercial relationships with a firm. Even when their future is unclear, the treatment of others offers insight to how they may be treated should another round of downsizing occur (Brockner and Greenberg, 1990; Datta *et al.*, 2010; Lewin *et al.*, 2010; Lewin and Johnston, 2008). But similar to research on the relationships between downsizing and a firm's financial performance, many questions regarding if and how the retained relationships realize their intended benefit remain empirically under-addressed. Did the firm (re)position itself to best leverage its resources and capabilities relative to market opportunities? Did the firm retain the most appropriate relationships? Did the firm appropriately modify the control and coordination mechanisms used to support those relationships? Do the firm's key partners in the creation and capture of value have an understanding of their future role? Are they predisposed to carry out that role?

It is the premise of this chapter that prudent and considerate implementation of downsizing can result in good downsizing. The emphasis is not on workforce reductions per se, but rather consideration of the cuts as a component of the firm's overall positioning in its markets. Good downsizing improves the firm's competitive position and its ability to realize returns from that position. Leaders pay attention to the effect of downsizing's implementation on the firm's ability to create and capture value by leveraging its talent internally and through boundary-spanning relationships.

For diversified corporations, good downsizing involves: (1) rebalancing the firm's portfolio of businesses (Nixon *et al.*, 2004), (2) aligning corporate control functions in support of the firm's mix of financial and strategic controls (Hoskisson and Hitt, 1994), (3) making appropriate competitive adjustments to the scale and scope of business units (DeWitt, 1998), (4) aligning business structure in support of those potentially altered business competitive postures (DeWitt, 1993; Freeman and Cameron, 1993; Zammuto and Cameron, 1985), and (5) implementing selective reductions of human resources and supplier and buyer relationships in a manner that sustains the commitment and willingness of these stakeholders to support the firm (Brockner, 1990; DeWitt, Harrigan, and Newman, 1998; DeWitt, Trevino, and Mollica, 2003; Lewin, 2001; Lewin and Johnston, 2008).

This chapter focuses on good downsizing at the level of a business unit: the last three components in the aforementioned sequence. It is at this level that the firm's revenues and input costs,[1] the essential elements in firm performance, are realized. Theoretically derived and normative in its orientation, the chapter identifies and elaborates upon the relationships between changes in the scale and scope of a business unit, the structural arrangements in support of those changes, and, most importantly, how downsizing affects the business's relationships with three key stakeholder groups: employees, suppliers, and buyers. Good downsizing comes from understanding this interplay and using this understanding to effect alignment between the multiple levels of downsizing implementation (Freeman, 1999; DeWitt, 1993).

The major contribution of this chapter is an extension of the lessons learned from the implementation of workforce reductions to other key relationships and consideration of those relationships as part of a downsizing gestalt. I extend our understanding of the reactions of remaining employees to the treatment of those let go (Brockner and Greenberg, 1990), to other individuals whose business relationships are built upon elements of psychological contracts (Rousseau and Anton, 1991), social exchange (Bandura, 1988), as well as more formal contracts (Williamson, 1975) to offer greater insight about a firm's ability to continue to create and capture value.

Each element of a relationship network is addressed in turn, beginning with a review of the available strategies, which incorporate: workforce reductions as a component of the selective resource reduction, structural changes, and the effect of these changes on individuals. These changes are put into perspective through a review of theory underlying the firm as an entity for creating and capturing value through its relationships with employees, suppliers, and buyers. Then, multi-level profiles of three business-level strategies that often incorporate workforce reductions – retrenchment, downscoping, and downscaling – are constructed to offer a more integrated, holistic perspective on the composition and effects of downsizing strategies from the perspective of employees, suppliers, and buyers. The chapter concludes with a discussion of the author's downsizing and public policy perspectives, research implications, and a consideration of the chapter's limitations.

## Good downsizing: Literature review

Downsizing can enhance a firm's performance when: (1) the approach taken fits the requirements for success in the firm's competitive context, (2) there is an alignment between the downsizing approach and the structure used in support of that approach, and (3) implementation of the selective reductions takes into consideration how the individuals, whose relationships with the firm are expected to continue, are affected by the downsizing. To apply extant literature to this claim requires recognizing that the first studies that incorporated consideration of selective resource reductions did not use the term "downsizing" but rather considered these reductions as a tool for addressing present or anticipated performance decreases. The use of the term downsizing likely emanated from the press's characterization of the human aspects of these changes.

The literature clearly suggests that there is no one best downsizing approach. Beginning with early frameworks that offered empirically tested alternatives to firms addressing mature and declining industries (Harrigan, 1980) to subsequent models that developed and elaborated upon alternatives for dealing with organization and environmental decline (Cameron and Zammuto, 1983; DeWitt, 1991; Freeman and Cameron, 1993), scholars have consistently argued that the most appropriate approach for making reductions in a firm's position and the internal arrangements used to support that position depends upon both the firm's competitive context and the firm's competitive capabilities relative to that context. Decision-makers were directed to evaluate the unattractiveness of the context for endgame (Harrigan, 1980) or the extent of environmental decline (Cameron and Zammuto, 1983;

DeWitt, 1991). They were also directed to conduct an unbiased evaluation of the firm's strengths and vulnerabilities. These analyses helped decision-makers understand the source of performance challenges and what alternatives were best suited to addressing these challenges. Enduring shrinkage in demand for an industry's core products was the primary indicator of unattractive endgames and significant environmental decline. When coupled with a firm's competitive inadequacies, that is higher levels of organizational decline (DeWitt, 1991; Freeman and Cameron, 1993), the recommended alternative was to significantly limit the firm's presence in an industry. Tactics included getting rid of products or withdrawing from markets supported by significant internal adjustments or exiting. But, when enduring pockets of price insensitive demand could be identified or environmental decline was expected to occur gradually over a long period of time, recommended alternatives included holding the investment (Harrigan, 1980) or "retrench the firm's domain" (DeWitt, 1991). These alternatives assumed that the firm's relative strength allowed it to make internal adjustments to support that positioning. Where the firm had larger competitive vulnerabilities, it would have to undertake more substantive changes to existing systems and processes and realistically recognize that even these changes might be insufficient to improve performance.

More details about the types of internal changes that would accompany the firm's positioning or repositioning were found in the descriptions of structural reorientation and structural retrenchment alternatives (Cameron and Zammuto, 1983; DeWitt, 1991) as well as the structural changes that were likely to accompany workforce reductions (Sutton and D'Aunno, 1989). DeWitt (1993) emphasized more precision in identifying, isolating, and addressing the internal causes of a firm's poor performance, distinguishing between circumstances by levels of environmental decline and organization decline. Where low levels of environmental and organization decline were present, it was proposed that firms would undertake a "mechanistic shift" and apply elements of organization structure to provide more fine-grained oversight of the firm's portfolio of products and markets. Increased horizontal differentiation in combination with increased vertical differentiation, increased standardization and formalization, and increased centralization would support stronger control and coordination of the firm's activities, prerequisites for improved performance. Where higher levels of organization decline were present in combination with low levels of environmental decline, a "mechanistic shift" was also proposed. But, instead of increasing the extent of vertical differentiation, further standardization and formalization would be used to obtain coordination and control; the argument being that the firm is not getting returns from its current use of authority structures (vertical differentiation) and policies, and procedures could supplant ineffective oversight.

While most of the literature on firms' responses to declining situations noted a predisposition of firms to use more mechanistic, threat-rigid approaches to regain control over the firm's performance with the possibility that a firm might utilize a more organic approach as workforce reductions evolved (Staw, Sandelands, and Dutton, 1981; Sutton and D'Aunno, 1989), others argued that "organic shifts" in a firm's structure as a first step were warranted (DeWitt, 1993). Noting that higher levels of environmental decline warranted domain reorientation, that is selective reductions in a firm's products or market withdrawal (DeWitt, 1993), a case was made for increased vertical differentiation, reduced horizontal differentiation, decreased formalization, and decreased standardization. The sloughing off of products and withdrawal from markets reduced the firm's complexity and warranted a reversal of the more elaborate bureaucracy to place greater responsibility on managerial review. The intent was, given the importance of the remaining products and markets to the firm's success, to revisit potentially outdated assumptions underpinning rules and procedures, and reinsert managerial judgment into realizing the revenue potential and cost implications related to pursuit of opportunities present in the remaining markets. Where higher levels of environmental decline were coupled with higher levels of organization decline, the organic shift also included reductions in vertical differentiation, that is fewer managers with broader oversight. More aggressive reductions were expected to take place all around.

At the same time that scholars were identifying the alternatives available for improving the positioning of the firm in its competitive environment and aligning the firm's structure with that positioning, other scholars were identifying alternatives for workforce reductions and studying the effect of the selective reductions on the firm's employees. Some chose to emphasize understanding the effect of downsizing on those who were let go, noting that variation in the experience was influenced by the coping strategies employed as well as the presence of alternative employment opportunities (Leana and Feldman, 1992; Newman, 1988). Others offered a unique perspective that has driven more than 25 years of inquiry. They noted that relative to affecting the ongoing viability of the firm, it was crucial to understand how downsizing affected the attitudes and behaviors of those who remained in the firm. In particular, their emphasis was on understanding how remaining employees' perceptions of the treatment of those let go influenced their feelings about the firm and their intention to stay with the firm. After all, a decision had been made that identified them as more vital to the future of the firm than the individuals who were let go. This research strongly and consistently indicates that the management of the perceived fairness of the workforce reduction, through severance arrangements made for departing employees in combination with the procedures used to make layoff decisions and the explanations offered for those decisions, affects remaining employees' attitudes toward the firm and their intentions to stay with the firm (Brockner, 1988; Datta *et al.*, 2010; Brockner and Greenberg, 1990).

Current research on downsizing, specifically workforce reductions, has been extended to more precisely consider the effect of downsizing on individuals who play boundary-spanning roles in the vertical value-added process (Lewin, 2001, 2003; Lewin *et al.*, 2010; Lewin and Johnston, 2008). These studies of employees' reactions to purchasing units' downsizing are evidence that employees' perceptions of the unit's structural attributes, role conflict, risk aversion, and organizational commitment are influenced by workforce reduction attributes including the size of the reduction, involuntary nature of the reduction, and expectations of the firm's future (Lewin, 2001). The results confirm that threat rigid and mechanistic predispositions are present when they perceive the workforce reduction to be more substantive and severe and when they hold negative expectations of the firm's future (Lewin, 2001).

In a study examining the effect of suppliers' downsizing on industrial buyers' satisfaction with supplier and their repeat purchase intentions, buyers were less satisfied and more predisposed to change the volume of business done with suppliers who downsized than with those who did not (Lewin and Johnston, 2008). This finding is not surprising; workforce reductions usually leave firms with less people to get the job done, and workforce reductions are still understood to be a negative event that makes it easy to find fault with the firm. More informative are the specific aspects of buyers' dissatisfaction with the downsized suppliers and the ways in which dissatisfaction varies as a function of the severity of the workforce reduction. Of the supplier attributes evaluated, the biggest differences between downsized and non-downsized suppliers were present in what could be referred to as an interpersonal dimension of the buyer–supplier relationship. Ability to reach support personnel, responses to special requests, and after-sale support evidenced greater differences in means between the two types of suppliers (Lewin and Johnston, 2008). In contrast, the differences in more transactional attributes such as price and quantity discounts, while still statistically significant, were not as great (Lewin and Johnston, 2008).

In addition, buyers' assessments and reactions varied as a function of the severity of the workforce reductions. As one would expect, the most severe workforce reductions were associated with the most negative reactions. But interestingly, an exploratory analysis of differences between three levels of downsizing severity evidences a curvilinear relationship between severity and reactions. The least (1–10 percent) and most severe (greater than 20 percent) workforce reductions were related to the most negative assessments, while workforce reductions that fell between 10 and 20 percent were perceived less negatively. The authors cautiously suggest that the suppliers' understanding of the need to make changes in customer service or their ability to make those changes vary as a function of the severity of the workforce reductions; intermediate levels of workforce reductions are large enough to trigger recognition that modifications in supplier practices are necessitated but higher levels leave the firm less room for maneuver to support those modifications (Lewin and Johnston, 2008, p. 253).

In summary, this in-depth overview of the downsizing literature identifies the building blocks for a more complete and integrated perspective of downsizing. It points to a range of selective resource reductions obtained through a combination of externally and internally directed changes. It notes that these domain and structural changes can be realized through a wide array of workforce reduction alternatives. It draws our attention to the effect of employment reductions on the employees themselves as well as on the suppliers and buyers that rely upon these employees' support to obtain their own desired commercial outcomes. It suggests that employee reductions may have a differential effect on the interpersonal and transactional aspects of these exchange relationships. In doing so, it becomes clear that "good downsizing" is a complex and rather daunting undertaking (Table 11.1). But, then again, establishing and sustaining a well-performing firm is not simple either. Revisiting our assumptions regarding how firms create and capture value by transforming inputs into outputs on a recurring basis and how that system evolves

Table 11.1 *Elements in good downsizing*[2]

| Key considerations | Requisite analytics | Likely challenges |
|---|---|---|
| Did the firm (re)position itself to best leverage its resources and capabilities relative to market opportunities? | Thorough understanding of the likely evolution of market and firm resources and capabilities *vis-à-vis* that market | Competitors are adjusting their own positioning at the same time requiring a dynamic, game theoretic analytic approach |
| Did the firm retain the most appropriate relationships? | Identification and prioritization of relationships with a strong consideration of the interpersonal composition of those relationships | Failure to consider the full array of within and between firm and partner value added relationships<br>Depersonalization of relationships<br>Overemphasis on the "costs" of the relationship as opposed to the revenue generation potential of the relationship<br>Loss of capabilities as a result of overemphasis on "who to let go" rather than on "who to retain" |
| Did the firm appropriately modify the control and coordination mechanisms used to support those relationships? | Thorough understanding of the advantages and disadvantages of various control and coordination tools and techniques | Predisposed to establish a "mechanistic shift" where policies and procedures signal a more transactional relationship |
| Do the key partners in the firm's value creation and capture process have an understanding of their future role in the firm's plans? | Understanding of the motives and interests of key partners as it pertains to their relationship with the firm | Overreliance on promotions, contract renewal, and business continuity to signal that firm has a viable future<br>Only talk when bad news is delivered |
| Are the key partners predisposed to carry out that role? | Baseline measures of partners' commitment to the firm so that likely effects of change can be discerned | Assume that key partners do not have other alternatives and should be thankful the firm retained the relationship |

over time provides a foundation from which we can more precisely consider why downsizing is necessary, where downsizing efforts are focused, how downsizing affects internal and boundary-spanning relationships, and the roles that employees and organization structure play in those relationships.

## Good downsizing: Leveraging talent and relationships to create and capture value

Alignment of the firm's transformation of inputs into outputs, with each other and with their competitive context, is central to the creation and capture of value (Brandenburger and Stuart, 1996; Porter, 1980). In the process of creating and capturing value, firms provide benefit to suppliers and buyers alike. As an intermediary, the firm adds benefit to its suppliers, both human capital and physical capital suppliers and buyers, by providing them access to markets they would otherwise be unable to directly reach (Porter, 1980). Satisfaction with the firm and its correlates, expressions of positive attitudes towards the firm, and intentions to continue the relationship are influenced by individual perceptions of the benefits and costs of the relationship in comparison to other opportunities (Bandura, 1988; Porter, 1980; Heskett, Jones, Loveman, Sasser, and Schlesinger, 1994). Employee satisfaction with the firm, whether mediated by perceptions of identification with the firm, personal control, or justice judgments, is evidenced in relationship loyalty, a willingness to disregard and not complain about minor inconveniences that arise in the workplace, and the willingness to exert ongoing effort to benefit the firm (Fassina, Jones, and Uggerslev, 2008; Mowday, Porter, and Steers, 1982; Organ, 1988). Supplier and buyer satisfaction with the firm is related to relationship loyalty, a willingness to engage in incomplete contracting, and a tolerance for minor, non-recurring relationship disruptions (Anderson, Fornell, and Rust, 1997; Heskett *et al.*, 1994; Kumar, Scheer, and Steenkamp, 1995; Sharma, Grewal, and Levy, 1995; Zhang, Henke, and Griffith, 2009).

Changes in the needs and preferences of the larger set of employees, suppliers, and buyers in combination with changes within the firm give rise to a dynamic interplay of relationships, and the evolution and adaptation of the firm as it aligns with evolving employee, supplier, and buyer needs and preferences (Brandenburger and Stuart, 1996; Chatain, 2010). As markets mature and inputs and outputs become more clearly understood or commodity-like, the firm's strategy and structure evolves. Firms may broaden the range of products offered and markets served (Ansoff, 1965) and may mix elements of process and product innovation in support of cost leadership and differentiation strategies (Rothaermel, Hitt, and Jobe, 2006). The firm's structural capital (Pinkham, Picken, and Dess, 2010) evolves with changes to the mix of: (1) formalized and standardized set of policies and procedures, often underpinned by machine-based systems, to support recurrent and predictable activities and obtain efficiencies, and (2) people-based practices and problem-solving capabilities to address uncertainty and ambiguity and obtain effectiveness (Galbraith, 1974). These structural arrangements are applied to support sharing of information within the firm as well as the sharing of information between the firm and its buyers and suppliers (Pinkham *et al.*, 2010).

Against this backdrop of the firm's strategy and structure is consideration of employee, supplier, and buyer expectations. Employee, supplier, and customer satisfaction with the firm – that is, this system of exchange relationships – is built upon an assumption that the relationships between the firm and its employees, buyers, and suppliers have imperfections due to uncertainty (March and Simon, 1958). These imperfections, occurring on both sides of the exchange relationship, may arise from ambiguous decision-making contexts driven by environmental dynamism (Dess and Beard, 1984), naturally occurring variations in partners' ability to exchange, as well as from the firm and its partners' more self-seeking intentions (Williamson, 1975). The firm and its employees', suppliers', and buyers' preferences for addressing these imperfections are reflected in the extent to which they utilize spot markets or pursue more enduring relationships. Exchange partners who seek to establish enduring relationships do so because of their strategic importance to their respective firms; enduring relationships are established in support of recurrent value-added activity or to assure access to scarce, valuable resources (Harrigan, 1983; Williamson, 1975). Ongoing conversations and co-dependent decision-making supported by a mix of formal contracting and informal arrangements result in interpersonally based commitments to the pursuit of shared interests (Bandura, 1988; Geyskens, Steenkamp, and Kumar, 1999). Boundary-spanning activities between the firm and its suppliers and buyers, in combination with the discovery, creation, diffusion, and application of knowledge throughout the firm, constitute the essence of the firm as a mechanism for resolving uncertainty, creating and capturing value, and hence persisting as a going concern (Grant, 1996).

Downsizing is a normal part of healthy business evolution. It is reasonable to expect that demand for extant products and services will be supplanted by new offerings and technological upheaval, and that skills and abilities are not perfectly transferable to new activity (Schumpeter, 1942). Internally, the need to handle exceptions (Galbraith, 1974) either in exchange between internal partners or in boundary-spanning roles becomes less prevalent as market preferences converge and standards emerge (McGahan, 2004). Furthermore, over time, the rules and procedures that once fostered information processing efficiency and supplanted human decision-making may become excessive, resulting in an overblown, inefficient organization design (Ford, 1980).

Downsizing's challenge, and potential detrimental effect, arises when it is counter to exchange partners' expectations of their ongoing relationship with the firm. In forming relationships with the firm, employees, suppliers, and buyers incorporate their expectations about the length of a relationship and the need for adjustments to the relationship. Downsizing is less disruptive when the relationship between the firm and its exchange partners is more transactional and episodic. Where concerns about a material effect of disruption on either party's performance are present, contracts will be established and are likely to incorporate how these types of changes shall be addressed ("advance notice" and "satisfaction for breach of contract" clauses). In contrast, where relationships between the firm and its exchange partners are less transactional – that is, are built upon collaborative value creation, incomplete contracting, and trust – downsizing can be devastating. Partners are likely to have foregone other opportunities and may have made a series of relationship-unique investments that are not readily transferable to other relationships. Consequently, advance consideration of the implications of change to exchange partners, communication about the anticipated changes, and identification of options for modifying the relationship are requisite to success.

Any workforce reduction, no matter how well anticipated or planned, has the potential to affect the relationship between the firm and its employees, suppliers, and buyers, irrespective of where within the firm's structure those cuts occur. When cuts involve the firm's support activities and/or internal linkages in the value chain (Porter, 1985), they can affect the firm's knowledge resources and internal social capital (Grant, 1996; Nixon *et al.*, 2004). Exchange partners may or may not be cognizant that informal practices underlying their relationship with the firm have disappeared, or, in the case of employees, that their role has become redundant. As an example, when computerized decision support systems replace human decision-making processes, the elimination of the redundancy between individual roles and the role of newly established computerized procedures severs human connections. To the extent that remaining employees are connected to the new system, they and the suppliers and buyers they serve may find that they are now supported by more consistent and enduring firm processes and systems (Galbraith, 1974). But, when downsizing programs are implemented before knowledge is captured and systematized, remaining employees, suppliers, and buyers are likely to experience significant erosion in their relationship with the firm. Not only are the individuals they connected with gone, but there is nothing to rely upon in their place.

When cuts affect employees holding boundary-spanning positions – the individuals who establish and build interpersonal connections with the exchange partners – the relationship between the firm and its exchange partners is potentially thrown into even greater disarray (Lewin, 2001, 2003; Lewin and Johnston, 2008). The extent of this disarray and exchange partners' likely reactions to those cuts depends upon the firm's efforts to manage the relationship, the severity of the cut (Lewin, 2001; Lewin and Johnston, 2008), and the nature of the ongoing relationship between the exchange partner. Cuts are especially detrimental and reactions are likely to be especially negative when there is no advance warning, when an exchange relationship is completely rather than partially severed, when exchange partners rely heavily upon a particular relationship for its role in value creation and have developed idiosyncratic skills and processes in support of that relationship, and when exchange partners have foregone building other value-creating relationships. Other exchange partners are likely to take note of the disruptive, value-destroying nature of the cut. As they reconsider the appropriateness of engaging in similar non-contractually bound relationship enhancing efforts that presume returns from relationship continuity, they will likely seek stronger assurances of returns either through more aggressive bargaining or contractual safeguards.

The capacity to incorporate downsizing as a tool in managing the firm's alignment with its markets requires leadership and managerial capabilities attuned to the interplay of the firm as an organizational concept and the firm as a repository of knowledge and social capital. Products, markets, technologies, units, departments, and the company names of suppliers and buyers serve as convenient shorthand for presenting the firm and its relationships. They help us focus our downsizing efforts by allowing us to draw boundaries around activities and outcomes. But, because they are conceptual, we may lose sight of the people, the faces, names, and intellectual capacity embedded in each. Considering two aspects of the human underpinning present in organizational concepts draws our attention to key roles of people in downsizing.

First, because people rely on these organizing concepts as a way of making sense of the firm and their role in the firm, when these organizing concepts are the focus of downsizing choices, care must be exercised as to how the cuts are portrayed and communicated. A relatively impersonal organizing concept, such as a product, may give rise to a highly emotionally charged reaction. Employees develop personal and workplace identities that are tightly linked to impersonal organizing concepts; that is, "I'm a product manager," or "I'm a purchasing specialist" (Ashforth and Mael, 1989). Buyers/suppliers develop attachments to the firm, but it may be a single conceptual connection that underlies the essence of that relationship and accounts for a broader construal of and attachment to the firm. The use of the organizing concept as a basis for performance evaluation, resource allocation decisions, and promotion and advertising of the firm further reinforces the organizing concept as a foundation for the individual's identification with the concept and the firm. When a decision is made to drop the concept – for example, a product – any communications that may be construed as diminishing or derogating the value of the product may be experienced by individuals, whose identity is strongly attached to that product, as derogatory and counter to human values of care and treatment with dignity and respect (Brockner, Tyler, and Cooper-Schneider, 1992). Consequently, what business leaders might have considered a relatively impersonal and safe downsizing decision, dropping a product line, becomes experienced as a highly personal, emotional, and value-laden decision with negative implications that may go far beyond the bounds of the loss of a specific product.

Second, because concepts are historical, incomplete, imperfect information artifacts, care must be exercised to ensure that people's knowledge and capacity is tapped and preserved when downsizing decisions are made and implemented. Organizing concepts are a codified, enduring set of attributes coupled to uniquely human capacities that address the ambiguity and uncertainty not economically addressed through rules or procedures. Over time, more rules and procedures are added, as emergent, recurrent decisions become captured. The remaining conceptually coupled human capacity becomes increasingly attuned to not only addressing the remaining ambiguity and uncertainty but to navigating the complex maze of rules, procedures, and coordinating devices. Even if the firm has an inventory of people's knowledge and capabilities, the tacit and individual-specific nature of these capabilities are often best revealed in downsizing decision-making that involves the individual's supervisor (DeWitt, Trevino, and Mollica, 2003). Furthermore, concerns for the retention of appropriate talent and knowledge should be prevalent when making choices between using involuntary and voluntary workforce reductions (Mollica and DeWitt, 2000).

## Good downsizing: Normative suggestions

To more fully and precisely consider the effect of downsizing on the firm's performance, human resource cuts should be considered in the context of the firm's downsizing strategy and the internal and boundary-spanning structural arrangements in support of that strategy. Each downsizing strategy, its likely effect on the structural arrangements, and the implications for the relationships between employees, suppliers, and buyers is examined below.

### *Retrenchment*

Retrenchment retains a firm's scope while maintaining or even augmenting its output (DeWitt, 1993). Retrenchment is focused on the firm's internal organization and is most commonly supported by centralization and specialization of production, alteration of supplier relationships, and realignment of managerial responsibilities (DeWitt, 1993). It is equivalent to the strategy that combines domain and structural retrenchment (DeWitt, 1993).

Retrenchment is undertaken to enhance firm performance when a firm has excessive and redundant internal control and coordination mechanisms or has a number of geographically dispersed production and/or distribution facilities that limit its ability to obtain scale, and to a lesser extent, economies. Excessive internal organization may arise from a failure to eliminate control and coordination roles that have been replaced by machine-based systems. Facility dispersion may arise from the firm's organic growth or from its merger and acquisition activity. Productivity improvements are driven by process reengineering and elimination of redundant facilities and jobs (Siegel and Simons, 2010). Line employee and staff employee relationships as well as supplier relationships unique to the closed facilities are commonly severed.

The firm becomes increasingly dependent on the machine-embedded solutions and the employee capabilities present in the retained facilities to support its suppliers and buyers; the laid-off employees and the shuttered facility no longer provides a backstop. To allow for a period of "machine replaces person" trial and error, employees whose positions are being eliminated may be given significant advance notice to provide for a period of purposive redundancy while the firm increasingly relies on information technology tools. To retain knowledge previously resident at the closed facility, line and staff employees with unique knowledge may be offered opportunities to relocate to the facilities where volume has been maintained or increased. For some ongoing suppliers, where they once provided inputs to a wide variety of locations, they may now obtain greater efficiency and lower costs as its volume remains the same but the need to ship inputs to a variety of locations is reduced. Some buyers will find that their source of supply is more distant but improved production and/or distribution efficiencies can offset potential distance disadvantages.

The firm may make use of the retrenchment event as an opportunity to reestablish its relationship with suppliers and buyers and negotiate for relationship changes that improve its ability to capture value. The potential for retrenchment to generate efficiencies for suppliers and buyers may encourage the firm to try to capture some of those gained efficiencies from its exchange partners. But, before it rushes headlong into an aggressive attempt to use its bargaining power to obtain even greater performance benefit, it is crucial for the firm to consider how retrenchment changes the nature of the firm's relationships with its suppliers and buyers.

Though retrenchment frequently involves more mechanistic structural attributes, because it potentially represents a resetting of the "organizational clock," it still requires an ability to perform non-routine tasks. At the core, administrators work to rearrange reporting and control processes to leverage machine-supported systems. Production managers work to incorporate the additional production into the production schedule making adjustments to accommodate the increased volume and variety of production. These efforts are likely to occur both within the work unit as well as between work and support units across the firm. At the boundary, purchasing managers work to incorporate production changes into the sourcing of inputs and distribution, and sales managers work to incorporate production changes into the inventory holding levels, shipping arrangements, and buyer replenishment. These processes are likely to have some fits and starts; interpersonal skills and trust will play an important role in employees, suppliers, and buyers working through the changeover.

To continue to use employee, supplier, and buyer relationships advantageously, managers responsible for these relationships must anticipate that a period of adjustment will be required. Any early attempts to bargain aggressively to obtain additional advantages will signal that a more transactional orientation is being initiated. Coupled with the early challenges the firm is likely to encounter in making transitions, it may give rise to a broader set of formal contractual expectations that require additional monitoring and oversight.

Opportunities will exist to modify relationships in both directions. But the firm may unwittingly negatively affect the very relationships they need to realize the benefits of the retrenchment. Integrating the operations of severed units into the remaining units is likely to have some challenges. Modification of the proximity of suppliers and buyers to facilities will likely create fulfillment delays. If the firm is predisposed to bargain aggressively with employees, suppliers, and buyers to try to take advantage of the change, they may unwittingly negatively affect the very relationships they need to realize the benefits of the retrenchment.

## *Downscoping*

Downscoping as a business strategy concept reduces a firm's vertical and/or horizontal scope (DeWitt, 1998). Downscoping may be obtained through a variety of approaches. Reductions in vertical scope, also known as de-integration or impartition (Barreyre, 1988; Kreiken, 1980; Porter, 1985), either eliminate upstream input products (backward de-integration) or eliminate distribution or retail facilities (forward de-integration). Reductions in vertical scope are warranted when the firm can more cheaply and/or effectively outsource the activities. Reductions in horizontal scope include product line pruning (Kotler, 1965), market withdrawal (Porter, 1985), or customer withdrawal (Porter, 1980).

Reductions in horizontal scope are warranted when the firm no longer generates sufficient returns from product, market, or customer variety. Downscoping is equivalent to domain reorientation (DeWitt, 1993).

## *Reductions in vertical scope*

Incentives to backward and/or forward de-integrate include growth in the number or quality of suppliers or buyers, changes in the context in which these suppliers and buyers operate that alter the relative cost advantages of being vertically integrated, and/or the ongoing investments required to support the vertically integrated firm. In backward and forward de-integration, vertical de-integration represents significant employment cuts at the jettisoned activities. It also requires structural changes; internal administrative support coordinating the flows of inputs and finished goods across a vertically integrated firm remains important but needs to be modified to control and coordinate a supply chain that has increased its reliance on external providers.

With backward de-integration the firm needs to strengthen its purchasing capabilities as activities that were once performed in house now are outsourced. If the firm had well-developed cost accounting practices in support of evaluating its capabilities, it has one component – comparative cost knowledge – that could be used in establishing further supply relationships. But, if the firm did not pursue a tapered integration strategy (Harrigan, 1983) and relied exclusively on its own inputs, it may lack the negotiation and purchasing prowess required to leverage that knowledge in making choices between using spot markets or developing more enduring supplier relationships. Employees who tracked the costs of the activities are likely to have strong analytic capabilities, but they may not possess the necessary boundary-spanning skills that allow them to effectively transition into roles that require more negotiation and purchasing acumen.

Similarly, with forward de-integration, the firm needs to strengthen its buyer-side relationship capabilities that it once performed in house. If the firm had well-developed cost accounting practices in support of evaluating its forward capabilities, that knowledge could be used in establishing expectations regarding markups and margins in distribution relationships. Again, without a tapered approach to forward relationships, it may lack the negotiation and selling prowess required to leverage that knowledge into a relationship advantage.

Thus, vertical de-integration implementation creates a number of challenges for establishing an appropriate mix of interpersonal and transactional elements in support of replacing a more internally based value chain with an external one. Positions with strong interpersonal boundary-spanning capabilities are likely required, especially early on as the firm transitions to outsourcing supplies or selling through others. Employees whose jobs have been most affected by the downsizing may be incapable of developing the requisite skills, or they may be unwilling. At a minimum, the firm should offer employees an opportunity to bid on those positions as hiring new employees in the context of letting others go to minimize negative employee reactions.

Purchasing processes, inventory control, accounts payable, and invoicing systems will also need to be updated to support the addition of supplier and buyer relationships. Here there is greater opportunity to reallocate employees to these administrative roles as they are built upon existing firm-specific routines. Non-routine work to incorporate the changes into the firm's administrative infrastructure, both jettisoning no longer needed policies and procedures and supplanting them with new policies and procedures, requires sufficient staffing to effect the changes. Depending upon the extent of changes represented by the de-integration, incorporation of additional activities into the existing administrative infrastructure may give rise to opportunities to modify the system.

As improved cost structures are the common motive for reductions in vertical scope, the firm must avoid the tendency to be overly transactionally oriented as it initially transitions. While it may possess the requisite information to bargain aggressively on price, it needs to recognize that it has yet to develop the interpersonal relationships that would allow it to address supply chain disruptions as it would have when it directly controlled them. Thus, it may take a while to realize the efficiency and flexibility benefits anticipated from vertical downscoping.

Finally, in transition the firm may seek a buyer for the upstream or downstream activity. It may include commitments to purchase goods or services from the new owner. This helps address its lack of negotiation or selling prowess as it pertains to seeking alternative suppliers or buyers and may provide sufficient incentive to a would-be buyer to acquire the activity (DeWitt, Harrigan, and Newman, 1998). But, it should recognize that its former activity, now owned and operated by another firm, may be perceived as increasing the competition between its other would-be suppliers and buyers, making them less favorably predisposed to develop a relationship with the firm.

## *Reductions in horizontal scope*

With horizontal downscoping, buyer relationships bear the brunt of the cuts, although supplier relationships are also likely altered. By withdrawing from selected products, markets, or customers, the firm decreases the volume and variety of needed inputs. An analysis of the contribution margins related to the variety of ways in which the firm could consider its horizontal scope and the interrelationships between those elements typically underpins the decision to cut products, markets, and/or customers. Product withdrawal looks for opportunities to jettison low-demand, low-margin products with an expectation that remaining items in the product portfolio will attract buyers' interests. Market withdrawal typically focuses on shrinking the firm's geographic breadth, while customer withdrawal severs relationships with customers who account for a small proportion of the firm's business or whose price sensitivity is out of line with the firm's capacity to manage costs.

In reducing the firm's horizontal scope, less variety needs to be accommodated by the firm's boundary-spanning buyer relationships and internal coordination and control mechanisms. Employees filling boundary-spanning roles associated with the products, markets, or customers are likely to be let go. These reductions in horizontal differentiation are likely to be combined with increased vertical differentiation as greater attention is placed on the contribution of the retained products, markets, or customers to the firm's performance (DeWitt, 1993).

Less precise is the effect of the horizontal reductions and the boundary-spanning supply relationships and internal coordination and control mechanisms. Where horizontal scope relationships have proven untenable to ongoing performance, it may be due to uneconomic supply relationships. It follows that these supply relationships will be severed hand in hand with the buyer relationships.

Concern for the reactions of buyers and suppliers in the case of horizontal downscoping is similar to that raised in the discussion of vertical downscoping above, with one important difference. In contrast to initiating new supplier and buyer relationships, the focus in horizontal downscoping is how remaining buyers and suppliers make sense about their own future based on their understanding of how the firm managed the severing of the buyer and supplier relationships. Where a firm's relationships with buyers and suppliers are considered to be spot markets, there is no expectation of an enduring relationship with either party. But where those relationships are expected to endure and are built upon more informal arrangements that have been used in lieu of more complete contracting, it is critical to take a cue from effective management of employee layoffs (Bies and Moag, 1986; Brockner, DeWitt, Grover, and Reed, 1990). Making a concerted effort to provide explanations regarding the reasons for the changes in the relationships and the implications of those changes for the ongoing relationships will help offset buyer and supplier concerns and help retain their commitment.

Finally, one should not lose sight of the potential value of the laid-off employees to the buyers who are directly or indirectly affected by horizontal downscoping. When products, markets, or customers and the people who sell those products, sell into those markets, or sell to those customers, are cut, the salesperson's knowledge can be valuable to the buyer who is left stranded or can be valuable to the competitor who now has an opportunity to fill the void. A firm should not expect that the buyer will easily switch to making purchases from the remaining product line nor should the firm underestimate how a competitor might use dropped markets or customers to strengthen their own presence.

### *Downscaling*

Downscaling is the use of permanent cuts in human and physical resources to maintain product line and market scope while reducing output to bring output in line with demand (DeWitt, 1998). In contrast to retrenchment, downscaling signals that the firm acknowledges that revenue potential has eroded but that profit potential remains, albeit at a more limited level. In contrast to downscoping, the firm holds its vertical and horizontal presence while reducing the volume of production available in support of that presence.

This approach may be undertaken for a number of reasons. First, it may be used because the firm is pursuing a "hold the investment" strategy (Harrigan, 1980) while waiting to see which product or market segments are less price sensitive. Second, it may be used because the firm lacks product or market diversification to allow it to "shrink selectively" (Harrigan, 1980). Or, the firm's production process may be highly physically or organizationally coupled, limiting its ability to sever particular products or markets without disrupting overall performance (DeWitt, 1998). Consequently, downscaling has more limited potential to stem further erosion in firm performance and further workforce reductions. First, for the firm who has limited product or market variety to begin with, downscaling confirms that the firm has limited sources of future viability. Second, for the firm with a broader range of products and markets, downscaling is likely to be a precursor to downscoping strategies of "shrinking selectively" as pockets of price insensitive demand are more clearly revealed. Finally, when downscaling is undertaken, the direct employee and supply relationship cuts and potentially indirect buyer relationship changes make it more difficult to extract the knowledge required to use more precise cuts in future relationship severing. Obtaining the more fine-grained understanding and measures of value-added opportunities present in relationships requires a willingness to share information. Employees, suppliers, and buyers are well aware that this information may be used to alter the firm in a manner that potentially threatens their relationship security. It should not be surprising that downscaling may increase employees', suppliers', and buyers' intentions to seek other more supportive relationships.

## Summary: Perspective and policy implications, suggestions for future research and limitations

### *Perspective and policy implications*

Consumer preferences evolve, new technologies emerge, and market dynamism makes it likely that once-valued skills and relationships will diminish in worth. Industries may persist with an underlying value creation and capture standard for decades but rarely for ever (McGahan, 2004). For leaders of firms in these industries, especially those who derive their performance from their talent and boundary-spanning relationships, an explicit, anticipatory consideration of how they will evolve and alter their strategy and structure and the role that talent and relationships play in these modifications are key to success. Policy-makers would also do well to consider industry evolution, how their employment policies contribute to or detract from the competitiveness of incumbent firms, and how these policies in combination with the country's talent influence the location decisions of would-be economic partners. Where employment security is valued, it may be more prudent for employers, worker organizations, and the government to work together towards assuring currency of employee skill sets than to establish requirements that give rise to persistent unemployment.

As long as we view the employment relationship with businesses as a sacred trust, involuntary reductions in force will be viewed as a violation of the trust between an employee and the employer (Mishra and Spreitzer, 1998). Legitimization of the use of involuntary reductions to enhance business performance has the potential to give rise to an increased transactional orientation between the firm and its employees, higher levels of employee turnover, and ultimately increased human resource costs. Yet, involuntary reductions offer far greater precision in talent retention than voluntary programs. Thus, firms should be encouraged to consider developing an array of employment solutions (Cascio, 2002, 2009). Fixed-term employment contracts, with or without renewal clauses, and staged retirements are but a couple of alternatives that would allow firms to sustain competitive viability through staffing flexibility to address the dynamism and uncertainty present in their markets. Modifications of unemployment and retirements policies would likely be required to assure a fair balance between the public's support of employment changes and the benefits individuals derive from these arrangements.

A failure to consider how downsizing actions at the level of changes in the scale and scope of the firm affect other relationships has the potential to have the same consequences. Buyers and suppliers may become increasingly transactional in their relationships with the firm. Contracts will increasingly either reflect aggressive up-front negotiation of supply accommodations, putting more pressure on margins and/or include specification of damages for disruptions to the relationship. But, to the extent that a downsizing firm can avoid early pressures to emphasize transactional aspects of their relationships with employees, suppliers, and buyers, it leaves itself in a better position to more appropriately leverage a mix of formal, routinized policies and procedures and interpersonal capacity in its internal and boundary-spanning efforts.

## *Suggestions for future research*

This chapter offers an overview to the many factors that must be managed to realize good downsizing. In contrast to the distinction drawn between downsizing and restructuring by Budros (1999), I argue that decisions about cutting employees affects the firm's ability to utilize the roles these individuals held and requires an explicit consideration of the relationship between the cuts and the firm's structure. Moreover, I argue that it is critical to place this in the context of the firm's strategy. Poor downsizing occurs when there is a mismatch between: (1) downsizing strategy and context, (2) downsizing strategy and structure, and (3) downsizing strategy, structure, and relationship management. Future studies could examine the interplay of these multiple levels to determine their relative influence on firm performance in the context of downsizing to determine if in fact the comprehensive set of relationships is required to explain downsizing performance.

It appears to be far easier to get downsizing wrong than to get it right. Perhaps more novel approaches to the study of downsizing are warranted. Instead of seeking to identify optimal practices and the predictors of those practices, we may be better served by studying downsizing failures. For, within those cases, we are likely to reveal the components of downsizing that are relatively easy to get right and those that are most difficult. We could then focus our attention on the downsizing implementation issues that are particularly intractable.

Furthermore, it would be useful to consider a more game-theoretic approach to the study of downsizing performance. This chapter suggests how the severing of relationships might not realize their intended benefits and might enhance the competitors' capabilities. In a context of competitive dynamics, especially in mature and declining industries where zero-sum interplay occurs and gives rise to consolidation (Harrigan, 1980; DeWitt, 1991), it is likely that the missteps of one firm provide the opportunity for others to be successful. Still others improve their position by doing nothing. We should not over-attribute success to what has been done – success may be due to what was not done and to what another firm did.

## *Limitations*

There are two main limitations to this chapter. First, it focuses on considering downsizing at the business unit level. Yet we also know that downsizing is often part of corporate level adjustments as corporations adjust their corporate staff. In some corporations, especially those that have the potential to realize economies of scope through centralized purchasing and sales organizations, the effect of downsizing may be experienced across multiple business units (Lewin, 2001). Reductions to corporate staff also have the potential to alter the relationships between the corporation and the business units as well as the corporate boundary-spanning relationships represented in shared services, such as government and financial market relations.

Second, this chapter presumes a rational, socio-economic approach, where a market-driven logic influences the choice of strategic, structural, and relationship adjustments in the pursuit of efficiency and effectiveness. It is very likely that where decisions about the actual cuts follow a firm's public commitment to make a particular level of cuts, external and internal political processes will intertwine with a rational, economic approach (McKinley, Sanchez, and Schick, 1995). Case studies of downsizing decision-making can inform our understanding of this interplay and could be used to develop theory about the conditions under which political and mimetic influences are more or less likely to affect downsizing decision-making.

*Notes*

* The author expresses her appreciation to David A. Jones and Chun Zhang for their guidance regarding the relationship between employee, buyer, and supplier involvement and their attitudes and behavioral intentions towards the firm.

1. It is recognized that corporations may centralize purchasing or selling activities at the corporate level to obtain efficiencies. These costs are then typically allocated to the business unit.
2. Note that these key considerations influence the likelihood that the downsized business unit will contribute to the performance of a corporation. Where the corporation has decided that the retention of the business unit, albeit in a modified form, is important to corporate performance, any corporate expectations of operational and/or strategic synergies between business units in the portfolio should be addressed by considering other business units and corporate offices as "key partners."

## References

Anderson, E. W., Fornell, C., and Rust, R. T. 1997. "Customers satisfaction, productivity, and profitability: Differences between goods and services." *Marketing Science* **16**(2): 129–145.

Ansoff, I. 1965. *Corporate Strategy: An Analytic Approach to Business Policy for Growth and Expansion*. New York: McGraw Hill.

Ashforth, B. E. and Mael, F. 1989. "Social identity and the organization." *Academy of Management Review* **14**: 20–39.

Bandura, A. 1988. *Social Foundations of Thought and Action: A Social Cognitive Theory*. Englewood, NJ: Prentice-Hall.

Barreyre, P. Y. 1988. "The concept of 'impartation' policies: A different approach to vertical integration strategies." *Strategic Management Journal* 9(5): 507–520.

Bies, R. J. and Moag, J. S. 1986. "Interactional justice: Communication criteria for fairness," in B. Sheppard (ed.), *Research on Negotiation in Organizations*, Vol. I. Greenwich, CT: JAI, pp. 43–55.

Brandenburger, A. M. and Stuart, H. 1996. "Value-based business strategy." *Journal of Economics and Management Strategy* **5**(1): 5–24.

Brockner, J. 1988. "The effects of work layoffs on survivors: Research, theory and practice," in B. M. Staw and L. L. Cummings (eds.), *Research in Organizational Behavior*, Vol. X. Greenwich, CT: JAI Press, pp. 213–255.

Brockner, J. 1990. "Scope of justice in the workplace: How survivors react to co-worker layoffs." *Journal of Social Issues* **46**: 95–106.

Brockner, J., DeWitt, R., Grover, S., and Reed, T. 1990. "When it is especially important to explain why: Factors affecting the relationship between managers' explanations of a layoff and survivors' reaction to the layoff." *Journal of Experimental and Social Psychology* **26**: 389–407.

Brockner, J. and Greenberg, J. 1990. "The impact of layoffs on survivors: An organizational justice perspective," in J. S. Carroll (ed.), *Applied Social Psychology and Organizational Settings*. Hillsdale, NJ: Erlbaum, pp. 45–75.

Brockner, J., Grover, S., Reed, T., DeWitt, R. L., and O'Malley, M. 1987. "Survivors reactions to layoffs: We get by with a little help for our friends." *Administrative Science Quarterly* **32**(2): 526–541.

Brockner, J., Tyler, T. R., and Cooper-Schneider, R. 1992. "The influence of prior commitment to an institution on reactions to perceived unfairness: The higher they are, the harder they fall." *Administrative Science Quarterly* **37**(2): 241–261.

Budros, A. 1999. "A conceptual framework for analyzing why organizations downsize." *Organization Science* **10**(1): 69–82

Cameron, K. and Zammuto, R. 1983. "Matching managerial strategies to conditions of decline." *Human Resource Management* **22**(4): 359–375.

Cascio, W. F. 1993. "Downsizing: What do we know? What have we learned?" *Academy of Management Executive* 7(1): 95–104.

Cascio, W. F. 2002. *Responsible Restructuring: Creative and Profitable Alternatives to Layoffs*. San Francisco, CA: Berrett-Koehler.

Cascio, W. F. 2009. *Employment Downsizing and Its Alternatives*. Alexandria, VA: Society for Human Resource Management.

Cascio, W. F., Young, C. E., and Morris, J. R. 1997. "Financial consequences of employment change decisions in major US corporations." *Academy of Management Journal* **40**: 1175–1189.

Chatain, O. 2010. "Value creation, competition, and performance in buyer –supplier relationships." *Strategic Management Journal* **32**: 76–102.

Datta, D. K., Guthrie, J. P., Basuil, D., and Pandey, A. 2010. "Causes and effects of employee downsizing: A review and synthesis." *Journal of Management* **36**(1): 281–348.

De Meuse, K. P., Bergmann, T. J., Vanderheiden, P. A., and Roraff, C. E. 2004. "New evidence regarding organizational downsizing and a firm's financial performance: A long-term analysis." *Journal of Managerial Issues* **16**(2): 155–177.

Dess, G. G. and Beard, D. W. 1984. "Dimensions of organizational task environments." *Administrative Science Quarterly* **29**: 52–73.

DeWitt, R. L. 1991. "Strategies for downsizing: Breaking up is hard to do." Unpublished Ph.D. dissertation. NY: Columbia University.

DeWitt, R. L. 1993. "The structural consequences of downsizing." *Organization Science* **4**(1): 30–40.

DeWitt, R. L. 1998. "Firm, industry and strategy influences on choice of downsizing approach." *Strategic Management Journal* **19**(1): 59–79.

DeWitt, R. L., Harrigan, K. R., and Newman, W. H. 1998. "Downsizing strategically," in D. L. Ketchen (ed.), *Advances in Applied Business Strategy*. Greenwich, CT: JAI Press, pp. 5, 21–36.

DeWitt, R. L., Trevino, L. K., and Mollica, K. A. 2003. "Stuck in the middle: A control-based model of managers' reactions to their subordinates' layoffs." *Journal of Managerial Issues* **15**(1): 32–49.

Fassina, N. E., Jones, D. A., and Uggerslev, K. L. 2008. "Relationship clean-up time: Using meta-analysis and path analysis to clarify the relationships among job satisfaction, perceived fairness, and citizenship behaviors." *Journal* of *Management* **34**: 161–188.

Ford, J. D. 1980. "The occurrence of structural hysteresis in declining organizations." *Academy of Management Review* **5**(4): 589–598.

Freeman, S. J. 1999. "The gestalt of organizational downsizing: Downsizing strategies as packages of change." *Human Relations* **52**(12): 1505–1541.

Freeman, S. J. and Cameron, K. S. 1993. "Organizational downsizing: A convergence and reorientation framework." *Organization Science* **4**: 10–29.

Galbraith, J. R. 1974. "Organization design: An information processing view." *Interfaces* **4**(3): 28–36.

Geyskens, I., Steenkamp, J.-B. E. M., and Kumar, N. 1999. "A meta-analysis of satisfaction in marketing channel relationships." *Journal of Marketing Research* **36**(2): 223–238.

Grant, R. M. 1996. "Toward a knowledge-based theory of the firm." *Strategic Management Journal* **17**: 109–122.

Greenhalgh, L., Lawrence, A. T., and Sutton, R. I. 1988. "Determinants of work force reduction strategies in declining organizations." *Academy of Management Review* **13**(2): 241–254.

Harrigan, K. R. 1980. *Strategies for Declining Businesses*. Lexington, MA: Lexington Books.

Harrigan, K. R. 1983. *Strategies for Vertical Integration*. Lexington, MA: Lexington Books.

Heskett, J. L., Jones, T. O., Loveman, G. W., Sasser Jr., W. E., and Schlesinger, L. A. 1994. "Putting the service profit chain to work." *Harvard Business Review* **72**(2): 164–174.

Hoskisson, R. E. and Hitt, M. A. 1994. *Downscoping: How to Tame the Diversified Firm*. New York: Oxford University Press.

Kotler, P. 1965. "Phasing out weak products." *Harvard Business Review* **43** (March/April): 108–118.

Kreiken, J. 1980. "Effective vertical integration and disintegration strategies," in W. F. Glueck (ed.), *Business Policy and Strategic Management*. New York: McGraw-Hill, pp. 256–263.

Kumar, N., Scheer, L. K., and Steenkamp, J.-B. E. M. 1995. "The effects of perceived interdependence on dealer attitudes." *Journal of Marketing Research* **32**: 348–356.

Leana, C. R. and Feldman, D. C. 1992. *Coping with Job Loss: How Individuals, Organizations, and Communities Respond to Layoffs*. New York: Lexington Books.

Lewin, J. E. 2001. "The effects of downsizing on organizational buying behavior: An empirical investigation." *Journal of the Academy of Marketing Science* **29**(2): 151–164.

Lewin, J. E. 2003. "An empirical investigation of the effects of downsizing on buyer–seller relationships." *Journal of Business Research* **56**(2): 283–293.

Lewin, J. E., Biemans, W., and Ulaga, W. 2010. "Firm downsizing and satisfaction among United States and European customers." *Journal of Business Research* **63**(7): 697–706.

Lewin, J. E. and Johnston, W. J. 2008. "The impact of supplier downsizing on performance, satisfaction over time, and repurchase intentions." *Journal of Business and Industrial Marketing* **23**(4): 249–255.

March, J. and Simon, H. 1958. *Organizations*. New York: John Wiley & Sons.

McGahan, A. M. 2004. *How Industries Evolve: Principles for Achieving and Sustaining Superior Performance*. Boston, MA: Harvard Business School Press.

McKinley, W., Sanchez, C., and Schick, A. 1995. "Organizational downsizing: Constraining, cloning, learning." *Academy of Management Executive* **9**: 32–42.

Mishra, A. and Spreitzer, G. 1998. "Explaining how survivors respond to downsizing: The roles of trust, empowerment, justice, and work redesign." *Academy of Management Review* **23**(3): 567–588.

Mollica, K. A. and DeWitt, R. L. 2000. "When others retire early: What about me?" *Academy of Management Journal* **43**: 1068–1075.

Mowday, R. T., Porter, L. W., and Steers, R. M. 1982. *Employee–Organization Linkages: The Psychology of Commitment, Turnover and Absenteeism*. New York: Academic Press.

Newman, K. S. 1988. *Falling From Grace*. New York: Free Press.

Nixon, R. D., Hitt, M. A., Lee, H., and Jeong, E. 2004. "Market reactions to announcements of corporate downsizing action and implementation strategies." *Strategic Management Journal* **25**(11): 1121–1129.

Organ, D. W. 1988. *Organizational Citizenship Behavior: The Good Soldier Syndrome*. Lexington, MA: Lexington Books.

Pinkham, B. C., Picken, J. C., and Dess, G. G. 2010. "Creating value in the modern organization: The role of leveraging technology." *Organizational Dynamics* **39**(3): 226–239.

Porter, M. E. 1980. *Competitive Strategy*. New York: Free Press.

Porter, M. E. 1985. *Competitive Advantage*. New York: Free Press.

Rothaermel, F. T., Hitt, M. A., and Jobe, L. A. 2006. "Balancing vertical integration and strategic outsourcing: Effects on product portfolio, product success, and firm performance." *Strategic Management Journal* **27**: 1033–1056.

Rousseau, D. M. and Anton, R. 1991. "Fairness and implied contract obligations in job terminations: The role of contributions, promises, and performance." *Journal of Organizational Behavior* **12**: 287–299.

Schumpeter, J. 1942. *Capitalism, Socialism and Democracy*. New York: Harper.

Sharma, A., Grewal, D., and Levy, M. 1995. "The customer satisfaction/logistics interface." *Journal of Business Logistics* **16**(2): 1–21.

Siegel, D. S. and Simons, K. L. 2010. "Assessing the effects of mergers and acquisitions on firm performance, plant productivity, and workers: New evidence from matched employer–employee data." *Strategic Management Journal* **31**(8): 903–916.

Staw, B. M., Sandelands, L. E., and Dutton, J. E. 1981. "Threat-rigidity effects in organizational behavior." *Administrative Science Quarterly* **26**(3): 501–524.

Sutton, R. I. and D'Aunno, T. 1989. "Decreasing organizational size: Untangling the effects of money and people." *Academy of Management Review* **14**(2): 194–212.

Uchitelle, L. 2006. *The Disposable American: Layoffs and Their Consequences*. New York: Alfred A. Knopf.

Wayhan, V. B. and Werner, S. 2000. "The impact of workforce reductions on financial performance: A longitudinal perspective." *Journal of Management* **26**(2): 341–363.

Williamson, O. E. 1975. *Markets and Hierarchies: Analysis and Antitrust Implications*. New York: Free Press.

Worrell, D. L., Davidson III, W. N., and Sharma, V. M. 1991. "Layoff announcements and stockholder wealth." *Academy of Management Journal* **34**: 662–678.

Zammuto, R. F. and Cameron, K. S. 1985. "Environmental decline and organizational response," in B. M. Staw and L. L. Cummings (eds.), *Research in Organizational Behavior*, Vol. VII. Greenwhich, CT: JAI Press, pp. 223–262.

Zhang, C., Henke, J. W., and Griffith, D. A. 2009. "Do buyer cooperative actions matter under relational stress? Evidence from Japanese and US assemblers in the US automotive industry." *Journal of Operations Management* **27**(6): 479–494.

# 12 Post-downsizing implications and consequences: A global perspective

FRANCO GANDOLFI, LISA M. RENZ, MAGNUS HANSSON, AND JOHN B. DAVENPORT

## Introduction

This book and the scholarly literature agree that firms engage in workforce downsizing for many reasons. Downsizing generates a myriad consequences and implications at organizational, subgroup, and individual levels of analysis (Gandolfi and Hansson, 2011; Datta, Guthrie, Basuil, and Pandey, 2010).

The body of literature on downsizing is substantial, reflecting the prevalence of this management practice in the United States, the United Kingdom, Canada, Europe, Australia, New Zealand, and Japan, and it is also spreading to other regions. The majority of the downsizing research has been conducted in the United States and Europe (Datta *et al.*, 2010). Still, the contraction of workforces has not been confined to US firms, but has occurred throughout the world (Ryan and Macky, 1998). Empirical evidence shows that downsizing and its many related concepts has been particularly pervasive in, for example, North America (Freeman, 1994), Britain (Thornhill and Saunders, 1998), Canada (Dolan, Belout, and Balkin, 2000), Japan (Griggs and Hyland, 2003; Mroczkowski and Hanaoka, 1997), Australia (Gandolfi, 2006a), New Zealand (Macky, 2004), South Africa (Littler, 1998), Western Europe (Lamsa and Takala, 2000) and several countries in Eastern Europe (Redman and Keithley, 1998; Filatotchev, Buck, and Zhukov, 2000). It is also evident that downsizing as a strategy has not been limited to established economies but has also been employed in developing countries, including African and Latin American countries (Jones, Jammal, and Gokgur, 1998) and transitioning economies (LaPorta and Lopes-de-Silanes, 1997).

Downsizing is also pervasive in countries that are moving from a state-regulated market system, with one or only a few market actors in each sector, to a market system based on competition and multiple actors in the majority of sectors. Examples of such countries are Russia, Belarus,

Ukraine, and countries in Eastern Europe, where privatization often brings about the need to reduce firms' headcounts (Appelbaum, Everard, and Hung, 1999; Filatotchev *et al.*, 2000). Cascio (2003) points out that downsizing has also affected China, which has become one of the world's foremost manufacturing hubs. In 2003 alone, over 25 million Chinese lost their jobs from the transformation and privatization of state-owned enterprises (SOE). Downsizing has even become common in industrialized countries, such as Japan and Sweden, which have historically displayed very stable employment practices.

As is evident from the literature, there is a wide range of downsizing causes and driving forces, yet no single cause seems to be able to explain and account for the emergence and pervasiveness of the phenomenon (Datta *et al.*, 2010). In fact, it is evident that popular management practices have a tendency to spread and to be adopted as management fashions or fads, thereby becoming isomorphic institutionalized in various countries, regions, and parts of the world (Abrahamson, 1996; Powell and DiMaggio, 1983; Barley and Tolbert, 1997). Consequently, contemporary firms have been shown to adopt similar or identical strategies and practices to handle challenges such as economic downturns, external threats, increased competition, or internal inefficiencies.

Across the globe, firms downsize their workforces for a multitude of reasons; still there are some common denominators that seem to recur in management's rhetoric. In the private sector, for instance, management often argues that organizations need to downsize to reduce costs (Sahdev, 2003; Gandolfi and Hansson, 2011), remain globally competitive (Macky, 2004; Levitt, Wilson, and Gilligan, 2008), maximize shareholder returns (Escalante, 2001), and improve efficiencies (Zyglidopoulos, 2003). Additional reasons cited include a reduction of profits, or poor management decisions that led to over-hiring (Downs, 1995). In the public sector, downsizing often occurs due to budget reductions and lost jobs derived from technology improvements (Escalante, 2001).

The downsizing literature reveals that executives adopt downsizing as a strategy due to financial pressures and financial losses (Cameron, Freeman, and Mishra, 1991; Cascio, 1991, 1993). Downsizing may occur because of demands by shareholders (Delorese, 1998), mergers and acquisitions (Kets de Vries and Balazas, 1997), privatization (Allen, 1997), and unacceptable profit margins (Allen, 1997). Ultimately, a common belief is that downsizing improves financial performance (Macky, 2004). Other examples of drives to downsizing that are frequently cited include pressures from rival firms (Luthans and Sommer, 1999), poor industry conditions (Espahbodi, John, and Vasudevan, 2000), deterioration of micro-niches (Cameron, Sutton, and Whetten, 1988; Hannan and Freeman, 1988, 1989), shrinking markets (Harrigan, 1982), severe loss of market shares (Hedberg, Nystrom, and Starbuck, 1978; Starbuck, Greve, and Hedberg, 1978), change in demographics (Mellahi and Wilkinson, 2004), divestments (Montgomery and Thomas, 1988), exit from international markets (Jackson, Mellahi, and Sparks, 2005), failing strategic initiatives and wrong investments (Ghemawat, 1991), and other types of failures (Mellahi and Wilkinson, 2004).

Downsizing has been shown to generate profound overall implications and consequences, as noted in the management literature as well as in the business press. A close study of the extensive body of literature on the consequences of downsizing presents a complex, yet rich picture. Despite the large body of research, there is scarce evidence regarding the overall success, effectiveness, and efficiency of this strategy when assessed from financial, organizational, and human resource perspectives (Burke and Greenglass, 2000; Littler and Gandolfi, 2008; Gandolfi, 2009). For example, downsizing produces a range of *financial* consequences. A multitude of studies – cross-sectional and longitudinal, North American, and international – have demonstrated that while some organizations have reported financial improvements, the majority of downsized firms have not been able to reap improved levels of efficiency, effectiveness, productivity, and profitability (Cascio, 1993; Sahdev, 2003; Macky, 2004; Love and Nohria, 2005; Gandolfi, 2008; Gandolfi and Neck, 2008; Guthrie and Datta, 2008).

Downsizing generates a range of *organizational* consequences. Downsizing consolidates decision-making at higher levels of the organizational hierarchy, and often produces a crisis mentality focused on immediate needs at the expense of long-term planning (Cameron, 1994). Downsizing generates a range of *socio-cultural* consequences. From the extant literature, it is possible to distinguish between three categories of people directly impacted by downsizing: victims, survivors, and executioners (Downs, 1995; Kettley, 1995; Allen, 1997; Littler, 1998). Each category experiences different effects of downsizing (Gandolfi, 2008). It has been reported that the human costs of downsizing are immense and far-reaching (Burke and Greenglass, 2000; Brockner 1988, 1992;

Brockner *et al.*, 1988). In fact, survivors often experience profound consequences (Macky, 2004) as a result of having limited resources and support following downsizing.

These consequences of downsizing are the focus of this chapter, which seeks to outline an international perspective of the consequences and implications of downsizing. The financial, organizational, socio-cultural, and human aspects will be examined, with a particular focus on Europe, Asia, and the United States. Along the way, this chapter reviews a broad array of downsizing literature to portray the consequences and implications of downsizing internationally. Specifically, we focus our attention on the impact of downsizing on: (a) the organization's financial performance, (b) the organization's culture and climate, and (c) employees as influenced by intrinsic and extrinsic motivation.

The chapter is structured as follows: First, we discuss downsizing as a strategy or process in order to frame the context of our discussion. In addition, we discuss the phases of downsizing because outcomes of downsizing may occur in different phases within organizations. Second, we review the literature on financial performance, identifying the various measures of financial performance used by researchers. Third, we discuss how downsizing influences the culture and climate of organizations, demonstrating the organization's response to training and development. Fourth, we discuss human and socio-cultural consequences, examining hierarchical differences in pay and benefits. The chapter concludes with a summary discussion and implications for future research.

## Downsizing – strategy or process?

In order to understand how downsizing affects financial performance, we revisit the fundamental question posed by Gandolfi (2006b) "Is downsizing a strategy or process?" This question is important to our discussion since it frames the context in which we will look at research to understand the relationship between downsizing and financial performance. According to Merriam Webster, *strategy* is the art of devising or employing plans toward a goal, while *process* is a series of actions or operations conducive to an end. Thus, if downsizing is viewed as a *strategy* then reducing the workforce by this definition should lead to increased financial performance. If, however, downsizing is a *process*, then reducing the workforce is part of a series of actions that, it is hoped, will ultimately lead to improved financial performance. Therefore, examining downsizing as a process rather than a strategy should help us identify if or how downsizing improves financial performance.

## Phases of downsizing

Gandolfi (2006b) examined large Australian banks to conceptualize the downsizing process. He concluded that while theoretically participants identified three phases of downsizing – *before, during*, and *after* or *post*-downsizing – for the most part they distinguished between *before* and *after* downsizing. Furthermore, participants identified the *before* phase as the period that immediately followed downsizing announcements and the *after* phase as that which occurred following implementation. His research suggested that organizations did not plan, prepare, and/or train employees prior to engaging in downsizing. Thus, he speculated that it was unlikely that firms had appropriate HR plans, policies, or programs in place. These findings were consistent with Cascio's (1993) assertions that organizations did not adequately prepare for downsizing, and surviving employees were largely ignored (Appelbaum, Delage, Labibb, and Gault, 1997; Gandolfi, 2006a).

Also, Gandolfi (2006b) concluded that *while* and *post*-downsizing phases were likely to have two subphases. The first phase, *while* downsizing, is referred to as a workforce reduction strategy (Cameron, 1994) and is frequently marked by dramatic cutbacks (Gandolfi, 2006b). The second phase requires more time and involves organizational redesign and systemic strategies (Gandolfi, 2006b). Post-downsizing has two subphases. The first phase, viewed as short term, occurs immediately following downsizing and involves preparing surviving employees to fill vacant positions. The second phase, post-downsizing, "consists of long-range activities that aim to foster employee empowerment and recommitment, such as counseling, training, professional advice, and support, and to focus on aligning remaining employees with the organization's new vision, mission, and strategic objectives" (Gandolfi, 2006b, p. 4). Thus, if downsizing is a process, then it is in the post-downsizing phase that we need to ask whether the downsized firm achieved its goal of reaping improved levels of financial performance derived from the adoption of downsizing activities. In order to begin to answer this question, we need to determine what measures researchers have examined to determine a change in financial performance.

## Financial implications and consequences of downsizing: A global overview

In this section, we outline a discussion on different ways to measure financial performance. This will serve as a base from which we continue our discussion regarding the financial outcomes following downsizing activities. Furthermore, we will also turn to a brief discussion of macro-economics and the implications of economic structures on organizations.

### *Measuring financial performance*

Researchers have used various measures to assess financial performance. For example, Kornecki (2010) examined nationwide outcomes in Europe by measuring changes in Gross Domestic Product (GDP). Megginson, Nash, and Van Randenborgh (1994) measured an increase in sales, while Love and Nohria (2005) examined change in organizational efficiencies and production processes. Mixed results and non-significant results have been found when measuring return on asset (ROA) ratio and return on equity (ROE) ratio (De Meuse, Vanderheiden, and Bergmann, 1994; Cascio, Young, and Morris, 1997; Dawkins, Littler, Valenzuela, and Jensen, 1999; De Meuse, Bergmann, Vanderheiden, and Roraff, 2004). Some empirical research has also found support for profitability, profit, margin, and EBDIT (earnings before depreciation, interest, and taxes) margin being improved from downsizing (Dawkins *et al.*, 1999; Morris, Cascio, and Young, 1999; De Meuse *et al.*, 2004; Macky, 2004). While researchers have used various methods to measure financial performance, many researchers have focused on the impact of downsizing on the value of stock in determining the impact on financial performance (Ballester, Livnat, and Sinha, 1999; Worrell, Davidson, and Sharma, 1991).

### *Stock valuation effects*

On a global scale, management within publicly traded companies can be motivated to undertake strategic initiatives that are believed to have positive effects on the valuation of the firm's stock. A review of the body of research on downsizing has attempted to explore the information effect of downsizing announcements and the follow-on effect on the underlying firm's stock price (Malatesta and Thompson, 1985). It has long been assumed that there is a positive market information effect on companies announcing downsizing efforts (Iqbal and Shetty, 1995). Management has long believed that announcements regarding downsizing efforts communicate that it is being proactive in attempting to control costs and in responding to organizational distress, and that equity markets react positively to these proactive measures. However, as with the research on the financial effects, the research on this topic has been shown to be just as inconclusive (Wertheim and Robinson, 2004).

Ballester *et al.* (1999) found a positive relationship of downsizing announcements and stock price effect within companies across 41 countries. Similar findings have been reported by Chalos and Chen (2002) within US-based firms. In contrast, there seems to be equal evidence suggesting a negative relationship between downsizing announcements and a firm's stock price. Indeed, a multitude of studies have reported negative stock price responses to downsizing announcements within a US context (Worrell *et al.*, 1991; Iqbal and Shetty, 1995; Abrahamson, 1996; Elayan, Swales, Maris, and Scott, 1998; Chen, Mehrotra, Sivakumar, and Yu, 2001). Lee (1997) found negative stock price action following downsizing announcements within companies in the United States and Japan, concluding that the stock market reacted negatively in both countries. However, Japanese stock price reactions were much smaller than the United States (Lee, 1997). Likewise, in Japan a single layoff announcement does not affect stock prices as much as it does in the United States. It appears that Japanese investors are not as quick to respond to layoff announcements as investors in the United States. Multiple announcements affect both countries more than a single announcement and temporary layoffs do not significantly affect market prices in either country.

In the United States, the size of layoffs tends to impact market performance. Lee (1997) speculated that large layoffs were perceived as signs of serious financial or operational problems. In contrast, the size of the stock price changes for Japanese firms does not vary with layoff characteristics. Hillier, Marshall, McColgan, and Werema (2007) reported similar negative effects in the United Kingdom.

What has emerged from the research on stock price effect seems to echo that of the studies on downsizing and financial performance. That is, the market tends to react negatively when downsizing announcements are perceived to be a reactive strategy to poor financial conditions (Hillier *et al.*, 2007). In particular, if the market has already identified poor financial conditions within an organization, the market appears to read the downsizing efforts as indicative of serious financial crises within the organization (Worrell *et al.*, 1991; Iqbal and Sekhar, 1995; Lee, 1997; Elayan *et al.*, 1998; Wertheim and Robinson, 2004).

It is important to recognize that companies do not reduce headcount only in response to financial distress; healthy companies often seek to revamp their workforces. The downsizing research indicates that while healthy firms may still experience a negative market reaction to downsizing announcements, the size of this reaction is 'decidedly less muted' than that of financially weaker companies (Iqbal and Shakhar, 1995).

To conclude, researchers have used various measures to identify a change in financial performance such as ROA, ROE, increase in sales, and GDP. Many researchers, though, have focused on the effect on stock value. While much research concludes a negative effect on stock value following downsizing activities, the findings are mixed on the other measures of financial performance. The following section discusses the mixed findings of the other measures of financial performance and shows the positive and negative outcomes related to downsizing.

## *Financial outcomes of downsizing*

As previously stated, the evidence from research around the globe is not entirely negative or as ambiguous on the financial performance of downsizing firms. Numerous studies in the United States (Bruton, Keels, and Shook, 1996; Cascio *et al.*, 1997; Wayhan and Werner, 2000; Love and Nohria, 2005) representing more than 3,000 companies found positive effects on financial performance after downsizing initiatives. De Meuse *et al.* (1994, 2004), for example, examined several financial measures of *Fortune* 100 firms over a five-year span, comparing financial aspects and reporting positive outcomes. Kang and Shivdasani (1997) found similar positive effects in a sample of 97 Japanese firms. Yu and Park (2004, 2006) made comparable observations in more than 500 downsized companies in South Korea.

In the absence of fundamental changes in the business system, much of the research suggests that financial improvements as a result of downsizing efforts remain elusive (De Meuse *et al.*, 1994; Cascio *et al.*, 1997; Munoz-Bullon and Sanchez-Bueno, 2008; Vanderheiden, De Meuse, and Bergmann, 1999). For instance, De Meuse *et al.* (1994) examined several measures of financial performance for 100 companies with workforce layoffs and without layoffs for a five-year period from 1987 to 1991. Specifically, they compared the financial performance of 35 companies without layoff announcements and 17 companies who announced layoff efforts. They found that profit margins, return on assets (ROA), return on equity (ROE), and market-to-book ratios for the companies without the layoff announcements were significantly better during the two-year period following the layoff announcements than those for the firms engaging in downsizing efforts over the same time frame.

Munoz-Bullon and Sanchez-Bueno (2008) examined profitability and productivity measures and reported that the size of the downsizing efforts of 96 Spanish firms that announced downsizing initiatives from 1995 to 2001 had no material effect on subsequent financial performance of the firms. It was evident that no improvement in ROA or return on sales occurred in the ensuing year for the downsizing companies relative to organizations without downsizing announcements. Other studies have found no statistically significant effects of downsizing on financial performance of the respective companies. Mentzer (1996) studied Canadian firms and reported no clear evidence that downsizing efforts improved organizations' net change in income or ROA relative to companies without downsizing. Krishnan and Park (1998) examined the financial performance of more than 100 *Fortune* 500 companies with more than $3 billion in revenue and that had made downsizing announcements between the years of 1984 and 1990. The researchers measured the return on sales for two years prior to the layoff announcements and for the subsequent two years. They found that the downsizing efforts had no positive impacts on the return on sales of the downsizing companies. Cascio (1998) studied the financial performance (return on assets) of US companies engaging in downsizing and examined 311 firms from *S&P* 500-list for the period of 1981 to 1990 and reported that there was no evidence of improved financial performance for those companies that had engaged in downsizing. In a similar vein, Vincente-Lorente and Suarez-Gonzalez (2007) found a negative effect on the financial performance of 297 Spanish companies that had embarked on downsizing. Similar negative financial impacts were observed in Carswell's (2005) study among 150 companies with more than 50 employees in New Zealand.

It is important, within this discussion, to make a clear distinction between downsizing and layoffs. Downsizing can be viewed as an involuntary employment adjustment that organizations implement in order to improve organizational performance. The implication is that there is an internal justification for the staff reductions. Organizations may have moved into a different lifecycle stage or they may have identified operational inefficiencies or redundancies that would be improved by fewer employees. The key point is that the firm takes on employment base redesign or reduction strategically as a means of improving organizational performance (Freeman and Cameron, 1993). Downsizing, by definition, includes all aspects of redesigning both the workforce and how it works. Layoffs, in contrast, are merely the personnel reductions that occur as part of the overall downsizing process. However, what is often seen in practice is management's propensity to equate downsizing with merely reducing headcount. Krishnan and Park (1998) assert that downsizing efforts will not be effective if downsizing is reduced to headcount reductions only. Firms that have adopted downsizing as one component of a broader approach to organizational redesign and to the management of human resources often experience more positive post-downsizing outcomes (Cascio *et al.*, 1997; Kase and Zupan, 2005). Organizations are further impacted by external factors, including the economic structure and the larger culture. The next two sections will examine how these factors influence downsizing and financial performance.

## Economic structure

Downsizing activity is not confined to shareholder-type economies such as the United States. Downsizing has been adopted in various countries for disparate reasons; a distinct thread of research on downsizing and financial performance explores instances where there is a fundamental shift in the host economic structure (Ahmdjian and Robbins, 2005). Therefore, the catalyst which begets downsizing may be an important factor in the financial outcomes of the different organizations. In Central and Eastern Europe, for example, fundamental excesses in staffing or other inefficiencies in the work processes due to the centrally planned structure of these former Soviet bloc economic systems served as a catalyst for downsizing (Kornecki, 2010).

As the Iron Curtain fell, these countries came to face competition in a global marketplace (Kornecki, 2010). As industries in formerly centrally planned governments struggled to remain relevant in the modern global marketplace, many management teams had to attempt to remedy the deep structural issues that plagued their industries. A key element in this struggle was management's ability to respond to environmental changes and substantial shifts in corporate governance as predicated by the privatization process (De Witt, 1998). Appelbaum *et al.* (1999) reported that privatization initiatives often result in the need to reduce headcount, since one goal of privatization is to improve areas where organizational inefficiencies are found (Aoki, 2001). Therefore, downsizing endeavors were undertaken as a response to a fundamental change in corporate governance, necessitated by inefficient employment and production practices of the state controlled industries. However, does privatization necessarily result in improved financial performance?

### *Privatization*

A comprehensive study of 61 firms in 18 countries demonstrated that companies that engaged in downsizing as a result of privatization experienced increased sales and even a subsequent rebound in employment levels (Megginson *et al.*, 1994). Kornecki (2010) extended the positive financial impacts of the privatization-related downsizing activities of companies within Central and Eastern Europe, contending that the downsizing efforts made positive overall contributions to the respective countries' economic growth as measured by gross domestic product (GDP). Still, on the organizational level of analysis, it has been evident that privatization, for example in Portugal, has led to reduction in the workforce, as well as the negative performance outcomes typically associated with downsizing (Campos de Cuhna, 2000).

Privatization efforts have not been confined to Eastern and Central Europe. Rather, as economies have opened up, privatization has often been the consequence. Chong and Lopez-de-Silanes (2002) note that privatization has occurred all around the world in the last few decades, often resulting in widespread labor restructuring efforts, including downsizing. Examples include Brazil, Argentina (Ramamurti, 1997), Côte d'Ivoire (Jones *et al.*, 1998), Mexico (La Porta and Lopez-de-Silanes, 1997), and China, all of which have engaged in similar downsizing efforts as a result of privatization. Megginson and Netter (2001) note that employment levels fall for nearly all firms in these transition economies.

It warrants reiteration that positive financial results were observed in firms that engaged in downsizing efforts as a result of fundamental changes within the economic system. As Aoki (2001) suggests, business systems are a result of the complementary institutions within the economic system itself. Aoki (2001) also asserts that changing any part of these existing systems can have adverse consequences if there is no change to the existing practices.

However, the unfortunate phenomenon that seems to emerge within the downsizing literature is that once downsizing finds its way into the toolbox of a particular management team, it becomes a staple response of that firm. Hamel and Prahalad (1994) describe the phenomenon as corporate anorexia. They suggest that while the disease of anorexia can make individuals thinner, it does not mean that such individuals are necessarily healthier. Hamel and Prahalad (1994) intimate that firms can be viewed in the same way. As such, whether the catalyst for downsizing is privatization, a response to globalization, or a response to various financial crises, the specter of downsizing has collateral effects on the entire workforce, beyond those that are downsized.

## What else may impact financial performance 'post-downsizing'?

Researchers have begun to speculate as to the underlying reasons why some firms experience positive results while others experience negative outcomes. Love and Nohria (2005) note that the effectiveness of downsizing on financial performance is largely contingent upon the conditions under which downsizing is undertaken. More specifically, firms that undertake downsizing as a proactive measure when they have excess capacity or inefficiencies in the workforce tend to experience positive results. However, in organizations where downsizing is adopted as a reactive response to external stimuli, such as a financial crises or fluctuations in the business cycle, the results seem to be less favorable (Yu and Park, 2004).

Whether downsizing occurs as a reaction to internal or external factors, the actual strategy and speed of implementation affect the organization's ability to achieve desired outcomes. Cameron *et al.* (1991, 1993) concluded that there are three distinct implementation strategies used by firms, that is workforce reduction, organization redesign, and systemic strategies. Organizations experienced increased organizational improvement when they engaged in continuous, gradual, and incremental downsizing (Cameron *et al.*, 1991). Additionally, a systemic approach with participation from middle- and lower-level employees increased organizational improvement. However, firms that implemented downsizing rapidly or discontinuously were less likely to have organizational improvements (Cameron *et al.*, 1993).

Thus far, we have examined the overall impact of downsizing on firms around the world. The results have been inconsistent; other factors, such as economic structure, cultural differences, and long-term orientation while engaging in the downsizing process, have proven to impact organizations differently. While downsizing often results in a negative reaction in the stock market, cultural differences cause different degrees of reactions.

At this point we shift our discussion on financial performance to see how downsizing impacts organizations and how organizations respond to changes.

## Organizational implications and consequences of downsizing: A global overview

As downsizing is an *intentional* endeavor, it should not be surprising that the organization's climate, culture, and surviving employees are impacted by management's decision to downsize (Cameron *et al.*, 1991). In this section, we discuss organizational outcomes following downsizing and discuss how organizations may cope with the lingering effects of downsizing.

Downsizing has been shown to generate a range of organizational effects. There is strong evidence suggesting that downsizing practices consolidate decision-making efforts at higher levels of organizational hierarchies and produce a crisis mentality focused on immediate needs at the expense of long-term planning (Cameron, 1994). Furthermore, downsizing activities produce a loss of innovation, with decreased tolerance for risk and failure associated with creative activity (Richtnér and Ahlström, 2006). Ironically, although overall communication tends to become more restricted, the organizational climate becomes more politicized as special interest groups organize and become more vocal (Burke and Cooper, 2000; Littler and Hansson, 2007). Other reported negative consequences following downsizing practices include decreased morale and productivity, increased numbers of conflicts, slower conflict resolution, and loss of trust (Cutcher-Gershenfeld, 1991; Hansson, 2008; Littler and Hansson, 2007). While increased levels of individualism and disconnectedness hinder teamwork, poor leadership (or its complete lack) and an increased level of resistance to change generate conservatism and a rigid, protectionistic stance (Cameron, 1994). In contrast, some studies have reported positive organizational outcomes, including lower overhead costs, less bureaucracy, faster decision-making, smoother communication, greater entrepreneurship, and increased employee productivity (Burke and Cooper, 2000).

## *Coping with organizational effects – the need for training and development*

Management must mitigate the effects of downsizing potentially caused when surviving employees lack the necessary knowledge, skills, and abilities needed to fill vacant positions. Likewise, management is often not prepared to adjust to the effects of downsizing (Gandolfi, 2006a). In fact, Gandolfi posits that firms engage in downsizing without appropriate human resource (HR) policies and plans in place. Ultimately, this impacts the organization's financial performance. Gutknecht and Keys (1993) indicate that firms are often resistant to investments in post-downsizing training programs due to the costs associated with training. Yet, training and development of existing employees has been shown to be pivotal to the organization's ability to recover post-downsizing (Nadeem, 2010).

Following downsizing activity, research has shown that surviving employees experience decreased organizational commitment, productivity, motivation, and job satisfaction, and often shifted to a purely transactional contract (Mihajlovic and Zivkovic, 2008). Employees often report feeling overwhelmed by an increased workload, guilt, anger, and/or relief (Gutknecht and Keys, 1993). Nadeem (2010) concluded that organizations that provided training for employees to improve employee knowledge, skills, and abilities had employees that were motivated, committed, and satisfied. Furthermore, training improved the organization's overall productivity and morale.

## *Training – as a national orientation*

According to Forrier and Sels (2003), some countries invest more in training than do others. For instance, Belgian organizations invest comparatively little in training (OECD, 1999), while Chinese firms make significant investments in training (Zhong-Ming, 1999). At a national level, China has developed management training programs in reaction to its changing economy. Zhong-Ming (1999) posits that economic transition increases the need for professional training and management education. In response, special management training programs emerged in 1978 (Zhong-Ming, 1999). Successful completion of the program was necessary for some managers and supervisors in certain industries in order to assume management responsibilities. A decade later a management training program was developed by the Chinese State Economic Commission in collaboration with organizations in the United States, United Kingdom, Germany, EU, Canada, and Japan. State-owned enterprises identified training opportunities by examining knowledge, skills, and abilities for positions. After managers completed the training program and were working in a position for a while, post-qualifications were assessed (Zhong-Ming, 1999). In the 1990s, organizations in China, including state-owned management, market-oriented shareholding systems, and state enterprises have expanded China's on-the-job training programs expansion in response to a nationwide downsizing movement that eliminated 16 million positions. On-the-job training was used for not only surviving employees, but also for the reemployed Chinese citizens (Zhong-Ming, 1999).

Zhong-Ming (1999) concluded that training in China was reoriented due to the changing economy to include:

1. From an academic to a professional orientation – shifting training to fit skills needed for management;
2. From general knowledge learning to competency development – universities and schools in China expanded education in organizational behavior and human resource management in MBA programs;
3. From technical orientation to managerial focus – rather than focusing on technical training, the focus shifted to learning "soft" skills such as process skills;
4. From a common program to an adaptive curriculum planning – management education went from a universal orientation to a flexible adaptive orientation that is customized to the needs of the organization;
5. From "one-shot" training to strategic distributive development – organizations began to subscribe to the value of longitudinal training programs instead of one-shot or one-time training.

The Belgian government has provided financial support to firms investing in training. Belgian firms have traditionally not warmed to providing training because of open contracts (Forrier and Sels, 2003). Organizations are reluctant to invest in training when employees can leave to work for competitors. Certain conditions are likely to support increased training. For instance, if a firm undergoes downsizing due to financial problems, it is not likely to reduce the amount of training investment. However, if an organization engages in downsizing as a systemic strategy, they train employees actively. Also, downsizing organizations invest less in training than turbulent organizations, which experience unstable inflow and outflow in the number of employees (Forrier and Sels, 2003). Furthermore, organizations that have an internal labor market are more likely to invest in training and monitor pre-training (assessing organizational needs) and post-training (assessing training effectiveness) than are firms lacking such a market. Finally, an internal labor market means that a firm mostly recruits from within, although it will externally recruit employees, but at a lower rate (Forrier and Sels, 2003).

## Socio-cultural and human implications and consequences of downsizing: A global overview

Downsizing generates a range of socio-cultural and human consequences. The literature review reveals similar patterns of explanations, implications, and outcomes on the individual level of analysis, irrespective of country of origin (Datta *et al.*, 2010; Gandolfi and Hansson, 2010). While downsizing processes might unfold differently in various countries, contingent on laws and regulations, still outcomes appear to be similar (Hansson, 2008).

It has been reported that the human costs of downsizing are far-reaching (Burke and Greenglass, 2000). Research depicts strong evidence of adverse psychological effects resulting from job loss, including psychological stress, ill health, family and marital problems, reduced self-esteem, depression, psychiatric morbidity, helplessness, anxiety, and feelings of social isolation (Gandolfi, 2007; Havlovic *et al.*, 1998). There is also evidence suggesting that job loss caused by downsizing generates permanent damage to the downsizing victims' careers (Dolan *et al.*, 2000), including a loss of earning power upon reemployment (Konovsky and Brockner, 1993) and decreased levels of employee commitment and loyalty that tend to carry over to the next job (Macky, 2004).

Downsizing survivors have been shown to display a variety of dysfunctional work behaviors and attitudes. This has been well documented in the literature and includes decreased levels of motivation (Kinnie *et al.*, 1998; Brockner *et al.*, 1986, 1988), morale (Smeltzer and Zener, 1994), commitment (Beylerian and Kleiner, 2003), job satisfaction (Redman and Keithley, 1998), and speed of conflict resolution (Hansson, 2008), as well as increased propensity to leave the firm (Appelbaum *et al.*, 1997), increased levels of resistance to change (Macky, 2004), and increases in conflicts (Cutcher-Gershenfeld, 1991). Further, downsizing survivor sickness pathologies include distrust towards management (Cascio, 1993), increased levels of absenteeism (Gandolfi, 2005) and employee turnover (Brockner *et al.*, 1988), as well as decreased levels of employee involvement (Beylerian and Kleiner, 2003), risk taking (Allen, 1997), and innovation (Gandolfi and Oster, 2009). Similarly, researchers have reported lowered productivity (Estok, 1996), work performance (Beylerian and Kleiner, 2003), efficiency (Lee, 1992), product and service quality (Fisher and White, 2000), learning (Sahdev, 2003), and competence level in the firm (Gettler, 1998). These outcomes are in several aspects fairly homogenous in an international context and have been reported from various countries, including Australia (Littler *et al.*, 1997), the United States (Macky, 2004), and Sweden (Hansson, 2008).

In the review of the socio-cultural and human consequences of downsizing, there is little evidence that the outcomes differ based upon nationality. Littler (2000) compared Australia, New Zealand, and South Africa in terms of correlation between frequency of downsizing and survivor syndrome scale (within country data). In Australia, there was a weak positive correlation between frequency of downsizing and the survivor syndrome scale, but this correlation was not found for New Zealand and South Africa. The results from New Zealand stood out, indicating a negative relationship – the higher the reported frequency, the more positive the human resource outcomes.

Littler (2000) concludes that there is little or weak evidence on the outcomes between downsizing practices in Australia, New Zealand, and South Africa compared to the reported human outcomes in downsizing firms in the United States. Still, Littler (2000) outlines a set of conclusions from the international comparison:

- Negative human resource outcomes and survivor syndrome are difficult to avoid in a post-downsizing context.
- Survivor syndrome is not inevitable and the processes can be managed.

- There are some signs of a recurring cycle of the survivor syndrome across the analyzed countries.

## *Cultural differences*

Cultural differences affect not only the decision to downsize, but also how downsizing victims, survivors, and executioners (Gandolfi, 2010) will be treated following downsizing and the tactics organizations will employ. For instance, a key distinction between the United States and Japan is their employment contracts with workers. Japanese firms have traditionally guaranteed lifetime employment in an implicit fashion (Lee, 1997). Thus, Japanese firms are historically averse to layoffs and are more likely to opt for creative forms of restructuring and cost savings. In contrast, firms in the United States often experience layoffs (Lee, 1997).

In addition to employment contracts, a firm's decision-making is influenced by corporate governance and involvement by a board of directors. Kang and Shivdasani (1997) examined banks in Japan and the United States from 1986 to 1990. These countries were selected because banks in the United States are restricted from owning equity of other firms, and Japanese banks can "own up to 5% of outstanding shares of their client firms." They concluded that during the two years surrounding a decrease in organizational performance, employment drops 15 percent in the United States and 4.7 percent in Japan. Japanese companies are also likely to respond to a drop in performance by expanding operations, often through diversifying activities. Japanese banks with greater equity ownership are more likely to experience layoffs, the removal of outside directors of the board, and a reduction of assets, discontinuations of operations, and plant closures (Kang and Shivdasani, 1997).

Staying with the same countries, differences can be seen in the way shareholders exert influence over executives and managers. For instance, in Japan shareholders often use passive threats and are effective because there is not a clear separation between board members and management (Wu and Delios, 2009). Banks in Japan are more directly influenced by board members because they often make significant investments in the organization. Japanese boards are often comprised of senior officials within the organization. However, in a more recent move, the number of outside board members has increased in Japan (Wu and Delios, 2009).

As demonstrated, cultural differences impact the decision to downsize and how employees will be treated. In addition to cultural differences, organizations also differ in how swiftly they implement downsizing strategies.

## *Compensation and benefits*

Reducing employee compensation and benefits during some stage of downsizing is often part of the strategy employed to improve financial performance (Kelly, 1996). In some instances, reductions in compensation and pay will occur in a pre-downsizing phase (Lin, Zu-Hsu, and Gibb, 2008). There is empirical evidence to suggest that firms see downsizing as an opportunity to reduce employee wages (Guiniven, 2001) and employment costs (Cascio, 1993). Furthermore, downsizing may trigger changes in health plans, life insurance programs, disability plans, retirement plans, non-qualified deferred compensation agreements, and severance plans (Kelly, 1996).

According to Kelly (1996), firms that downsize may actually experience an increase in the cost of employee benefits in the short term, due to an increase in demand for employee benefits by survivors. Improving benefits provides survivors with a sense of security, increases retention, and reduces productivity distractions. The organization can also increase tax efficiencies and obtain lowered premiums by taking advantage of group purchasing (Kelly, 1996). Likewise, executive pay is likely to increase as surviving executives receive increased compensation in order to encourage restructuring activities (Dorata, 2008).

Much of the research regarding compensation and downsizing has focused on executives. Research on executive pay has mostly focused on CEOs of US organizations. These studies typically employ agency theory (Buck, Liu, and Skovoroda, 2008) and use pay as a dependent variable (Tosi *et al.*, 2000), suggesting performance drives pay. According to agency theory, shareholder principals impose executive compensation packages that are likely to align with their own interests. Therefore, executive pay increases when shareholder wealth increases. In the United States, it is suggested that CEOs are able to do this because they are able to manipulate board structures (Bebchuk and Fried, 2004). Buck *et al.* (2008) posited that executive pay in other countries is influenced by corporate governance, institutional contexts, and cultural environments. Thus, it would not be expected that executives in other countries would experience the changes in compensation and benefits common in US organizations (Buck *et al.*, 2008).

## *Executive pay*

Executives are pivotal to a firm's ability to recover from downsizing (Dorata, 2008). Executive support for changed goals is critical for an organization to achieve its new goal of improving financial performance (Buck *et al.*, 2008). Executive pay may be changed either to encourage executives to achieve the organization's new goals (Buck *et al.*, 2008) or to adjust for ineffective leadership (Lin *et al.*, 2008). They posited that changes in executive compensation and benefits may be initiated to correct past inefficiencies, diversifications, or missteps. Also, executive compensation and benefits may be changed prior to or after downsizing in order to reduce conflict between shareholders and executives (Lin *et al.*, 2008). Thus, executive compensation and benefits may be changed to reward positive outcomes post-downsizing or to adjust for prior poor performance.

Downsizing that results from mergers and acquisitions impacts compensations packages and often reflects both firms' statuses. Montmarquette, Rulliere, Villeval, and Zeiliger (2004) conducted an experiment to identify executive compensation schemes and performance after a merger. They examined two pharmaceutical companies – one French and one German – that recently consolidated and underwent post-merger downsizing. They concluded that the use of differing compensation packages among executives reduces team cooperation. Financial incentives improved output (Prendergast, 1999), however; financial incentives were not effective with heterogeneous groups (Montmarquette *et al.*, 2004). Thus, it is likely in firms with mixed cultures that other factors, such as norms and social behaviors, impact team cooperation and output.

Singh and Agarwal (2002) compared the impact of union and non-union metal-mining firms on executive compensation levels and structure in Canada. They proposed that unions can produce two divergent outcomes during downsizing by negotiating executive pay concessions. The first outcome produces a dampening effect by reducing executive compensation due to pressure from collective bargaining and media exposure. The second outcome produces a ratcheting effect by increasing executive compensation and by increasing wages at lower levels within the firm. They found a significant positive relationship between union presence and executive higher salaries, bonuses, short-term compensation, cashed/exercised stock options, other long-term incentives, and total compensation when conducting bivariate analyses (one way ANOVA and zero order correlations). These findings were not found when conducting hierarchical regression analyses. Thus, after downsizing occurs, executive compensation is likely to increase in firms with union representation compared to organizations without union representation.

Andre, Magnan, and St-Onge (2008) found that following a merger and acquisition in Canada between Abitibi-Consolidated and Donohue, the CEO's compensation increased despite underperformance. Therefore, an executive who survives downsizing may experience an increase in salary, bonuses, stock options, and enhanced value to a retirement plan (Andre *et al.*, 2008). This disparity in treatment of executives and non-executives has shown negative effects. Flint (2003) examined the impact of downsizing in hospitals in Canada. The hospitals reduced non-management positions only and did not cut executive pay. Not surprisingly, lower level employees at these hospitals expressed resentment.

Fisher, Lee, and Johns (2004) examined company turnaround following retrenchment, replacement of the chairman or chief executive, and ownership change in Australia and Singapore. Retrenchment was defined as asset divestment and cost reduction, often by downsizing (Fisher *et al.*, 2004). These countries were selected because they have similar governance transparency yet different cultures. They concluded that there was no significant difference in the speed of change of the CEO or Chairman in either country and no indication that Australian companies were likely to change the CEO or Chairman faster than Singaporean companies. Likewise, there was no support that Australian companies would undertake retrenchment faster than Singaporean companies. Support was found for change in ownership for Australian companies compared to Singaporean companies. Thus, Australian companies were more likely to change ownership than Singaporean companies. Furthermore, there was no difference in organizations that engaged in any of the four actions and their turnaround performance (Fisher *et al.*, 2004).

Singh and Agarwal (2002) posit that executives are likely to be impacted differently from the effects of downsizing compared to lower-level employees. Certainly, in some instances executives seem to fare better with compensation and benefits post-downsizing. Still, research indicates that it is not guaranteed (Feldman, Leana, and Bolino, 2002). Executives, like employees at lower levels, may find themselves either unemployed, or underemployed, making less money than before. Yet, an advantage executives have over other employees is they often negotiate their severance packages before entering an organization (Jones, 2006).

## *Non-executives*

A review of the downsizing literature suggests little research has been conducted regarding non-executive employees post-downsizing. Zimermanova (2010) examined how the 2009 economic crisis affected pay in small- and medium-sized organizations in the Slovak Republic and in the European Union. In the Slovak Republic, the government establishes a minimum wage by industry. Members of the European Union, on the other hand, legally enforce nationwide minimum wages to a majority of full-time employees in each country (Zimermanova, 2010).

During the economic crisis in 2009, in the Slovak Republic and in the European Union, 66.83 percent of small business owners paid at the level of minimum wage (Zimermanova, 2010). One third of small business owners also reported that they pay part of the wages as "black money" in order to reduce the amount of money they would have to pay for individual insurance funds. While the study did not indicate how many firms participated in downsizing specifically, organizations reduced the workforce as the primary strategy to save costs. Three quarters of the businesses in the study indicated that the economy forced them to reduce employees' wages. Some of the organizations reduced wages at the same time they reduced the workforce. Additionally, bonuses were cut by many organizations (Zimermanova, 2010).

Employees that survive the first round of downsizing are not guaranteed that they will not fall victim to a second round of cuts. Unlike for executives, who are likely to have severance packages no matter where they are located, entitlements for lower-level employees vary by country. According to the OECD (1999), many countries, such as Australia, Belgium, and Finland, do not require firms to pay severance. Denmark provides severance for white-collar but not for blue-collar workers. The United States, Germany, and Sweden, for instance, do not offer legal entitlement to severance unless it is included in a collective agreement. If workers are dismissed due to redundancy in Australia and in the Czech Republic, they are entitled to severance. The amount of severance varies drastically between countries. Austria, for instance, by far offers the most in the amount of severance by providing 12 months of pay for employees that work for the organization for at least 25 years. Most countries pay a percentage of pay based on the amount of time worked. Thus, non-executive employees are not likely to fare as well as executives. These lower-level employees will most likely experience a reduction in pay and benefits if they survive downsizing and little severance if they do not (Gandolfi, 2006a).

## Concluding thoughts

In this chapter, we have demonstrated that there are patterns in downsizing practices irrespective of country of origin. Internationally oriented firms adopt similar strategies and practices in order to handle external threats or internal inefficiencies and experience similar outcomes. In the scholarly literature, there has been a strong focus on the strategies and practices employed in North America and Europe. It is evident that popular management practices have a tendency to spread and be adopted as management fashions or managerial fads thereby becoming isomorphic institutionalized in various parts of the world. As a consequence, modern-day firms have adopted similar or identical strategies and practices in order to handle, for example, downturns, external threats, increased competition, or internal inefficiencies.

There is substantial empirical evidence, from multiple countries, suggesting that executives have adopted downsizing activities as a strategy driven by a deep-seated belief that these strategies will improve organizational efficiency, effectiveness, and overall financial performance. Still, as scholars, we have stressed that downsizing has the propensity to generate negative performance outcomes and harmful psychological effects for downsizing executioners, victims, and survivors.

This chapter has highlighted that, in privately held firms and in multiple countries, downsizing is frequently used to reduce costs, remain globally competitive, maximize shareholder value and returns, improve organizational efficiencies, or in response to changed patterns of organizational profitability. There is evidence suggesting that poor management may lead to an over-hiring of employees during profitable years. This seems to be in contrast to the public sector where downsizing has occurred in organizational entities affected by new governmental mandates, budget and regulatory changes, as well as changes in the political structures on both the local and federal levels.

Research from across the globe depicts a mixed picture regarding the success of downsizing on the financial performance of a firm. A noteworthy observation made in the 1990s was that workforce reduction announcements engendered positive stock market responses when downsizing was first announced and when downsizing activities were perceived to be a reactive strategy to poor financial conditions. This pattern was discontinued in the first decade of this millennium, with firms reaping little or no stock price appreciation following downsizing news. Overall, and on a global scale, there is scant empirical research demonstrating positive support for profitability, profit margins, and EBDIT margins being improved from the use of downsizing.

Finally, as demonstrated throughout the chapter, the adoption of downsizing has not yielded the highly anticipated organizational and financial rewards. So why is this likely to have occurred? Cameron (1994), a downsizing authority, concluded that managers often experience a crisis mentality following the implementation of downsizing and fail to make effective long-term plans for the organization and its constituencies. Furthermore, executives have neglected to adequately prepare for the aftermath of downsizing and have failed to understand how downsizing survivors will be affected by workforce reduction activities. The chapter has shown that firms have mitigated some of the negative effects by providing training for survivors and introducing human resource policies and plans to mediate the after effects of downsizing.

## References

Abrahamson, E. 1996. "Management fashion." *Academy of Management Review* **21**(1): 254–285.

Ahmadjian, C. and Robbins, G. 2005. "A clash of capitalisms: Foreign shareholders and corporate restructuring in 1990s Japan." *American Sociological Review* **70**(3): 451.

Allen, R.K. 1997. "Lean and mean: Workforce 2000 in America." *Journal of Workplace Learning* **9**(1). http://www.emerald-library.com/brev/08609ae1.html.

Andre, P., Magnan, M., and St.-Onge, S. 2008. "Analysis of a merger from a governance perspective: The case of Abitibi-Consolidated and Donohue." *Canadian Journal of Administrative Sciences* **25**(2): 153–169.

Aoki, M. 2001. *Toward a Comparative Institutional Analysis*. Cambridge, MA: MIT Press.

Appelbaum, S.H., Delage, C., Labibb, N., and Gault, G. 1997. "The survivor syndrome: Aftermath of downsizing." *Career Development International* **2**(6): 278–286.

Appelbaum, S.H., Everard, A., and Hung, L. 1999. "Strategic downsizing: Critical success factors." *Management Decision* **37**(7): 535–559.

Ballester, M., Livnat, J., and Sinha, N. 1999. "Corporate reorganizations: Changes in the intensity of labor and capital expenditures." *Journal of Business Finance and Accounting* **26**(9/10): 1205–1238.

Barley, S. R. and Tolbert, P. 1997. "Institutionalization and structuration: Studying the links between action and institution." *Organization Studies* **18**(1): 93–117.

Bebchuk, L. and Fried, J. 2004. *The Unfilled Promise of Executive Renumeration*. Cambridge, MA: Harvard University Press.

Beylerian, M. and Kleiner, B. H. 2003. "The downsized workplace." *Management Research News* **26**: 97–108.

Brockner, J. 1988. "The effects of layoffs on survivors: Research theory and practice." *Research in Organizational Behavior* **10**: 213–255.

Brockner, J. 1992. "Managing the effects of lay-offs on survivors." *California Management Review* **34**(2): 9–28.

Brockner, J., Greenberg, J., and Grover, S. 1988. "The impact of layoffs on survivors: Insights from interpersonal and organizational justice theory," in J. Carrol (ed.), *Advances in Applied Social Psychology: Business Settings*. Hillsdale, NJ: Erlbaum, pp. 45–75.

Brockner, J., Greenberg, J., Brockner, A., Bortz, J., Davy, J., and Carter, C. 1986. "Layoffs, equity theory and work motivation: Further evidence for the impact of survivor guilt." *Academy of Management Journal* **29**: 373–384.

Bruton, G. D., Keels, J. K., and Shook, C. L. 1996. "Downsizing the firm: Answering the strategic questions." *Academy of Management Executive* **10**(2): 38–45.

Buck, T., Liu, X., and Skovoroda, R. 2008. "Top executive pay and firm performance in China." *Journal of International Business Studies* **39**(5): 833–850.

Burke, R. J. and Cooper, C. L. 2000. *The Organization in Crisis*. Oxford: Blackwell Publishers.

Burke, R. J., and Greenglass, E. R. 2000. "Organizational restructuring: Identifying effective hospital downsizing processes," in R. J. Burke and C. L. Cooper (eds.), *The Organization in Crisis*. Malden, MA: Blackwell Publishers, pp. 284–303.

Cameron, K. S. 1994. "Strategies for successful organizational downsizing." *Human Resource Management* **33**(2): 189–211.

Cameron, K., Freeman, S., and Mishra, A. 1991. "Best practices in white collar downsizing: Managing contradictions." *Academy of Management Executive* **5**(3): 57–73.

Cameron, K. S., Freeman, S. J., and Mishra, A. K. 1993. "Downsizing and redesigning organizations," in G. Huber and W. Glick (eds.), *Organizational Change and Redesign*. New York: Oxford University Press, pp. 19–63.

Cameron, K, S., Sutton, R, I., and Whetten, D. A. (eds.). 1988. *Readings in Organizational Decline: Frameworks, Research and Prescriptions.* Cambridge, MA. Ballinger.

Campos de Cunha, R. 2000. "Impact of privatization in Portugal," in R. J. Burke and C. L. Cooper (eds.), *The Organization in Crisis.* Malden, MA: Blackwell Publishers, pp. 44–57.

Carswell, P. 2005. "The financial impact of organisational downsizing practices – the New Zealand experience." *Asia Pacific Journal of Management* **22**(1): 41.

Cascio, W. F. 1991. *Costing Human Resources.* Boston: PWS-Kent Publishing.

Cascio, W. F. 1993. "Downsizing: What do we know? What have we learned?" *Academy of Management Executive* 7(1): 95–104.

Cascio, W. F. 1998. "Learning from outcomes: Financial experiences of 311 firms that have downsized," in M. K. Growing, J. D. Kraft and J. C. Quick (eds.), *The New Organizational Reality: Downsizing, Restructuring Revitalization.* Washington, DC: American Psychological Association, pp. 55–70.

Cascio, W. F. 2003. "Responsible restructuring: Seeing employees as assets, not costs." *Ivey Business Journal Online*, November 2003.

Cascio, W., Young, C., and Morris, J. 1997. "Financial consequences of employment-change decisions in major US corporations." *Academy of Management Journal* **40**(5): 1175–1189.

Chalos, P. and Chen, C. 2002. "Employee downsizing strategies: Market reaction and post announcement financial performance." *Journal of Business Finance and Accounting* **29**(5/6): 847–870.

Chong, A. and Lopez-de-Silanes, F. 2002. "Privatization and labor force restructuring around the world." Policy Research Working Paper Series 2884, The World Bank.

Cutcher-Gershenfeld, J. 1991. "The impact on economic performance of a transformation in workplace relations." *Industrial and Labor Relations Review* **44**(2): 241–260.

Datta, D. K., Guthrie, J. P., Basuil, D., and Pandey, A. 2010. "Causes and effects of employee downsizing: A review and synthesis." *Journal of Management* **36**(1): 281–348.

Dawkins, P., Littler, C. R., Valenzuela, M. R., and Jensen, B. 1999. "The contours of restructuring and downsizing in Australia." Melbourne Institute of Applied Economic and Social Research, Melbourne University.

Delorese, A. 1998. *Healing the Downsized Organisation.* New York: Three Rivers Press.

De Meuse, K. P., Bergmann, T. J., Vanderheiden, P. A., and Roraff, C. E. 2004. "New evidence regarding organizational downsizing and a firm's financial performance: A long-term analysis." *Journal of Managerial Issues* **16**(2): 155–177.

De Meuse, K. P., Vanderheiden, P. A., and Bergmann, T. J. 1994. "Announced layoffs: Their effect on corporate financial performance." *Human Resource Management* **33**(4): 509–530.

De Witt, R. L. 1998. "Firm, industry, and strategic influences on choice of downsizing approach." *Strategic Management Journal* **19**: 59–79.

Dolan, S., Belout, A., and Balkin, D. B. 2000. "Downsizing without downgrading: Learning how firms manage their survivors." *International Journal of Manpower* **21**(1): 34–46.

Dorata, N. 2008. "The shielding of CEO cash compensation from post-acquisition earnings' charges." *Managerial Finance* **34**(5): 288–303.

Downs, A. 1995. *Corporate Executions*. New York: Amacom.

Elayan, F. A., Swales, G. S., Maris, B. A., and Scott, J. R. 1998. "Market reactions, characteristics, and the effectiveness of corporate layoffs." *Journal of Business Finance and Accounting* **25**(3/4): 329–351.

Escalante, M. F., Jr. 2001. "Government reform and diversity: The value of incentive buyout programs as downsizing strategies at the Port Hueneme Division of the Naval Surface Warfare Center." D.P.A. dissertation, University of La Verne, California, United States.

Espahbodi, R., John, T. A., and Vasudevan, G. 2000. "The effects of downsizing on operating performance." *Review of Quantitative Finance and Accounting* **15**: 107–126.

Estok, D. 1996. "The high cost of 'dumbsizing'." *Macleans's* **109**(23): 28–29.

Feldman, D., Leana, C., and Bolino, M. 2002. "Underemployment and relative deprivation among re-employed executives." *Journal of Occupational and Organizational Psychology* **75**: 453–471.

Filatotchev, I., Buck, T., and Zhukov, V. 2000. "Downsizing in privatized firms in Russia, Ukraine, and Belarus." *Academy of Management Journal* **43**: 286–304.

Fisher, G., Lee, J., and Johns, L. 2004. "An exploratory study of company turnaround in Australia and Singapore following the Asia crisis." *Asia Pacific Journal of Management* **21**: 149–170.

Fisher, S. R. and White, M. A. 2000. "Downsizing in a learning organization: Are there hidden costs?" *Academy of Management Review* **25**(1): 244–251.

Flint, D. 2003. "Downsizing the public sector: Metro-Toronto's hospitals." *Journal of Health Organization and Management* **17**(6): 438–456.

Forrier, A. and Sels, L. 2003. "Flexibility, turnover and training." *International Journal of Manpower* **24**(2): 148.

Freeman, S. J. 1994. "Organizational downsizing as convergence or reorientation: Implications for human resource management." *Human Resource Management* **33**(2): 213–238.

Freeman, S.J. and Cameron, K.S. 1993. "Organizational downsizing: A convergence and reorientation framework." *Organizational Science* **4**(1): 10–29.

Gandolfi, F. 2005. "Australian and New Zealand banks and the implementation of downsizing." *Sasin Journal of Management* **11**(1): 25–35.

Gandolfi, F. 2006a. *Corporate Downsizing Demystified: A Scholarly Analysis of a Business Phenomenon.* Hyderabad, India: The ICFAI University Press.

Gandolfi, F. 2006b. "The downsizing process: Conceptual frameworks." *The Business Review* **6**(2): 1–7.

Gandolfi, F. 2007. "How do large Australian and Swiss banks implement downsizing?" *Journal of Management and Organization* **13**(2): 145–159.

Gandolfi, F. 2008. "Cost-reductions, downsizing-related layoffs, and HR practices." *SAM Advanced Management Journal* **73**(3): 52–58.

Gandolfi, F. 2009. "Where did downsizing go? A review of 30 years of a strategic business phenomenon." *The Australasian Journal of Business and Social Inquiry* 7(1): 40–65.

Gandolfi, F. 2010. "Organizational downsizing: A review of two decades of a strategic phenomenon." *Sasin Journal of Management* **16**(1): 85–108.

Gandolfi, F. and Hansson, M. 2010. "Reduction-in-force (RIF): New developments and a brief historical analysis of a business strategy." *Journal of Management and Organization* **16**(5): 727–743.

Gandolfi, F. and Hansson, M. 2011. "Causes and consequences of downsizing: Towards an integrative framework." *Journal of Management and Organization* **17**(4): 517–540

Gandolfi, F. and Neck, P. 2008. "Consequences, payoffs, and fallout of downsizing (a literature review of corporate downsizing: Part 3)." *Review of International Comparative Management* **9**(1): 55–78.

Gandolfi, F. and Oster, G. 2009. "Sustaining innovation during corporate downsizing." *SAM Advanced Management Journal* **74**(2): 42–53.

Gettler, L. 1998. "Survey: Downsizing doesn't cut costs." *Sydney Morning Herald* June 16: 27.

Ghemawat, P. 1991. *Commitment: The Dynamic of Strategy.* New York: Free Press.

Griggs, H.E. and Hyland, P. 2003. "Strategic downsizing and learning organizations." *Journal of European Industrial Training* **24**(2–4): 177–187.

Guiniven, J. 2001. "The lessons of survivor literature in communication decisions to downsize." *Journal of Business and Technical Communication* **15**(1): 53–71.

Guthrie, J.P. and Datta, D.K. 2008. "Dumb and dumber: The impact of downsizing on firm performance as moderated by industry conditions." *Organization Science* **19**(1): 108–123.

Gutknecht, J. and Keys, J. 1993. "Mergers, acquisitions and takeovers: Maintaining morale of survivors and protecting employees." *The Academy of Management Perspectives* 7(3): 26.

Hamel, G. and Prahalad, C. K. 1994. *Competing for the Future*. Boston, MA: Harvard Business School Press.

Hannan, M. T. and Freeman, J. H. 1988. "The ecology of organizational mortality: American labor unions 1863–1985." *American Journal of Sociology* **94**: 25–52.

Hannan, M. T. and Freeman, J. H 1989. *Organizational Ecology*. Cambridge, MA: Harvard University Press.

Hansson, M. 2008. "On closedowns: Towards a pattern of explanation to the closedown effect." Unpublished doctoral Dissertation, Örebro Studies in Business, Örebro University, Örebro, Sweden.

Harrigan, K. R. 1982. "Exit decisions in mature industries." *Academy of Management Journal* **25**: 707–732.

Havlovic, S. J., Bouthillette, F., and Van der Wal, R. 1998. "Coping with downsizing and job loss." *Canadian Journal of Administrative Sciences* **15**: 322–332.

Hedberg, B. L. T., Greve, H., and Starbuck, W. 1978. "Camping on the seesaws: Prescriptions of a self-designing organization." *Administrative Science Quarterly* **21**(1): 41–65.

Hillier, D., Marshall, A., McColgan, P., and Werema, S. 2007. "Employee layoffs, shareholder wealth and firm performance: Evidence from the UK." *Journal of Business Finance and Accounting* **34**(3/4): 467–494.

Iqbal, Z. and Shetty, S. 1995. "Layoffs, stock price, and financial condition of the firm." *Journal of Applied Business Research* **11**(2): 67–72.

Jackson, P., Mellahi, K., and Sparks, L. 2005. "Shutting up shop: Understanding the international exit process in retailing." *Service Industries Journal* **25**: 252–273.

Jones, L. P., Jammal, Y., and Gokgur, N. 1998. "Impact of privatization in Côte d'Ivoire." Draft Final Report, Boston Institute for Developing Economies, Boston, MA.

Jones, R. 2006. "Don't be caught unaware – severance and change-in-control policies need to be reviewed now more than ever." *Benefits Quarterly* **22**(3): 48–52.

Kang, J. K. and Shivdasani, A. 1997. "Corporate restructuring during performance declines in Japan." *Journal of Financial Economics* **46**(1): 29–65.

Kase, R. and Zupan, N. 2005. "Strategic human resource management in European transition economies: Building a conceptual model on the case of Slovenia." *International Journal of Human Resource Management* **16**(6): 882.

Kelly, P. 1996. "Downsizing and other related workforce trends: An employee benefits perspective." *Benefits Quarterly* **12**(3): 8–42.

Kets de Vries, M. and Balazs, K. 1997. "The downsizing of downsizing." *Human Relations* **50**: 11–50.

Kettley, P. 1995. "Employee morale during downsizing." Institute of Employment Studies, Report 291.

Kinnie, N., Hutchinson, S., and Purcell, J. 1998. "Downsizing: Is it always lean and mean?" *Personnel Review* **27**(4): 296–311.

Konovsky, M. A. and Brockner, J. 1993. "Managing victim and survivor layoff reactions: A procedural justice perspective," in R. Cropanzano (ed.), *Justice in the Workplace: Approaching Fairness in Human Resource Management*. Hillsdale, NJ: Lawrence Erlbaum, pp. 133–153.

Kornecki, L. 2010. "Foreign direct investment and macroeconomic changes in CEE integrating in to the global market." *Journal* of *International Business and Cultural Studies* **3**: 1–12.

Krishnan, H. A. and Park, D. 1998. "Effects of top management team change on performance in downsized US companies." *Management International Review* **38**(4): 303–319.

La Porta, R. and López-de-Silanes, F. 1997. "The benefits of privatization: Evidence from Mexico." NBER Working Paper 6215, National Bureau of Economic Research, Cambridge, MA.

Lamsa, A. M. and Takala, T. 2000. "Downsizing and ethics of personnel dismissals: The case of Finnish managers." *Journal of Business Ethics* **23**: 389–399.

Lee, C. 1992. "After the cuts." *Training*, July: 17–23

Lee, P. M. 1997. "A comparative analysis of layoff announcements and stock price reactions in the United States and Japan." *Strategic Management Journal* **18**(11): 879–896.

Levitt, K., Wilson, T., and Gilligan, E. 2008. "Corporate downsizing: An examination of the survivors." *Journal of Global Business Issues* **2**(2): 13–21.

Lin, B., Zu-Hsu, L., and Gibbs, L. 2008. "Operational restructuring: Reviving an ailing business." *Management Decision* **46**(4): 539–552.

Littler, C. R. 1998. "Downsizing organisations: The dilemmas of change." *Human Resources Management Bulletin*. Sydney: CCH Australia Limited.

Littler, C. R. 2000. "Comparing the downsizing experiences of three countries: A restructuring cycle?" in R. J. Burke and C. L. Cooper (eds.), *The Organization in Crisis*. Malden, MA: Blackwell Publishers, pp. 58–77.

Littler, C. R., Dunford, R., Bramble, T., and Hede, A. 1997. "The dynamics of downsizing in Australia and New Zealand." *Asia Pacific Journal of Human Resources* **35**(1): 65–79.

Littler, C. R. and Gandolfi, F. 2008. "What happened to downsizing? Organizational continuity, managerial fashion, and signaling." Academy of Management Conference, Paper presentation, Anaheim.

Littler, C. R. and Hansson, M. 2007. "Closure and downsizing: Integrating overlapping literatures." The Academy of Management annual conference, Philadelphia.

Love, E. F. and Nohria, N. 2005. "Reducing slack: The performance consequences of downsizing by large industrial firms, 1977–1993." *Strategic Management Journal* **26**(12): 1087–1108.

Luthans, B. C. and Sommer, S. M. 1999. "The impact of downsizing on workplace attitudes." *Group and Organization Management* **24**(1): 46–70.

Macky, K. 2004. "Organisational downsizing and redundancies: The New Zealand worker's experience." *Journal of Employment Relations* **29**(1): 63–87.

Malatesta, P. H. and Thompson, R. 1985. "Partially anticipated events: A model of stock price reactions with an application to corporate acquisitions." *Journal of Financial Economics* **14**(2): 237.

Megginson, W. L., Nash R., and van Randenborgh, M. 1994. "The financial and operating performance of newly privatized firms: An international empirical analysis." *Journal of Finance* **49**(2): 403.

Megginson, W. and Netter, J. 2001. "From state to market: A survey of empirical studies on privatization." *Journal of Economic Literature* **39**(2): 321.

Mellahi, K. and Wilkinson, A. 2004. "Organizational failure: A critique of recent research and a proposed integrative framework." *International Journal of Management Review* **5**(1): 21–41.

Mentzer, M. S. 1996. "Corporate downsizing and profitability in Canada." *Revue Canadienne des Sciences de l'Administration* **13**(3): 237–250.

Mihajlovic, I. and Zivkovic, Z. 2008. "Factors influencing job satisfaction in transitional economies." *Journal of General Management* **34**(2): 71–87.

Montgomery, C. A. and Thomas, A. R. 1988. "Divestments: Motives and gains." *Strategic Management Journal* **9**(1): 93–97.

Montmarquette, C., Rulliere, J., Villeval, M., and Zeiliger. 2004. "Redesigning teams and incentives in a merger: An experiment with managers and students." *Management Science* **50**(10): 1379–1389.

Morris, J., Cascio, W., and Young, C. 1999. "Downsizing after all these years: Questions and answers about who did it, how many did it and who benefited from it." *Organizational Dynamics* **27**(3): 78–87.

Mroczkowski, T. and Hanaoka, M. 1997. "Effective rightsizing strategies in Japan and America: Is there a convergence of employment practices?" *The Academy of Management Executive* **11**(2): 57–67.

Munoz-Bullon, F. and Sanchez-Bueno, M. 2008. "Downsizing implementation and financial performance." *Business Economic Series 06*, Working Paper 08–29.

Nadeem, M. 2010. "Role of training in determining the employee corporate behavior with respect to organizational productivity: Developing and proposing a conceptual model." *International Journal of Business Management* 5(12): 206–211.

OECD. 1999. *Employment Check*. Paris: OECD.

Powell, W.W. and DiMaggio, P.J. 1983. "The iron cage revisited: Institutional isomorphism and collective rationality in organizational fields." *American Sociological Review* **48**(2): 147–160.

Prendergast, C. 1999. "The provision of incentives in firms." *Journal of Economic Literature* **37**(1): 7–63.

Ramamurti, R. 1997. "Testing the limits of privatization: Argentine railroads." *World Development* **25**(12): 1271–1993.

Redman, T. and Keithley, D. 1998. "Downsizing goes east? Employment restructuring in post-socialist Poland." *The International Journal of Human Resource Management* **9**(2): 274–295.

Richtnér, A. and Ahlström, P. 2006. "Organizational downsizing and innovation." *SSE/EFI Working Paper Series in Business Administration*, January 1. Retrieved from http://swoba.hhs.se/hastba/papers/hastba2006_001.pdf

Ryan, L. and Macky, K.A. 1998. "Downsizing organizations: Uses, outcomes and strategies." *Asia Pacific Journal of Human Resources* **36**(2): 29–45.

Sahdev, K. 2003. "Survivors' reactions to downsizing: The importance of contextual factors." *Human Resource Management Journal* **13**(4): 56–74.

Singh, P. and Agarwal, N. 2002. "Union presence and executive compensation: An exploratory study." *Journal of Labor Research* **23**(4): 631–647.

Smeltzer, L.R. and Zener, M.F. 1994. "Minimizing the negative effect of employee layoffs through effective announcements." *Employee Counseling Today* **6**(4): 3–9.

Starbuck, W.H., Greve, A., and Hedberg, B.L.T. 1978. "Responding to crisis." *Journal of Business Administration* **9**: 111–137.

Thornhill, A. and Saunders, M.N.K. 1998. "The meanings, consequences and implications of the management of downsizing and redundancy: A review." *MCB Personnel Review*, **27**(4). (http://www.emerald-library.com/brev/01427da1.html)

Tosi, H., Werner, S., Katz, J., and Gomez-Mejia, L. 2000. "How much does performance matter? A meta analysis of CEO pay studies." *Journal of Management* **26**(2): 301–339.

Vanderheiden, P., De Meuse, K., and Bergmann, T. 1999. "Response to Haar's comment – and the beat goes on: Corporate downsizing in the 21st century." *Human Resource Management* **38**(3): 261–267.

Vincente-Lorente, J. D and Suárez-González, I. 2007. "Ownership traits and downsizing behaviour: Evidence for the largest Spanish firms, 1990–1998." *Organizational Studies* **28**(11): 1613–1638.

Wayhan, V. B. and Werner, S. 2000. "The impact of workface reductions on financial performance: A longitudinal perspective." *Journal of Management* **26**: 341–363.

Wertheim, P. and Robinson, M. 2004. "Markets reactions to company layoffs: Evidence on the financial fistress versus potential benefit hypothesis and the effect of predisclosure information." *Journal of Applied Business Research* **20**(1): 51–62.

Worrell, D. L., Davidson III, W. N., and Sharma, V. M. 1991. "Layoff announcements and stockholder wealth." *Academy Management Journal* **43**: 662–678.

Wu, Z. and Delios, A. 2009. "The emergence of portfolio restructuring in Japan." *Management International Review* **49**(3): 313–335.

Yu, G. C. and Park, J. S. 2004. "The effect of downsizing on the employee productivity and financial performance of Korean firms after 1997 economic crisis: An analysis of longitudinal data of listed firms." IIRA, 5th Asian Regional Congress, Seoul.

Yu, G. C. and Park, J. S. 2006. "The effect of downsizing on the financial performance and employee productivity of Korean firms." *International Journal of Manpower* **27**(3): 230–250.

Zhong-Ming, W. 1999. "Current models and innovative strategies in management education in China." *Education and Training* **41**(6/7): 312–318.

Zimermanova, K. 2010. "Selected actual aspects of employees' remuneration in small and medium-sized companies." *E and M Ekonomie a Management* **3**: 33–44.

Zyglidopoulos, S. C. 2003. "The impact of downsizing on the corporate reputation for social performance." *Journal of Public Affairs* **4**(1): 11–25.

# 13 *Exploring the etiology of positive stakeholder behavior in global downsizing*

SHAY S. TZAFRIR, HILA CHALUTZ BEN-GAL, AND SIMON L. DOLAN

*Studies have tracked the performance of downsizing firms versus nondownsizing firms for as long as nine years after a downsizing event. The findings: as a group, the downsizers never outperformed the non-downsizers.*

(Cascio, 1993)

## Introduction

Downsizing is commonplace in present-day industrialized markets. Between 1995 and 2007, approximately 11.5 million people lost their jobs to downsizing in the United States alone (Lewine, Biemans, and Ulaga, 2010). Furthermore, according to data from the US Bureau of Labor Statistics (2005), sales and marketing personnel have been hit harder than many other groups of employees. Not only are reductions in workforce size becoming more frequent, organizations are changing their rationale for downsizing as well. In the past, layoffs were the last resort for employers. More recently, however, healthy firms around the world have been using downsizing as a preemptive way to cut costs.

Downsizing has become an international phenomenon, and it is not limited to North America or Europe. In the United States, more than 6.5 million jobs have been lost from downsizing since the recession began in December 2007, with numbers expected to grow in the foreseeable future (Datta, Guthrie, Basuil, and Pandey, 2010). Other countries have engaged in their share of downsizing activities, including countries whose tradition does not include such events. For example, recent times have witnessed significant employee reductions in economies such as Japan, Hong Kong, South Korea, and Taiwan. Even China has been affected, with major layoffs in a number of sectors; between 1993 and 2001 about 43 million urban employees were laid off, with most dismissals happening in the service sector and such industries as mining, weaving, and military production. European countries have suffered as well. For example, in Ireland, the unemployment rate jumped from 5.6 percent to 10.6 percent between 2008 and 2009, while in Spain the figure went from 9.5 percent to 17.4 percent over the same period (Datta *et al.*, 2010, p. 282).

Although downsizing can involve reductions in various combinations of physical, capital, and human resources, much research has focused on downsizing in employment, entailing personnel reductions in the organizational context (Cascio, 1993; Iverson and Zatzick, 2011). There is a wide variety of definitions of the term "downsizing" (Cameron, 1994; Cameron, Freeman, and Mishra, 1993; Cascio, 1993; DeWitt, 1998; Freeman and Cameron, 1998). For example, "an organization's conscious use of permanent personnel reductions in an attempt to improve its efficiency and/or effectiveness" (Cascio, 1993; Lanciano and Nitta, 2010). Others have defined employee downsizing as "a planned set of organizational policies aimed at workforce reduction with the goal of improving firm performance" (Datta *et al.*, 2010, p. 282). Over the years, this changed management strategy has generated a great deal of interest. As a result, companies suffering from low performance over a long period of time and ongoing financial problems often choose to implement a downsizing strategy (Hareli and Tzafrir, 2006).

The historical roots of downsizing lie in the capitalist world and globalization trends. The second half of the last century was characterized by transition and transformation (Raich and Dolan, 2008; Fasenfest, 2010). Modern capitalism and the Fordist accord between labour and capital changed into postmodern capitalism and "post-Fordism" (Fasenfest, 2010, p. 629) in the context of economic growth. The economic growth experienced by the world economy in the past two decades can be attributed to trade liberalization or globalization (Anwar, 2009), and increased competition. Accelerated international trade between nations enabled corporate reach and resulted in multinational companies, some more successful than others. With globalization[1] came tough competition, creating the expectation that workers everywhere would have to rethink wage demands and renegotiate working conditions. Some of the consequences of globalization include the increasing alienation of workers as a result of downsizing and job losses (Fasenfest, 2010).

Globalization and the opportunity to increase markets for services and products, as well as to reduce taxes and other incentives, led many organizations to become multinational corporations (MNCs) in the manner of an "octopus" (Koerber and Fort, 2008). According to UNCTAD's

2009 *World Investment Report*, an estimated 82,000 transnational firms now span the globe (UNCTAD, 2009, ch. 1). Thus, the power of these firms on economies at the global and national levels is unprecedented. With so much economic power, the managerial behavior and activities of MNCs can have both harmful and beneficial effects within and between countries. In the face of global economic competition, rapid changes in markets, and a consistent desire for effectiveness and efficiency, downsizing in MNCs has become a mode of adjustment widely used by corporate management (Lanciano and Nitta, 2010; Van Buren and Greenwood, 2011).

This chapter offers an integrated view between a universal model of downsizing and a country-specific perspective. It is organized in the following manner. We start by providing a review of the global perspective on downsizing, as well as of the main causes and origins; in the following sections we propose a multilevel (Klein and Kozlowski, 2000), multifactor approach as a framework for analyzing the consequences of downsizing in cross-cultural terms; and finally, we point out some practical implications. In order to provide a wider perspective on the topic of downsizing among MNCs, we conducted semi-structured interviews with professionals who had participated and/or led downsizing initiatives in their professional careers in multinational corporations.[2] We believe that analyzing these interviews and presenting their outcomes may shed new light on the topic and its practical implications in both the short and the longer term.

## Downsizing: A global perspective

A globalized managerial strategy of downsizing has different consequences on employees in various countries, ranging from the western (Makela and Nasi, 2010) to the eastern hemisphere (Sturgeon and Van Biesebroeck, 2010). Industries such as information technology are relocated according to efficiency, effectiveness, and cost–benefit analysis. The positive side focuses on new jobs, relatively higher wages, and other income-earning opportunities for the local economy, which can be used to enhance prosperity. Nevertheless, the results are not always positive. As Kochan (2005) mentions, one of the roles of government is to ensure that opportunities to learn and gain access to good jobs are open to men and women of all races, family backgrounds, and cultures. And perhaps most of all, we need to renew our sense of solidarity by working together for the common good so that the gains and hardships of the economic booms and busts to come are shared in an equitable fashion. This may not turn out to be the case.[3] Negative sides of downsizing are losses of jobs in the country of origin, as well as a deterioration in employment conditions.

Datta *et al.* (2010) attempted to depict the causes and origins of the downsizing phenomenon by focusing on environmental and organizational factors. Studies generally support the idea that employee downsizing is likely to be more prevalent when there is a downturn and change in market demand (Wagar, 1997; Filatotchev, Buck, and Zuhkov, 2000). However, not all scholars share the same view. For example, Budros (1997, 2000, 2002) did not find any significant relationship between economic conditions and employee downsizing. On the contrary, he found that firms in the utility and industrial sectors often engaged in employee downsizing during economic peaks. Others report that industry deregulation and privatization often trigger employee downsizing. This is specifically true in the case of manufacturing firms. An interesting finding of a different strand of research indicates that firms are likely to be involved in employee reduction when the firms they relate to go through massive downsizing (Tsai, Wu, Wang, and Huang, 2006; Datta *et al.*, 2010).

Looking at firms with globalization opportunities, Coucke, Pennings, and Sleuwaegen (2007), who studied layoff trends in the Belgian market, found that manufacturing firms were more likely to downsize than those in the service sector. Different wage levels and employment conditions help to explain why some industries are more prone than others to downsize on one side of the globe and build up operations on the other side. For example, in many countries, manufacturing was found to be prone in this way, compared to non-manufacturing firms (Budros, 2004).

Two important factors in global–local interaction are government (Haiyong and Weiwei, 2010) and national culture (Hofstede, 2001). The global movement towards MNCs bringing foreign investment into a local country accentuated the role of government in this process, on the one hand, and the role of national culture, on the other hand. Government plays a role in the local economy and serves as an actor in the industrial relations system, as well as being a major influence in the legal system. For example, government may decide on levels of taxes, subsidies, and modes of collective bargaining, and act as a major employer, etc. The result is administrative, economic, and legal power in the economy and the employment market. The ascendancy of government in relation to these systems, however, is confronted by a growing tendency to consider

MNCs as a new form of government (Willke and Willke, 2008). Therefore, there is a need to reconfigure the "balance between institutions that together make up both national and global governance constellations" (Jamali and Mirshak, 2010). People need jobs and MNCs want to demonstrate revenue, so that finding the equilibrium between these two may affect downsizing strategies.

The second factor in the context of MNCs is the issue of national culture, and this cannot be ignored; human behavior and attitudes will almost certainly arise out of an interaction between the local national culture and the imported culture of the MNCs. Culture is what distinguishes between different groups of people. Culture is not an attribute of an individual; it is an attribute of a group, manifested through the behavior of its members. There are four ways in which a culture manifests itself: it filters observation; it sets expectations about the context for interpersonal communications; it sets norms for what constitutes an appropriate partner; and it determines the kind of action that is most appropriate in the light of the three former modes (Hofstede, Jonker, Meijer, and Verwaart, 2006). Culture is a moderating variable, which establishes the meaning of constructs, and the strength and direction of relationships among constructs (Aycan, Kanungo, Mendoca, Yu, Deller, Stahl, and Kurshid, 2000). Thus, the upper echelons of MNCs need to pay attention to culture when they make global managerial decisions such as downsizing.

Ample research has explored the organizational factors that influence and drive downsizing. Common to many of these studies is the underlying assumption that the key role of downsizing is to achieve a more effective and efficient performance within a predetermined and restricted level of resources, therefore using human resources more efficiently. In the context of underperforming firms, employee downsizing is seen as an important signal communicating organizational intentions and efforts to bridge the gap between stakeholders' expectations and achieved performance (Datta *et al.*, 2010). For example, a vice president for human resources (HR) in a global and fast-moving consumer goods company states:

> The corporation decided to cut back on human resources functions. The global trend was towards 'shared services', therefore eliminating almost 50% of local HR functions, while keeping this function centralized in our European headquarters.

The organizational efficiency perspective has also been used to justify downsizing following mergers and acquisitions (M&As). Using longitudinal employer–employee data for 1985–98 on Swedish workers and plants and the firms that employ them, Siegel and Simons found that "M&As are associated with downsizing of the workforce. Employment declined faster than output, which resulted in a productivity increase" (2010, p. 909). Previously, Horn and Persson (2001) had explained how globalization increases cross-border M&As, and when similar firms merge, consolidation of operations usually generates personnel redundancies. Conyon, Girma, Thompson, and Wright (2004) found that downsizing is more likely to appear following a hostile merger, rather than a friendly one. It has also been found that when acquisition premiums have been high for the shareholders of the acquired firm, this has led to greater reductions in the workforce (Krishnan, Hitt, and Park, 2007). In this context, employee downsizing represents a vehicle by which the merged entity can eliminate slack and realize organizational effectiveness in the long term.

In referring to governance, we refer to board characteristics, ownership structure, and compensation systems. Research outcomes vary in their conclusions on this topic (Datta *et al.*, 2010). For example, in a study of layoffs among firms in Russia, Ukraine, and Belarus, the authors found a link between institutional ownership and downsizing (Filatotchev *et al.*, 2000). In a study of foreign ownership among Japanese firms, no significant relationship was found. Additionally, family-owned businesses were found to engage less in severe downsizing activities (Datta *et al.*, 2010). Firms with independent boards are more likely to engage in downsizing. Moreover, the size of boards does not seem to have a significant effect. Interestingly enough, some studies focus on CEO characteristics and their effect on downsizing initiatives and decisions. In examining the role of the functional background of CEOs, Budros (2000, 2002, 2004) found that CEOs with a stronger finance or operations background were more likely to decide on downsizing initiatives. These data are sensitive to industry type. Additionally, a negative relationship was found between the age of CEOs and downsizing. A country manager in a large international consulting firm gave her perspective on a possible dilemma during a global downsizing initiative of the firm. She pointed out:

> There was a dilemma in regards to who would be appointed for the top role in the local company. The issue of whether to appoint the local guy, who knows the market better, or the international guy, who is more experienced, remained a big question mark.

Concerning human resources policy, Wagar (1997) found that when firms are more committed to employee job security, the likelihood of employee layoffs is diminished.

Thus, it is argued that in order to address downsizing and MNCs as a global phenomenon that affects the private and public sectors, with major impacts on people, corporations, and economies, a multifactor approach is needed. The overall spread of globalization has opened up new markets and has increased competition in various markets for most of the MNCs within different industry sectors (Makela and Nasi, 2010). A number of organizational models of MNCs have addressed the issue of how they should organize in order to utilize their dispersed resources (Bresman, Birkinshaw, and Nobel, 1999). Growing globalization is a challenge for MNCs, especially from a managerial perspective (Kristensen and Zeitlin, 2005). In the longer term, however, it enables global businesses to close facilities in one country and open up new facilities in another as part of the corporation's global strategy (Lehman, 1999). From a global perspective, the term "organizational downsizing" is used to describe the adjustment of firms to global competition and technological innovation by eliminating jobs and closing down facilities.

## Downsizing globally: Different countries, different approaches

Globalization and its impact on international downsizing usually affect western industrial countries. For example, similar downsizing processes in the steel industry in Japan and France have reflected differences in pace and focus, as well as in restructuring of the internal labor market (Lanciano and Nitta, 2010). Cascio mentions a good example of global downsizing that worked well in Taiwan. There, a semiconductor manufacturing company (TSMC), which commands half of the global market in contract chip-making and employs 23,000 people, faced a record drop in revenue in the first quarter of 2009. To contain costs, TSMC implemented obligatory unpaid leave, as well as employment downsizing of about 3 percent of the workforce. The result was that in the second quarter, revenue was 80 percent higher than in the first quarter, and the factory utilization rate rose from below 40 percent to 70 percent. TSMC rehired 700 workers who had been previously dismissed, and offered additional compensation to those who did not wish to return (Cascio, 2010, p. 3).

Global downsizing has important legislative implications. In many cases, the determination of which employee goes, and in what order, is determined by statute. In the Netherlands, for example, the rule is "last in, first out." In other countries, social criteria determine layoffs (Cascio, 1993). Some countries have taken a different approach to preserving jobs which contrasts with the downsizing technique. For example, Singapore has assembled a "resilience package" that includes cuts in corporate tax, subsidies to companies that do not lay off workers, and payments that cover 90 percent of the costs of employee training. This has kept unemployment low, at least in the short run. At Kato Spring, for example, a company which bends wires into springs for consumer electronics, the program kept workers busy learning new skills even as the company cut managers' pay and laid off 15 percent of its 200 workers. Six months later, orders bounced back and the company no longer needed the program (Cascio, 2010). Lanciano and Nitta (2010, p. 17) found that management in the Anglo-Saxon countries has tended to respond by shifting certain employees into the external labor market through mass redundancies, contrary to the French approach that tries to organize transitions from one market to the other. The authors summarize: "these labor flows, organized on the basis of age, perhaps reveal the existence of transitional labor markets organized in turn by the public authorities or by firms."

Denmark's approach allows liberal hiring and firing, and the country has imposed limits on the duration of its high unemployment benefits. Denmark also invests more than any other country, as a percentage of its GDP (4.4 percent), in retraining those who have lost their jobs. The Danes call this approach "flexicurity." The cost is covered by tax revenue, which accounts for 50 percent of GDP, second only to Sweden. About two-thirds of Danes who are laid off have a new job within one year. This helped Denmark to cut its unemployment rate in half, from about 10 percent in the early 1990s to less than 5 percent in 2006 (Cascio, 2010, p. 15). In Japan, a different system was created in order to cope with the problem of the large supply of employees, the 'shukko' system, shifting older employees into subcontracting companies and subsidiaries (Lanciano and Nitta, 2010). In general, therefore, MNCs need to pay attention to Harzing's (2004) assertion that differing institutions, laws, and regulations may limit the coordination of human resources management (HRM) practices, leading to the implementation of different downsizing strategies among the various subsidiaries. (For more detailed comparisons concerning the antecedents and outcomes of employee downsizing, see Datta *et al.*, 2010.)

Looking at globalization, Cascio (1993) suggested that it is important to consider the country in which expatriate employees are working, as well as any employment agreements they have apart from what they are entitled to under local laws. It is especially important to have expatriates sign releases of legal claims for all of the jurisdictions in which they have worked during their tenure with the company. The author pointed out that institutional infrastructures vary considerably across countries. This also applies to some of the costs associated with downsizing, such as severance pay, accrued vacation, sick pay, supplemental unemployment, outplacement pension, and other benefits, and administrative processing of rehiring (direct costs). Recruitment, decreased productivity, start-up costs, voluntary termination of the remaining employees, potential lawsuits, etc. (indirect costs) may also vary. Dolan and his colleague (Dolan and Garcia, 2002) noted that downsizing costs more in Europe than in the United States. Most countries in the European Union have laws that require firms to provide severance pay for laid-off employees that can range from six to 24 months of salary for employees who have worked for more than ten years in an organization.

Understanding and accepting that downsizing as a labor phenomenon originated in the United States, it would be very interesting to explore some points of comparison from a global perspective. Comparing downsizing initiatives as a global phenomenon, Redman and Keithley (1998) focus on the "western approach to downsizing" in relation to what we take as the "eastern approach to downsizing." For example, culture plays an important role in people's interpretation of information and their perception of security-related issues, such as feeling safe, protecting privacy, and having trust (Karvonen, Cardholm, and Karlsson, 2000). As a result, the downsizing phenomenon, like other intercultural issues (Rodriguez and Wilson, 2002), can be very unique to a country and involve very specific challenges, such as the number of downsizing events per country, legal restraints on the downsizing initiatives faced by each country, and personnel management following downsizing events, as well as different individual interpretations (Dirks and Ferrin, 2001). Cultural differences between East and West exist (Buchan, Johnson, and Croson, 2006; Hofstede, 1980) and are synchronized with some universalistic practices.

In navigating our comparison in relation to Hofstede's model for cross-cultural comparison (Hofstede, 1980), we propose that the cultural dimensions offered in that model (power distance, uncertainty avoidance, masculinity versus femininity, individualism versus collectivism, and time dimensions) may help us draw some differences between the western approach to downsizing and the eastern approach to downsizing. Some studies of downsizing in the United States and the United Kingdom (Lewine *et al.*, 2010; Mellahi and Wilkinson, 2010) offer a picture which represents a strong individualistic approach by organizations, with time management throughout the process being very well kept. The motives of American or "western" downsizing are strictly economic, business oriented, etc. (For the intensification of managerial work in the USA, UK, and Japan, see Hassard, McCann, and Morris, 2009.) In this respect, the "eastern approach" tends to be more paternalistic. For example, Japanese and Korean downsizing tends to be much more "family oriented and proactive" (Hassard *et al.*, 2009; Yu and Park, 2006; Alakent and Lee, 2010). Looking at some European countries such as Poland (Redman and Keithley, 1998), Germany (Badunenko, 2007), and others (Falk and Wolfmayr, 2010), it seems there is a certain schizophrenia which has not yet been settled by downsizing practices and each country behaves differently. For example, in Poland (Redman and Keithley, 1998) there is a strong feeling that "Polish managers appear to be tackling the problem of employment re-structuring in a less draconian way than their western counterparts." "As Koubek and Brewster note in their survey of HRM in the Czech Republic, Central and Eastern European managers prefer 'less painful' methods of downsizing" (Redman and Keithley, 1998, p. 291). Summarizing all of the above, one may suggest that some cultural differences come into play between the western world, with the United States at the top, and the eastern world, simultaneously with some universalistic patterns.

## Consequences of downsizing: A multilevel, multifactor approach

HR matters enormously in good times. It defines you in the bad. (Jack and Suzy Welch, *Business Week*, 11 March 2009)

The consequences of downsizing are enormous. In the ensuing discussion, we will trace these, focusing on some cross-cultural consequences of downsizing by presenting a multilevel, multifactor approach for analyzing them in order to achieve positive stakeholder behavior (PSB) among

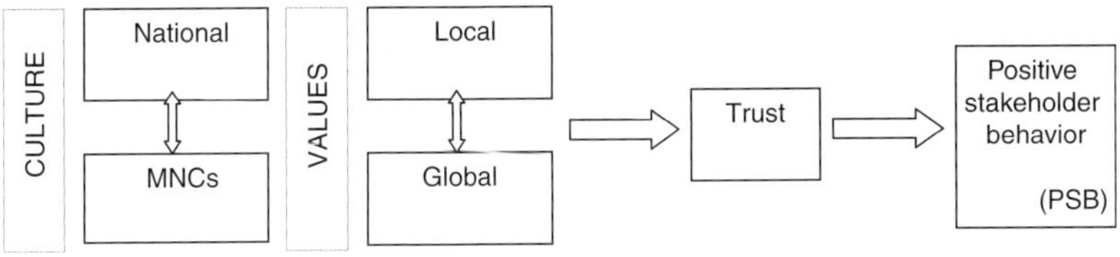


**Figure 13.1** Downsizing: Multinational, multi-level, multi-factor, and cross-cultural perspectives of the effects of downsizing on PSB

customers, employees, unions, managers, etc. (see Figure 13.1). The model presents the importance of fit (Tushman and Nadler, 1978) between different stakeholder groups and different levels (Klein and Kozlowski, 2000). Stakeholders are persons or groups that have, or claim, ownership, rights, or interests in a corporation and its activities, past, present, or future (Clarkson, 1995). In trying to determine the parameters that influence the possibility of cooperation between organizations, we must remember the importance of defining the characteristics of each interest group and stakeholder, in order to try to predict the results of efforts to achieve cooperation between the different groups (Malvey, Fottler, and Slovensky, 2002). Thus it is extremely important to anticipate their behavior, as well as increase the probability for positive behavior. A global compensation and benefits manager, in a global and very active consumer goods company, mentioned the importance of stakeholder satisfaction:

> The stakeholders involved in the downsizing activities were numerous throughout the process. Throughout the change process, we had to double check that each and every stakeholder remained satisfied.

Positive stakeholder behavior is defined as the sum of actions on behalf of the various stakeholders that contribute to the success of the downsizing process. In this chapter we focus on the global versus the local level of analysis; thus, we will particularly single out the organizational and the individual at these two levels. At the organizational level, we consider the relationship between the culture of MNCs versus national culture. At the individual level, we are trying to bridge between universal values (etic) and different values with meaning to different people (emic). Underlying these four variables are two comparisons measuring how they affect the level of trust (Smith and Schwegler, 2010). For example, a smaller gap between universal values and country values (for a closer fit, see Tushman and Nadler, 1978, and for a cultural perspective see Leung, Bhagat, Buchan, Erez, and Gibson, 2005) results in a higher level of trust between parties (Dietz, Gillespie, and Chao, 2010). This increased trust in the organization corresponds to the fact that under these circumstances the MNC is likely to be seen as fair and just. Such a connection is expected from the relation between justice and trust (Brockner, Siegel, Daly, Tyler, and Martin, 1997). The higher the level of trust between parties (managers from different countries and employees), the more likely will be the appearance of positive stakeholder behavior concerning strategic decisions (Tzafrir, Harel, Baruch, and Dolan, 2004).

MNCs need to have an economic rationale for their activities, so that economic measurements focusing on efficiency and effectiveness are a necessity. Surprisingly, this topic remains unresolved among scholars, and they have not found a consistent relationship between downsizing and financial performance. The economic impact of downsizing on firms is controversial and the long-term effect of downsizing on firm effectiveness is questionable (Dolan, Belout, and Balkin, 2000). For example, some studies suggest that firms choose to downsize in order to cut costs and/or to improve financial performance (Espahbodi, John, and Vasudevan, 2000) on the assumption that a firm's profitability will be increased with fewer employees. Another strand of research finds that the effect of personnel reductions on organizational profitability is non-existent or even negative (Cascio, 1993; Datta *et al.*, 2010), because of such aspects as feelings of guilt and negative attitudes (for example, job insecurity and low morale and motivation) towards the organization among the surviving employees. More recent studies claim that positive effects on firm performance from excessive downsizing may be low. Limits on reductions in employee levels may result from a top manager's recognition that protecting the organization's core competencies is important for its long-term success (Munoz-Bullon and Sanchez-Bueno, 2010). A call suggests that downsizing as an organizational phenomenon has a large impact on innovation initially, but the magnitude of the impact declines over time, so that "the results show that the level of downsizing does not have a significant impact on innovation" (Mellahi and Wilkinson, 2010, p. 501).

It needs to be acknowledged that within the context of downsizing, different kinds of stakeholder behavior have an impact on success in terms of revenue (Espahbodi *et al.*, 2000), for example, and customer satisfaction is very important (Lewine *et al.*, 2010). For example, when positivity is missing on the part of the service provider (Brockner, Grover, Reed, De Witt, and O'Malley, 1987), the customer may complain and even leave. More specifically, "in global business environments where cultural values and norms vary among customer groups, the issue of understanding how cultural differences affect perceptions of performance and quality becomes crucial, and especially with regard to how global suppliers allocate resources within diverse cultural regions" (Lewine *et al.*, 2010 p. 697).

## *Cross-cultural consequences*

The world is being flattened. I didn't start it, and you can't stop it, except at a great cost to human development and your own future. (Thomas Friedman, *The World is Flat*)

Coleman (1988) has argued that human capital has to do with people's ability to associate with each other. The ability to associate depends on the degree to which communities share norms and values. According to Fukuyama (1995, p. 12), in low-trust "familistic" societies, like China, France, Italy, and South Korea, the family constitutes the basic unit of economic organization, and therefore each of these societies has experienced difficulties in creating large organizations that go beyond the family; consequently, the state has had to step in to promote durable, globally competitive firms. High-trust societies, like Germany and Japan, in contrast to the familistic societies, have found it much easier to generate large-scale firms not based on kinship. Not only did these societies move to modern professional management early on, but they have been able to create more efficient and satisfying workplace relationships on the factory floor. Holtbrugge and Mohr (2010) studied the values of 939 students in eight countries for cultural determinants of preferences in learning style. The authors found mixed results; while individualism and masculinity (Hofstede, 2001) related to learning style preferences, the data did not provide support for a relationship concerning uncertainty avoidance and long-term orientation.

The fact that MNCs have expanded their reach and now extend into every corner of the globe obliges them to understand the way people perceive, judge, interpret, and behave, in order to be effective. For example, culture plays an important role in people's interpretation of information and their perception of security-related issues, such as feelings of security, privacy and trust (Karvonen *et al.*, 2000). Misunderstanding these differences, with the resulting conflict and tension, is one of the main reasons for the failure of acquisitions to achieve their predicted performance levels (Buono and Bowditch, 1989).

MNCs choose to downsize their operations for diverse reasons, but one of them is the notion of synergy when they buy firms across the globe. Downsizing-related activities in a multinational context may have an immense impact on the relationship between the global company and the local company. Our approach, depicted in Figure 13.1 above, stems from the idea that *positive stakeholder behavior* (PCB) is a crucial element in the success of any international downsizing activities in which a global company and its local subsidiary are involved. PCB exists in cases where *trust*, or a trusting relationship (More and Tzafrir, 2009), exists between the two sides, the global downsizing firm and the local company being cut. The achievement of positive results may be analyzed by comparing the *fits* between local and global values (Schwartz, 1992) as well as between national culture (Hofstede, 2001) and the MNC's culture. The need for alignment between parties is the focus of one human resources vice president who summarized the factors for a successful global process:

> One of the key success factors to this whole initiative was very strong communication between sides throughout the process. This phase took us three years to complete, and without strong and healthy communication, it would have been a complete failure.

## *Values: Local and global*

Values are the building blocks of culture and are therefore key in the cultural design of both global and local companies (Dolan, Garcia, and Richley, 2006). A common denominator among people rests on a convention that "a specific mode of conduct or end-state of existence is personally or socially preferable to an opposite or converse mode of conduct or end-state existence" (Rokeach, 1973, p. 5). The values in Schwartz's (1992) theory represent three universal requirements of human existence to which all individuals and societies must be responsive: biological needs; requirements of social interaction; and the survival and welfare needs of groups. The role of values and their organizational contribution has long been studied in the academic world. Values have been defined as the principles or standards that people use, individually or collectively, to make judgements about what is important or valuable in their lives (McEwan, 2001). Moreover, they are described as constructs representing generalized behaviors or states of affairs that are considered by the individual to be important (Yukl, 2002). They are broad feelings, often unconscious and taken for granted, about what is good and what is evil, beautiful or ugly, rational or irrational, normal or abnormal, natural or paradoxical, decent or indecent. These feelings are present in most members of a culture, or at least in those who occupy pivotal positions (Pucik, Ticy, and Barnett, 1993, p. 141).

Rokeach (1973) defines an individual value system as an "enduring organization of beliefs concerning preferable modes of conduct or end-states of existence along a continuum of relative importance." Ashkanasy (2000) writes that one issue that has received major attention in the values literature has to do with the distinction between values (in a general sense) and work values – a concept that implies the existence of particular sets of values governing an employee's work-related behavior, in all of its forms. Most definitions of work values, although consistent with definitions of values in the broader sense, focus strongly on work, work behavior, and work-related outcomes. Connor and Becker (1994) have emphasized the important role of values in people's behavior and attitudes expressed when they are acting in groups. Actors enter the downsizing process with stable values and conceived notions of what "ought" and what "ought not" to be. Thus, the interactions between actors in this process lay the foundation for an understanding of other actors' behavior and attitudes, as well as influencing them. Therefore, such values help us to predict, interpret, and act accordingly in order to achieve better performance.

Research has given much attention to values and their utmost importance within the organizational arena. Additionally, links have been examined between human values and organizational values; and it has also been noted that an organization's values have a relative influence on its overall culture, and even performance (Schwartz and Bilsky, 1987; 1990). For example, values such as well-being and sustainability may influence the organizational culture and even long-term organizational performance.

In more recent research, values are described as a management tool in modern organizations. For example, Dolan and Garcia introduce the management by values (MBV) concept, which contributes to cultural redesign to assist strategic organizational change at the outset of the twenty-first century. The authors claim that "the system of beliefs and values that shaped the model for management and organizations during the twentieth century is just not good enough today. In order to keep a business functioning well and competing successfully in markets that are increasingly more global, complex, professionally demanding, constantly changing and oriented towards quality and customer satisfaction, a new model is needed" (2002, p. 101). In these organizations, and especially in multinational firms, where cultural complexity exists, key stakeholders want to get a clear understanding of which values and beliefs need to be changed, as well as how to go about the process of change, more specifically in downsizing, in a successful manner. The authors introduce the MBV concept as a "strategic leadership tool" (2002, p. 102), whose added value is specifically useful throughout the change process in a downsizing context.

A better fit (Nadler and Tushman, 1980) between global and local values focuses on how closely local values match the global values. The basic assumption (O'Reilly, Chatman, and Caldwell, 1991) is that the closer the fit the lower the conflict inherent in the particular situation (downsizing, for example). Summarizing all of the above, downsizing processes within MNCs are founded on a set of both universal and particularistic work values that derive from the beliefs and perceptions inherent in culture and that guide interactions between actors from different countries. The better the fit between the levels, the higher the probability of success. One of the resources for these values is the national culture within which an individual operates.

## *Culture: Local and global*

Culture is defined as what a group learns over a period of time as that group solves its problems of survival in an external environment and its problems of internal integration (Schein, 1992; Erez and Gati, 2004). In this context, one of the greatest challenges in successfully leading a global downsizing initiative is overcoming cultural diversities. From a cross-cultural perspective, global downsizing initiatives may be complex because of the need to navigate wisely between three dimensions: the organizational culture dimension; the national culture dimension; and the global culture dimension. Organizational culture is defined as "the sense of common identity and purpose across the whole organization"

(McNulty and De Cieri, 2010, p. 21). Organizational culture, it has been suggested, influences the commitment of employees, with implications for retention strategies. Organizational culture has also been shown to influence the transfer of management practices across subsidiaries, particularly in post-merger or downsizing operations (McNulty and De Cieri, 2010).

National cultures and their influence both in the external business arena and in the internal organizational context have been widely discussed in the literature (Leung *et al.*, 2005). Since the seminal study by Hofstede (1980), there have been a significant number of large-scale projects investigating dimensions of cultural variability at the country level (Fischer and Mansell, 2009; House, Hanges, Javidan, Dorfman, and Gupta, 2004; Schwartz, 1994). Across these various projects, three consistent dimensions of cultural variability have emerged: individual/collective, power distance, and mastery/harmony. These dimensions are of particular importance in the context of downsizing at the global level, on the one hand, and for the local integration of a downsized firm in local operations in a post-merger scenario (Fischer and Mansell, 2009).

In the course of global downsizing processes, local cultures are increasingly "contaminated and penetrated by elements of global culture" (Lin and Ke, 2010, p. 638). Western nations are economically advanced and often perceived to be the representatives of global culture. However, many studies support the idea that some aspects of local culture will survive the erosive effects of globalization. Since cultures are often classified in a dichotomous way (Hofstede, 1980), cultural pluralism and hybridization result when global culture enters the local, as it does in global downsizing (Lin and Ke, 2010). This emphasizes the economic interdependence among countries that develops through cross-national flows of goods and services, capital, know-how, and people (Erez and Gati, 2004).

The global work environment is highly diverse when it crosses cultural borders. In downsizing initiatives, this increases as the level of sensitivity rises. Therefore, one of the challenges for global organizations, particularly at times when there are cuts to be made, is to develop an awareness of cultural variations, and to respect cultural diversity. Tolerance for diversity enables companies to operate effectively across cultural borders, and to motivate employees from different cultures to join forces in strengthening the sustainable competitive advantage of their global corporation (Erez and Gati, 2004, p. 592).

## *Positive stakeholder behavior: Trust as a tool for overcoming the gap*

> One of the key success factors of the change process as a whole was that there was open communication and trust between sides as the change process emerged. It took us three years. Of course every country has its local culture. However, this strong feeling of trust enabled us to create a global culture, our culture, and everyone was willing to accept that, wherever trust exists. (Global Compensation and Benefits Manager, multinational firm)

A global downsizing scenario can be a long and painful process. It entails a reshuffling of organizational resources on a multinational basis. We believe that trusting behavior, or a relationship built on trust between the global and local companies, is the key for successfully overcoming the constraints inherent in the decision to downsize employees. Coleman (1990) mentions that trustworthiness has important implications for the social environment, especially in enabling the norm of reciprocity to flourish. Following the logic that people's social environment, and especially trust, has an important role in people's health and behavior, Suzuki and his colleagues (2010) found that an environment of workers' distrust relates to poor health, and Chen, Aryee, and Lee (2005) found that organizational trust is a key concept in achieving better work outcomes.

The role of trust in collaborative inter-firm ties, as well as in cooperative relationships, is of fundamental importance (Zaheer *et al.*, 1998, p. 141). A substantial amount of theoretical and empirical work has suggested that trust is also a critical factor in interorganizational collaboration (Alter and Hage, 1993; Cummings and Bromiley, 1996; Fichman and Levinthal, 1991; Jarillo, 1988; Currall and Judge, 1995). It has been argued that trust has a positive effect because it strengthens dyadic ties (Fichman and Levinthal, 1991), speeds up contract negotiations, and generally reduces transaction costs (Cummings and Bromiley, 1996). Additionally, research has revealed that trust affects managerial problem-solving (Zand, 1972), openness and receptivity (Butler, 1991), affective commitment (Herscovitch and Mayer, 2002), and risk-taking (Mayer, and Davis, and Schoorman, 1995).

Researchers have shown that national culture has affected trust through macro factors such as national health, education, democracy, etc. (Ferrin and Gillespie, 2010, p. 65). Nevertheless, MNCs wanting to promote effectiveness and efficiency (Dolan *et al.*, 2000) will try to close the cultural gap (Gould and Grein, 2009) between the parties involved.

These MNCs, through their managers (Ferrin and Gillespie, 2010), will have a willingness to increase their resource investment in local organizations with positive expectations over time. These dynamic interactions that build and develop trust over time (Tzafrir and Dolan, 2004) reciprocate (Gouldner, 1960) with positive stakeholder behavior, which in turn facilitates the existence of an MNC's global culture.

A company which successfully adopts a strong global culture has a set of core values and practices that are shared worldwide. This culture often reflects a deep connection to global sources. It serves as a yardstick to guide operations and actions worldwide. This does not mean that local values and differences are ignored. In fact, failing to adapt the global culture to local realities may hinder the company's success. Respect and trust in local knowledge are often key. This allows companies to localize the company's core values in a way that evolves into effective local practices (Levy, Taylor, and Boyacigiller, 2010). As one of the interviewees commented:

> I felt that the reason that trust was not hurt between sides throughout the downsizing process was because of this amended global culture that our company wisely developed internationally and locally. (Global Compensation and Benefits Manager)

## Conclusion and implications

The fact that MNCs have expanded their reach and now extend into every corner of the globe creates the need to better understand different stakeholder needs and requirements. The point of departure in creating a positive environment between the various stakeholders rests on trusting behavior. The way to build, develop, and achieve trusting behavior is first by understanding each other and taking into account others' interests (Tzafrir and Dolan, 2004). De Cieri, Wolfram, and Fenwick (2007, p. 14) suggest that the "cultural" values of an MNC's home country may help to explain the types of international human resource management strategies and practices that it tries to extend to its international subsidiaries. We propose that MNCs need to bridge between different values rather than enforcing similar values everywhere; thus, organizational processes will be implemented in a way that fits between values and culture.

Gould and Grein concluded that 'for International Business cultural theory and research is to avoid confounding or conflating national culture with other cultural forms and processes' (2009, p. 250). We suggest that implementing a decision for major organizational change, such as downsizing in MNCs, needs to take into account the different levels of fit between various forms of culture and values. Does the universalistic part of the model answer the question of the preferred approach when implementing such decisions around the globe? We suggest that MNCs need to create equilibrium between culture and values at the two levels of analysis by eliminating part of the gap that focuses on non-standardized principles while using the constructive separate national and organizational values. This framework provides a common logic that enables CEOs and HR leaders to reorganize and focus their strategic planning and behavior in respect of the three challenges: operational, cultural, and behavioral.

The PAP (Policy, Alignment, Prioritization) operational challenge concerns the upper echelon's prior decision on the downsizing process (Battistoni and Longo, 2009; Gandolfi, 2009; Munoz-Bullon and Sanchez-Bueno, 2010). We suggest that the optimal strategy is to build bridges between country, organization, and individuals. Thus, three main issues need to be raised in order to achieve efficiency and effectiveness. The downsizing policy will involve a glocal (global-local) national and organizational culture (Levy *et al.*, 2010) as well as analysis comparing values in order to get an answer for three questions: (1) Have the main policy issues of centralization versus decentralization in the process and implementation of downsizing been considered? (2) Is global versus local alignment being considered? For example, Erez and Gati (2004) have proposed an idea for calculating the commonly used phrase "think global, act local." (3) Has consideration of the prioritization of needs followed a clear distinction between "must do" and "nice to have"?

The second core challenge concentrates on cultural differentiation between individuals and groups (Fischer and Mansell, 2009; Schwartz and Bilsky, 1990). Charts and scripts help in evaluating and making sense of incoming information such as the reasons to downsize. A perception of national, organizational, and individuals' values would influence the organizational evaluation of the reasons, process, and consequences of downsizing, and therefore the formation of related attitudes. However, the question remains: do all employees fall into the same category? Research has already pointed out that different employees have different perceptions and expectations (Cook and Crossman, 2004). Thus, we suggest that managers must use a proactive and systematic tool to build and develop reliable benevolence (Mayer *et al.*, 1995) and harmony (Tzafrir and Dolan, 2004) within the organization (Dolan and Garcia, 2002). Management by values is proposed as a management tool to overcome several cultural gaps; the methods proposed by Dolan and colleagues are designed to audit the gap (Dolan and Garcia, 2002; Dolan *et al.*, 2006) and then coach people and teams (or entire organizations) to narrow it (Dolan, 2011), which is at the core of the concept of value and culture reengineering.

Finally, as in every organizational decision, the aspect of behavior is a significant challenge. Our suggestion is to focus on building and developing trusting relationships (Tzafrir, 2005). Some suggest that trust is the meta-value, or the "value of Values" (Dolan, 2011). Creating positive cultural behavior based on international flexibility, openness (Tzafrir and Dolan, 2004), concern (Mishra, 1996), empathy, and sensitivity (Dolan and Garcia, 2002) will help managers to implement the downsizing process with low costs, overcoming resistance and sabotage, and meeting important timeline constraints, eventually leading to a greater degree of sustainability and higher levels of productivity.

*Notes*

1. "Globalization" even ranks ahead of "technology" as a force for change (Connell, 2010).
2. Our method in the examination of this subject has two phases. The first is the collection and integration of the downsizing literature, with a focus on the global perspective. The second includes some fieldwork in the form of semi-structured interviews.
3. Our model, presented in the following, accounts for these important variables.

## References

Alakent, E. and Lee, S.H. 2010. "Do institutionalized traditions matter during crisis? Employee downsizing in Korean manufacturing organizations." *Journal of Management Studies* **47**(3): 1–50.

Alter, C. and Hage, J. 1993. *Organizations Working Together*. Newbury Park, CA: Sage.

Anwar, S. 2009. "Wage inequality, welfare and downsizing." *Economics Letters* **103**: 75–77.

Ashkanasy, N. M., Wilderom, P. M., and Peterson, M. F. 2000. "Introduction," in N. M. Ashkanasy, P. M. Wilderom, and M. F. Peterson (eds.), *Handbook of Organisational Culture and Climate*. Newbury Park, CA: Sage, pp. 1–18.

Aycan, Z., Kanungo, R. N., Mendoca, M., Yu, K., Deller, J., Stahl, G., and Kurshid, A. 2000. "Impact of culture on human resource management practices: A 10-country comparison." *Applied Psychology: An International Review* **49**: 192–221.

Badunenko, O. 2007. "Downsizing in German chemical manufacturing industry during the 1990's: Why small is beautiful?" Working Paper, Discussion Papers of DIW 722, German Institute for Economic Research, pp. 1–28.

Battistoni, R. M. and Longo, N. V. 2009. "Acting locally in a flat world: Global citizenship and the democratic practice of service-learning." *Journal of Higher Education Outreach and Engagement* **13**(2): 89–108.

Bresman, H., Birkinshaw, J., and Nobel, R. 1999. "Knowledge transfer in international acquisitions." *Journal of International Business Studies* **30**(3): 439–462.

Brockner, J., Grover, S., Reed, T., De Witt, R., and O'Malley, M. 1987. "Survivors' reactions to layoffs: We get by with a little help for our friends." *Administrative Science Quarterly* **32**: 526–541.

Brockner, J., Siegel, P. A., Daly, J. P., Tyler, T., and Martin, C. 1997. "When trust matters: The moderating effect of outcome favorability." *Administration Science Quarterly* **42**: 558–583.

Buchan, N. R., Johnson, E. J., and Croson, R. T. A. 2006. "Let's get personal: An international examination of the influence of communication, culture and social distance on other regarding preferences." *Journal of Economic Behavior and Organization* **60**: 373–398.

Budros, A. 1997. "The new capitalism and organizational rationality: The adoption of downsizing programs, 1979–1994." *Social Forces* **76**: 229–250.

Budros, A. 2000. "Organizational types and organizational innovation: Downsizing among industrial, financial and utility firms." *Sociological Forum* **15**(2): 273–306.

Budros, A. 2002. "The mean and lean firm: Causes of involuntary and voluntary downsizing strategies." *Sociological Forum* **17**(2): 307–342.

Budros, A. 2004. Causes of early and later organizational adoption: The case of corporate downsizing. *Sociological Inquiry* **74**: 355–380.

Buono, A. F. and Bowditch, J. L. 1989. *The Human Side of Mergers and Acquisitions*. San Francisco, CA: Jossey-Bass.

Bureau of Labor Statistics Data. 2005. US Department of Labor, www.bls.gov.

Butler, J. K., Jr. 1991. "Toward understanding and measuring conditions of trust: Evolution of a conditions of trust inventory." *Journal of Management* **17**(3): 643–663.

Cameron, K. S. 1994. "Strategies for successful organizational downsizing." *Human Resource Management* **33**(2): 189–211.
Cameron, K. S., Freeman, S. J., and Mishra, A. K. 1993. "Downsizing and redesigning organizations," in G. Huber and W. Glick (eds.), *Organizational Change and Redesign*. New York: Oxford University Press, pp. 19–63.
Cascio, W. F. 1993. "Downsizing: What do we know? What have we learned?" *Academy of Management Executive* 7(1): 95–104.
Cascio, W. F. 2009. "Use and management of downsizing as a corporate strategy." SHRM Foundations Executive Briefing, pp. 1–4. https://www.shrm.org/about/foundation/products/Documents/609%20Exec%20Briefing-%20Downsizing%20FINAL.pdf
Cascio, W. F. 2010. "Employment downsizing and its alternatives: Strategies for long-term success." Right Management Foundation's Effective Practice Guidelines Series, 1–33.
Chen, Z. C., Aryee, S., and Lee, C. 2005. "Test of a mediation model of perceived organizational support." *Journal of Vocational Behavior* **66**(3): 457.
Clarkson, M. B. E. 1995. "A stakeholder framework for analyzing and evaluating corporate social performance." *Academy of Management Review* **20**(1): 92–117.
Coleman, J. S. 1988. "Social capital in the creation of human capital." *American Journal of Sociology* **94**: 95–120.
Coleman, J. 1990. *Foundations of Social Theory*. Cambridge, MA/London: The Belknap Press of Harvard University Press.
Connell, R. 2010. "Building the neoliberal world: Managers as intellectuals in a periphery economy." *Critical Sociology* **36**(6): 777–792.
Connor, E. P. and Becker, B. W. 1994. "Personal values and management: What do we know and why don't we know more?" *Journal of Management Inquiry* **3**(1): 67–73.
Conyon, M. J., Girma, S., Thompson, S., and Wright, P. W. 2004. "Do wages rise or fall following merger?" *Oxford Bulletin of Economics and Statistics* **66**: 847–862.
Cook, J. and Crossman, A. 2004. "Satisfaction with performance appraisal systems: A study of role perceptions." *Journal of Managerial Psychology* **19**(5): 526–541.
Coucke, K., Pennings, E., and Sleuwaegen, L. 2007. "Employee lay-off under different modes of restructuring: Exit, downsizing or relocation." *Industrial and Corporate Change* **16**: 161–182.
Cummings, L. and Bromiley, P. 1996. "The organizational trust inventory (OTI): Development and validation," in R. M. Kramer and T. R. Tyler (eds.), *Trust in Organizations*. Thousand Oaks, CA: Sage, pp. 302–330.

Curral, S. C. and Judge, T. A. 1995. "Measuring trust between organizational boundary role persons." *Organizational Behavior and Human Decision Processes* **64**(2): 151–170.

Datta, D. K., Guthrie, J. P., Basuil, D., and Pandey, A. 2010. "Causes and effects of employee downsizing: A review and synthesis." *Journal of Management* **36**(1): 281–348.

De Cieri, H. J., Wolfram, C., and Fenwick, M. 2007. "A review of international human resource management: Integrations, interrogation, imitation." *International Journal of Management Reviews* **9**(3): 1–22.

Dietz, G., Gillespie, N., and Chao, G. T. 2010. "Unraveling the complexities of trust and culture," in M. N. K. Saunders, D. Skinner, G. Dietz, N. Gillespie, and R. J. Lewick (eds.), *Organizational Trust: A Cultural Perspective*. Cambridge: Cambridge University Press, pp. 3–41.

DeWitt, R. L. 1998, "Firm, industry, and strategy influences on choice of downsizing approach." *Strategic Management Journal* **19**: 59–79.

Dirks, K. T. and Ferrin, D. L. 2001. "The role of trust in organizational settings." *Organization Science* **12**: 450–467.

Dolan, S. L., Belout, A., and Balkin, D. 2000. "Downsizing without downgrading: Learning how firms manage their survivors." *International Journal of Manpower* **21**(1): 34–46.

Dolan, S. L. and Garcia, S. 2002. "Managing by values: Cultural redesign for strategic organizational change at the dawn of the twenty-first century." *Journal of Management Development* **21**(2): 101–117.

Dolan, S. L., Garcia, S., and Richley, B. 2006. *Managing by Values: Corporate Guide to Living, Being Alive and Making a Living in the XXI Century*. London: Palgrave-Macmillan.

Dolan, S. L. 2011. *Coaching by Values*. iUniverse (in press).

Erez, M. and Gati, E. 2004. "A dynamic, multi-level model of culture: From the micro level of the individual to the macro level of a global culture." *Applied Psychology: An International Review* **53**(4): 583–598.

Espahbodi, R., John, T. A., and Vasudevan, G. 2000. "The effects of downsizing on operating performance." *Review of Quantitative Finance and Accounting* **15**: 107–126.

Falk, M. and Wolfmayr, Y. 2010. "The substitutability between parent company and foreign affiliate employment in Europe." *Empirica* **37**: 87–100

Fasenfest, D. 2010. "Neoliberalism, globalization and the capitalist world order." *Critical Sociology* **36**(5): 627–631.

Ferrin, D. L. and Gillespie, N. 2010. "Trust differences across national-societal cultures: Much to do, or much ado about nothing?" in M. N. K. Saunders, D. Skinner, G. Dietz, N. Gillespie, and R. J. Lewicki (eds.), *Organizational Trust: A Cultural Perspective*. Cambridge: Cambridge University Press, pp. 42–86.

Fichman, M. and Levinthal, D. A. 1991. "Honeymoons and the liability of adolescence: A new perspective on duration dependence in social and organizational relationships." *Academy of Management Review* **16**(2): 442–468.

Filatotchev, I., Buck, T., and Zuhkov, V. 2000. "Downsizing in privatized firms in Russia, Ukraine and Belarus." *Academy of Management Journal* **43**(3): 286–304.

Fischer, R. and Mansell, A. 2009. "Commitment across cultures: A meta analytical approach." *Journal of International Business Studies* **40**: 1339–1358.

Freeman, S. J. and Cameron, K. S. 1993. "Organizational downsizing: A convergence and reorientation framework." *Organization Science* **4**: 10–29.

Fukuyama, F. 1995. *Trust: The social Virtues and the Creation of Prosperity*. New York: The Free Press.

Gandolfi, F. 2009. "Executing downsizing: The experience of executioners." *Contemporary Management Research* **5**(2): 185–200.

Gould, S. J. and Grein, A. F. 2009. "Think glocally, act glocally: A culture-centric comment on Leung, Bhagat, Buchan, Erez, and Gibson 2005." *Journal of International Business Studies* **40**: 237–254.

Gouldner, A. W. 1960. "The norm of reciprocity: A preliminary statement." *American Sociological Review* **25**(2): 161–179.

Haiyong, M. and Weiwei, Z. 2010. "Cross border merger and acquisition in BRICs." *Research in World Economy* **1**(1): 43–46.

Hareli, S. and Tzafrir, S. S. 2006. "The role of causal attribution in survivor's emotional reaction to downsizing." *Human Resources Development Review* **5**(4): 400–421.

Harzing, A. W. 2004. 'Strategy and structure of multinational companies,' in A. W. Harzing and J. Van Ruyssevel (eds.), *International Human Resource Management* (2nd edn.). London: Sage.

Hassard, J., McCann, L., and Morris, J. 2009. *Managing in the Modern Corporation: The Intensification of Managerial Work in the USA, UK and Japan*. Cambridge: Cambridge University Press.

Herscovitch, L. and Meyer, J. P. 2002. "Commitment to organizational change: Extension of a three-component model." *Journal of Applied Psychology* **87**(3): 474–487.

Hofstede, G. 1980. *Culture's Consequences: International Differences in Work-related Values*. Beverly Hills, CA: Sage.

Hofstede, G. 2001. *Culture's Consequences: Comparing Values, Behaviors, Institutions and Organizations across Nations*. California, CA: Sage Publications.

Hofstede, G. J., Jonker, C. M., Meijer, S., and Verwaart, T. 2006. "Modeling trade and trust across cultures," in Ketil Stølen *et al.* (ed.), *Trust*

*Management, 4th National Conference, iTrust 2006, Lecture Notes in Computer Science*, 3986, Berlin: Springer-Verlag, pp. 120–134.

Holtbrugge, D. and Mohr, A. T. 2010. "Cultural determinants of learning style preferences." *Academy of Management Learning and Education* **9**(4): 622–637.

Horn, H. and Persson, L. 2001. "The equilibrium ownership of an international oligopoly." *Journal of International Economics* **53**: 307–333.

House, R. J., Hanges, P. J., Javidan, M., Dorfman, P. W., and Gupta, V. (eds.). 2004. *Culture, Leadership, and Organizations: The GLOBE Study of 62 Societies*. London: Sage Publications Inc.

Iverson, R. D. and Zatzick, C. D. (2011). "The effect of downsizing on labor productivity: The value of showing consideration for employees' morale and welfare in high performance work systems." *Human Resource Management* **50**(1): 29–44.

Jamali, D. and Mirshak, R. 2010. "Business–conflict linkages: Revisiting MNCs, CSR, and conflict." *Journal of Business Ethics* **93**: 443–464.

Jarillo, J. C. (1988). "On strategic networks." *Strategic Management Journal* **9**(1): 31–41.

Karvonen, K., Cardholm, L., and Karlsson, S. 2000. "Cultures of trust: A cross-cultural study on the formation of trust in an electronic environment." *Proceedings of the Fifth Nordic Workshop on Secure IT Systems*, **12**: 89–100.

Klein, K. J. and Kozlowski, S. W. J. 2000. *Multilevel Theory, Research, and Methods Organizations: Foundaions, Extensions and New Directions*. San Francisco, CA: Jossey-Bass.

Kochan, T. A. 2005. *Restoring the American Dream: A Working Families' Agenda for America*. Cambridge, MA: MIT Press.

Koerber, C. and Fort, T. 2008. "Corporate citizenship and global conflicts: The baboon moment," in A. Scherer and G. Palazzo (eds.), *Handbook of Research on Global Citizenship*. Cheltenham: Edward Elgar, pp. 208–221.

Krishnan, H. A., Hitt, M. A., and Park, D. 2007. "Acquisitions premiums, subsequent work force reductions, and postacquisition performance." *Journal of Management Studies* **44**: 709–732.

Kristensen, P. and Zeitlin, J. 2005. *Local Players in Global Games: The Strategic Constitution of a Multinational Corporation*. Oxford: Oxford University Press.

Lanciano, E. and Nitta, M. 2010. "How do Japanese and French firms in steel industry address the institutional change and the globalization? Employment adjustment and age management in downsizing context." Working Paper, International Sociology Association, Goteborg, pp. 1–19.

Lehman, G. 1999. "Disclosing new worlds: a role for social and environmental accounting and auditing." *Accounting, Organizations and Society* **24**(3): 217–241.

Leung, K., Bhagat, R. S., Buchan, N. R., Erez, M., and Gibson, C. B. 2005. "Culture and international business: Recent advances and their implications for future research." *Journal of International Business Studies* **36**(4): 357–378.

Levy, O., Taylor, S., and Boyacigiller, N. A. 2010. "On the rocky road to strong global culture." *MIT Sloan Management Review* **51**(4): 19–23.

Lewine, J. E., Biemans, W., and Ulaga, W. 2010. "Firm downsizing and satisfaction among United States and European customers." *Journal of Business Research* **63**: 697–706.

Lin, S. and Ke, X. 2010. "Chinese glocalization – a study of intergenerational residence in urban China." *Journal of Consumer Marketing* **27**(7): 638–644

Makela, H. and Näsi, S. 2010. "Social responsibilities of MNCs in downsizing operations." *Accounting, Auditing and Accountability Journal* **23**(2): 149–174.

Malvey, D., Fottler, M. D., and Slovensky, D. J. 2002. "Evaluating stakeholders management performance using a stakeholder report card: The next step in theory and practice." *Health Care Manage Review* **27**(2): 66–79

Mayer, R. C., Davis, J. H., and Schoorman, F. D. 1995. "An integrative model of organizational trust." *Academy of Management Review* **20**(3): 709–734.

McEwan, T. 2001. *Managing Values and Beliefs in Organisations*. Englewood, NJ: Prentice Hall.

McNulty, Y. and De Cieri, H. 2010. "Determinants of expatriate return on investment in global firms: Advancing the conceptual framework." *Proceedings of the 2010 Academy of Management Annual Meeting*, Montreal, Canada: 6–10 August

Mellahi, K. and Wilkinson, A. 2010. "A study of the association between level of slack reduction following downsizing and innovation output." *Journal of Management Studies* **47**(3): 483–508

Mishra, A. 1996. "Organizational responses to crisis: The centrality of trust," in R. M. Kramer and T. Tyler (eds.), *Trust in Organizations: Frontiers of Theory and Research*. London: Sage.

More, V. K. and Tzafrir, S. S. 2009. "The role of trust in core team employees: A three-nation study." *Cross Cultural Management: An International Journal* **16**(4): 410–433.

Munoz-Bullon, F. and Sanchez-Bueno, M. J. 2010. "Downsizing implementation and financial performance." *Management Decision* **48**(8): 1181–1197.

Nadler, D. and Tushman, M. 1980. "A model for diagnosing organizational behavior: Applying a congruence perspective." *Organizational Dynamics* **9**(3): 35–51.

O'Reilly III, C. A., Chatman, J., and Caldwell, D. F. 1991. "People and organizational culture: A profile comparison approach to assessing person-organization fit." *Academy of Management Journal* **34**(3): 487–516.

Pucik, V., Ticy, N., and Barnett, C. 1993. *Globalizing Management, Creating and Leading the Competitive Organisation.* New York: John Wiley & Sons.

Raich, M. and Dolan S. L. 2008. *Beyond: Business and Society in Transformation.* London: Palgrave-Macmillan.

Redman, T. and Keithley, D. 1998. "Downsizing goes east? Employment restructuring in post-socialist Poland." *The International Journal of Human Resource Management* **9**(2): 274–295.

Rodriguez, C. M. and Wilson, D. T. 2002. "Relationship bonding and trust as a foundation for commitment in US–Mexican strategic alliances: A structural equation modeling approach." *Journal of International Marketing* **10**: 53–76.

Rokeach, M. 1973. *The Nature of Human Values.* New York: The Free Press.

Schein, E. H. 1992. *Organizational Culture and Leadership.* San Francisco, CA: Jossey-Bass.

Schwartz, S. H. 1992. "Universals in the content and structure of values: Theoretical advances and empirical tests in 20 countries," in M. Zanna (ed.), *Advances in Experimental Social Psychology*, vol. XXV. Orlando, FL: Academic, pp. 1–65.

Schwartz, S. H. 1994. "Beyond individualism and collectivism: New cultural dimensions of values," in U. Kim, H. C. Triandis, C. Choi, S.-C. Choi, and G. Yoon (eds.), *Individualism and Collectivism: Theory, Method, and Applications.* Newbury Park, CA: Sage, pp. 85–122.

Schwartz, S. H. and Bilsky, W. 1987. "Toward a universal psychological structure of human values." *Journal of Personality and Social Psychology* **53**(3): 550–562

Schwartz, S. H. and Bilsky, W. 1990. "Toward a theory of the universal content and structure of values: Extensions and cross-cultural replications." *Journal of Personality and Social Psychology* **58**(5): 878–891

Siegel, D. S. and Simons, K. L. 2010. "Assessing the effects of mergers and acquisitions on firm performance, plant productivity, and workers: New evidence from matched employer–employee data." *Strategic Management Journal* **31**: 903–916.

Smith, R. L. and Schwegler, U. 2010. "The role of trust in international cooperation in crisis area: A comparison of German and US-American NGO partnership strategies," in M. N. K. Saunders, D. Skinner, G. Dietz, N. Gillespie, and R. J. Lewicki (eds.), *Organizational Trust: A Cultural Perspective.* Cambridge: Cambridge University Press, pp. 281–310.

Sturgeon, T. J. and Van Biesebroeck, J. 2010. "Effects of the crisis on the automotive industry in developing countries: A global value chain perspective." World Bank Working Paper 5330. Available at http://www.iadb.org/intal/intalcdi/PE/2010/05542.pdf

Suzuki, E., Takao, S., Subramanian, S. V., Komatsu, H., Doi, H., and Kawachi, I. 2010. "Does low workplace social capital have detrimental effect on workers' health?" *Social Science and Medicine* **70**: 1367–1372.

Tsai, C., Wu, S., Wang, H., and Huang, I. 2006. "An empirical research on the institutional theory of downsizing: Evidence from MNCs subsidiary companies in Taiwan." *Total Quality Management and Business Excellence* **17**: 633–654.

Tushman, M. L. and Nadler, D. A. 1978. "Information processing as an integrating concept in organizational design." *Academy of Management Review* **3**: 613–624.

Tzafrir, S. S. 2005. "The relationship between trust, HRM practices and firm performance." *International Journal of Human Resource Management* **16**(9): 1600–1622.

Tzafrir, S. S. and Dolan, L. S. 2004. "Trust ME: A scale for measuring employee manager trust." *Management Research* **2**(2): 117–134.

Tzafrir, S. S., Harel, G., Baruch, Y., and Dolan, L. S. 2004. "The consequences of emerging HRM practices for employees trust in their managers." *Personnel Review* **33**(6): 628–647.

UNCTAD. 2009. United Nations Conference on Trade and Development, World Investment Report 2009: Vol I Transnational Corporations, Agricultural Production and Development, available at: www.unctad.org/en/docs/wir2009_en.pdf.

Van Buren, H. J. III and Greenwood, M. 2011. "Bringing stakeholder theory to industrial relations." *Employee Relations* **33**(1): 5–21.

Wagar, T. 1997. Factors affecting permanent workforce reduction: Evidence from large Canadian organizations. *Canadian Journal of Administrative Sciences* **14**: 303–314.

Willke, H. and Willke, G. 2008. "The corporation as a political actor? A systems theory perspective," in A. Scherer and G. Palazzo (eds.), *Handbook of Research on Global Citizenship*. Cheltenham: Edward Elgar, pp. 552–574.

Yu, G. C. and Park, J. S. 2006. "The effect of downsizing on the financial performance and employee productivity of Korean firms." *International Journal of Manpower* **27**(3): 230–250.

Yukl, G. A. 2002. *Leadership in Organisations* (5th edn.). Englewood, NJ: Prentice-Hall.

Zaheer, A., McEvily, B., and Perrone, V. 1998. "Does trust matter? Exploring the effects of interorganizational and interpersonal trust on performance." *Organization Science* **9**(2): 141–159.

Zand, D. E. 1972. "Trust and managerial problem solving." *Administrative Science Quarterly* **17**(2): 229–239.

# Index